VARIORUM COLLECTED STUDIES SERIES

Immortals, Festivals and
Poetry in Medieval China

Donald Holzman

Immortals, Festivals and Poetry in Medieval China

Studies in Social and Intellectual History

Routledge
Taylor & Francis Group

LONDON AND NEW YORK

First published 1998 in the Variorum Collected Studies Series by Ashgate Publishing

Reissued 2018 by Routledge
2 Park Square, Milton Park, Abingdon, Oxon, OX14 4RN
52 Vanderbilt Avenue, New York, NY 10017

Routledge is an imprint of the Taylor & Francis Group, an informa business

Publisher's Note
The publisher has gone to great lengths to ensure the quality of this reprint but points out that some imperfections in the original copies may be apparent.

Disclaimer
The publisher has made every effort to trace copyright holders and welcomes correspondence from those they have been unable to contact.

A Library of Congress record exists under LC control number:

ISBN 13: 978-1-138-38675-4 (hbk)
ISBN 13: 978-0-429-42661-2 (ebk)

VARIORUM COLLECTED STUDIES SERIES CS623

CONTENTS

Preface   vii-x

Acknowledgements   xi

IMMORTALS

I   Immortality-Seeking in Early Chinese Poetry   103-118
        The Power of Culture: Studies in Chinese Cultural
        History, eds. W. J. Peterson, A. H. Plaks, Y.-s. Yü.
        Shatin, N.T., Hong Kong: The Chinese University Press, 1994

II   The Wang Ziqiao Stele   77-83
        Rocznik Orientalistyczny 47, no. 2. Warsaw, 1991

III   Ts'ao Chih and the Immortals   15-57
        Asia Major, Third Series, 1, no. 1. Princeton, 1988

IV   From Scepticism to Belief in Third-Century China   311-317
        A Festschrift in Honour of Professor Jao Tsung-i on the Occasion
        of His Seventy-Fifth Anniversary. Hong Kong: The Institute of
        Chinese Studies, The Chinese University of Hong Kong, 1993

FESTIVALS

V   The Cold Food Festival in Early Medieval China   51-79
        Harvard Journal of Asiatic Studies 46, no. 1. Cambridge, Mass., 1986

VI   Songs for the Gods: The Poetry of Popular Religion
        in Fifth-Century China   1-19
        Asia Major, Third Series, 3, no. 1. Princeton, 1990

VII   Une fête chez Su Shih à Huang chou en 1082   121-137
        Études Song. In memoriam Étienne Balazs, Sung Studies, éd.
        Françoise Aubin (série II, civilisation 2). Paris: EHESS, 1980

POETRY

VIII   La poésie de Ji Kang   107-177, 323-378
        Journal Asiatique 248, nos. 1/2, 3/4. Paris, 1980

IX   Folk Ballads and the Aristocracy   345-358
      Études chinoises 13, no. 1/2. Paris: Association
      Française d'Études Chinoises, 1994

X   Xie Lingyun et les paysans de Yongjia   115-127
      Hommage à Kwong Hing Foon: Études d'histoire culturelle
      de la Chine, éd. J.-P. Diény. Paris: Institut des Hautes
      Études Chinoises, 1995

XI   The Image of the Merchant in Medieval   92-108
      Chinese Poetry
      Ganz allmählich : Festschrift für Günther Debon, ed. R. Ptak
      and Siegfried Englert (Heidelberger Bibliotheksschriften 23).
      Heidelberg, 1986

Addenda and Corrigenda   1-3

Index   1-9

PREFACE

All of the articles that make up this second Variorum volume of my writings concern medieval China (except one, VII), and all of them (again, except for one, article XI), concern early medieval China. After I began my study of Chinese history, I was soon attracted to the period extending from the third to the seventh centuries AD because, it seemed to me,) that a new type of spirituality had entered Chinese civilization during those centuries, a new concern for a type of religious salvation unkown in Antiquity. In most of the articles contained in this volume I have attempted to bring to light different aspects of this new type of religiosity.

The first four articles are directly concerned with "immortals" in early medieval China, those strange beings who begin to figure so prominently in popular religion and in literature around the third century BC. The first article is really a general introduction in which I try to define the role that immortals played in poetry from the Former Han dynasty to the mid third century AD. I attempt to show that, although it seems clear that belief in the immortals was wide-spread in all classes of society throughout this period, in poetry the immortal seems to figure solely as an allegorical figure. When they say they want to "follow the imortal", the poets are actually saying they are unsatisfied with the world of politics. I deal in detail with this problem in article III.

The second article is built around the translation of an inscription by Cai Yong that describes the cult held in honor of one of the most famous and earliest of the "immortals" named Wangzi Qiao. It shows us that in AD 165 Wangzi Qiao was honored by the emperor and adored by the common people who came in droves to the place of his apparition in order to worship him and benefit from his aura.

In the third article I have attempted to analyze in detail the attitude of a single poet, Cao Zhi, toward the immortals as they are described in his verse. Cao Zhi has not only left us with a considerable number of poems that sing of the immortals, but also leaves a long essay telling us that not only did he not believe in their existence, but that, even if they did exist, he had no desire to become one. There can be little doubt that in his poetry the immortals play an allegorical role, but there is some possibility that, toward the end of his relatively short life, he mellowed and that the idea of seeking immortality became more appealing to him as he finally realized that he would be unable to achieve his political ideals.

The last article in this first group (article IV) shows that belief in immortals was so wide-spread around the mid third century AD that even literate men

viii

were convinced that they actually existed. I translate a group of texts that describe what is purported to be a liaison between a mortal man, a lowly scribe in a provincial yamen, and an immortal woman, sent down from heaven as a favor for her good works as handmaiden to the gods so that she can enjoy connubial bliss here below. The tale appears in collections of stories of the occult, but there is no doubt in my mind that it represents a faithful portrayal of contemporary beliefs in all levels of society.

Article V, on the origins of a festival still celebrated throughout China, the Cold Food Festival, is the first of three articles that have festivals as their main theme. I was particularly interested in this festival because of the large number of theories that have been elicited as to its origin by, among others, Frazer, de Groot, Eberhard, and Lévi-Strauss. These theories, all different and, in the main , contradictory, made me curious to find out which, if any of them, were valid. I felt that only through a thorough history of the festival and, especially, of the reasons the Chinese themselves have formulated for celebrating it throughout the centuries could we hope to find the answer or, more probably, the answers. The wealth of allusions to and descriptions of the festival I was able to find in a great number of old histories show that its origins and history are extremely complicated and do not permit any easy answer, but I believe they make it impossible to accept any of the theories formulated by the anthropologists I have named. The fact that this festival cannot be proved to be typical of what pass for being "universal" myths— sun worship or purification ceremonies or the like— but that it celebrates the exemplary morality of a loyal official tells a great deal about the originality of Chinese civilization.

"Songs for the Gods"(article VI) studies eleven popular songs from the early fifth century A.D. Only a few of the songs in themselves have literary value, but, taken together, they give us a precious glimpse of early medieval popular religion whose forms of worship were so successfully combatted by the three established religions, Confucianism, Daoism and Buddhism, that we know next to nothing of them today.

The last article in the group devoted to festivals again treats the Cold Food Festival, but this time rather late in its history because it concerns the festival as Su Shi celebrated it in 1082 when in internal exile in Huangzhou (today called Huanggang in Hubei province). Over five hundred years separate the celebration of the festival by Su Shi and the festival as I left it in article V. By Su Shi's time the festival had become inextricably entwined with the ritual visit to the family tombs on the 105th day after the winter solstice (called qingming), a practice that appeared only during the Tang dynasty and is still flourishing today among the Chinese.

The last four articles grouped under the rubric "Poetry" concern the whole of the period that is today generally considered to be China's Middle Ages, the period from the fall of the Han to the fall of the Tang, roughly from the third to the end of the ninth centuries. The first of these articles (article

VIII) is a study and translation of the whole corpus of the the poetry (excluding his *fu*) of Ji (also called Xi) Kang. Although better known for his philosophical essays than for his poetry, Ji Kang was, after Ruan Ji (210-263), the most important poet of the mid third century and his poetry is interesting not only for the light it throws upon his biography and thought but as an early example of philosophical poetry that had its influence on the great mode for "Metaphysical Poetry" that flourished during the following century. A translation by Peter Rushton of Ji Kang's eighteen poems written to his elder brother appeared in the *Journal of the American Oriental Society* 99, no. 2 (1979) at about the same time my own translation appeared.

The next article (article IX) studies poetry that dates from around the mid fifth century, two centuries after Ji Kang, a new type of popular poetry that sang of the joys and sorrows of the common people with total disregard of the Confucian gentleman's moral commitment to his role as a state official considered to be an essential quality in earlier poetry. It is perhaps not strange that some of this quite un-political, folk poetry should be attributed to members of the ruling class, often to men in the forefront of political life, because poetry was a natural form of expression for the literati in China, but I found it impossible to understand why there should be so many far-fetched and conflicting political explanations of why these men wrote what looks like innocent verse describing the lives of humble peasants. I reach a conclusion that may sound like it belongs to reasoning of the type *se non è vero è ben' trovato*, but I believe some sort of explanation is necessary for what looks like special pleading to find a place for this new sort of folk poetry within the great Confucian tradition of literature committed to service of the state.

The subject of the next article (article X), Xie Lingyun, has been considered since the times of his earliest critics to be a spoiled aristocrat, interested only in participating in goverment as a close associate of the emperor and disdainful of any less prestigious employment in the government. However, three poems written while he was employed as a lowly local official far from the capital in 422/3 show a quite different side of his character. These poems reveal a real interest in the welfare of the peasants in his charge and provide proof that, despite the aristocratic haughtiness that he presented to the world when he was unemployed in state affairs, he was thoroughly conscious of his duties when placed in a position that required him to look after peasants suffering from natural catastrophes that occurred during his tour of duty.

The last article in this volume (article XI) discusses merchants as they appear in poetry during the Middle Ages. Towards the beginning of the ninth century, in the works of Bai Juyi and his circle, merchants are mercilessly decried as fierce and soulless exploiters of the innocent peasantry. Nevertheless, a study of earlier and later poetry shows that this attitude was far from the only one held by the literati. On the contrary, in earlier and later verse the merchants are portrayed with sympathy.

Finally I would like to thank those who have helped me in the preparation of the articles collected here: Celia Hoare and John Smedley in London and Hubert Delahaye and Paul Leu in Paris.

DONALD HOLZMAN

Triel-sur-Seine, France,
21 March 1998

ACKNOWLEDGEMENTS

Grateful acknowledgement is made to the following persons, journals, institutions and publishers for their permission to reproduce the articles included in this volume: the Chinese University Press (for article I); *Rocznik Orientalistyczny* (II); *Asia Major* (III and VI); The Institute of Chinese Studies, Chinese University, Hong Kong (IV); *Harvard Journal of Asiatic Studies* (V); the École des Hautes Études en Sciences Sociales (VII); the Société Asiatique (VIII); *Études Chinoises* (IX); the Institut des Hautes Études Chinoises (X); and the Heidelberger Verlagsanstalt u. Druckerei GmbH (XI).

PUBLISHER'S NOTE

The articles in this volume, as in all others in the Variorum Collected Studies Series, have not been given a new, continuous pagination. In order to avoid confusion and to facilitate their use where these same studies have been referred to elsewhere, the original pagination has been maintained wherever possible.

Each article has been given a Roman number in order of appearance, as listed in the Contents. This number is repeated on each page and is quoted in the index entries.

Corrections noted in the Addenda and Corrigenda have been marked by an asterisk corresponding to the relevant text to be amended.

I

Immortality-Seeking in Early Chinese Poetry

The theme of immortals from its inception in Chinese poetry around the middle of the second century B.C. until the end of the third century A.D. superficially seems not to change much at all. In a larger time frame, from the earliest texts in the *Chuci* down to the poets in the Middle Ages, the immortals mentioned remain the same. In the vast majority of cases, they are Wangzi Qiao 王子喬, "Prince Qiao," and Chisongzi 赤松子, "Master Red Pine" or "Red Pine Cone". The astral voyages, nostrums of Long Life granted by strange figures, Taoist allusions, and mountain itineraries vary only slightly. And yet there is a subtle but important change that shows that poets during the third century A.D. have accepted new values and come to look upon the immortals in an almost completely new light,. *

Perhaps the best way to begin is to ask just what the "immortals" were and why I, and most sinologues, have chosen that translation of their name. The Chinese word I am translating is *xian* 僊, or 仙, which the earliest dictionaries gloss as "To fly away, having attained Long Life" 長生僊,[1] or "To live to an old age without dying" 老而不死曰仙.[2] For us "Long Life" or "old age" are quite a different matter from "immortality," but for the Chinese, with their innate distaste for metaphysical concepts, it is, I believe, as close as they are willing to come to our absolute definition of the term. I believe the term "immortal," that is *xian*, first appears around the third century B.C. when immortality-seeking becomes a widespread religious phenomenon. With the decay of the ancient religions on both sides of the Old World, the search for some kind of personal salvation gave rise to a new kind of religiosity in which the search for immortality played a predominant role. Men in the Mediterranean world were no longer willing to descend to some Sheol of Hades after death, nor were the Chinese satisfied any more with travelling to the Yellow Springs below the earth at the end of their lives. The Mediterraneans

---

[1] Xu Shen 許慎 (30–124), *Shuowen jiezi* 說文解字, (Peking: Zhonghua shuju, 1963), 8A, p. 13b (p. 167). I accept the emendation by Duan Yucai (1710–1803) that the word I have translated as "fly away" should be written without the "Man" radical, that is 僊 should be 䙴; see *Shuowen jiezi zhu* 說文解字注 (Shanghai: Feiyingguan 蜚英館, 1888) 8A, p. 10a.

[2] Liu Xi 劉熙 (fl A.D. 200), *Shi ming* 釋名, (Congshu jicheng ed.), 3(10), p.43. The explanation continues: "The word 'immortal' means to remove [*qian* 遷] into the mountains. Thus the character is formed by writing a 'mountain' next to a 'man.'"

sought for some kind of transcendence, an eternal new life in heaven; the Chinese, whose view of what constituted the soul was more psychosomatic, sought a corporeal Long Life which could be terrestrial or celestial, or a bit of both at once.[3] The religion of the immortals was invented to replace the Old Religion, sometimes converting the old gods and goddesses such as Xiwangmu 西王母, the Queen Mother of the West, into immortals, but more often inventing new ones whose only claim to fame was precisely that they had attained Long Life or "immortality."[4]

The problem is of course not as simple as I have stated it here. Some scholars believe the search for immortality existed from earliest times.[5] The earliest kings are, like the Japanese emperor, wished "ten thousand years" or "ten thousand longevities without end" in the Book of Poetry,[6] and they are treated like gods after their death, interceding for their descendants with the Sovereign-on-High (Shang-di). There are other reasons adduced that would have us believe in the existence of "immortality" in archaic China, but I find none of them convincing. I agree with Gu Yanwu 顧炎武 (1613–1682) who says, in a terse phrase: "Immortals begin to be mentioned only at the end of the Zhou dynasty".[7] Sima Qian 司馬遷 (145–86 B.C.) dates immortality-seeking to the fourth century B.C., in the northeast of China, and I think his testimony is the best we have today.[8]

The first poems to use immortals as their subject are also mentioned by Sima

[3] Some of these questions are discussed by Joseph Needham in his *Science and Civilisation in China*, (V2), pp. 71–85 (Cambridge University Press, 1974); his discussion of the early history of the immortals on pp. 93–113 is the best and most complete I have found. The ambiguous attraction of adepts, sometimes towards celestial immortality, sometimes towards terrestrial immortality, is discussed in the second chapter of Wolfgang Bauer's interesting *China and the Search for Happiness*, (New York: The Seabury Press, 1976), pp. 89–109. See also Yü Ying-shih, "Life and Immortality in the Mind of Han China," *HJAS* 25 (1964–65), pp. 80–122, and "'O Soul, Come Back!': A Study in the Changing Conceptions of the Soul and Afterlife in Pre-Buddhist China," *HJAS* 47/2 (1987), pp. 363–395.

[4] Here I part company with David Hawkes who, in a remarkable essay called "The Supernatural in Chinese Poetry," *University of Toronto Quarterly* 30.3 (April, 1961), pp. 311–324, does not distinguish between what he calls the "Old Religion" and the religion of the immortals. He quite correctly emphasizes the allegorical element in the poetry I am about to discuss, but he does not distinguish the ways allegory is used in the *Chuci* from the ways it is used in the poets of the third century A.D. or even in Tang poets such as Li Bo and Li He.

[5] See the discussion in Nakagome Kisou 中込競, "Yūsen bungaku genryū kō" 遊仙文學源流考, *Tōkyō gakugei daigaku kenkyū hōkoku* 8 (1957), pp. 32–35 (pp. 428–431), and Tang Yizhang 唐亦璋, "Shenxian sixiang yu youxian shi yanjiu" 神仙思想與遊仙詩研究, *Danjiang xuebao* (Taibei) 14 (1976), pp. 122–124.

[6] See, for example, *Shi jing* 154, 166, 172, 209–211.

[7] *Ri zhi lu* 日知錄 30, p. 28 (Wanyou wenku edition); Gu makes a similar statement in his "Laoshan zhi xu" 勞山志序 (Sibu congkan edition), 2, p. 18b.

[8] *Shi ji* 史記 28, pp. 1368–1370 (of the Peking: Zhonghua shuju, 1975 edition; these punctuated editions of the dynastic histories will be quoted throughout this paper); E. Chavannes, *Les mémoires historiques de Se-ma Ts'ien*, (Paris: Adrien-Maisonneuve, 1967), vol. 3, pp. 435–437.

Qian: "The First Emperor of the Qin was unhappy; he ordered the Erudite Scholars to compose poems on the immortals and True Men."[9] These poems are lost.[10]
The First Emperor and Emperor Wu of the Han dynasty (reigned 141–87 B.C.)
were both ardent immortality-seekers. The latter, after having heard the story of
the apotheosis as an immortal of the Yellow Emperor, carried to heaven on the
back of a dragon, said: "Ah! If I could really do what the Yellow Emperor did, I
would leave my wife and children as easily as I slough off a pair of straw sandals!"[11]
These are strong words and show that immortality-seeking was of the greatest
interest for the Han emperor, as it had been for the First Emperor of the Qin.[12]

The first poems still in existence that actually use the names of the immortals
appear in the *Chuci* 楚辭, "The Songs from the South,"[13] but not in the earliest
poems of that collection, not in the "Lisao" 離騷, "On encountering sorrow", nor
"Jiu ge" 九歌, "The nine songs," nor "Tian wen" 天問, "Heavenly questions," nor
in any of the other early poems. This in itself is interesting: the earliest poems to
use the theme of the immortals still in existence are of Han date and probably no
earlier than around 140 B.C., at the beginning of the reign of Emperor Wu. The
theme is used in these poems in two ways: either to describe a mystical voyage in
which the hero is indistinguishable from the True Men of the *Zhuangzi*, more
interested in experiencing union with the *dao* than in immortality-seeking, or to
serve as an allegory for a pure official retreating from public life, unable to bear the
corruption of the court or the lack of understanding of his sovereign.

The first theme is represented by only one poem, the "Distant voyage," "Yuan
you" 遠遊, a poem that imitates the "Lisao," but is quite original. It became the
model for most of the poems on the immortals that appeared after it, and there are
allusions to it in many of them. Although the poem is concerned with a religious
experience, it actually begins in the same manner as the allegorical poems, saying
that the basic impetus for the "distant voyage" is flight from "the parlous state of

---

[9] *Shi ji* 6, p. 259; Chavannes, *Mémoires historiques*, 2, p. 183.

[10] The earliest hymns of this type still in existence are those written for Emperor Wu of the Han
dynasty, perhaps in imitation of those ordered by the First Emperor. They are found in the *Han shu*
漢書 22, pp. 1052–1070; translation by E. Chavannes, *Mémoires historiques*, 3, pp. 612–629. The
resemblances in these hymns to the ballads on immortality-seeking are discussed in Konishi
Noboru 小西昇, "Kandai gafu shi to shinsen shisō" 漢代樂府詩と神仙思想, *Mekata Makoto
hakase kanreki kinen: Chūgokugaku ronshū*, (Tokyo, 1964), pp. 137–141.

[11] *Shiji* 28, p. 1394; Chavannes, MH 3, p. 489.

[12] And for, among many others, Zhang Liang 張良 (d. 189 B.C.), who, at the end of his life,
"wanted to give up human affairs and spend all his time roaming with [the immortal] Red Pine-
cone"; *Shiji* 55, p. 2048; translation in B. Watson, *Records of the Grand Historian of China*, (New
York and London; Columbia University Press, 1961), vol. 1, p. 150.

[13] Poems from the Chuci will be quoted from David Hawkes, *The Songs of the South: An* ✱
Anthology of Ancient Chinese Poems by Qu Yuan and Other Poets, (Harmondsworth, Eng.: Penguin
Books, 1985), but the translations may sometimes be modified to fit my terminology.

this world's ways" (1.1), from the "time of foulness and impurity" (1.5) in which the poet lived. At least four immortals are mentioned: Red Pine Cone (1.23), Han Zhong 韓衆 (1.30), the Yellow Emperor (Xuanyuan 軒轅, 1.53), and Wangzi Qiao (11.54–56), and there are references to immortality-seeking practices, to the Feathered Men on Cinnabar Hill (1.71), etc. The general tenor of the poem is in the more philosophical vein of the *Zhuangzi*, and the main aim of the author seems not to be immortality at all, but mystical experience. The poem ends with the poet in a stupor, transported out of heaven and earth, hearing nothing and seeing nothing.

I contend that this grandfather of all the "wandering immortal" poems to come is closer to philosophical Taoism than it is to the immortality-seekers. The relations between the two are, of course, close. Zhuangzi's True Men, *zhenren* 眞人, are very close to being immortals. Xu Shen 許慎 (30–124), in his invaluable diction-ary, the *Shuowen jiezi* 說文解字, goes so far as to define the word for "true," *zhen*, as meaning "immortal,"[14] but I believe there is an important difference between True Men in philosophical Taoism and the immortals. Zhuangzi is not interested in immortality-seeking as such; on the contrary, he "equates life and death," which has, in fact, earned him the opprobrium of the medieval immortality-seekers such as Ge Hong 葛洪.[15] The word "immortal" (*xian*) is only used once in his work (in Chapter 12),[16] and I believe the traditional critics are right in seeing this reference, and other references to immortal-like creatures, to be allegorical. The First Emper-or and Emperor Wu perhaps conceived of their immortality in Taoist terms, but what they were after was not the mystical experience, but Long Life, life without end. The difference is an important one, and must be kept in mind if we are to discover the meaning behind the poems we are going to read: Zhuangzi and the ancient philosophers in general were simply not interested in immortality and, in

[14] *Shuowen jiezi* 8A, p. 15a (p. 168): "an immortal who transforms his body and rises to heaven." Since the word *zhen* is used in early texts and found in bronze inscriptions, this is enough to per-suade Duan Yucai (*loc. cit.*, note 1 above) that "'true men' [i.e., immortals] existed before the times of [the legendary inventor of writing] Cang Jie." I disagree; the non-existence of the word for immortal (*xian*) in ancient texts seems to me stronger proof of the non-existence of the concept than this arbitrary definition by Xu Shen that is not generally accepted today as the real etymol-ogy. Cf., e.g., Tōdō Akiyasu 藤堂明保, *Kanji gogen jiten* 漢字語源辭典, (Tokyo: Gakutōsha, 1976), pp. 743–745.

[15] *Baopuzi* 抱朴子, "Neipian" 8, translation by J.R. Ware, *Alchemy, Medicine and Religion in the China of* A.D. *320: The Nei P'ien of Ko Hung*, (New York: Dover Publications, Inc., 1981; first edition, 1966), p. 142; Ch. 14, p. 229.

[16] Translation in B. Watson, *The Complete Works of Chuang-tzu*, (New York and London: Columbia University Press, 1968), p. 130. A.C. Graham, *Chuang-tzu: The Seven Inner Chapters*, (London: George Allen and Unwin, 1981), pp. 176–180, devotes a short chapter to the "cult of immortality" in *Zhuangzi*. He finds "only two passages which recommend the pursuit of immortality" and insists upon the probability of their being of late date, and in any case contrary to the spirit of philosophical Taoism.

spite of the fact that they have chosen to describe their heros in Taoist garb, the immortality-seekers differ considerably from the philosophical Taoists on this crucial point.

Thus I believe this first poem to mention the immortals is not primarily interested in immortality at all, and I believe the very similar poem by Sima Xiangru 司馬相如 (179–117 B.C.), the "Great man fu" ("Daren fu"), helps support my argument. Sima Qian tells us, in his biography of Sima Xiangru, that the latter wrote (or, more exactly, revised) the poem to flatter Emperor Wu's liking for the "way of the immortals" (xian dao 僊道). He also tells us that Sima Xiangru felt that the traditional view of xian half starved to death and lurking in the wilderness was not in keeping with imperial ideas of what immortals should be like, and wrote his poem with this in mind. In fact, Sima Xiangru's poem has none of the names of the immortals found in the "Distant voyage," and it includes two lines against immortality-seeking that the best Western interpreter of Sima Xiangru thinks reveal the meaning of the entire work.[17] After showing the Queen Mother of the West, an ancient goddess become patron of the immortality-seekers, crouching in a cave, the poet adds:

> If not to die means we must live out our Long Lives
> > like this [in a damp cave],
> We would have no joy were we to live ten thousand ages.[18]

His poem is, in fact, the description of a mystical journey very similar to the "Distant voyage," and closer, I believe, to the philosophers than to the Long Life seekers.

The second way the theme of the immortals is used in the Chuci, as political allegory, is even more common and has even less to do with immortality-seeking. The poet leaves on a mystical voyage, feels the exhilaration of astral swooping, the joys of listening to heavenly music and of frequenting the Jade Maidens, but these things are, in the final analysis, unpleasing to him. What the poet really wants is a good job in the government under a ruler who will understand him. The poem "Sorrow for Troth Betrayed" ("Xi shi 惜誓"), probably written about the same time as the "Distant voyage," is an example. It begins with a long and beautiful description of a mystical voyage which takes the poet beyond the western Kunlun Mountains, the habitual haunt of the immortals, as far west as Da Xia 大夏, Bactria in

---

[17] Yves Hervouet, Un poète de cour sous les Han: Sseu-ma Siang-jou (Bibliothèque de l'Institut des Hautes Etudes Chinoises, vol. XIX), (Paris: Presses Universitaires de France, 1964), p. 300. In these two lines, according to Hervouet, "Le poète a ainsi glissé dans son texte . . . la leçon qui fait le sens principal de son poème."

[18] Cf. Y. Hervouet, Le chapitre 117 du Che-ki (Bibliothèque de l'IHEC, vol. XXIII), Paris: Presses Universitaires de France, 1972, p. 200.

I

Central Asia, north of Afghanistan today. But his exaltation does not satisfy him, and he ends the mystical first half of his poem with the statement (11.33–34):

> But then I thought I would rather return to my old home
> Than enjoy Long Life forever among the immortals.[19]

The last half of the poem laments the plight of an honorable man in a dishonest world. There can be no doubt that the poet is using the immortals and the theme of the "Distant voyage" in this poem allegorically. By saying that he will "follow the immortals" he is declaring he can no longer live in the corruption of the capital. He is (as he himself puts it) like the phoenix or the unicorn, legendary beasts who are symbols of a saintly man, and they, like him, can only live in a virtuous environment. And so it is with the other poems in the *Chuci* that describe immortals and mystical voyages. The poet is telling us he wants to leave the world of politics because he is slandered and misunderstood; he is not interested in the pursuit of immortality itself.

We find this same lack of interest in the poets who lived a century or so later, in spite of continued imperial patronage of immortality-seeking. Huan Tan 桓譚 (43 B.C.?–A.D. 28?) wrote a "*Fu* on the immortals," "Xian fu" 仙賦, for the emperor Cheng 成 (reigned 33–7 B.C.), but it is a formal description made to amuse or perhaps amaze an emperor by a poet who had little interest and no belief in the immortals.[20] A little over a century later still we find another, and greater poet, Zhang Heng 張衡 (78–139), writing on this same theme in a *fu* called "Pondering the Mystery," "Sixuan fu" 思玄賦.[21] Zhang Heng was a great scientist, the inventor of a seismograph, and astronomer, and a rationalist. It would be strange to find him a fervent believer in the immortals and a fellow-traveller on the mystical voyage. As David Knechtges has clearly shown, Zhang Heng is writing allegory, or, more precisely, satire. Knechtges says: "Chang [i.e., Zhang Heng] manipulates his description of it [the mystical journey] to show that mystical escape is an unsatisfying and ineffective solution to his dilemma. In two of the directions that his travels take him he not only fails to find solace for his grief, but he experiences great discomfort (the south is unbearably hot, and the north freezing cold)."[22]

---

[19] D. Hawkes, *The Songs of the South*, p. 240.

[20] Translations by Timoteus Pokora, "Huan T'an's '*Fu* on Looking for the Immortals' (*Wang-hsien fu*)," *Archiv orientalni* (Prague) 28 (1960), pp. 353–367, and *Hsin-lun and other Writings by Huan T'an* (Michigan Papers in Chinese Studies, No. 20), (Ann Arbor: Center for Chinese Studies, 1975), pp. 231–232.

[21] Text in *Hou Han shu* 後漢書 59, pp. 1914–1938, and in *Wenxuan* 文選 15, pp. 1a–19b (of the Hu Kejia edition, Taibei, 1967).

[22] "A Journey to Morality: Chang Heng's The Rhapsody Pondering the Mystery," *Essays in Commemoration of the Golden Jubilee of the Fung Ping Shan Library (1932–1982)* (Hong Kong, 1982), p. 181. Zhang Heng's interest in the immortals is perhaps similar to that of Ban Gu (32–92). At the very end of the bibliographical monograph of the *Han shu* 30, p. 1780, the latter underlines

In all the immortal wanderings we have looked at so far, we find only allegory and satire or, in the "Distant voyage," a description of the mystical experience for itself. This disaffection for the immortals is all the more remarkable when we realize how widespread the religion was. The number of representations of immortals at this period on bronze mirrors, lacquer bowls, tomb paintings, and stone reliefs is truly impressive.[23] The resistance of the intellectuals to all this shows how strongly they were inspired by Confucian rationalism, and how conservative they were, how unwilling to accept new ideas, even when they were ideas cherished by the emperor. This intellectual atmosphere began to change in the second century, as can be seen by the fact that the court had official rituals performed in honor of the Taoist saints, for Laozi in 165 in Ku (or Hu) xian 苦縣, his supposed birthplace in Henan, and for Laozi and the Yellow Emperor the following year in the imperial palace itself, accompanied by the most solemn ritual music and elaborate ritual trappings.[24] There can be no doubt that among the common people fervor for the Taoist religion was extraordinary. An inscription of 165 attributed to Cai Yong 蔡邕 (133?–192) describes the site of an apparition of Wangzi Qiao in what is today eastern Henen in terms that, with only slight changes in vocabulary, could ✳ be applied to Lourdes or Czestochowa: "The Taoist adepts came from far and wide. Some strummed zithers and sang of the Great Unity; others meditated [so that they seemed] to soar over Cinnabar Mountain. The sick and weak were cured straight away when they bowed and prayed in silence, but those who lacked respect were struck down immediately."[25] The "meditations" that led to "soaring over Cinnabar Mountain" were surely popular versions of the mystical voyages we have been reading about in the writings of the literati.

I imagine, too, that they are the source of the popular ballads (yuefu 樂府) that take up the theme of wandering immortal. Most of these ballads are extremely hard to date. There are hints of the theme among the earliest of them that can be dated to the reign of Emperor Wu around 100 B.C.,[26] and there are popular ballads

the hygienic and psychological benefits of immortality-seeking, but he is very severe against "those who devote all their time to it and who have brought about the proliferation of texts full of extravagant lies and far-fetched tales, a far cry from the teachings of the saintly kings of antiquity."

[23] The representations of immortals on bronze mirrors have been studied by Zhang Jinyi 張金儀, Han jing suo fanying de shenhua shuo yu shenxian sixiang 漢鏡所反映的神話說與神仙思想, (Taibei: Gugong bowuyuan, 1981).

[24] See Qing Xitai 卿希泰, Zhongguo daojiao sixiang shigang 中國道教思想史綱 1: Han Wei liang Jin Nanbeichao shiqi 漢魏兩晉南北朝時期, (Chengdu: Sichuan renmin chubanshe, 1981), pp. 54–55.

[25] Text contained in Quan shanggu sandai Qin Han Sanguo Liuchao wen 全上古三代秦漢三國六朝文: Quan Hou Han wen 全後漢文, pp. 3ab (Peking: Zhonghua shuju, 1958); translated in D. Holzman, "The Wang Ziqiao Stele," to appear in Rocznik orientalistyczny (Warsaw) 47,2 (1991), pp. 77–83, dedicated to J. Chmielewski.

[26] See above, note 10, and Chavannes, 3, pp. 620–621.

using the theme in various ways, sometimes allegorical or satirical, sometimes more straightforward. I would like to quote only one as an example, a relatively simple one, that will not require much annotation. It is probably not one of the oldest, because its title bears the name of a city gate of Loyang which was the capital of the latter Han in the first centuries of the Christian era, but it is typical of the genre of popular poetry that probably served as a model for later literati writers.

As I Stepped Out Summer Gate

1   On a side-path I passed an empty hut
          Where a virtuous man once had lived.
      He at last learned to be an immortal
          And rose to take his place in heaven.
5   Then in passing I called on Father King and Mother Queen,
          For I was on the side of Mt. Tai.
      A mile or two from heaven
          I met, on the way, with [Master] Red Pine.
      He grasped the reins and became my coachman,
10   Taking me up to roam through heaven.
      And what did I find there?
          White elms clearly planted out;
      Osmanthus trees growing on each side of the road;
          Green dragons facing one another as they crouched.[27]

Since "white elms," "osmanthus trees," and "green dragons" are all also names of constellations in the sky, this charming poem ends on a conceit that adds a note of humor. The Father King and Mother Queen are famous Taoist deities, the former the patron of the east and the latter the Queen Mother of the West whom we have already met.

This poem, it seems to me, is a variation on the kind of mystical meditation practiced at Wangzi Qiao's family tomb. This time the adept soars to heaven aided by Master Red Pine instead of "soaring over Cinnabar Mountain" with Wangzi Qiao. This ballad reflects popular Taoist religion. It is no longer the distortion of it to permit the literati poets to express their dissatisfaction with the world of politics. The poet here is using the theme of the immortals to celebrate an ideal world. Other ballads (such as "Shanzai xing" 善哉行, "How good it is!") describe the sadness of life on earth and seek solace in wine before finally escaping to the world

[27] Text in *Yuefu shiji* 樂府詩集 37, p. 545 (Peking: Zhonghua shuju, 1979 edition; translation in Sawaguchi Takeo 澤口剛雄, "Kan no gafu ni okeru shinsen dōka no shisō 漢の樂府における神山道家の思想, *Tōhō shūkyō* (Kyoto) 27 (1960), pp. 2–3, and Obi Kōichi 小尾郊一 and Okamura Sadao 岡村貞雄, *Kogafu* 古樂府, (Tokyo: Tōkai daigaku, 1980), pp. 163–165.

of the immortals. Still others end in celebration, wishing long life to the reader or to the assembled guests at a banquet where the ballad was sung ("Changge xing" 長歌行, "Long song", or "Dong Tao xing" 董逃行).[28] The theme of the immortals has thus had a new facet added to its meanings, but even this more straightforward, popular verse remains somewhat formal, less interested in immorality-seeking or Long Life than in the perhaps completely imaginary joys of heaven.

Literati reticence with the theme, however, has by no means been vanquished, even in the second century. The idea of attaining corporeal immortality seemed absurd to the intellectuals, as it seems to us today, and the excesses of religious fervor must have made religious Taoism extremely hard to take for the ruling class at the end of the Han dynasty. Two famous examples of their incredulity are to be found in Poems Nos. 13 and 15 of the Nineteen Old Poems:

> Those who take pills seeking to become immortals
> Are often duped by the drugs they take.

and

> Who can hope to equal the life span
> Of the immortal Wangzi Qiao?

But the very fact that the possibility of immortality has been questioned in verse is important here. It means that immortality-seeking has become a subject that can no longer be ignored or contorted; personal religion was at last imposing its presence on the Confucian literati.

Cao Cao 曹操 (155–220), Cao Pi 丕 (186–226), and Cao Zhi 植 (192–233), the founder of the Wei dynasty and his two sons, are the most important poets of the early third century and they are also the first known poets (the Nineteen Old Poems are anonymous) to have discussed the subject of the immortals in their verse. Each poet in this extraordinary family has a different attitude toward the subject: Cao Cao seems seriously attracted to immortality-seeking; Cao Pi rejects it out of hand; Cao Zhi, after having written a violent diatribe against it in his youth, seems to have mellowed in old age and used the theme in his verse with sympathy.

Cao Cao's two sons insist that their father's interest in immortality was purely political. According to them he gathered the most famous among the entire nation's Long Life seekers in the capital solely in order to keep them from fomenting another rebellion similar to the Yellow Turbans' that brought the Han dynasty to its end and caused more bloodshed than China had probably ever seen.[29] Other

---

[28] See the article by Sawaguchi Takeo mentioned above.

[29] For Cao Pi, see *Quan Sanguo wen* 8, p. 6b, where he quotes his brother's "Analysis of Taoism," "Bian dao lun" 辯道論, translated by D. Holzman, "Ts'ao Chih and the Immortals", *Asia Major* 1.1 (1988), pp. 47–48.

texts insist that Cao Cao was interested in these magicians' "art of prolonging life" for itself and that he actually practiced it.[30] The *Hou Hanshu* tells us that three magicians "were chosen for official posts by Cao Cao, who questioned them about their arts in order to put them into practice. . . . All these men were aged over a hundred years, and some attained two hundred years of age."[31] I suppose we could discount these texts by saying their authors surely knew less about Cao Cao's beliefs than his own sons or that his interest in Long Life was purely hygienic, his desire to prolong his years being not religious but political, to permit him to live long enough to be able to reunite the empire.[32]

A look at Cao Cao's own poetry, however, shows us that these secondary sources are credible.[33] He has written four ballads[34] on the theme of immortality. The first, which bears a Taoist-sounding title, is called " A song of vital breath exhaled," "Qichu chang" 氣出唱, and was probably written, like the other three, towards the end of Cao Cao's life. It is, like all his poetry, a ballad, and is very much like the ballad we just read, showing, in the first stanza, the poet driving six flying dragons and wandering about in immortal haunts. Finally, after calming his heart and taming his desires, he flies up to the Gate of Heaven where, kneeling in deep reverence, he receives divine drugs that will grant him immortality. In the last two stanzas we see that the ballad is a drinking song in which the poet celebrates his host and wishes him long life. A second ballad, "Mulberry trees at the side of the path," "Moshang sang" 陌上桑, is in the same vein.

The other two ballads are more interesting and more complex. The first, called "Dissolution of the vital essence," "Jing lie" 精列, sandwiches lines which express immortal longings ("I would like to live in the Kunlun and see the marvels there;/ My will is to reside in Penglai [immortal isles in the eastern sea]") between statements saying immortality is impossible. And the last ballad, the most interesting of all, is called "Qiu Hu" 秋胡, a man's name which has nothing to do with the contents of the poem. It is the longest Cao Cao wrote and the most complex and one of the most intimate. In the first stanza he shows himself in deep meditation, seated on a stone slab in the mountains, caressing the strings of a zither. A strange and

[30] See the quotation from the *Bowu zhi* 博物志 by Zhang Hua 張華 (232–300) in the commentary to *Sanguo zhi* 1, p. 54, and a text called "Order given to Huangfu Long 皇甫隆," attributed to Cao Cao by Sun Simiao 孫思邈 (581–682) in his *Qianjin fang* 千金方, "Priceless prescriptions," and found in *Quan Sanguo wen* 3, pp. 5b–6b.

[31] *Hou Han shu* 82B, p. 2750.

[32] See Komori Ikuko 小守郁子, "Sō Shaku ron" 曹植論, *Nagoya daigaku bungakubu kenkyū ronshū (Tetsugaku)* 69 (1976), pp. 291–292.

[33] And make me wonder if his sons were not attempting to whitewash what some Confucianists might take to be a dangerous penchant that could lead Cao Cao down the ruinous road pursued by the First Emperor of the Qin and Emperor Wu of the Han.

[34] For the texts see Lu Qinli 逯欽立, *Xian Qin Han Wei Jin nanbei chao shi* 先秦漢魏晉南北朝詩, (Peking: Zhonghua shuju, 1983), pp. 345–346, 348, 349–351.

extraordinary old man comes up to him and, after having asked Cao Cao why he is so melancholy, the old man says he is a True Man, an immortal, who lives in the Kunlun and visits the sacred peaks in the four quarters. Then Cao Cao continues:

> I hesitated, undecided,
>> And thus he rose to heaven. . . .
> He left me and I could not pursue him.
>> I will regret forever to have been pulled back
>> [by my worldly affairs]. . . .
> Night after night I seek sleep in vain,
>> Frustrated, full of self-pity. . . .

The poem continues and meanders from topic to topic, including a verse on immortal longing at the beginning of the second stanza, and ends on a singularly upbeat note as the poet assumes his duties as a national leader and spurns any other use of his talents as frivolity.[35] But the lines I have quoted, and, indeed, this entire poem, are very serious in tone. Cao Cao seems to be showing us his innermost thoughts as they come to him, and immortality-seeking occupies a place of honor.

Cao Pi, on the contrary, seems completely hostile in his prose and in his poetry to immortality-seeking. His most radical hostility is expressed in a ballad that has come down to us in two different versions with three or four different titles. The first two stanzas of the poem are a typical "wandering immortals" poem (which is one of the titles given to these first two stanzas); the last two stanzas condemn the search for immortality as a vanity that pleases only fools. They end with a rejection of unorthodoxy in any form. The last line declares: "What I observe is the Way of the Saints,"[36] meaning the saints of Confucianism.

[35] There are translations of this poem (or these poems, because the two stanzas are sometimes considered separate poems) by E. Balazs, *Chinese Civilization and Bureaucracy*, translation H.M. Wright, (New Haven: Yale University Press, 1964), pp. 182–186. (This is an English translation of an article in German which first appeared in *Monumenta serica* 2, 1936–1937); D. von den Steinen, "Poems of Ts'ao Ts'ao", *Monumenta serica* 4 (1939), pp. 153–156, 177–179; and (of the second stanza only), Frances LaFleur Mochida, "Structuring a Second Creation: Evolution of the Self in Imaginary Landscapes," in R. E. Hegel and R. C. Hessney, eds., *Expressions of Self in Chinese Literature*, (New York: Columbia University Press, 1985), pp. 92–95. There is a formal analysis of the ballads on the immortals of Cao Cao by Funazu Tomihiko 般津富彦, "Gi no butei no yūsen bungaku ni tsuite" 魏の武帝の遊仙文學について, *Yoshioka hakase kanreki kinen Dōkyō kenkyū ronshū*, (Tokyo, 1977), pp. 165–192, and articles concerning the subject appear almost every year in China. I have been able to read only Chen Feizhi 陳飛之 and He Rouxiong 何若雄, "Cao Cao de youxian shi" 曹操的遊仙詩, *Xueshu yuekan* (Shanghai) 1981, 5, pp. 43, 78–81, which gives a very traditional interpretation, refusing to recognize Cao Cao's aspiration towards immortality-seeking as sincere.

[36] Text in Lu Qinli, *Xian Qin* . . ., pp. 393–394, under the title "Zhe yangliu xing" 折楊柳行, "Picking a willow branch."

Cao Zhi is different from both his brother and his father. He devoted close to one quarter of his ballads to the theme of the immortals, that is, ten poems in all. This in itself is surprising in a man who wrote that even if he believed it possible to become an immortal (which was by no means the case) he would still prefer to remain as he was rather than be transformed into one of those strange feathered creatures (some kind of Papageno) who one could not be sure was a human being at all.[37] Of these ten ballads I believe five belong to the most ancient tradition of allegory as found in the *Chuci*; that is, Cao Zhi has used the theme of the immortals in them allegorically to describe his political fears and aspirations. The other five poems are less easy to define. They seem to spring directly from the celebratory popular ballads and to describe a purely imaginary world. But the *tone* of these poems is not humorous, and they do not end, as so many of the popular ballads do, on a set formula wishing long life to the assembled guests or to the emperor. They seem to me to be solemn, almost pathetic, and to spring directly from Cao Zhi's own biography, showing him attempting to free himself, in spirit if not in the flesh, from what amounted to imprisonment imposed upon him by his brother the emperor and then, after his brother's death, by his nephew, Emperor Ming. He is still using the immortals as symbols, as symbols of absolute freedom (as Sima Xiangru used them). He and his father and brother have, in the final analysis, rejected the pursuit of immortality as a goal, but their usage of the theme shows an evolution from the earlier, more formal and allegorical usage. The immortals now are a subject of debate in poetry and are treated for themselves.

They figure prominently again in the poetry of Ruan Ji 阮籍 (210–263) and Ji Kang 嵇康 (223–262), the two greatest poets of the Zhengshi 正始 (240–249) era. Over one fourth of Ruan Ji's eighty-two "Intimate poems," "Yonghuai shi" 詠懷詩, take the immortals as their theme. There can be no doubt that by the mid third century, when Ruan Ji wrote, immortality-seeking impinged itself upon the minds of the literary figures, however they used the theme. A superficial reading of Ruan Ji's verse gives the impression that he was himself an immortality-seeker, and, if we can believe an anecdote told about him, he did go into the mountains and seek out a strange immortal-like character called Sun Deng 孫登 and conversed with him. But actually they did not get on well together at all — until Ruan Ji started whistling. Ruan Ji's philosophical chit-chat bored Sun Deng to death, but his whistling, a non-conceptual art similar to the sounds of nature, pleased this Taoist figure.[38] Ruan Ji's poetry parallels this meeting: it shows him at heart a traditional philosopher, imbued with traditional values, but also an amateur Taoist, capable of mystical flights of fantasy. When we look closely into Ruan Ji's verse, we

---

[37] I have translated the diatribe and all the ballads in the article to mentioned in note 29 above.

[38] See D. Holzman, *Poetry and Politics: The Life and Works of Juan Chi*, (Cambridge: Cambridge University Press, 1976), pp. 150–151.

see that the immortals play a complicated role, but one that is not completely different from the role they played in the *Chuci*. They are used allegorically in most cases to show Ruan Ji wants to flee from the political corruption he sees about him, not to show that he actually wants to seek immortality. Ruan Ji's allegory is still different from that practiced by the poets of the *Chuci*. Although they never reject it, the *Chuci* poets seem ultimately uninterested in immortality-seeking. Although Ruan Ji ultimately rejects immortality-seeking as a possibility, he does so with a heavy heart. This heavy-heartedness shows Ruan Ji to be more deeply attracted to the immortals than were the poets of the *Chuci*. In the first twelve lines of Poem 41, for example, he describes the immortals enjoying Long Life far from the vicissitudes of the inconstant world. Then he alludes to the missions sent by the First Emperor and Emperor Wu to the Blessed Isles in the Eastern Sea to look for immortals that ended in failure. This proves to him that the accounts in the histories that describe immortals living in these isles are untrustworthy. He ends his poem with the lines:

> This has so oppressed me and filled me with doubt
> That I have been hesitant for a long time.[39]

In poem 78, again, after a quatrain that is typical of "wandering immortals" poems and shows the immortals driving dragons and nibbling jade flowers, Ruan Ji adds:

> That they can be heard of, but cannot be seen,
> Makes me sigh and groan with pent up passion.
> Pained that I am not of their kind,
> I feel sadness and bitterness well up within me.[40]

It is hard to reconcile this passion with artificial allegory. In the poetry of Cao Cao, Cao Zhi and Ruan Ji we see immortality-seeking gradually entering into the conscience of the poets, and in Ruan Ji we see it becoming a problem that can be called a religious dilemma.

Ji Kang also went to see Sun Deng — and he stayed with him for three years![41] More than any poet we have considered until now, Ji Kang was a believer in and practioner of immortality-seeking. He tells us so repeatedly in his prose, and the very last lines of the long poem he wrote before his execution reaffirm his desire to live the life of a Taoist adept in the mountains "nourishing his years."[42] It is not surprising, then, to find references to immortals in his poetry. What is more surprising is to find that these references are relatively few and that they lack

---

[39] *Ibid.*, pp. 180–181.

[40] *Ibid.*, p. 176.

[41] See D. Holzman, *La vie et la pensée de Hi K'ang*, (Leiden: E.J. Brill, 1957), pp. 42–43.

[42] D. Holzman, "La poésie de Ji Kang", *Journal asiatique* 218 (1980), pp. 354–356.

originality. One would expect that a man who says he has dedicated his life to the search for immortality would have exploited the subject more fully. One of his poems, the only one actually entitled "Wandering immortals," comes close to being allegorical. It begins with the description of a solitary pine, remaining green and faithful in the coldest weather, but growing so high up on the mountainside that it was impossible for the poet to approach it. The pine is obviously a symbol, but what it symbolizes is less clear. Ji Kang, when he realizes he cannot reach the pine, flies away with Wangzi Qiao and lives among the immortals. The last two lines again seem to suggest that he is writing allegorically. He ends his poem saying:

> I will leave the world of common men forever;
> No one will see where I have gone.[43]

Chen Zuoming 陳祚明 says that in this poem Ji Kang "is not expressing a real desire to become an immortal. All that he wants is to 'leave the world of common men forever.'"[44] Ji Kang has used the theme of the immortals in other poetry (in poems 6 and 7 of his ballads on the theme of Qiu Hu, for example),[45] but again without much originality, following his popular models very closely.

The Jian'an and Zhengshi eras mark a turning point in the treatment of immortals in poetry. The ancient allegorical tradition of course is still present, and will continue to exist, but the search for immortality as a valid subject for poetic expression has begun to appear in the works of such innovative poets as Cao Cao and Ruan Ji, and will become even more explicit in the poets of the Jin Dynasty soon to follow. Chenggong Sui 成公綏 (231–273), only eighteen years younger than Ji Kang, has written a suggestive poem entitled "The Immortal" in some editions, "Wandering Immortals" in others, in which he describes his longings for immortality ("my one desire is to live forever"[46]) in a new way, as something that seems a good in itself, unattached to political concerns. In the next generation, Guo Pu 郭璞 (276–324) has mixed allegorical tradition and straightforward description of immortality-seeking to create what is generally conceded to be the masterpiece of the "wandering immortals" genre.[47] But these works belong to another chapter in the history of Chinese literature.

My main interest here has been to show the origins of immortality-seeking in poetry, and to show how the poets for centuries refused to use the theme for itself,

---

[43] *Ibid.*, pp. 342–344. Zhuang Wanshou 莊萬壽, *Ji Kang nianpu* 稽康年譜, (Taibei: Sanmin shuju, 1981), p. 159, assigns this poem to 254, but gives no reason for doing so.

[44] *Caishutang gushi xuan* 采菽堂古詩選, quoted in Dai Mingyang 戴明揚, *Ji Kang ji jiaozhu* 稽康集校注, (Peking: Renmin wenxue chubanshe, 1962), p. 40.

[45] "La poésie de Ji Kang," pp. 339–341.

[46] Text in Lu Qinli, *Xian Qin . . .*, p. 584.

[47] Text in ibid., pp. 865–867.

I

preferring to see in it matter for allegory, either of the mystical experience or of retreat from political life. But why did they refuse to use the theme for itself, while immortality-seeking was so widespread, probably permeating the whole of society, from the emperor himself down to the peasants who went to pray at Wangzi Qiao's family tomb? There is no doubt in my mind that the reason for this refusal is to be found in the intellectual atmosphere of the times.

I believe that the poets whose work we have been studying shared a certain number of values with the philosophers of Antiquity in China, values that made it impossible for them to envisage the theme of immortality-seeking in their poetry as anything other than allegory. The ancient Chinese philosophers, from the sixth to the third centuries B.C., beginning with the first and greatest of them, Confucius, were single-mindedly interested in the state, in government, in politics, and, more widely, in the external world, the truth as it manifests itself objectively in the universe. They were hardly interested in religion, in man's fate as an individual, in his psychology, in his salvation from death. One of the most striking illustrations of the one-sidedness of the thinkers of the ancient period is the fact that, for something like three centuries, during the brilliant Golden Age of Chinese philosophy, from Confucius to the end of the fourth century, not a single poem worthy of the name has been preserved. I find it hard to believe none was written. I feel rather that the men of the period simply did not think poetry was worth being preserved, and when, around the beginning of the third century, it began to be preserved again, they made sure its themes were worthwhile. The *Chuci* illustrates this choice; the poets in it describe their political aspirations, their search for the absolute truth in the universe, or the shamanistic religion which is more concerned with the welfare of the state than it is for the salvation of the poet. At this time, when philosophers or writers happen to talk about the value of literature, they place it very low, insisting upon it as a vehicle for morality, or to keep a wayward emperor in tow. Yang Xiong 揚雄 (53 B.C.–A.D. 18), the greatest writer of his times, rejected his youthful literary output as childishness, "something that a grown man would not indulge in,"[48] and Cao Zhi, who was the greatest writer of his times, regarded his own poetry as frivolous, not worthy of comparison with political philosophy. Even Cao Pi, the author of a "declaration of independence" for literature, still sees it as "the great profession by which the state is governed."[49] All these men, and all those we have considered here, seem to have been interested almost exclusively in the external world, at least until the third century, when we see members of the Cao family, Ruan Ji, and Ji Kang questioning the veracity of immortality-seeking and toying with the idea of indulging in it themselves. They come closer than any

[48] *Fayan yishu* 法言義疏 3, p. la (Taibei: Yiwen yinshuguan, 1968).
[49] D. Holzman, "Literary criticism in China in the early third century A.D.", *Études asiatiques* (Bern) 28, 2 (1974), pp. 119, 131.

earlier poet to forsaking the allegorical tradition and actually using the theme to describe their search for personal salvation.

The poets of the next generation and those who follow them have no such prejudices. The grip politics held on men's minds was slowly loosening, as the centralized state itself lost its power, and the search for spiritual values began to ignore man's role in politics. Something like two generations after Cao Pi wrote his "Essay on Literature," in which he rather timidly showed the way towards autonomy while still insisting upon the role literature plays in the governing of the state, Lu Ji 陸機 (261–303) wrote a long poem, "On Literature," in which he ignores *completely* its role in politics.[50] Our long wandering among the immortals has allowed us to see how Chinese poets slowly and subtly altered their ideas of what was most important in their lives and in their poetry. After centuries of reluctance they finally welcomed the "new religion" into their verse and at the same time broadened and enriched the Chinese poetic tradition.[51]

[50] Paradoxically, Lu Ji's own poems on the theme of the wandering immortals are in the main allegorical.

[51] In an excellent article that I discovered only after I had written my own, Li Fengmao 李豐楙, "Liuchao daojiao yu youxian shi di fazhan" 六朝道教與遊仙詩的發展, *Zhonghua xueyuan* 中華學苑 28 (Taibei, Zhengzhi University, 1983), pp. 97–118, describes the development of the "wandering immortals" poetry from the end of the Han until the Sui, touching on the importance of the evolution of religious Taoist doctrine in this development. Isabel Robinet, "The Taoist Immortal: Jesters of Light and Shadow, Heaven and Earth," *Journal of Chinese Religions* 13/14 (1985–86), pp. 87–105, on the contrary, sees no changes in the conception of the immortal throughout the ages, from Zhuangzi (*sic*) to the Zhao Song dynasty. Finally, Wei Fengjuan 韋鳳娟, "Youxian shi de 'renjianhua' ji qi yuanyin" 遊仙詩的 "人間化" 及其原因, *Guangming ribao* 光明日報 (Peking) 11 August 1983 ("Wenxue yichan" No. 611), sees a "subtle change" in the description of the immortals in poetry in the penultimate decade of the third century (the Taikang 泰康 era), a "humanization."

II

The Wang Ziqiao Stele

It is well known that religious Taoism flourished in the first centuries of the Christian era in China and a good deal of scholarly work has been done to describe it. But, aside from a few pregnant remarks by M a s p e r o[1] and an excellent book by Anna S e i d e l on the deification of L a o z i[2], the relations of Taoism with the state and with the élite have been practically ignored, all the interest being focussed upon the popular, unofficial movements, the Yellow Turbans or the Taiping   ✱ jing. It is the aim of this paper to present and translate a short inscription that describes the establishment of an official cult to a Taoist saint in A. D. 165. The inscription is fairly well known to specialists, but, to my knowledge, it has never been studied or translated before.

The inscription is called "Wang Ziqiao bei" 王子喬碑 or "Xianren 仙人 Wang Ziqiao bei" and describes the apparition of the immortal Wang Ziqiao at the tomb next to which it was erected. There was a historical personage named Wang Qiao, a near homonym of the immortal, who lived under Emperor Ming (A. D. 58–75), about a century before the stele was erected, but I do not believe he has anything to do with this stele. Wang Qiao came from Hedong (present Shanxi),· and his tomb was in Ye 葉 (central Henan, about two hundred km to the east of the Wang Ziqiao stele). It is true that he was identified, at the end of his biography in the *Hou Hanshu*[3], as an incarnation of the immortal Wang Ziqiao, but his place of origin,

---

[1] See, for example, Henri M a s p e r o, *Le taoïsme et les religions chinoises*, Gallimard, Paris, 1971, pp. 463–466.

[2] Anna K. S e i d e l, *La divinisation de Lao tseu dans le taoïsme des Han* (Publications de l'Ecole Française d'Extrême-Orient, Vol. LXXI), Paris 1969.

[3] Hou Hanshu 82, p. 2712 of the Peking: Zhonghua shuju, 1973 ed.; good transla-   ✱ tion in N g o Van Xuyet, *Divination, magie et politique dans la Chine ancienne*, Presses Universitaires de France, Paris 1976, pp. 86–87, where Ye is romanized as „Che" (should be „Chö"), an old reading of the character.

Hedong, and his tomb were both so far from this stele, which was said to be located on the site of the Wang Ziqiao family tomb, that I believe he has nothing to do with the events described on it.

The stele was erected north of the city of Meng 蒙 (northeast of the present Shangqiushi 商丘市, Henan, near the Shandong border). Some three and a half centuries after it was erected Li Daoyuan 酈道元(d. 527) saw it there.[4] He does not tell us the name of the author of the insciption, but it appears in the works of C a i Yong 蔡邕 (133?-192) who was without doubt the greatest of the earliest writers of stele inscriptions.[5] Thirty inscriptions attributed to him are still in existence[6] and two were thought of high enough literary merit to be included in *Wenxuan* 58. The form used is typical of C a i Yong's other inscriptions, except that he is not interested here in writing a eulogy of Wang Ziqiao, only in describing the history of the tomb, the circumstances surrounding the apparition of the immortal, and the unofficial and then official ceremonies that took place at the site and turned it into a Taoist shrine. The trimeter verses that follow and recapitulate the prose are also typical of C a i Yong's inscriptions, although he usually prefers tetrameters.[7]

Wang Ziqiao's hagiography in the *Liexianzhuan* 列仙傳 [8] calls him a prince of the Zhou dynasty which may account for the fact that some versions of the inscription begin with the words, "the prince, *wangsun* 王孫, Ziqiao".[9]

---

[4] *Shuijingzhu* 水經注 23, p. 64 of the Guoxue jiben congshu edition Commercial Press, (Shanghai 1936).

[5] „From the Latter Han, when stele inscriptions appeared in great number, no one has written inscriptions with more trenchancy than C a i Yong", L i u Xie, *Wenxin diaolong* 12.

[6] And can be found in Yan Kejun 嚴可均, *Quan shanggu sandai Qin Han sanguo liuchao wen, Quan Hou Hanwen* 75-79 (Zhonghua shuju, Peking 1958).

[7] Two exceptions, also in trimeters, can be found in *Quan Hou Hanwen* 75, p. 8a, and 76, p. 6a.

[8] Translation in M. K a l t e n m a r k, *Le Lie-sien tchouan*, Centre d'Etudes Sinologiques de l'Université de Paris, Peking 1952, pp. 109-114.

[9] The text of the inscription presents considerable problems that I have not always had space enough to discuss in the notes. Aside from the editions mentioned in notes 3 and 6, I have consulted the Shuijing zhushu 疏 (Zhongguo Kexue yuan tushuguan, Peking 1955), the *Cai Zhonglang ji* 蔡中郎集 (in the Sibu congkan edition) and in the *Han Wei liuchao baisan mingjia ji* (Shanghai Saoye shanfang, 1925 ed.), and the *Li shi* 隸釋 20, pp. 16b-17b (Hongshi Huimuzhai congshu, 1871). I have used the *Shuijingzhu* as my basic text, printing the passages that only appear in the *Cai Zhonglang ji* version in italics.

The Wang Ziqiao Stele

Wang Ziqiao would seem to be the name of an antique Perfect Man. It is not known during which dynasty he first appeared as an immortal. Among the numerous Taoists I consulted some say he was from Yingchuan, some say he was born in Meng.[10] This tumulus has been here since the founding of the city and it has been called "the Wang family tomb" by word of mouth since early times. B u t t h e
f a m i l y l i n e w a s n o t c o n t i n u e d; t h e t o m b h a s b e e n
a b a n d o n e d w i t h o u t a n i n h e r i t o r f o r y e a r s b e y o n d
c o u n t i n g.

In the twelfth month of the first year of the Yonghe era, during the night of the All Saints Festival (17 January 137)[11], very plaintive crying was heard on the tomb.
Wang Bo王伯, who lived nearby, thought it strange, and when it became light he
ascended the tomb and investigated. There had been a heavy snowfall and no path had yet formed, but there were tracks of a large bird where sacrifices had been held, and the onlookers all took them to be supernatural.[12] Later a man wearing an official's hat and a scarlet unlined robe stood before the sepulture leaning upon a bamboo
staff. He called to the young wood-gatherer, Yi Yongchang 伊永昌, and said: "I am
Wang Ziqiao. You must not take the trees on our[13] grave mound!" In an inkling he disappeared.

The local magistrate, Wan Xi 萬熹 of Taishan[14], looked into what the elders
had to say about this and felt that there had been an extremely favorable supernatural
occurrence. H e h e l d a n i n q u e s t a n d b e l i e v e d t h e r e w a s
s u f f i c i e n t e v i d e n c e p r o v i n g t h a t m i r a c l e s h a d t r u l y
t a k e n p l a c e. He then had an ancestral temple built to rejoice the god [i.e. Wang Ziqiao]. Thereupon those who took delight in the *dao* came from distant places to assemble there. Some strummed zithers and sang of the Great One[15]; others practiced meditation to visit their Cinnabar Fields.[16] T h o s e w h o w e r e

---

[10] Yingchuan was a large commandery in central Henan, with its capital in the present Yuxian; Meng is the site of the Wang Ziqiao stele, in eastern Henan near the Shandong border.

[11] The All Saints (La 臘) festival is described in D. B o d d e, *Festivals in Classical China*, Princeton University Press, Princeton 1975, pp. 49–138.

[12] Wang Ziqiao is said to have risen to heaven on a white crane; cf. M. K a l-
t e n m a r k, op. cit., pp. 110–113.

[13] As will soon become clear, this is not Wang Ziqiao's own tomb; the other versions of the text say „my ancestors' tomb".

[14] Unknown.

[15] An important divinity since early Han times; see, for example, H. M a s-
p e r o, op. cit., pp. 398–400.

[16] Cinnabar Fields, *dantian* 丹田 , are points in the body upon which the Taoist adept concentrates during his meditations; see H. M a s p e r o, op. cit., pp. 360–363, 491–495.

sick or crippled and who silently bowed and prayed for good fortune were granted it straight away, but those who were lacking in respect were struck down immediately. Thus it was known that this was a tomb of great virtue, in truth the tomb of the ancestors of the Perfect Man.[17]

In the eighth month, in autumn, of the eighth year of the Yanxi era (165) the emperor sent an envoy to offer a sacrificial victim and perform a ritual. The purification [?] was accomplished with utmost reverence and dignity. The Counselor-

* Delegate Wang Zhang王璋 zi Boyi, of Donglai[18], felt that the place of origin of a divine saint required the erection of an inscription that would make it known to succeeding generations. It is thus that in Laixiang賴鄉 they venerate the vestiges of Laozi and that the people living near the Pass admire the remaining aura of Yin i Xi尹喜.[19]

[Wang Zhang] then, with his Aide, Bian Qian邊乾[20], had this stele set up to com-

---

[17] These two paragraphs have been translated by Patricia E b r.e y, „Later Han Stone Inscriptions", Harvard Journal of Asiatic Studies 40/2 (1980), p. 337.

[18] Meng was part of the principality of Liang during the Latter Han dynasty so that the reigning official there was called *xiang* 相 , not "governor", *taishou*太守. Wang Zhang was one of the officials who were outlawed in this same year (165) for their factional activity against the eunuchs. Little is known of his life, except that he rose to the high rank of Shaofu qing少府卿 , Chamberlain for the Palace Revenues; see *Hou Hanshu* 67, pp. 2190 and 2187.

[19] Laixiang is said in the *Shiji* 63, p. 2139 (Zhonghua shuju, Peking 1975 ed), to be the native place of Laozi. It was located near the present Luyi in eastern Henan, about 60 km south of the Wang Ziqiao stele. Yin Xi is said to have been the Guardian of the Pass when Laozi left China for the West; see their hagiographies in the *Lie-xianzhuan*, K a l t e n m a r k, op. cit., pp. 60–67. A. S e i d e l, op. cit., pp. 36 ff., discusses the cult rendered to Laozi at his supposed place of origin.

[20] Bian Qian is otherwise unknown. He probably belonged to the same family as Bian Shao 韶 , the author of an inscription to Laozi written in the same month as this inscription to Wang Ziqiao, and as Bian Rang 讓, a writer and a protégé of C a i Yong, his compatriot from Chenliu. The *Cai Zhonglang ji* version of this line reads "[Wang Zhong] then had Bian Qian consult with the officials, following which they erected this stele." It is perhaps this version that prompts A. S e i d e l, op. cit., pp. 58–59, n. 6, to say this inscription is not by Cai Yong, but by Bian Qian himself. C a i Yong often mentions, at the end of the prose sections of his stele inscriptions, in passages that strongly resemble these lines, the circumstances that led to the erection of the stele in question and the names of the men involved; there is no reason to believe Bian Qian is mentioned here because he was the author of the stele. Of course it is always possible that the attribution to C a i Yong is false. The earliest mention of C a i Yong as the author of a "Wang Qiao lu" is late, in *Taiping yulan* 33, p. 6b. (Wang Ziqiao is often called "Wang Qiao"; I do not believe the title attributed to C a i Yong refers to the Wang Qiao who lived under Emperor Ming mentioned above.) However the fact that educated and eminent men like the Bians (if they are related, as seems probable) and C a i Yong are seen associated in the organization of Taoist religious cults is interesting.

memorate and glorify the great acts of the past and for the inspection of those men who have set their hearts on the *dao*.

"Lord Wang,
So virtuous he could commune with the spirits,
Shone with internal brightness,
Keeping himself perfectly pure.
In tune with the great dao,
He longed for eternal youth.
Rejecting the world and its customs,
He flew away, his body made divine.
Soaring in the highest clouds,
Floating in the Great Purity,
He would ride on a hornless dragon,
Or drive in a car pulled by a crane,
Wearing a multicolored bamboo hat,
Making his metallic bells ring out,
Waving a flag of plumes,
Brandishing a rainbow banner.
His joys know no limits
As he lives for ever and ever, without end.
To manifest his fervent filial piety,
He thought of those who had given him life.
As the year drew to its close
He showed his sincere feelings.
In attendance near the tomb
He sang forth his doleful chant.
By leaving bird tracks
He alerted the old town,
And wearing a scarlet robe,
With purple hat-strings dangling,
He called to the child
And announced his name.
At this men understood
And reacted with fear and surprise.
They rebuilt the shrine
And returned the altars and bamboo mats.
They presented sacrificial foods
That spread forth sweet-smelling odors.
As all looked on [?],
A far-wafting fragrance arose from the pure sacrifice,
Adding to the stream of good fortune
And to the glory of the imperial court.[21]
[Thus it is that] heaven will protect our land,
Aid our common people,
Make our great blessings glow,
Shining to the ends of the earth."

---

[21] The text seems extremely corrupt here and the *Cai Zhonglang ji* version (Sibu congkan ed.) is even harder to construe.

II

82

It was appropriate for W a n g Ziqiao to visit the family tomb during the All Saints Festival because the worship of one's ancestors played a significant role in this all-important festival.[22] We do not know exactly when the W a n g s' family tomb was rebuilt, nor do we know anything about Wang Xi, the local magistrate, but the crowds that assembled at the miraculous site and their conduct—singing hymns to a great deity, meditating, seeking deliverance from sickness—all look very familiar and might describe religious manifestations almost anywhere. The sacrifice made in the name of the emperor in 165 should be seen in the context of similar sacrifices made around this same time. In February a powerful eunuch was sent to Ku 苦 [23] to perform a sacrifice to L a o z i; in September the inscription to L a o z i was written and the sacrifice to W a n g Ziqiao performed; in January of 166 another eunuch performed the same ceremony to L a o z i in Ku[24]; and on 25 September 166 "a sacrifice was performed by the emperor to Huang Lao in the Bright Dragon Palace".[25] "The emperor personally sacrificed to L a o z i in the Bright Dragon Palace. The altars were covered with patterned rugs; the vessels were of pure gold; flower-canopied thrones were erected and the music used was the music performed at the suburban sacrifices to Heaven".[26] Thus the cult of L a o z i was considered important enough to be accompanied by the music performed during the most solemn imperial civil ceremonies!

This short inscription shows us that, less than twenty years before the revolt of the Yellow Turbans, the Taoist religion had permeated all classes of Chinese society, as M a s p e r o saw so clearly[27], and was not a purely "popular" or lower-class phenomenon. The fact that the inscription was written by C a i Yong, one of the very greatest scholars of his time, a calligraphist of genius, a ritualist and musician, is another sign that Taoism was accepted by the élite, much as Christianity was accepted by the élite in the Mediterranean world, as well as by the common

---

[22] This is underlined by T' u n g - t s u Ch'ü, Han social structure, University of Washington Press Seattle and London 1972, p. 31, and William G. B o l t z, *Philological footnotes to the Han New Year rites*, "Journal of the American Oriental Society" (Baltimore) 99 (1979), pp. 427–428.

[23] Near Laozi's birth place, Laixiang.

[24] Cf. A. S e i d e l, op. cit., p. 37, and Q i n g Xitai 卿希泰 , *Zhongguo daojiao sixiang shigang* 中國道教思想史綱 , Sichuan renmin chubanshe, Chengdu 1981, pp. 54–55.

[25] *Hou Hanshu* 7, p. 317. The Bright Dragon Palace and Park were in the eastern-most part of the palace grounds in Luoyang; see Hans B i e l a n s t e i n, *Lo-yang in Later Han times*, "Bulletin of the Museum of Far Eastern Antiquities" (Stockholm) 48 (1976), p. 38 and notes 177–179. B i e l a n s t e i n translates the name of the palace as "Sleek Dragon Palace".

[26] *Hou Hanshu zhi* 8, p. 3188.

[27] H. M a s p e r o, op. cit., pp. 465–466.

people.[28] The cataclysmic results of the revolt of the Yellow Turbans put an end to imperial patronage of the Taoist religion for over a century, but it probably remained an important religious phenomenon in all classes of society even when it was hardly seen in the historical records.

---

[28] This is one of the leitmotifs of the book of Peter B r o w n , (*The Cult of the Saints* (University of Chicago Press, Chicago 1981, pp. 12–22), in which he castigates early scholars (such as H u m e and G i b b o n) for seeing religion in late Antiquity as a "two-tiered" system, one tier for the "ignorant masses" and one for the (very small) educated class.

III

Ts'ao Chih and the Immortals

Ts'ao Chih 曹植 (192–232 A.D.) has left us a number of remarks, including a whole essay, in which he denies the existence of immortals (*hsien*
仙) or of immortality in general, and he does so with such scorn that it seems
strange to find ten ballads (*yüeh-fu* 樂府) in his works that take immortals as
their theme and present them in a very favorable light. This anomaly has
struck generations of critics who have tried, often contradicting one another,
to explain it away. My aim here is to present the complete dossier, that is, all
of Ts'ao Chih's prose and verse concerning immortals, and attempt to see
which, if any, of the various explanations accounting for the existence of
these contradictory works is the right one. In other words, I will attempt to
discover just how we are to interpret the ballads in question, in order to find
out what Ts'ao Chih was actually getting at. His poems of immortals have
the added interest of being one of the very first treatments by a known author
of a theme that would become a permanent fixture of Chinese poetry.

TS'AO CHIH'S ESSAYS ON IMMORTALS

Perhaps the best way to begin our study is to read what Ts'ao Chih has
to say about immortals in a prose essay he must have written sometime
between 217, when his brother was established as crown prince, and the
death of his father in 220. I deduce this because he speaks in the essay of "the
crown prince" and his father ("the king") as if they were both still alive.

My translation is based on the new (and now indispensable) edition of
Ts'ao Chih's works by Chao Yu-wen 趙幼文,[1] which takes as its basic text
the standard edition by Ting Yen 丁晏 (1794–1875).[2] This text, in its turn,
is actually a rifacimento by Sun Hsing-yen 孫星衍 (1753–1818),[3] who used
as his basic text the version given in *Pien-cheng lun* 辨正論 by Fa-lin 法琳
(572–640),[4] to which he added fragments from *Kuang hung-ming chi* 廣弘明集

THIS ARTICLE has benefited from comments by J. R. Hightower, E. G. Pulleyblank, and H. H.
Frankel, all of whom I would like to thank here.
    [1] Chao Yu-wen 趙幼文, ed., *Ts'ao Chih chi chiao-chu* 曹植集校注 (Peking: Jen-min wen-
hsüeh, 1984; hereafter cited as *TCCC*), pp. 186–96.
    [2] Ting Yen, comp., *Ts'ao chi ch'üan-p'ing* 曹集銓評, pref. dated 1865.
    [3] Included in Sun Hsing-yen, comp., *Hsü ku-wen yüan* 續古文苑 (pref. dated 1807), ch. 9,
pp. 462–68 of the Ts'ung-shu chi-ch'eng edn.
    [4] Included in *Taishō shinshū Daizōkyō* 大正新修大藏經, no. 2110, pp. 500c–01a.

by Tao-hsüan 道宣 (596–667)[5] and from the commentary to *San-kuo chih* 三國志, *ch.* 29.[6] As Ting Yen says,[7] Sun Hsing-yen's editing is extremely well done and it is hard to see where one text is joined to another. Ts'ao Chih's essay was used by Buddhists in their polemics against Taoism, but there is no reason to believe that it was fabricated by them.

Here is a translation of the essay. It will give us a good idea of what Ts'ao Chih thought of immortals and of the search for immortality when he was in his late twenties.

An Analysis of Tao[ism]

We find the following in the Taoists' books about immortals: Fu Yüeh 傅說 rose up to become a star in the lunar mansion of the Tail[8] and the year star (Jupiter) came down to earth to become Tung-fang Shuo 東方朔;[9] the prince of Huai-nan, Liu An 劉安, was executed in his fief, but these books say he obtained the Way (*tao* 道) and ascended in an apotheosis;[10] [Lady] Kou-i 鉤弋 died in Yün-yang and these books say her corpse passed on, leaving her coffin empty.[11] What is all of this but a pack of lies!

[5] *Taishō*, no. 2103, pp. 118c–19b.

[6] Ch'en Shou 陳壽 (233–297), *San-kuo chih* 三國志 (Peking: Chung-hua, 1975; hereafter *SKC*) 29, p. 805.

[7] Ting Yen, comp., *Ts'ao chi ch'üan-p'ing* (Peking: Wen-hsüeh ku-chi k'an-hsing-she, 1957), *ch.* 9, p. 155.

[8] See *Chuang-tzu* 6; trans. Burton Watson, *The Complete Works of Chuang-tzu* (New York: Columbia U.P., 1968), p. 82. Fu Yüeh is said to have been minister of the Shang king Wu-ting 武丁 (r. 1324–1266 B.C.) and to have been translated to the heavens as a star in the constellation Scorpio (i.e., Wei 尾, the Tail, in China). See also *Ch'u-tz'u*, "Yüan-yu"; David Hawkes, trans., *Ch'u Tz'u, The Songs of the South: An Ancient Chinese Anthology* (London: Oxford U.P., 1959), p. 82.

[9] See *Lieh-hsien chuan*; trans. Max Kaltenmark, *Le Lie-sien tchouan* (Peking: Univ. de Paris, Centre d'Etudes Sinologiques, 1953), p. 138: "The scholars suspected he was the spirit, *ching* 精, of the planet Jupiter." Chao Yu-wen, *TCCCC*, p. 190, n. 3, quotes *Feng-su t'ung-i*, which says Tung-fang Shuo was popularly thought to have been the spirit of the planet Venus, but the *Feng-su* cannot be in Ts'ao Chih's mind here because it is not one of the "Taoist" books.

[10] This is the version of *Shen-hsien chuan* 4; trans. Sawada Mizuho 沢田瑞穗, in *Chūgoku koten bungaku taikei* 8 (Tokyo: Heibonsha, 1969), pp. 374, 378. Wang Li-ch'i's 王利器 *Feng-su t'ung-i chiao-chu* 風俗通義校注 (Peking: Chung-hua, 1981) 2, pp. 115–18, explodes this myth as being the fabulation of Liu An's followers ashamed of the fact that their master, as seeker of immortality, had actually died. It is impossible today to know exactly to which of the "Taoists' books" Ts'ao Chih refers in these examples; the work *Lieh-hsien chuan* may well have been in existence during his lifetime, but *Shen-hsien chuan* is attributed to Ko Hung 葛洪, who lived a century later.

[11] Yün-yang 雲陽 was probably another name for the Sweet Spring Palace, northwest of the present Ch'un-yang 淳陽, Shensi. Ssu-ma Ch'ien 司馬遷 (145–86? B.C.), *Shih-chi* 史記 (Peking: Chung-hua, 1962; hereafter *SC*) 49 (in Edouard Chavannes, trans., *Les mémoires historiques de Se-ma Ts'ien* [Paris: E. Leroux, 1895–1905; rpt. Paris: Adrienne-Maisonneuve, with supp. vol., 1969; hereafter *MH*] 6, pp. 62–64) says Lady Kung-i was allowed to commit suicide there by

Among the serious essayists who lived at the time of the restoration [of the Han dynasty] was one called Huan Chün-shan [Huan T'an],[12] whose writings are often quite good. Liu Tzu-chün 劉子駿 [i.e., Liu Hsin 歆, d. 23 A.D.] once asked him: "If a man can truly repress his desires, and close his ears and eyes [to external distractions], can he preserve himself from physical decay?" At the time, there was an old elm tree in the courtyard; Huan T'an pointed to it and said: "This tree has no sentiments it could suppress, no ears or eyes to close, and yet it will wither and rot; thus when Liu Hsin says it is possible to preserve oneself from physical decay, he is speaking nonsense!"

Huan T'an was not quite right to use the elm tree for his comparison. Why?[13] ... "I [Huan T'an] was grandee of the Directorate of Music under Wang Mang.[14] There were documents on the musicians there which said that Emperor Wen [r. 180–157 B.C.] was able to procure the services of the musician named Aged Tou 竇公, who had been a musician attached to the Marquis Wen of Wei [424–387 B.C.]. He was 180 years old[15] and blind in both eyes. The emperor was amazed and asked him what he had done [to be able to live so long]." Aged Tou answered: "I lost my eyesight at the age of twelve, and my parents, distressed by the fact that I could not cope with any business, taught me

---

Emperor Wu, who feared she would dominate her young son, the future Emperor Chao (cf. Pan Ku 班固 [32–92 A.D.], *Han shu* 漢書 [Peking: Chung-hua, 1962; hereafter *HS*] 97A, pp. 3956–57). But *Lieh-hsien chuan* (and not *Shen-hsien chuan*, as said by Chao Yu-wen, *TCCCC*, p. 190, n. 5), adds that "her corpse remained warm and fragrant for a month and when later the Emperor Chao had her reburied they found only silk slippers in her coffin" (trans. Kaltenmark, *Le Lie-sien tchouan*, p. 140).

[12] Huan T'an (Chün-shan) 桓譚 (君山) was a well-known thinker born toward the end of the Western Han; he died at the beginning of the Eastern Han. He has been studied by Timoteus Pokora, *Hsin-lun (New Treatise) and Other Writings by Huan T'an (43 B.C.–28 A.D.)*, Michigan Papers in Chinese Studies 20 (Ann Arbor: U. of Michigan P., 1975); for a translation of another version of this section, see Pokora, *Hsin-lun*, no. 156, p. 156 and p. 162, n. 34. This section about Huan T'an is quoted and discussed in Hou Wai-lu 侯外廬 et al., *Chung-kuo ssu-hsiang t'ung-shih* 中國思想通史 (Peking: Jen-min ch'u-pan-she, 1962) 3, pp. 339–40.

[13] As Sun Hsing-yen points out (*Hsü ku-wen yüan*), something has dropped out here because the following words obviously quote Huan T'an himself. This whole section has a number of versions all showing differences; see Pokora, *Hsin-lun*, pp. 74–75, n. 82, for all references and translations.

[14] The official title given, *tien-yüeh ta-fu* 典樂大夫, did not refer to the Directorate of Music under Wang Mang's reign but to the Directorate of Foreign Affairs; cf. *HS* 99B, p. 4103 (trans. Homer Dubs, *History of the Former Han Dynasty* 3 [Baltimore: Waverly Press, 1955], p. 269). Either there is an error in the text here or the title used is an anachronism, but I believe the reference is to Huan T'an's appointment in the Directorate of Music.

[15] He was at least 200 years old. If he served the marquis in the last year of his life, 387 B.C., and the emperor in the first year of his reign, 180 B.C., he would have been 207 years old at the time.

to play the zither. I do not know Taoist gymnastics (*tao-yin* 道引),[16] nor do I know what strength has enabled me to live so long!"

Huan T'an discussed this and said: "He was helped by the fact that he was rather young when he became blind. He was able to concentrate on his inner self and not let his feelings be influenced by exterior things." Previously, when criticizing Liu Hsin, Huan T'an said inner concentration was to no avail, but here, on the contrary, when discussing Aged Tou, he invokes the fact that the latter had no external influences as a reason for his achieving longevity. I just wonder what his final judgment on this subject was.

Huan T'an has also said: "There was a magician named Tung Chung-chün 董仲君 who was imprisoned because of a crime he had committed. He pretended to die and, after a few days, his eyes sank into his head and worms came out of them. He had died and was reborn. Later he finally died once and for all." A superior man knows full well that what is born must die: why try to explain it further? Even the most godlike of the things of the universe[17] could not be greater than the universe itself; it could not make insects who hibernate in the winter hide away in summer, nor produce a peal of thunder in winter. It is seasonal changes that make the creatures in nature bestir themselves, and movements in the [*yin* and *yang*] breaths of the atmosphere that elicit responses in nature. Isn't it simply too strange to believe that this fellow named Tung Chung-chün was able to conceal his breathing, turn his body into a corpse, make his skin rot, and let worms come out of him?

All the magicians that can be found today have been brought [to the capital] by our king [Ts'ao Ts'ao 曹操]: Kan Shih 甘始[18] of Kan-

[16] Some texts say, on the contrary, that Tou did practice Taoist gymnastics (*HS* 30, p. 1712; and *Kuang hung-ming chi* 廣弘明集), while two texts in the *T'ai-p'ing yü-lan* 383, p. 10b and 740, pp. 5a–b, agree with the version translated here.

[17] According to the "Hsi-tz'u" (the "Great Treatise" commentary to the *I-ching*), it is the *I-ching* that is "the most god-like thing under heaven"; see James Legge, trans., *The Yi King* (Oxford: Clarendon Press, 1899), p. 370. In these sentences Ts'ao Chih is presenting a mechanistic view of the universe which has no place for the occult or for the supernatural prowesses claimed by Taoist magicians.

[18] Kan Shih shares a three-line biography with two other magicians in Fan Yeh 范曄 (398–445), *Hou Han-shu* 後漢書 (Peking: Chung-hua, 1963; hereafter *HHS*) 82B, p. 2750. Trans. in Ngo Van Xuyet, *Divination, magie et politique dans la Chine ancienne* (Paris: Presses Univ. de Fr., 1976), pp. 141–42, and Kenneth J. DeWoskin, *Doctors, Diviners and Magicians of Ancient China: Biographies of Fang-shih* (New York: Columbia U.P., 1983), pp. 87–88. The portion of Ts'ao Chih's essay concerning Kan Shih is quoted in the commentary and is translated in DeWoskin, *Doctors, Diviners*, pp. 151–52. Scholars from the Hunan Provincial Museum and from the Institute for Chinese Medicine, writing in a booklet devoted to the painting found in

ling (Hopei), Tso Tz'u 左慈[19] of Lu-chiang (Anhwei), Ch'ieh Chien 郤儉[20] of Yang-cheng (Honan). Kan Shih knows how to circulate his breath through his body and perform Taoist gymnastics; Tso Tz'u is versed in the arts of the bedchamber; Ch'ieh Chien excels in abstaining from eating grain. All of these men declared they were centenarians many times over. The main reason they were gathered together in Wei was in fact because it was feared that they and men like them would band together with wrongdoers and liars to cheat the masses, and carry out their magical evil to befuddle the people. That is why [Ts'ao Ts'ao] has gathered them together and restrained them from action. It is not that he too, [like the First Emperor of the Ch'in dynasty], wanted to see the immortals on the Isle of Ying or seek An-ch'i on the seashore,[21] or that he rejected the royal golden carriage looking for an [immortal's] coach made of clouds and threw away the six coursers [used by a king] in envy of the flying dragons [used by immortals]! From the king in our family [Ts'ao Ts'ao] and the crown prince [Ts'ao P'i 曹丕] down to me and my brothers, we all consider these men to be laughable and do not believe in them at all!

But Kan Shih and the others know that they can depend upon regular treatment from the authorities: their salaries will not exceed those of the lowest officials and they will receive no rewards without rendering services. [They know that at the time of the First Emperor of Ch'in the men he sent out found it] hard to swim to the isles [of the immortals] in the sea, and that it would be hard to wear the six cords for official seals [like those given to Luan Ta by Emperor Wu of the Han dynasty],[22] and so in the end they have not dared present their empty and fallacious words to the throne or hold forth any extravagant discourses.

Ma-wang-tui showing Taoist gymnastics, called *Tao-yin-t'u lun-chi* 導引圖論集 (n.p.: Wen-wu ch'u-pan-she, pref. dated 1978), p. 13, refer to Ts'ao Chih's remarks on Kan Shih, whom they cite as an example of a Han dynasty practitioner of Taoist gymnastics.

[19] Tso Tz'u's "biography" is also in *HHS* 82B, pp. 2747–48. It contains nothing but examples of his magical powers; trans. in Ngo, *Divination*, pp. 138–39 and DeWoskin, *Doctors, Diviners*, pp. 83–86.

[20] The name Ch'ieh 郤 or 郄 is sometimes written Hsi 卻. There seem to have been two men of this name. One was governor, *tz'u-shih*, of I-chou (Ssu-ch'uan) who was killed in 188 A.D., before Ts'ao Chih was born. The other is our magician who appears in the commentaries to *SKC* 1, p. 54 (which quotes Chang Hua's *Po-wu chih*) and 29, pp. 805–06 (quoting Ts'ao P'i's *Tien-lun* and this essay).

[21] The Isle of Ying and An-ch'i refer to the search for immortals by the First Emperor; see *MH* 3, pp. 465–66.

[22] *MH* 3, pp. 481–82.

I once tried to test Ch'ieh Chien to see if he could refrain from eating grain for one hundred days. I personally stayed with him [even] while he slept [and saw] that he was able to live normally [without eating]. Now, a man dies when he doesn't eat for a week, but Ch'ieh Chien was actually able to [live on] as described! This does not mean, however, that he was necessarily able to live any longer, even if, by his art, he could cure his sicknesses and not fear hunger during times of famine. Tso Tz'u excelled in the practice of the arts of the bedchamber, which should enable him, more or less, to accomplish his allotted span of life. But one cannot carry out [these arts] if one does not want it with all one's might.

The man named Kan Shih was old, but he looked like a young man. The other magicians all looked upon him as their master. Kan Shih talked a lot but had little real accomplishment to show for it. He was quite a weaver of tall tales. I once got rid of the people around us and talked to him *tête-à-tête*, asking him questions about his activities. I made myself as pleasant as I could to draw him out, leading him on with fine words. Kan Shih told me the following:

"My first master was named Han Shih-hsiung 韓世雄. I once was with him at the Southern Sea making gold. All in all, from the beginning to the end of our work, we threw tens of thousands of pounds of gold into the sea." He also said: "At the time of the Liang 梁 [influential family around 150 A.D.], a foreigner from Central Asia presented belts of perfumed wool and knives that cut jade to the court.[23] At the time I regretted not having taken them." He said again: "In the Western Country of Chü-shih 車師,[24] when a boy is born, they open his back and take his spleen out, so that he will eat less and work harder."[25] He said again: "Take a pair of carp around five inches long and put a drug in the mouth of one of them; then throw both of them into boiling oil. When the one that has swallowed the drug is still wriggling its tail and working its gills, swimming about up and down as if it were in a deep pool filled with water, the other carp will be cooked and ready to bite into." At the time I asked him: "Can all this be tested?" He answered:

[23] This is the famous *k'un-wu* 昆吾 knife; see Joseph Needham et al., *Science and Civilisation in China* 3 (Cambridge: Cambridge U.P., 1959), pp. 656, 667–68.

[24] Chü-shih was a confederation of six states in what is now Sinkiang.

[25] The idea that the removal or shrinkage of the spleen permits men or animals to run fast seems to be very old and may actually have come to China from the West via Chü-shih; see Pliny, *Natural History* 26.83.13. It would seem that at the end of the 16th century surgeons attempted to remove the spleens of dogs to see if they would run faster!

"This drug is over 10,000 *li* from here, beyond the frontiers. Only I could get it." And that's not all he said; it would be very difficult to write down all of it, so I have sketched in only the most extraordinary of his stories. If Kan Shih and the others had lived during the times of the First Emperor of the Ch'in and Emperor Wu of the Han, they would have been followers of Hsü Shih and Luan Ta.[26] [The arch-villains] Chieh 桀 and Chou 紂 lived in different periods but were equally bad; the dynasty may change, but dishonest behavior is equally false whatever the period, and so it is with these [charlatans of our own times]!

And, now, we have theories about immortals based on thin air. What is an immortal? Is it a kind of ape? Are men who obtain the *tao* transformed into immortals? When pheasants go into the sea they become clams.[27] When, [before their transformation], these birds flew around, flapping their wings together,[28] they recognized one another still. But once they had plunged headlong into their spiritual and material transformations and become members of the race of turtles, how could they remember the joy they had soaring over the forests or nesting in hedges and roofs? Niu Ai fell sick and became a tiger. When he met his elder brother, he ate him.[29] When confronted with such examples, what can we find to esteem in such transformations?

Now an emperor's position is higher than that of any of his innumerable vassals; his riches comprise the entire universe; his majesty is clear to all, his brilliance the equal of the sun's and moon's. His palaces and courtyards sparkle like the stars in heaven. Why should he long for the palaces of the Queen Mother [of the West] or the K'un-lun region [where the immortals' palaces are found]? Her three [blue] birds on

[26] Hsü Shih 徐市 (*SC* 6; *MH* 2, pp. 151–52, 180, 190) and Luan Ta 欒大 (*SC* 28; *MH* 3, pp. 477–81) were both magicians. The former tried to delude the First Emperor, the latter Emperor Wu of the Han dynasty.

[27] These two transformations are typical prescientific attempts at explanations of natural phenomena; there is some confusion as to which bird becomes which bivalve, and I doubt that it would serve any useful purpose to try to clear up the confusion. The *Huai-nan-tzu* 5, p. 11a (SPTK edn.) says "a pheasant entering the sea becomes a clam 蛤." The Chu-tzu chi-ch'eng edn. of the *Huai-nan-tzu* (Peking: Chung-hua shu-chü, 1954), p. 79, has "sparrow." The *Li chi*, "Yüeh-ling" section (trans. S. Couvreur, *Li Ki, ou mémoires sur les bienséances et les cérémonies*, 2nd. edn. [Ho Kien Fou: Impr. de la Mission Catholique, 1913] 1, p. 385) also says "sparrows ... become clams." It is in the apocrypha quoted in the *TCCCC* notes to Ts'ao Chih's essay that we find confirmation of his statements. There is an interesting discussion of similar theories of transmutation by Joseph Needham and Lu Gwei-djen, "Ancient Chinese Oecology and Plant Geography: The Case of the *Chü* and the *Chih*," in F. Aubin, ed., *Etudes Song, Sér. II (Civilisation)* (Paris: Ecole des Hautes Etudes en Sciences Sociales, 1984), pp. 249–65.

[28] These lines are near quotations of *Shih ching*, Poem 28.

[29] Cf. *Huai-nan-tzu* (Chu-tzu chi-ch'eng edn.), p. 20.

mission are not as fine looking as the whole corps of his officials;[30] the White Girl or Ch'ang-o were not as beautiful as the [women] in the pepper room [of his palace];[31] cloud robes and feather skirts cannot compare with the *fu-fu* 黼黻 embroideries that ornamented [imperial uniforms]; to drive a hornless dragon bearing a rainbow [as a flag] is not so splendid as to ride in the imperial carriage; carnelian pistils and jade flowers are not as pure as jade scepters. And yet [emperors] let themselves be duped by ignoramuses, accepting falsehoods, giving credence to misleading theories. They heap up presents to invite men who are not their subjects,[32] and dilapidate their goods to seek for vanities. They distribute royal titles to glorify [these charlatans] and clean great halls to house them. This they do year in and year out, with nothing to show for it. One of them, [the First Emperor of Ch'in], died at Sha-ch'iu [Hopei]; another, [emperor Wu of the Han], died in the Palace of Five Oaks [Shensi]. When the time came, [the emperors had these charlatans] put to death with their entire families, causing the whole empire to laugh out loud!

If the various colors of the spectrum are there to delight the eyes, if there are musical sounds to give pleasure to the ears, if there are beautiful wives to perpetuate our family lines, meats of grass- and grain-fed animals to please our palates, why must we satisfy ourselves with tastes that have no taste, listen to music that has no sound, or look at beauty without color?[33] But the truth of the matter is that each person's

[30] Hsi-wang-mu 西王母 is a famous figure in Chinese folklore; in his commentary to *Shan-hai ching* 16 (SPPY edn.), p. 3b, Kuo P'u says the three "blue birds" on the Wang-mu mountain of the West were all in attendance upon Hsi-wang-mu's messengers. In *ibid., ch.* 12, p. 1a, it is said that three blue birds nourished Hsi-wang-mu; see also the references by R. Mathieu, *Etude sur la mythologie et l'ethnologie de la Chine ancienne: traduction annotée du Shanhai jing*, Mémoires de l'IHEC 22 (Paris: Coll. de Fr., 1983) 1, p. 100, n. 3, to which should be added Homer H. Dubs, "An Ancient Chinese Mystery Cult," *Harvard Theological Review* 35 (1942), pp. 221–40.

[31] The White Girl, Su-nü 素女, and Ch'ang-o 嫦娥 are both well-known Taoist immortals; the former was famous as a musician (see *Ch'u-tz'u*, "Chiu huai" and "Chao shih"; trans. Hawkes, *Ch'u Tz'u*, p. 145) or as a specialist in the bedroom arts (cf. R. H. van Gulik, *Sexual Life in Ancient China* [Leiden: E.J. Brill, 1961], pp. 74–75). The latter (originally Heng-o 姮娥) was the Lady in the Moon (see *Huai-nan-tzu* 6, p. 98 and Edward Schafer, "Ways of Looking at the Moon Palace," *AM* 3rd ser. 1.1 [1988], pp. 1–14). The "pepper room" was a bedchamber in the palace in which the walls were plastered wih mud and pepper, creating warmth and a pleasant odor. See *HS* 66, p. 2885, n. 8 by Yen Shih-ku, who treats the term as the name of a Han palace.

[32] This is an allusion to *SC* 28 (*MH* 3, pp. 478, 481), according to which Luan Ta, who said he was despised by the immortals he met "because he was a subject" (and thus not an absolutely free man), was given an official seal in a strange night ceremony "to show that he was not a subject."

[33] These are of course allusions to Taoist mysticism as found in *Lao tzu* 63 and *Chuang tzu* 12 (Watson, *The Complete Works of Chuang-tzu*, p. 128, etc.).

longevity has a predestined limit, just as his body has just so much strength. Those who nourish themselves intelligently will reach the limit allotted to them; those who tire themselves out or are dissolute, will cut that limit in half; and those who neglect to use what was given to them[34] die young. This is the truth of the matter!

It would be difficult to write a more thorough, or a more contemptuous demolition of the idea of Taoist immortality. Whatever we may think of the literary quality of this essay,[35] Ts'ao Chih here shows not only that he does not believe in the possibility of achieving Taoist immortality, but that the very idea of transformation into some sort of winged creature, half-human, half-ape, is distasteful to him. He is contemptuous, too, of the "miracles" performed by Kan Shih, although he does seem to believe in Ch'ieh Chien's ability to go without eating. Furthermore, he extends this aversion to his whole family, insisting upon the fact that Ts'ao Ts'ao's assembling of the magicians in the capital had been for political reasons — to keep them from fomenting the kind of disorder that had occurred under the Taoists' Yellow Turban Rebellion just before the writing of this essay. He insists at such length, that indeed some critics have seen this disavowal of imperial interest in immortality-seeking as the main motive for writing the essay.[36]

Actually, we know from other texts and from some of Ts'ao Ts'ao's own writings that his interest in the quest for immortality was more complex than Ts'ao Chih's essay would have us believe, and we will soon see that Ts'ao Chih's attitude toward immortals became more complex and less categorically negative as he grew older.

Complaints against immortality-seeking were already commonplace by Ts'ao Chih's time, as were immortals in literature. Seeking immortality, in fact, although often decried, had become a legitimate aim in life. Just

---

[34] Chao, in *TCCCC*, suggests that 虛用 is inspired by *SC* 30, p. 3289: "Too great usage 大用 of the spirit brings on exhaustion." I believe Ts'ao Chih's usage of the word 虛 is closer to that in *Lü-shih ch'un-ch'iu* 3, "Yüan-tao" (see Ch'en Ch'i-yu 陳奇猷, *Lü-shih ch'un-ch'iu chiao-shih* 呂氏春秋校釋 [Shanghai: Hsüeh-lin, 1984], p. 172), in which it is said that "it is wrong to concentrate on only one of man's 'nine orifices' [organs of the senses and private parts] to the exclusion of the eight others; to leave them 虛, 'empty,' 'unused,' leads to death."

[35] Liu Hsieh 劉勰, *Wen-hsin tiao-lung* 文心雕龍, rpt. of the Fan Wen-lan 范文蘭 commented version (Hong Kong: Commercial Press, 1960) 18, p. 328, is extremely harsh: "Ts'ao Chih's 'Analysis of Taoism' is no more than a series of extracts from other books; when one's talents are not up to holding an argument, it is better to stop, and not to write at all!"

[36] Chao, *TCCCC*, and Ch'ing Hsi-ta'i 卿希泰, *Chung-kuo tao-chiao ssu-hsiang shih-kang* 中國道教思想史網 (Ch'eng-tu: Ssu-ch'uan jen-min ch'u-pan-she, 1981) 1, pp. 167–71, insist upon this. T'ang Ch'ang-ju 唐長孺, *Wei Chin Nan-pei-ch'ao shih-lun shih-i* 魏晉南北朝史論拾遺 (Peking: Chung-hua shu-chü, 1983), p. 219, on the basis of Ts'ao Ts'ao's poetry, states rightly, I believe, that Ts'ao Ts'ao's motives in assembling the magicians in the capital were not just political. See also Ngo, *Divination*, pp. 61–62.

when men began to pursue immortality it is hard to say. There is evidence of it as early as the end of the fourth century B.C., although the word for "immortal," *hsien* 僊 or 仙, seems to appear for the first time in the *Ch'u-tz'u* and there seems to be no evidence of a cult of the immortals much earlier than the earliest of the poems in that collection.[37] The word does not appear in "Li-sao," although the end of the poem sees Ch'ü Yüan off on a quest for immortals and long life; but in the later poems in *Ch'u-tz'u* the word "immortal" appears frequently, as do the names of the most famous of them: Wang Ch'iao 王喬, Ch'ih-sung-tzu 赤松子, and the others. At the very beginning of the Han dynasty, Chang Liang 張良 (d. 189 B.C.), one of the dynasty's most important founding generals, said late in life: "I would like to put aside the affairs of men and spend all my time following Ch'ih-sung-tzu." Pan Ku 班固, the author of the *Han shu*, adds: "He then studied the *tao* with the desire to rise into the air" as an immortal.[38] Moreover, it is well known that Emperor Wu of the Han and many other emperors were fervent immortality-seekers. In fact, since its inception and until the time of Ts'ao Chih, searching for the immortals accelerated rather than diminished.

Proof of this acceleration of interest in immortals can be seen in the importance given to them in tomb decorations and more clearly still in the images and inscriptions on the bronze mirrors that abound during the Han dynasty. Most of these inscriptions are in verse, and some of them can be seen as forerunners of the ballads by Ts'ao Chih that I discuss here. Former Han mirror inscriptions do not mention immortals and limit their interest in immortality to wishes of long life for the recipient of the mirror. But beginning with the Later Han we find more and more mirrors that supplement these wishes with evocations of the immortals, in particular of Hsi-wang-mu and, later, Tung-wang-fu 東王父 (or Tung-wang-kung 公).[39] In fact the end of the Later Han dynasty would seem to be the most flourishing period for mirrors that depict immortals, and the period that corresponds with Ts'ao Chih's essay and other poems that doubt the existence of the immortals

[37] There is a good résumé of the origins of the cult of the immortals in Needham, *Science and Civilisation* 2, pp. 93–113. See also Yü Ying-shih, "Life and Immortality in Han China," *HJAS* 25 (1964–65), pp. 88–107.

[38] *HS* 40, p. 2037. Chang Liang is said to have been the eighth-generation ancestor of Chang Tao-ling (2nd century A.D.), the founder of the T'ien-shih sect of Taoism; see *MH* 2, p. 157, n. 1.

[39] See Tamada Tsugio 玉田継雄, "Kandai ni okeru gafu no shinsen kaji to kyomei" 漢代における楽府の神僊歌辞と鏡銘, *Ritsumeikan bungaku* [Shirakawa Shizuka 白川静 Festschrift] 430–43 (1981), pp. 310–36. Translations from two of these poems engraved on mirrors can be found in Michael Loewe, *Ways to Paradise* (London: Allen and Unwin, 1979), p. 200.

represents a sudden, sharp decline.[40] The end of the Han was surely *the* crucial period in the formation of the Taoist religion, and we should not be surprised to find reflections of this religious activity in contemporary poetry.

Ts'ao Ts'ao 曹操 and Ts'ao P'i 曹丕, Ts'ao Chih's father and elder brother, both wrote poems about immortals, and both show a certain ambiguity in their attitudes. Ts'ao P'i in his *Tien lun* 典論 insists, like his brother, that the idea of human physical immortality is a myth.[41] But Ts'ao P'i devotes the first half of one poem, sometimes called "Breaking Off a Willow Branch" and sometimes called "Wandering Immortals," to the description of his transformation into an immortal, and the last half to a complete negation of immortality-seeking, ending in an affirmation of the "Way of the Saints" of Confucianism.[42] Ts'ao Ts'ao's ambiguity seems even more pronounced. He surrounded himself with magicians and immortality-seekers, but his poems sometimes show him sympathetic to the search for immortality and sometimes show him hostile to it. Ch'en Tso-ming 陳祚明 (fl. 1670) contrasts the two by saying that Ts'ao Ts'ao "pondered seriously" about immortals, while Ts'ao P'i's usage of them in his poem is decorative and insincere; he has, therefore, produced inferior poetry.[43]

Ts'ao Chih is equally ambiguous, and, to complicate matters even more, he seems to have mellowed later in life and to have written an essay called "Resolving Doubts," "Shih-i lun" 釋疑論, in which he refutes many of the ideas he put forward in his "Analysis of Taoism." This essay is found only in *Pao-p'u-tzu* 抱朴子 by Ko Hung 葛洪 (fourth century) and it contains a certain number of anomalies, but let us read it before attempting to decide whether or not it is trustworthy. I begin with Ko Hung's prefatory remarks on Ts'ao P'i.

> Emperor Wen of the Wei [Ts'ao P'i] had seen all there was to see and heard all there was to hear and said there was nothing he did not know. He said there was no such thing as a knife that cuts jade or a cloth

[40] Tamada, "Kandai," pp. 332–33, believes the falling off in the number of inscriptions describing immortals should be attributed precisely to the kind of skepticism found in the works of Ts'ao Chih, Ts'ao Ts'ao, and Ts'ao P'i.

[41] See Yen K'o-chün 嚴可均, *Ch'üan shang-ku san-tai Ch'in Han San-kuo Liu-ch'ao wen* 全上古三代秦漢三國六朝文 (rpt. Peking: Chung-hua shu-chü, 1958), *ch.* 8, pp. 5a–7b.

[42] Reproduced in Lu Ch'in-li 逯欽立, *Hsien Ch'in Han Wei Chin Nan-pei-ch'ao shih* 先秦漢魏晉南北朝詩 (Peking: Chung-hua shu-chü, 1983), pp. 393–94.

[43] Ch'en Tso-ming, *Ts'ai-shu-t'ang ku-shih hsüan* 采菽堂詩選, *ch.* 5; quoted in Ho-pei Shih-fan hsüeh-yüan chung-wen-hsi ku-tien wen-hsüeh chiao-yen tsu 河北師範學院中文系古典文學教研組, comp., *San Ts'ao tzu-liao hui-pien* 三曹資料彙編 (Peking: Chung-hua shu-chü, 1980; hereafter, *San Ts'ao*), p. 79.

cleansed by fire,[44] and then included both these declarations in his *Tien-lun*. Before long both these objects arrived [in China]. The emperor sighed and hastily destroyed his essay on the subject. One may apply here [the prescriptions of Confucius in *Analects* 9, 4]: "Be not obstinate; have no foregone conclusions."

The Thoughtful Prince of Ch'en [Ts'ao Chih] said in his "Shih-i lun," "At first I said that it was certain that the arts of the Taoists were simply words without meaning aimed at fooling the unenlightened common people. But when I saw Emperor Wu [Ts'ao Ts'ao] experiment with Tso Tz'u and the others, keeping them in an enclosed space and having them stop eating cereals for a whole year, and when I saw that the color in their cheeks did not diminish, nor did their vitality, and that they said repeatedly that they could go on like that for fifty years, then really what doubts could I still harbor that these arts were not real?"

He said again: "He [Ts'ao Ts'ao] had Kan Shih give medicine to live fish and then had them fried in boiling fat. When those fish who received no medicine [and were fried at the same time] were cooked and ready to eat, those who had absorbed the medicine were still happily swimming about as if they were in water. [Kan Shih] also fed silkworms on mulberry leaves powdered with medicine and the silkworms lived for ten months without becoming old [i.e., without turning into chrysalises]. He also gave a medicine that stops aging to chicks and newborn puppies and they all stopped growing. A medicine for changing the color of white [hair] was fed to white dogs whose fur turned completely black in one hundred days.

"Thus we can see that we cannot know all there is to know in the world, and that we cannot allow ourselves to decide arbitrarily whether things exist or not. My only regret is that I cannot renounce the pleasures of the flesh and give myself up wholeheartedly to the study of the way of long life."

These two Ts'ao [brothers] had read all there was to read and were famous in their generation for their talents, and yet they both first said all these things did not exist, admitting late in life that they did. This shows how difficult it is "to get to the bottom of all truths and exhaust

[44] Ts'ao P'i's skepticism about the existence of a jade-cutting knife (see n. 23, above) seems to appear only in *Pao-p'u-tzu*; for the fire-cleaned cloth, see Yen K'o-chün, *Ch'üan San-kuo wen* 8, p. 14b, and n. 47, below.

III

TS'AO CHIH AND THE IMMORTALS

all that can be known of human nature."[45] It is not surprising that men who do not come up to these two do not believe in immortality.[46]

Can we believe Ko Hung? Did these two Confucian rationalists actually recant later in life and become "believers in immortality"? It is obvious that Ko Hung has got much of his information wrong. Ts'ao P'i did not himself destroy his essays on asbestos and the jade-cutting knife; it was his son, Ts'ao Jui 曹叡, Emperor Ming 明, who in 239 had the engravings of the essay concerning asbestos scraped off the tablets that had been set up in front of the Ts'ao family ancestral temples when real asbestos was brought to the court as tribute from the Western Regions.[47] We have seen, too, that it was not Tso Tz'u who refrained from eating grains, but Ch'ieh Chien, and for one hundred days, not "a whole year."[48] Ts'ao Chih also seems to have been skeptical of Kan Shih's "fish preserver," and in general of all his nostrums.

But are these anomalies sufficient to invalidate Ko Hung's testimony altogether and prove the "Shih-i lun" an out-and-out forgery? Certainly Ts'ao Chih's firsthand observation of Tso Tz'u's ability to live without eating grain (which probably means without eating at all) must have been striking. It is possible that he was haunted by the thought ten years or so later, even to the extent of accepting many of the "miracles" he refused to believe earlier; but Ko Hung's judgment as to the value of historical texts is so manifestly bad (as can be seen by his belief that Liu Hsin wrote *Hsi-ching tsa-chi* 西京雜記), that it is probably better to treat this text with caution.[49] But let us not condemn the work utterly. Ko Hung has not made an immortality-seeker out of Ts'ao Chih, as he most probably would have if he had created this essay out of his own mind. The essay does not ring false and only shows us that Ts'ao Chih mellowed when he became older.

[45] *I-ching*, "Shuo-kua," sect. 1; Legge, *The Yî King*, p. 422.
[46] *Pao-p'u-tzu* 2, p. 15; cf. James Ware, *Alchemy, Medicine, and Religion in the China of A.D. 320: The Nei P'ien of Ko Hung* (rpt. New York: Dover Publications, 1981), pp. 39–40, and Honda Wataru 本田済, *Hōbokushi* 抱朴子, in *Chūgoku koten bungaku taikei* 8, pp. 10–11, but I have followed the Tun-huang ms. given in Wang Ming 王明, *Pao-p'u-tzu nei-p'ien chiao-shih* 抱朴子內篇校釋 (Peking: Chung-hua shu-chü, 1980), pp. 14–15 and notes pp. 28–29, which makes my translation differ from the others at a few places.
[47] See Donald Holzman, "Literary Criticism in China in the Early Third Century A.D.," *Etudes Asiatiques* 28.2 (1974), p. 126.
[48] It is the Tun-huang ms. version of *Pao-p'u-tzu* that reads "a whole year" 朞; the other versions read "one month" 一月.
[49] Chung Yu-min 鍾優民, *Ts'ao Chih hsin-t'an* 曹植新探 (Ho-fei: Huang-shan shu-she, 1984), pp. 73–77, thinks the "Shih-i lun" is an out-and-out forgery, typical of Ko Hung, and he refers to a similar attempt to enroll a dyed-in-the-wool Confucianist, Chung-ch'ang T'ung 仲長統 (179–219), in the immortality-seekers' ranks (see *Pao-p'u-tzu* 5; in *Pao-p'u-tzu nei-p'ien chiao-shih*, p. 104; and Ware, *Alchemy, Medicine, and Religion*, pp. 107–08).

27

III

In fact, aside from this essay, Ts'ao Chih seems to have been an unbeliever. All his works show him to be a rationalistic Confucianist and there are couplets and phrases denouncing or rejecting immortality. The most famous is probably the couplet in the last stanza of his masterpiece, "To Piao, Prince of Pai-ma," dated 223, in which he says: "It is in vain that we search for the immortals; / [Ch'ih]-sung-tzu has cheated us for a long time" 虛無求列仙 / 松子久吾欺.[50] In another, probably fragmentary, work called "Ch'iu-ssu fu" ("Autumn Thoughts"), he ends with the lines:

> We live in a single generation,
>> The days of our youth pass on.
> It is hard to emulate [Chih]-sung-tzu and [Wang-tzu] Ch'iao:
>> Who can become an immortal?
> Our destiny has a certain length;
>> Who can add to it?[51]

It is possible that in his essay he is particularly severe against the Taoists because he is eager to disassociate himself, his father, and the dynasty in general, from the taint of immortality-seeking that had been associated with the imperial court since the First Emperor of the Ch'in and Emperor Wu of the Han. But the fact is that Ts'ao Chih in all his works that treat the subject, except the "Shih-i lun" and those we are about to read, is hostile to immortality-seeking, and we must take that hostility into account when we read his ballads on the theme of the immortals.

TS'AO CHIH'S TEN BALLADS ON IMMORTALS

The ten ballads on the theme of the immortals are written within a fairly tight-knit tradition which stems from the *Ch'u-tz'u* and in particular from the poem in the *Ch'u-tz'u* entitled "Distant Voyage" ("Yüan yu" 遠遊). Whatever date is ascribed to that poem,[52] Ts'ao Chih probably thought the original attribution to Ch'ü Yüan correct, and he knew that the poem was, by his time, many centuries old.

Did he believe in the traditional interpretation of the poem by the compiler of the *Ch'u-tz'u*, Wang I 王逸, who died fifty or so years before Ts'ao Chih was born? That is something more difficult to determine. Wang I tells

---

[50] *TCCCC* 2, p. 300.
[51] *TCCCC* 3, p. 471.
[52] The most complete and best discussion is in Yves Hervouet, *Un poète de cour sous les Han: Sseu-ma Siang-jou*, BIHEC 19 (Paris: Presses Univ. de Fr., 1964), pp. 288–302, who suggests an early Han date.

III

us, in his preface to the poem,[53] that the "distant voyage" is only an allegory. Ch'ü Yüan, he says, although pure and honest, was calumniated and rejected from the court. Although he still "wanted to save the world, he felt frustrated in his heart and, with baroque splendor, set forth his marvellous thoughts. He pretended to accompany the immortals in their playful wanderings, traveling through the entire universe, visiting every corner. But he kept his native country of Ch'u in his heart and thought longingly of his old friends and relatives: he was truly loyal, thoroughly good and righteous."

When we read the poem today we find some support for Wang I's interpretation, but also room to wonder if he has not "Confucianized" what is, at bottom, a mystical, Taoist voyage of the soul to the absolute. It is true that the poet begins with a rejection of the corruption of the world and turns toward a mystical leap into the heights as an escape, and that later in the poem, when the poet is close to his mystical goal, he remembers his loved ones with sadness,[54] but the rest of the work is in a purely mystical vein, and it ends in a true apotheosis, a state of union with the cosmos. It is hard for us today to agree with Wang I and see "Distant Voyage" as a pure allegory showing Ch'ü Yüan as a politician manqué out on an imaginary jaunt simply to proclaim that he wants to keep out of the corrupt world of politics. Did Ts'ao Chih see the poem as we do, or was his understanding closer to Wang I's? Perhaps it would be better to attempt to answer that question when we have studied his own adaptations of "Distant Voyage."

In a way, this whole "tight-knit tradition" of ballads taking immortals as their theme is made up of adaptations of "Distant Voyage," just as that poem itself is a mystical version of the shamanistic, heavenly wanderings described earlier in the "Li-sao." Originality shows up (as is often the case in Chinese poetry) only as small variations that only the reader practised in the genre can appreciate. Just how many poems on the theme existed when Ts'ao Chih sat down to write, and just when the first were written, are of course impossible to know. The earliest ones still extant in which elements of the tradition can be observed seem to be the sacrificial hymns composed for Emperor Wu and conserved in *Han shu*, ch. 22.[55] A few of these poems only hint at the theme here and there, but the filiation with the later tradition seems clear. It can be seen in such poems as "Hymn No. Ten," which celebrates the capture of "Heavenly Horses" in the Western Regions in 101

[53] In Hung Hsing-tsu 洪興祖 (fl. Sung), ed., *Ch'u-tz'u pu-chu* 楚辭補注, rpt. of SPPY edn. (Taipei, 1978) 5, pp. 1a–b.
[54] *Ch'u-tz'u pu-chu* 11, pp. 69b–71b; cf. Hawkes, *Ch'u Tz'u*, p. 85.
[55] *MH* 3, pp. 605–29.

29

B.C. At the very end of this poem the horse and its rider are said to "reach the K'un-lun, ... wander in the gates of Heaven and see the Jade Terrace" of the Emperor-on-High.[56] In these poems the immortals do not actually appear, but the desire to reach their abodes (the K'un-lun or P'eng-lai) and wander through the heavens is very much the same as in the later ballads.

Such ballads are extremely difficult to date, our earliest text for some of them being the monograph on music in *Sung shu* (c. 500 A.D.)[57] and some of them are found for the first time only in the Northern Sung *Yüeh-fu shih-chi* 樂府詩集. They show us the immortal Wang-tzu Ch'iao, mounted on a carriage pulled by a white deer, riding among the clouds over the Four Seas and the Five Peaks ("Wang-tzu Ch'iao"),[58] or another unnamed immortal, mounted on a white deer, who distributes drugs in a jade box that give health and blacken white hair ("Ch'ang ko-hsing" 2),[59] or a hermit who, together with Ch'ih-sung-tzu, can drive us up to heaven ("Pu ch'u hsia-men hsing").[60] These are all themes that appear again and again in the "wandering immortals" poems and, whether they are older or younger than Ts'ao Chih's poems, they are surely written in the same tradition. In their rusticity and naiveté they seem closer to Ts'ao Ts'ao's ballads of immortals than to Ts'ao Chih's, which makes me feel that they are earlier.

These different themes that appear and reappear in Ts'ao Chih's poetry could probably be traced to their origins and catalogued. This would provide us with a convenient method of formal analysis.[61] But an analysis will not tell us enough about just what Ts'ao Chih is getting at. I know I am treading on delicate ground even to suggest such a question, but I believe I

[56] *MH* 3, pp. 620–21. For a discussion of these early "immortals" ballads, see Konishi Noboru 小西昇, "Kandai gafushi to shinsen shisō" 漢代楽府詩と神仙思想, *Mekada Makoto hakase kanreki kinen: Chūgoku gaku ronshū* 目加田誠博士還暦記念中国学論集 (Tokyo: Daian, 1964), pp. 137–60, esp. pp. 140–49; and Sawaguchi Takeo 沢口剛雄, "Kan no gafu ni okeru shinsen dōka no shisō" 漢の楽府における神仙道家の思想 *Tōhō shūkyō* 東方宗教 27 (1966), pp. 1–22.

[57] From the observance of the taboos for the names of the late Ch'i and early Liang emperors, it can be seen that the monograph on music in the *Sung shu* was not completed in 488 with the biographical part of the work: see Su Chin-jen 蘇晉仁 and Hsiao Lien-tzu 蕭煉子, *Sung-shu yüeh-chih chiao-chu* 宋書樂志校注 (Shan-tung: Ch'i Lu shu-she, 1982), p. 4.

[58] Trans. in Sawaguchi Takeo, *Gafu* 樂府, Chūgoku koten shinsho (Tokyo: Meitoku shuppansha, 1969), pp. 114–17. Sawaguchi (p. 117) suggests that this poem dates from the time of Emperor Wu of the Han. The text can also be found in Lu, *Hsien Ch'in*, pp. 261–62.

[59] Lu, *Hsien Ch'in*, p. 262; trans. in Obi Kōichi 小尾郊一 and Okamura Sadao 岡村貞雄, *Kogafu* 古楽府 (Tokyo: Tōkai daigaku shuppansha, 1980), pp. 130–31.

[60] Lu, *Hsien Ch'in*, p. 267 (under the title "Lung-hsi hsing" 隴西行); Obi and Okamura discuss the problems this poem presents in *Kogafu*, pp. 158–63, and translate it on pp. 163–65.

[61] This has been done by Funazu Tomihiko 船津富彦, "Sō Shoku no yūsenshi ron: Toku ni setsuwa no tenkai o chūshin ni shite" 曹植の遊仙詩論（特に説話の展開を中心にして）, *Tōyō bungaku kenkyū* 東洋文学研究 13 (1965), pp. 49–65, in order to date the poems, without much success in my opinion.

can prove, in the words of the poetry itself, that Ts'ao Chih's interest in using
the theme of the immortals is not always simple or straightforward, that he
is not always interested in immortals as such, and that his main interest in the
theme is complex, sometimes satirical, sometimes personal and emotional. It
is only by a close reading that we can arrive at a conclusion, and although I
agree that extraneous biographical material cannot be used to explain or
even to contradict what the poem itself tells us, I do believe that it is only
against what we know of Ts'ao Chih's biography and what he tells us in his
other poetry that we will be able to approach the true meaning or, more
exactly, the true "feeling" of his ballads that deal with immortals.

About half of Ts'ao Chih's ten "immortals" ballads seem clearly to be
satires, that is, they seem to use the *Ch'u-tz'u* tradition to describe not a
mystical journey or wandering immortals, but the political concerns of their
author. The clearest of these is the only one of the ten that can be dated with
any assurance. It is a ballad describing a trip to Mount T'ai in Shan-tung
which, as Chao Yu-wen has shown, can only have taken place after Ts'ao
Chih had become Prince of Tung-a 東阿 in 229, and probably shortly after
he was granted the title.[62] Only the last six lines of the ballad conform to the
"immortals" poetic tradition; the first twenty-two lines are concerned more
with a description of Mount T'ai and a history of the *feng* 封 and *shan* 禪
ceremonies held upon it.

I Speed in My Carriage

I speed in my carriage, urging on my aging nags,
And in the east arrive at the walls of Feng-kao.
How divine is Mount T'ai,
The most preeminent of all the Five Peaks!
5   Its exalted heights thread the clouds and rainbows,
And jut into the Vast Purity of the heavens.
A dozen watchtowers surround it completely,
And twelve relay stations are placed at intervals about it.

[62] *TCCCC*, p. 406. The poem concerns the performance of the great *feng* and *shan* rituals on
Mount T'ai which had been suggested by Chiang Chi 蔣濟 to Emperor Ming in 228 (*SKC* 25,
p. 717). Ts'ao Chih became Prince of Tung-a in 229 and would only then have been close
enough to have been able to voyage to Mount T'ai, some 55 miles east of Tung-a, although even
this voyage would have been considerably longer than the "thirty *li*" allowed to feudal lords for
their hunting expeditions. (For this see *Yüan-tzu* 袁子, quoted in *SKC* 20, pp. 591–92, trans. A.
Fang, *The Chronicle of the Three Kingdoms* 1, Harvard-Yenching Institute Studies 6 [Cambridge,
Mass.: Harvard U.P., 1952], p. 114; also p. 100.) One gets the impression from *SKC* that the
discussion of the opportunity for holding the ritual on Mount T'ai was halted in 230 with the
death of the Empress Dowager, Mme. Pien 卞, Ts'ao Chih's mother, so that 229 is the most
probable date for this poem.

Above and below sweet springs gush forth,
10   Where rough jade stones shine brightly.
[From?] the northeast we look toward the wilds of Wu;
And [from?] the west we contemplate the sun's rays far away.
It is here that our souls will be bound;
So that those who pass away feel moved that they too will voyage
         hither.

15   It is here our rulers place their trust in heaven
And here they [announce] that their great work has been achieved.
For dynasty after dynasty all have followed this custom,
Their rituals and sacrifices performed according to proper number
         and order.
Here the divining sticks may predict a long or a short life:
20   Only the virtuous will enjoy advantage and constancy.
Seventy emperors have performed the *feng* ceremony,
But the first and only to become a spirit was the Yellow Emperor.

He ate rosy vapors and rinsed his mouth with midnight dew;
Feathers covered his body.
25   He rose up and trod upon the void,
Straightway ascending to the empyrean.
His longevity was like that of the Father of the East,
Prolonging his life for generation upon generation.[63]

Feng-kao 奉高, literally "offering to the heights," was located to the
east of Mount T'ai in Shan-tung. A sacred hall, Ming-t'ang 明堂, was located
there, for imperial sacrifices to the sacred mountain.[64] The description of the
mountain emphasizes its height and circumference (since the watchtowers
and relay stations were placed at regular intervals, to say there were twelve
of each presupposes a circumference of something like 120 *li*). I do not
understand why Ts'ao Chih, in lines 11 and 12, speaks of the "northeast"
and the "west." I have attempted to account for this in my translation by
implying that Mount T'ai is to the northeast of Wu (actually it is to the
northwest), and that the sun's rays are looked at from the west, for the
tradition (still observed) is to watch the sun rise from the top of Mount
T'ai.[65] But I fear I have not understood something here; Chinese poets
seldom confuse their directions in this way.

[63] *TCCCC*, pp. 404–06.   [64] *MH* 3, pp. 510–11.
[65] See the *Han kuan-i* 漢官儀 and *T'ai-shan chi* 泰山記, quoted in *T'ai-p'ing yü-lan* 39,
pp. 6a–b. Different "observatories" or "towers," *kuan* 觀, are mentioned from which one can see
Ch'ang-an, Wu, Ch'i, and the Yellow River.

Beginning with lines 13–14, Ts'ao Chih describes the spiritual role of Mount T'ai, which housed the souls of the dead[66] and was the scene (lines 15–21) of the all-important *feng* and *shan* ceremonies, during which emperors who founded a dynasty or achieved great peace were to announce their deeds to the gods.[67] According to one account, Emperor Wu of the Han had his fortune told while on Mount T'ai (line 19): he learned he would live another eighteen years.[68] Line 21 refers to a remark attributed to Kuan Chung 管仲 in *Shih-chi* where he says that seventy-two men had performed the *feng* and the *shan* sacrifices.[69] The following line also refers to a passage in this chapter of *Shih-chi*[70] which says (contradicting the previous passage) that the Yellow Emperor was the only one of the seventy-two kings who performed the *feng* and *shan* sacrifices to do so on Mount T'ai. The passage continues by describing his apotheosis as a Taoist immortal.

The last lines of the poem ostensibly describe the Yellow Emperor, but can be taken as a form of flattery for Ts'ao Chih's nephew, who was thinking of performing the *feng* and *shan* sacrifices on Mount T'ai at the time this poem was probably written. It is possible, of course, that the poem was not written during an actual trip to the sacred mountain and that Ts'ao Chih wrote it before he became Prince of Tung-a, but unless the *feng* and *shan* ceremonies were envisaged at some other period during Ts'ao Chih's life, it would be hard to imagine that this poem could have been written at any other time or for any other reason.

In spite of its "wandering immortal" ending, then, "I Speed in My Carriage" is not basically a poem that takes immortals as its real subject. In the following poem, on the contrary, it is the ending that shows us the real meaning; the rest, including the title, is in fact, strictly in the "wandering immortals" tradition.

Immortals

I

The immortals hold the six counters in their hands
And play face to face on the slopes of Mount T'ai.
O, the nymph of the Hsiang, strums the zither,
As the Princess of Ch'in blows the reed organ.
5   The jade jars are filled with osmanthus wine;
The Count of the Yellow River has offered divine fish.

---

[66] See Edouard Chavannes, *Le T'ai Chan: Essai de monographie d'un culte chinois* (Paris: Ernest Leroux, 1910).
[67] Described in *SC* 28; see *MH* 3, pp. 413–519.   [68] *Feng-su t'ung-i chiao-chu*, p. 65.
[69] *MH* 3, p. 423.   [70] *MH* 3, p. 487.

2

How narrow the confines of the Four Seas seem to me!
There is nowhere to go in the Nine States!
Han Chung and Wang Ch'iao
10 Invite me on the road to Heaven.
I cover infinite distances in less than a pace
As I float upward, high into the Great Void.

3

Flying in a single leap beyond the many-colored clouds,
I am blown about by the winds on high.
15 I turn my carriage to pass through the celestial region of Tzu-wei
Where I will join my magic tally to the Emperor's.
The Heavenly Gates jut high into the firmament,
Their two towers looming up without end.

4

Jade trees grow on either side of the road;
20 White tigers flank the hinges of the gate.
Driving the wind I wander over the Four Seas;
In the east I pass before the hut of the Queen Mother.
Looking down among the Five Peaks,
The men there seem to be no more than passing guests.

5

25 I will hide my light and try to grow my wings,
And proceed slowly, slowly.
Until I see the Yellow Emperor
Come out from Cauldron Lake mounted on a dragon,
I shall pace back and forth above the Nine Heavens,
And await his coming as long as it takes.[71]

This poem divides itself nicely into five sections of six lines each. The first section describes a scene commonly depicted on Han bronze mirrors and bas-reliefs which Ts'ao Chih must have seen since his childhood: two men or (more often) immortals surrounded by other mortal or immortal personages,[72] playing at a game which superficially resembles backgammon, called

[71] *TCCC*, pp. 263–65.
[72] See the two articles by L. S. Yang, "A Note on the So-called TLV Mirrors and the Game *liu-po*," *HJAS* 9 (1947), pp. 202–06, and "An Additional Note on the Ancient Game of *liu-po*," *HJAS* 15 (1952), pp. 125–39; rpt. in Yang's *Excursions in Sinology*, Harvard-Yenching Institute

liu-po 六博. Here the accompanying figures are ancient gods and goddesses: O 娥, the nymph of the River Hsiang 湘, was the elder daughter of Yao and wife of Shun who, after his death, drowned with her sister in the Hsiang and became a goddess or nymph.[73] The princess of Ch'in was named Lung-yü 弄玉 and was the daughter of Duke Miao (659–621 B.C.), who married her to the virtuoso of the panpipes, Hsiao-shih 蕭史. They were carried off by phoenixes.[74] The Count of the Yellow River, Ho-po 河伯, is a famous and fearful ancient deity who appears in many texts.[75]

The sight of this idyllic group of immortals and deities seems to provoke an epistemological shock: Ts'ao Chih realizes that ordinary life in the ordinary world is narrow and useless. He decides to attempt to follow the immortals and roam with them to the ends of the universe. Han Chung 韓終 (also written 衆) was an adept at the time of the First Emperor of the Ch'in[76] and Wang Ch'iao (or Wang-tzu Ch'iao) we have already seen. They will teach Ts'ao Chih to navigate in the heavens where he will be able to see the celestial emperor who resides in the region of Tzu-wei 紫微, "Purple Sub-tlety," north of the Big Dipper (thus including the Pole Star). The tally he joins to the emperor's is the proof of his status as a vassal. The description of the heavenly scenery is stereotyped; still, it is strange, in line 22, to see the Queen Mother, Wang-mu 王母, presumably Hsi 西 Wangmu, the Queen Mother of the West, in the east. Chao Yu-wen quotes *Wu-yüeh ming-shan t'u* 五岳名山圖, otherwise unknown to me, which says that the Queen Mother's palace was in the eastern corner of the K'un-lun Mountains. But the K'un-lun are in the west and this line is obscure unless Ts'ao Chih is attempting to show that his cosmic view of the universe is so all-enfolding and unifying that east and west no longer have any meaning.

The first four stanzas present no real problems: Ts'ao Chih declares that he is opting for the life of a Taoist immortal in order to leave the imper-manence and relativity of the ordinary world. But the last stanza is strange.

Studies 24 (Cambridge, Mass.: Harvard U.P., 1969), pp. 138–65. L. S. Yang quotes the first two lines of the poem by Ts'ao Chih on p. 206 of his earlier article. Ts'ao Chih is credited with the invention of a *liu-po* gameboard in *Hsü shih-shih* 續事始, quoted in Hu San-hsing's com-mentary to the *Tzu-chih t'ung-chien* (Peking: Chung-hua shu-chü, 1956), *ch.* 162, p. 5006. See also Loewe, *Ways to Paradise*, pp. 145–46, nn. 40–46.

[73] See the numerous references to O found in Mathieu, *Etude sur la mythologie* 1, pp. 363–64, and Yüan K'o 遠珂, *Chung-kuo shen-hua ch'uan-shuo* 中國神話傳說 (Peking: Chung-kuo min-chien wen-i ch'u-pan-she, 1984), p. 272, n. 17, p. 276.

[74] See Kaltenmark, *Le Lie-sien tchouan*, pp. 125–27. Ts'ao Chih has presented her here as a mouth organist, while her hagiography mentions her only as a panpipe virtuoso.

[75] Given in Mathieu, *Etude sur la mythologie*, p. 492, n. 3, and Yüan K'o, *Chung-kuo shen-hua ch'uan-shuo*, p. 306, n. 6, and other references in his index.

[76] *MH* 2, pp. 167, 180.

His conversion, which seemed complete and sudden, here becomes something to be achieved slowly and in secret, and it is only after he sees the apotheosis of the Yellow Emperor, described in *Shih-chi*,[77] that he will cease his "pacing back and forth," that is, his inactivity far above mundane existence, above the highest heavens. However we interpret the earlier stanzas (his journey to the celestial court could be wishful thinking, an imaginary journey to his brother's or nephew's court), this waiting and pacing back and forth in the last stanza suggests some kind of allegory. Ts'ao Chih is saying he will retire from politics and wait until a wise sovereign appears who will be worthy of his services.[78] This poem would thus be very much in the allegorical tradition of the *Ch'u-tz'u*, and the "religious" quality of Ts'ao Chih's "conversion" should accordingly be taken with a grain of salt, although it would be wrong to discount the religious element entirely.

The previous poem, "I Speed in My Carriage," with its allusions to the *feng* and *shan* ceremonies could, I believe, be dated; can this poem? A Ch'ing critic, Sung Ch'ang-pai 宋長白, rather incongruously, gives the date as "when Ts'ao Chih moved from Jen-ch'eng to Tung-a." Ts'ao Chih was in Jen-ch'eng in 221 and moved to Tung-a only in 229, after three other removals.[79] Chao Yu-wen assigns it to the middle of Ts'ao P'i's reign when the latter put into force his restrictions against his brother.[80] These dates seem fairly convincing. One would expect Ts'ao Chih to have written such a poem when he realized that he could expect no cooperation from the reigning monarch and that he would have to wait for a succession before he would be able to serve. I doubt that one can get closer than that. He was disappointed by both his brother and his nephew, but would he have had the courage and the hope to serve another sovereign after the death of his nephew?

The following poem is in irregular meter and rhyme. I think it is also a statement of Ts'ao Chih's feelings about his place in the world of politics.

Hard Thinking

The green creeper hugs the tree of jade;
They shine together, glittering brightly.

[77] *MH* 3, pp. 488–89.
[78] See Chu Ch'ien 朱乾, *Yüeh-fu cheng-i* 樂府正義, quoted in *San Ts'ao*, p. 202. Wang Yün-hsi 王運熙, *Yüeh-fu shih lun-ts'ung* 樂府詩論叢 (Shanghai: Ku-tien wen-hsüeh ch'u-pan-she, 1958), pp. 137–38, criticizes Chu Ch'ien's forced readings of these texts, but still concludes that his work is the richest in material and in insights among all the works dedicated to the study of the *yüeh-fu* written during the Ming and Ch'ing dynasties.
[79] Sung Ch'ang-pai, *Liu-t'ing shih-hua* 柳亭詩話 ch. 2, quoted in *San Ts'ao*, p. 172.
[80] *TCCCC*, p. 265.

Below there are two Perfect Men
Who raise their wings to beat them and fly in the heights.
5   How my heart leaps up for joy!
I would like to climb the clouds and follow them.
How verdant is the summit of the Western Peak
Whose dark blue stone caves reach to the heavens!
In one of them lives an ancient hermit
10   Whose beard and hair are all shining white.
Leaning on his staff he follows me as I roam,
To teach me that I must "forget about words." [81]

The first two lines of this poem may simply be a short description that introduces the world of the immortals with its eternal "jade trees," or it may be more significant, a metaphor (*hsing* 興) that gives the clue to the meaning of the whole poem. If it is the latter, then I suspect that the "creeper," *lo* 蘿, in line 1, whatever it may be in the natural world (perhaps some kind of dodder — which is not green — or spanish moss?) has symbolic significance derived from Poem 217 of the *Shih-ching*. In that poem the "creeper" symbolizes a sovereign's brothers or close relatives who cling to him as the *lo* clings to the pine tree. These first two lines, if they are metaphorical, would thus be a message to his brother or nephew, saying that the emperor would gain added luster by surrounding himself with his brothers and uncles.

The Perfect Men are immortals whom Ts'ao Chih does not seem to be able to follow when they fly off to heaven (or the imperial court?). Instead he finds an ancient wise man on Mount Hua (the Western Peak) who teaches him Chuang-tzu's lesson that "words are there to preserve meaning; when you get the meaning, you must forget the words." [82] But in the context of the poem, and especially of a poem entitled "Hard Thinking," "forgetting words" must mean "learning to keep one's mouth shut to avoid calamity." In fact it is these two characters that give the poem its "hard" or "bitter" meaning, as the Ch'ing critic Cho Erh-k'an 卓爾堪 (Pao-hsiang shan-jen 寶香山人) has pointed out. [83] The title is a *yüeh-fu* title and therefore may not actually be meaningful, but, since it is the only *yüeh-fu* with such a title, [84] it is probable that he chose it to tell us something about the

[81] *TCCCC*, p. 316; previous trans., George W. Kent, *Worlds of Dust and Jade* (New York: Philosophical Library, 1969), p. 79.

[82] *Chuang-tzu* 26; see Watson, *The Complete Works of Chuang-tzu*, p. 302.

[83] Quoted in *San Ts'ao*, p. 165. See also Chang Ch'ao 張潮, quoted in Chao Fu-t'an 趙福壇, *Ts'ao Wei fu-tzu shih-hsüan* 曹魏父子詩選 (Hong Kong: Joint Publishing Co., 1982) 63, p. 205.

[84] Kuo Mao-ch'ien 郭茂倩, comp., *Yüeh-fu shih-chi* 樂府詩集 (mod. edn.; Peking: Chung-hua shu-chü, 1974), *ch.* 63, p. 919.

poem. A straightforward reading of the poem, seeing it as a description of a man who yearns to follow immortals, but makes do instead with an ancient professor of Taoist philosophy, simply does not live up to the title. The first two lines, if my theory is correct, hinting at the joy of fraternal union as described in Poem 217 of the *Shih-ching*, are contradicted by the end of the poem. There the poet must learn to keep silent. The subtlety of the allusion in line 1 is already an application of "disguising," if not exactly "forgetting," his words.

The last ballads exalting immortality which I believe not to be "pure" poems both have the title "Ascending to Heaven." [85] They should be treated as separate poems, but they both concern mythological themes and share a slightly melancholic mood.

Ascending to Heaven

1

I will mount on my stilts to follow the magicians
Far away to Mount P'eng-lai.
On the sacred waters white waves fly up;
The magnolias and osmanthus grow to the heavens.
5   The black leopard roams at the foot [of the mount],
And soaring cranes play at its crest.
Rising on the wind I suddenly leap into the sky
And it is as if I could see the immortal throng.

2

Where the Fu-sang tree grows,
Is in the Morning-bright Torrent.
The tree's trunk rises to the blue heavens;
Its leaves cover all to the ends of the earth.
5   When the sun rises, it climbs the eastern trunk,
And as night falls, the sun sinks into the western branches.
I would like to be able to turn the reins of the sun's [chariot]
And make it rush back toward the east![86]

---

[85] Two lines of the first poem, reduced to tetrameters, under the title "K'u-han-hsing" 苦寒行 are quoted by Li Shan in *Wen-hsüan*, rpt. of a Sung edn. (Peking: Chung-hua shu-chü, 1974), *ch.* 21, p. 27a.

[86] *TCCCC*, pp. 266–67; previous trans., Kent, *Worlds of Dust and Jade*, p. 80, and Ronald C. Miao, *Sunflower Splendor* (Garden City, N.Y.: Anchor/Doubleday, 1975), p. 42 (second poem only).

The "stilts" of the first poem are *ch'iao* 蹺 which all the commentators understand as some kind of seven-league boots or magic sandals.[87] Whatever they are, they allow the poet to travel to the legendary haunts of the immortals in the Eastern Sea. Here he sees fantastic plants and animals and seems to see the immortals themselves. It is in the "seems" that the melancholy of the poem lies, for the word reminds us of the attempts made by the First Emperor of the Ch'in and Emperor Wu of the Han to reach this island mountain, which they "seemed" to see floating on the sea but were always unable to find.[88]

The second poem is even more melancholic. It begins with an innovative description of the famous mythological Fu-sang tree, which the *Shan-hai ching* and all other sources consulted claim to have been in the east, "where the sun rises." However, Ts'ao Chih wants us to believe it is a tree whose leaves reach to the eastern and western ends of the earth and in whose branches the sun both mounts to the heavens in the morning and sinks to the earth at the end of day. The "Morning-bright Torrent" in line 2 also seems original; the Fu-sang is usually said to rise in T'ang 湯 or Yang 暘 Valley.[89] The belief that the Fu-sang has more than one trunk is, however, not unique to Ts'ao Chih, for it appears also in *Hai-nei shih-chou chi* 海內十洲記, a work attributed to Tung-fang Shuo, but probably by an author from the Six Dynasties period; there the Fu-sang is said to have two trunks on a single root.[90]

But the most striking part of this poem is the last couplet. It is wrong for the true Taoist immortality-seeker to want to turn back the sun, to alter nature in any way. His immortality comes from living in harmony with nature, not from stopping the sun (and time). If Ts'ao Chih wants to turn back the sun (and the clock) it can only be, as Chao Yu-wen says,[91] because he felt "the times were against him." His plea to set back the sun is one made by a positive, active man who desires to accomplish something in society, not by a religious spirit attempting to save his soul.

---

[87] They refer to *Pao-p'u-tzu* 15 (*nei-p'ien*); cf. Ware, *Alchemy, Medicine, and Religion*, pp. 258–59. See also the excellent remarks on this subject by Kaltenmark, *Le Lie-sien tchouan*, pp. 46–47, 111–14, and his "Un procédé de vol magique dans le taoïsme," in *Suzuki hakase koki kinen tōyōgaku ronsō* 鈴木博士古稀記念東洋学論叢 (Tokyo: Meitoku shuppansha, 1972), pp. 5–13.

[88] *MH* 3, pp. 436–38, 465–66.   [89] Cf. Mathieu, *Etude sur la mythologie*, p. 439, n. 6.

[90] Cf. *Shih-chou chi* as quoted in *Wen-hsüan* 15, p. 6a. For the date of the composition of the *Hai-nei shih-chou chi*, see *Ssu-k'u ch'üan-shu tsung-mu t'i-yao* 142, p. 71 (Wan-yu wen-k'u edn.). I accept the emendation made by Chao Fu-t'an, *Ts'ao Wei fu-tzu shih-hsüan*, p. 92, of 兩 into 幹 of the text of the *Shih-chou chi* quoted in *Wen hsüan*; the original has 兩兩同根.

[91] *TCCCC*, p. 267.

III

These two poems, then, both seem to be the kind of "distant roaming" that Taoists like to describe, full of extravagant braggadocio and exotica. But, more precisely, they are lamentations, the first for a paradise impossible to find, the second for time, which leaves Ts'ao Chih behind. It seems to me that Chu Ch'ien is reading too much into the second poem when he says that Ts'ao Chih shows his "unflagging devotion to his sovereign." But I think he is right in underlining the fact that Ts'ao Chih is lamenting his lack of success in the world of politics (and thus his failure to achieve merit for the dynasty).[92] Or has Chu Ch'ien put his finger on an explanation of Ts'ao Chih's innovative mythology: that Ts'ao's extended Fu-sang tree is a symbol of universal sovereignty?

In the six remaining poems one looks in vain for the kind of "allegorical" or satirical elements seen in the preceding poems. Here Ts'ao Chih speaks the language of immortality-seekers, as if he were one of them. The following translation is the first example; in it his conversion is still conditional.

Wandering Immortals

The life of man does not last a century.
And year after year his joys diminish.
I would like to stretch out the shafts of my wings
And pushing aside the mist, rise up to the purple void.
5   I would slough off my old form as Ch'ih-[sung-tzu] and [Wang-tzu]
       Ch'iao did,
    Leave behind all traces of my former self and rise up from Cauldron
       Lake,
Soaring above the Nine Heavens,
Loosening the reins to undertake a long wandering.
In the east I will observe the brightness of the Fu-sang tree;
10 In the west approach Jo River's current;
    In the north I will go as far as one can go and climb up the Dark
       Islands;
In the south I will soar and mount Cinnabar Hill.[93]

The first line is a near quotation of line 1 of Poem 15 of the Nineteen Old Poems and, in the reading I have followed, the second line seems to be a comment, or a revision of the second line of that "old poem" ("And yet

---

[92] Chu Ch'ien, *Yüeh-fu cheng-i* 12, quoted in *San Ts'ao*, p. 201.
[93] *TCCCC*, pp. 265–66; previous trans., Miao, *Sunflower Splendor*, p. 48.

we keep within us one thousand years of woe"). A textual variant would read "we live in solitude with few joys."

It is because of the first two words in line 3, *i-yü* 意欲, literally, "In my mind I would like to...," that I have put parts of the poem into the conditional tense. We have already seen almost all the elements in the lines that follow: Ch'ih-sung-tzu, Wang-tzu Ch'iao, Cauldron Lake, the Nine Heavens; but here the Fu-sang tree regains its traditional site in the east, and the River Jo, while it has many locations according to different sources, here probably refers to the river of the immortals in the K'un-lun Mountains.[94] The Dark Islands, Hsüan-chu 玄渚, appear in the "Hsi-ching fu" of Chang Heng, in a context full of allusions to immortal haunts,[95] and the Cinnabar Hill, Tan Ch'iu 丹丘, in the "Distant Voyage" of the *Ch'u-tz'u*.[96]

On first reading, I found the last four lines of this poem rather abrupt and wondered if it were not fragmentary. But, although both Pao-hsiang shan-jen and Ch'en Tso-ming think this ending particularly satisfying,[97] the poem seems to elicit questions like the following. Why has Ts'ao Chih chosen this theme for his poem? Is it, as Ch'en Tso-ming says, "again" simply "a pretext" or allegory?[98] What in the poem tells us that Ts'ao Chih was thinking of something else when he wrote? Line 3, as I have said, makes one think that this is a poem of wishful thinking, but even "wishful thinking" would be a complete reversal of Ts'ao Chih's scorn of the immortals and would seem to show that he adopted a new attitude toward them in some of his (late?) poems. It may very well be that the near-misery of his life after his brother's accession made him want to renounce the world and seek solace in religion, but this is not to take immortality-seeking as a "pretext" or "allegory;" it may be a last resort, but then religion often is.

Another poem shows this same positive attitude toward immortals with, as far as I can see, no conditional tense implied in the words of the poem itself. This poem is in tetrameters.

The Flying Dragon

In the morning I wandered on Mount T'ai
When the mist made all silent and mysterious.
I suddenly met two youths,
Whose faces were fresh and fair.

---

[94] See *SC* 123, pp. 3163–64, for a discussion of the location of the River Jo.

[95] *Wen-hsüan* 2, p. 12a; trans. David Knechtges, *Wen xuan, or Selections of Refined Literature, Volume One: Rhapsodies on Metropolises and Capitals* (Princeton: Princeton U.P., 1982), p. 201.

[96] Hawkes, *Ch'u Tz'u*, p. 178.   [97] *San Ts'ao*, pp. 164, 195.

[98] Ch'en Tso-ming, *Ts'ai-shu-t'ang ku-shih hsüan* 6, quoted in *San Ts'ao*, p. 195.

III

5   They rode white deer
And bore magic mushrooms in their hands for shade.
I knew they were Perfect Men,
So I fell to my knees and asked them about the Way.
In the west we climbed to the Hall of Jade
10   With its golden towers and two-tiered galleries.
They gave me drugs of immortality
Prepared by the Divine Emperor,
And taught me how to take them,
And to turn backward my sperm to restore the brain.
15   I shall live as long as metal or stone,
Generation after generation I will not grow old![99]

Why has Ts'ao Chih given this little fantasy the title "Flying Dragon" when no dragon appears in it? Kuo Mao-ch'ien 郭茂倩 suggests that the title comes from the "Li-sao," and that the search for immortals is the common bond that ties the two together.[100] Is he also suggesting that Ts'ao Chih's poem, like the "Li-sao," has political overtones? He does not say so specifically and it would be hard to follow him if he did, because the poem seems so straightforward and transparent, perhaps too transparent for the traditional critic's taste. Ting Yen says, "this poem is a satire against (*sic*) the immortals. In the closing lines he does not speak out clearly [against them] and that is the most remarkable thing of all: you must seek his meaning beyond his words." There are two fragments, one of four words, one of four tetrameter lines,[101] which do not appear in the poem as we have it and do not seem to have much to do with it, but I don't think they are sufficient reason to doubt the poem's authenticity, or perhaps even to doubt its being complete as it stands. The poem does not present any difficulties, except perhaps line 14 which refers to sexual techniques aiming at preventing emission of semen ("essence") and sending it back up through the body to the brain.[102]

[99] *TCCCC*, pp. 397–98.
[100] *Yüeh-fu shih-chi* 64, p. 926.
[101] Found in the commentary to the *Wen-hsüan* 28, p. 14b; and in *Pei-t'ang shu-ch'ao* 北堂書鈔 (Taipei: Wen-hai ch'u-pan-she, 1962), *ch.* 158, p. 23a.
[102] Ts'ao Chih's line appears verbally in *Pao-p'u-tzu* 8, p. 137, and 5, p. 101; cf. Ware, *Alchemy, Medicine, and Religion*, pp. 140, 103. It is briefly discussed by Henri Maspero, *Le Taoïsme* (Paris: Gallimard, 1971), p. 575. The poem has been translated by Hugh Dunn, *Cao Zhi: The Life of a Princely Chinese Poet* (Peking: New World Press, 1983), pp. 51–52. Line 8 does not mean (as Dunn would have it) "long knelt," but refers to kneeling with the torso erect, less honorific than bowing the head to the ground from a kneeling position on the floor. He has not caught the allusion in l. 14, which he translates, "to renew your spirit and remake your mind." He gives the second half of the poem, from l. 9, as the answer of the two youths to the questions "about the Way" in l. 8. This is clever and can be defended, but the first-person pronoun in ll. 11 and 13 makes me translate as I have.

III

TS'AO CHIH AND THE IMMORTALS

The poems that I have put into the next group present the same straightforward, unsatirical descriptions of immortals as were seen above. The next short poem in irregular lines speaks twice of "flying dragons," making that phrase much better suited logically to be the title, ironically unlike the case of the previous poem.

East of P'ing-ling

The celestial gates unfold
Opening the Road to Heaven.
I don my feathered robe and mount the flying dragon.
I mount the flying dragon
5   To meet with the immortal.
In the east I climb P'eng-lai and gather magic mushrooms,
Gather magic mushrooms that can be eaten
To make our years, like the King Father [of the East's], without
     end.[103]

The title of this poem is taken from an old ballad which, according to traditional commentaries, describes the sadness of the local population when an official loyal to the Han was arrested by Wang Mang's policemen. As far as I can see, the title has nothing to do with this poem, although the prosody of the two poems shows some similarity.[104] The poem, like the preceding, is a fantasy showing the poet's achievement of Taoist immortality.

The following poem in irregular lines is again exactly in the same vein.

Isabelle Robinet, *La révélation du Shangqing dans l'histoire du Taoïsme*, Publications de l'EFEO 137 (Paris: Ecole Française d'Etrême Orient, 1984) 1, p. 158, n. 1, remarks that this line and other lines of poetry from this period date some of the Taoist practices for the first time. She here and elsewhere (e.g., p. 151, n. 2) takes me to task for ignoring the esoteric meanings given to terms used by poets of this period (Chi K'ang in particular). But many of these meanings appear only centuries later and she is wrong to attempt to extrapolate them anachronistically. The term *nieh-ching* 顳景, as she would have it, is not used in a mystical sense by Chi K'ang or by Ts'ao Chih. In the latter's "Ch'i-ch'i" 七啓, for example (*TCCC*, p. 9), it is used in reference to the hunt, exactly as it is in Chi K'ang's poem. (Erwin von Zach, *Die chinesische Anthologie*, Harvard-Yenching Institute Studies 18 [Cambridge, Mass.: Harvard U.P., 1958], p. 621, translates: "Plotzlich galoppieren wir so schnell, wie wenn die Sonnenstrahlen verfolgten.") This proves, to me in any case, that Chi K'ang's use of this term is not mystical and that his poem at this point describes a hunting scene. The term is also said to have been the name of one of the horses of the First Emperor of Ch'in (see Ts'ui Pao 崔豹 [*ca.* 300], comp., *Ku-chin chu* 古今註, *chung*, Pai-tzu ch'üan-shu edn. [Shanghai: Sao-yeh shan-fang, 1931], p. 2b), again underlining its original hunting overtones. We are in for some surprises if this kind of naive interpretation of early terms by later esoteric usage catches on.
[103] *TCCC*, p. 400.
[104] Chu Ch'ien would have us believe that Ts'ao Chih is using this title to tell his brother (or nephew) that if the court ("celestial gates") were open to him (and he were not taken away, as the official in the old ballad was), he and the emperor would protect one another and preserve their longevity. See his *Yüeh-fu cheng-i* 5, quoted in *San Ts'ao*, p. 196.

43

The Osmanthus Tree

The osmanthus tree,
The osmanthus tree,
How beautiful it has grown!
Unfolding crimson blooms and blue green leaves
5   It wafts its fragrance to the ends of the earth.
In its branches nests the phoenix
And at its foot coils the dragon.
At the osmanthus tree
The Perfect Men who have attained the Way all come to discourse
        on the immortals
10   And to teach us how to swallow the sun's rays.
The essence of the Way is very simple, uncomplicated:
Tranquility, inactivity, spontaneity.
Riding on stilts we go beyond the longest distances,
Leaving or staying according to the heart's desire.
15   Either in the highest spheres, reaching beyond all things,
Or in the lowest, reaching to the ends of heaven and earth.[105]

I have translated "osmanthus" instead of "cinnamon" or "cassia," because in line 4 its flowers are described as "crimson,"[106] whereas cassia flowers are white. Why has Ts'ao Chih chosen this tree for his poem? Chu Ch'ien, Chu Hsü-tseng 朱緒曾, and Huang Chieh[107] all believe Ts'ao Chih is alluding to the poem "Seeking for the Hermit," "Chao yin-shih" 招隱士, in the *Ch'u-tz'u* in which the first line refers to the osmanthus (or cassia) growing in the recess of the mountains. Wang I glosses this by saying that the osmanthus's fragrance symbolizes Ch'ü Yuan's loyalty and steadfastness, and the fact that it grows in the wilderness, his exile from the court. It is impossible to prove or disprove this kind of symbolism, but it is very possible that Ts'ao Chih had both "Chao yin-shih" and such personal matters in mind when he chose his title.[108] But does this "explain" the whole poem? Are

---

[105] *TCCCC*, pp. 399–400; previous trans., Kent, *Worlds of Dust and Jade*, p. 77.

[106] This is also the reasoning of Itō Masafumi 伊藤正文 in his translation of this poem in *Sō Shoku* 曹植, Chūgoku shijin senshū 中国詩人選集 3 (Tokyo: Iwanami shoten, 1958), p. 158.

[107] The first quoted in *San Ts'ao*, p. 200; the second in Itō, *Sō Shoku*, p. 185; the last in Huang Chieh 黃節, *Ts'ao Tzu-chien shih chu* 曹子建詩註 (Peking: Jen-men wen-hsüeh ch'u-pan-she, 1957), p. 100.

[108] The title of this poem is said by Chao Yu-wen (*TCCCC*, p. 400) to be based on a ballad of the P'i-wu ko-tz'u 鼙舞歌辭 category named "The Osmanthus Grow before the Hall" (Tien ch'ien sheng kuei-shu 殿前生桂樹), a poem Ts'ao Chih had already imitated, according to *Sung shu* 22 (Chung-hua edn.), p. 626, with his "Ling chih p'ien" 靈芝篇, a poem on filial piety in regular pentameters.

the references to Perfect Men, Taoist philosophy, and all the rest simply allegorical statements of the fact that Ts'ao Chih has left the world of politics? I find it hard to believe this.

"Swallowing the sun's rays" in line 10 refers to actual Taoist regimen, to the adepts' penchant for nibbling the rosy vapors of the early morning, and the other references to Taoist practices and thought in the poem are equally coherent. There is a serious, meditative strain, and the last four lines seem pathetic in the context of Ts'ao Chih's life. Soon after the establishment of the dynasty in 220, Ts'ao Chih and his brother princes had been assigned to their fiefs in what amounted to house arrest, surrounded by spies sent by the central government.[109] As he said in a famous memorial: "I live like a bird or a beast ... ," like an animal fed in a pen.[110] The absolute liberty of movement expressed in the last two couplets takes on added meaning in the context of his life, and the "Taoism" in lines 9–12 becomes more credible as a true search for some kind of liberation when we know he was a near-prisoner at the end of his life.

The following poem is again one that sings of freedom of movement; it seems to continue the last poem.

The Five-fold Wandering

The Nine Provinces are too small for my steps;
I want to be able to soar in the clouds
And wander beyond the world's eight directions,
Letting my eyes roam over the distant wildernesses.
5   I put on a tunic made of rosy clouds
And a skirt made of a colorless rainbow.
My flowered parasol embalms the air about;
My six dragons raise their heads and gallop toward the heavens,
And before the sun moves its bright rays
10 We have, in a twinkling, reached the blue sky.
The Gates of Heaven open their vermilion doors;
The twin jade towers shine with a reddish glow.
I walk to and fro in the Wen-ch'ang Palace
And ascend to T'ai-wei Hall.
15 God on high leans upon the railing
While his vassals gather in the eastern chambers.
They give me a sash of precious jade

[109] See *Yüan-tzu*, cited in n. 62, above.
[110] *TCCCC*, p. 370; memorial dated 228.

And have me rinse my mouth with midnight dew.
I dally, playing with magic mushrooms
20 And loiter, handling perfumed flowers.
Wang-tzu offers drugs of immortality,
Hsien-men presents rare nostrums.
By taking them I will enjoy a long lifetime,
Longevity prolonged without end.[111]

The "five" or "five-fold" of the title can be explained by the first couplet: the four directions of the known world are not enough, so the poet decides to leave in a fifth direction, straight up into the sky. Almost all the critics are agreed that here Ts'ao Chih is imitating the "Distant Voyage" of the *Ch'u-tz'u* and that his interest in immortals is only allegorical.[112] In the very first line they find evidence that Ts'ao Chih, unable to find satisfaction in the world, has written this poem to tell us his sorrow. The whole poem, according to this view, should be read "ironically," that is, with opposite intent, just as Wang I would have us read "Distant Voyage." Such an attitude can only be held by men who have a very monolithic view of life, who feel that we can realize our lives only by devoting them to public service, to the state, to the emperor. Once we have been obliged to renounce such service, *tout le reste n'est rien*, and whatever solace we attempt to find is not even second best; it is misery, failure, a kind of moral suicide. Ts'ao Chih's sidereal swooping would thus be his way of telling us how sad he is not to be able to participate in the government. As improbable as this sounds, it is not impossible, especially since, from all we know of Ts'ao Chih, he was a very single-minded, Confucianist, "monolithic," committed public servant, and such an interpretation would explain away nicely what we know to be Ts'ao Chih's low esteem of immortals.

There is, however, another explanation that has been put forward for these poems, first by Yü Kuan-ying 余冠英 in 1956, and in a more elaborate form by Hsü Kung-ch'ih 徐公持 in 1979.[113] This explanation says that these poems are actually written as drinking songs; if they speak of immortals and

---

[111] *TCCCC*, pp. 400–02. There are translations of this poem in Arthur Waley, *Chinese Poems* (London: Allen and Unwin, 1948), pp. 80–81, Hans H. Frankel, "Fifteen Poems by Ts'ao Chih," *JAOS* 84 (1964), pp. 6–7, and Frances LaFleur Mochida, "Structuring a Second Creation: Evolution of the Self in Imaginary Landscapes," in R. E. Hegel and R. C. Hessney, eds., *Expressions of Self in Chinese Literature* (New York: Columbia U.P., 1985), pp. 97–98.

[112] *San Ts'ao*, pp. 191, 201–02.

[113] Yü Kuan-ying, *San Ts'ao shih-hsüan* 三曹詩選 (1956; rpt. Peking: Jen-min wen-hsüeh ch'u-pan-she, 1979), p. 55. Hsü Kung-ch'ih, "Ts'ao Chih shih-ko te hsieh-tso nien-tai wen-t'i" 曹植詩歌的寫作年代問題, *Wen shih* 文史 [Peking] 6 (1979), pp. 158–60. Itō, *Sō Shoku*, p. 185, agrees with their interpretation of "The Osmanthus Tree."

46

III

TS'AO CHIH AND THE IMMORTALS

of long life, it is a way of pledging the health of one's guest or host. Hsü Kung-ch'ih singles out the preceding three poems ("East of P'ing-ling", "The Osmanthus Tree," and "Five-fold Wandering") as of this type, and there-fore belonging to the early period of Ts'ao Chih's life, when he caroused with his friends in Ts'ao Ts'ao's capital of Yeh. Hsü Kung-ch'ih stresses the fact that the Wen-ch'ang Palace, while actually the name of a celestial, stellar palace, was also the name of a hall in the Yeh palace.

At first glance, this theory is appealing. Some of the songs of immortals may very well have been used as drinking songs (the dream of immortality goes well with intoxication), and the poem by Ts'ao Ts'ao singled out by Hsü Kung-ch'ih does end in the description of guests and hosts pledging one another in the palace of the Queen Mother of the West. But is this scene in Ts'ao Ts'ao's poem proof that the poem itself was used as a drinking song? One of Ts'ao Ts'ao's three poems, moreover ("The Osmanthus Tree," explained by Yü Kuan-ying as a drinking song), does not end in, nor indeed does it contain, wishes for long life, which seems to me to make it the least likely candidate for a "drinking song." One wonders, too, how Hsü Kung-ch'ih divided these "wandering immortal" poems into "early" (drinking songs) and "late"; surely "Flying Dragon" is as good a candidate as any for an "early" drinking song, and yet he declares it to be late. However *ben trovato*, I find it difficult to admit the "drinking song" theory.

But before we look into another explanation, we have one more poem on immortals to read, a poem that clearly refutes the ending of Ts'ao Chih's "Analysis of Taoism," and indeed the whole of his Confucian aspirations.

Distant Voyage

On a distant voyage over the Four Seas
My eyes follow the gigantic waves as they rise and fall.
Great fish, like winding hills,
Pass one another on the billows.
5   A magic tortoise holds Mount Fang-chung on its head
As the sacred mountains rise soaring into the sky.
Immortals swoop about their crags;
Jade maidens play upon their slopes.
Carnelian flowers appease my hunger;
10 Lifting my head, I suck in the rosy mists of morning.
The K'un-lun Mountains are my native land;
The Middle Kingdom is not my home.
When I return to visit the Eastern Father,

47

In one bound I will jump over the deserts.
15 Flapping my wings and dancing in the seasonable wind,
    I shall whistle and pierce the air with my vibrant song.
    Metal and stone decay so fast:
    My splendor shall vie with the sun and the moon.
    For one who can live as long as heaven and earth.
20 The wealth of an empire is as naught.[114]

This poem can again be divided into quatrains. The first sets the stage: heroic scenery on the edge of the world (which is, in traditional geography, surrounded by four seas). The Isles of the immortals, Mount Fang-chung (and P'eng-lai) among them, are said, in the *Lieh-tzu* and other texts[115] to rest on the heads of giant tortoises. "Jade maidens" are variously identified, sometimes simply as immortal maidens, sometimes as the goddess of Mount Hua.[116] The Eastern Father is the King Father of the East whom we have already met. The "deserts" in line 14 are presumably the Gobi, which lies between the K'un-lun and the east. Metal and stone are of course things that decay most slowly, but they are also the material upon which the most ancient texts were preserved. Ts'ao Chih here not only renounces any desire for political glory (in line 20), but even suggests that in becoming an immortal he will have more lasting and more brilliant glory than the greatest historical figures whose high deeds are inscribed on stone and bronze. In the last couplet he rejects even the imperial rank, which previously (in "An Analysis of Taoism") he said was superior to any "immortality." The whole poem can thus be read as a triumphant declaration of liberation from and transcendence of the world as we know it.

Or can it? As far as I have been able to see, no critic sees the poem in that light. They all insist that it is a sad poem, a poem whose title, "Distant Voyage," shows that Ts'ao Chih was thinking of Ch'ü Yüan when he wrote it, and that his "distant voyage" was undertaken because, as Wang I said of Ch'ü Yüan, he was "rejected by society," calumniated and left without any possibility except "to throw in with the immortals and roam with them throughout the universe." There can be no doubt that Ts'ao Chih's condition resembles Ch'ü Yüan's. He has been rejected from the court and totally

---

[114] *TCCCC*, pp. 402–03. There are translations by Dunn, *Cao Zhi*, pp. 87–88, Mochida, "Structuring a Second Creation," p. 96, Kent, *Worlds of Jade and Dust*, p. 68, and J. D. Frodsham and Ch'eng Hsi, *An Anthology of Chinese Verse: Han Wei Chin and the Northern and Southern Dynasties* (Oxford: Clarendon Press, 1967), pp. 44–45.

[115] *Lieh-tzu* 5; trans. in A. C. Graham, *The Book of Lieh-tzu* (London: John Murray, 1960), p. 97. Cf. *Ch'u-tz'u*, "T'ien wen"; trans. in Hawkes, *Ch'u Tz'u*, p. 51.

[116] See the references in David Knechtges, *The Han Rhapsody* (Cambridge: Cambridge U.P., 1976), p. 130, n. 50.

III

frustrated in political activity, but where, in these six poems, does he give us any hint of his dissatisfaction, as he did in the title and last two words of "Hard Thinking," or in the last quatrain of "Immortals," or when he very un-taoistically tried to stop the sun in the second of the "mounting to heaven" poems? Should we light on lines 1 and 2 of "Five-fold Wandering" and lines 11 and 12 of "Distant Voyage," as so many critics have, and say that Ts'ao Chih can only be satirical when he says he cannot live in China, which, after all, is the only civilized country in the world? The problem may seem an artificial one to the Western reader, and even an improper one to the New Critic, but it is a problem we must face when we read any of the innumerable poems of immortals that were written after Ts'ao Chih's times.

I believe three answers have thus far been given to the question, "what was Ts'ao Chih getting at when he wrote his 'immortals' poems?" (1) He was satirically expressing dissatisfaction with his life, his interest in immortality being secondary or of no importance. (2) He was writing drinking songs. (3) He actually was searching for immortality and fervently hoped to achieve it.

Those who hold the second view actually believe in the first as well. Yü Kuan-ying adds, after giving his new interpretation: "Ts'ao Chih wrote this kind of poem as a means of pouring out his anguish."[117] He, as well as Hsü Kung-ch'ih, adheres to traditional interpretations of these poems as allegories mourning the sad state of the world and of Ts'ao Chih's own affairs in it. Thus, our three answers are actually two: either satire or religious conviction.

As far as I have been able to see, *all* the commentators except one have subscribed to the first answer. Perhaps the very earliest critic to have commented on this poem actually combines the two attitudes. This is what Wu Ching 吳兢 (670–749) does in his work on *yüeh-fu* ballads, *Yüeh-fu ku-t'i yao-chieh* 樂府古題要解 (*Explication of the Essential of Old Ballad Titles*). Under the title "Mounting to Heaven" he lists seven ballad titles by Ts'ao Chih: "Flying Dragons," "Immortals," "Five-fold Wandering," "Distant Voyage," and three others that no longer exist. He says that "all these poems," and another by Lu Chi, "lament the fact that man is not eternal, that the sentiments of the common run of mankind are pernicious and dangerous; they believe we must seek the immortals to swoop beyond the universe. The model for these texts can be found in 'Distant Voyage' of the *Ch'u-tz'u*."[118]

[117] Yü, *San Ts'ao shih-hsüan*, p. 55.
[118] Wu Ching, *Yüeh-fu ku-t'i yao-chieh*, pt. 3, pp. 3a–b, in Ting Fu-pao 丁福保, *Li-tai shih-hua hsü-pien* 歷代詩話續編 (pref. 1915; rpt. I-wen yin-shu-kuan, n.d., n.p.). The last sentence does not appear in the version of this extract given in *Yüeh-fu shih-chi* 63, p. 919.

III

Wu Ching cannot be said, when read in the context of Chinese criticism, to be suggesting that Ts'ao Chih's motives are purely religious, but he is at least not ignoring the religious aspect of Ts'ao Chih's turning away from the inconstancy of man and time. Another relatively early critic, Cho Erh-k'an, commenting on Ts'ao Chih's "Distant Voyage" says: "Men of superior intelligence talk freely about death and grieve much about life. When they think of these things, it is not simply because 'they have been rejected by society' [as Wang I said of Ch'ü Yüan]." [119] The way Cho Erh-k'an has phrased this comment shows that he is speaking against critics who held too strictly to the first attitude and who attempt to reduce this poetry to pure political allegory.

But it is the allegorists who seem to have won out during the Ch'ing dynasty, and even in our own day. Chu Ch'ien,[120] Ch'en Tso-ming, and in our own day Chao Fu-t'an 趙福壇, Hsü Kung-ch'ih, and Yü Kuan-ying all hold this position. As far as I know, only Chao Yu-wen in the invaluable notes to his new edition of the complete works of Ts'ao Chih has come out resolutely in favor of a new interpretation. He has attempted to present Ts'ao Chih's work in a chronological sequence and places those poems that I have considered lacking in allegory toward the end of Ts'ao Chih's life, after the essay "Resolving Doubts." [121] Of "East of P'ing-ling" he says: "This poem contains sentiments of longing for long life (i.e., Taoist immortality)." [122] Of "Five-fold Wandering" he says, "Ts'ao Chih has taken elements that he has assimilated from ancient stories of immortals to write this poem, using them to express his longing for long life." [123] Of "The Osmanthus Tree," he refers to the bas-reliefs of religious motifs found in I-nan that are probably contemporary with Ts'ao Chih and says that the poem "reflects the governing class's ardent desire to seek long life." [124]

This explanation seems to me to correspond very well to what we know of Ts'ao Chih's biography, especially if we accept the authenticity of the essay "Resolving Doubts." But it is not completely satisfying. In the first place, at the end of this essay Ts'ao Chih says he is too attached to carnal pleasures to be able to "give himself up wholeheartedly to the study of the way of long life" (see the full translation above). In the second place, most of his works at the end of his life show him to have remained passionately

---

[119] Quoted in *San Ts'ao*, p. 165.   [120] See above, n. 92.

[121] With the exception of "Wandering Immortals," which he places after "Immortals," *TCCCC*, pp. 263–66, probably because of superficial resemblances in vocabulary between the two poems. Chao does not call into question the authenticity of "Resolving Doubts," *TCCCC*, pp. 396–97.

[122] *TCCCC*, p. 400.   [123] *TCCCC*, p. 402.   [124] *TCCCC*, p. 400.

attached to political life and to have desired to serve his dynasty to the end. Finally, the *tone* of his "immortals" ballads sets them apart from his other poems and makes them seem at first reading like set pieces (thus the appeal of the "drinking songs" theory).

Komori Ikuko 小守郁子 has underlined this last aspect of Ts'ao Chih's ballads. She insists upon the fact that the tone of the poems is too glib, that there is no "expression of doubt about the reality of the way of the immortals," no "expression of the inevitable and natural complications in his thinking that would accompany the change in his aspirations when he was removed from the center of political life.... It is all so single-minded.... The poem lacks sincerity ..." She goes so far as to say that the last couplet of "Distant Voyage," which is the poem she uses as her example, is "the expression of his attachment to the values of the real world turned inside out ... no more than an empty, vain bluff. Ts'ao Chih himself was probably conscious of its emptiness and that is why there are no contradictory complications in his 'wandering immortals' poems and why they lack urgency, poignancy." [125]

Komori Ikuko has done us great service in underlining the fact that these poems simply do not give the impression of describing a sincere religious conversion to Taoism. But is she right in reading these poems as meaning the opposite of what they say? Is this Taoist fantasy a proof of "Ts'ao Chih's attachment to the values of the real world"? This sounds very much like the reasoning of the traditional critics who read "white" for "black" simply because "white" agrees better with what we know of Ts'ao Chih's biography.[126] Are these poems really so glib and superficial? As we shall see, the critics have given them fairly high marks, and the poems seem to me to express real, heartfelt yearnings for liberation. I cannot help finding her analysis of these poems as "empty bluff" gratuitous, not clearly enough based upon what we know of Ts'ao Chih's ideas and upon the poems themselves.

[125] Komori Ikuko, "Sō Shoku ron" 曹植論, *Nagoya daigaku bungakubu kenkyū ronshū (Tetsugaku)* 名古屋大学文学部研究論集 (哲学) 69 (1976), pp. 293–94.
[126] Mochida, "Structuring a Second Creation," pp. 95–100, studies "The Five-fold Wandering" and "Distant Voyage," which she contrasts with songs in the *Ch'u-tz'u* to show how Ts'ao Chih's attitude toward religion differs from the attitude expressed there: Ts'ao being an "alchemist" "restructuring the world," not a "shaman-poet," like the *Ch'u-tz'u* narrators. Her arguments are very sophisticated attempts at placing Ts'ao Chih's poems in the perspective of intellectual history, but her conclusions as to Ts'ao Chih's attitudes in the poetry are very traditional; for her, in Ts'ao's wandering immortal poems, it is "conviction that is lacking" (p. 99). Concerning ll. 11–12 of "Distant Voyage," she comes very close to Komori's paradox: "But the mention of the Central Land belies the poet's attachment to earth. In his vociferous denial, he in a sense asserts it."

TAOISM IN TS'AO CH'IH'S LATE WORKS

What do we know of Ts'ao Chih's last years? Chao Yu-wen lists fifty pieces as having been written after "I Speed in My Carriage" (220 A.D.). I find most of his datings quite convincing, the inevitable room for debate notwithstanding. Among these pieces there are memorials that concern current politics and in which Ts'ao Chih shows clearly that he has by no means lost all interest in serving his dynasty and that he remains, indeed, very clear-sighted about the events at court and the disastrous effects they could have in due course.[127] These memorials are hardly the work of a man who has turned his back on the world and who has been converted to religious Taoism. But there is a short piece that does give us some idea of what he thought about Taoism; it is a piece that Chao Yu-wen assigns, most likely correctly, to this period.

Freedom from Melancholy

Suffering from melancholy, I walked along the roadside sighing. I was emaciated and sick at heart with my sadness when Master Dark Emptiness saw me and asked: "What malady has brought you to such an extremity?" I answered: "My sickness is melancholy." "What is melancholy that it has made you so sick?"

"Melancholy
    "Is undefinable:
"It comes without calling
    "And does not leave when chased away.
"Seek it and you will not see even its outline;
    "Hold it in your hand and it will not even fill your palm.
"When I am solitary during the long night
    "It assails me in hordes and droves,
"Coming and going irregularly,
    "Wracking havoc with my nervous stamina.
"When it comes, it is hard to chase away;
    "When it leaves, it comes back so easily!
"When I eat, it makes my throat contract;
    "When I am beset by worries, it worsens them with headache.
"Try to disguise it with ornaments and it will not shine;

---

[127] Extracts from two of the best known of these memorials are translated in Dunn, *Cao Zhi*, pp. 78–86; the complete original texts can be found in *TCCCC*, pp. 436–54.

"Fine food will not make it pleasant to bear;
"Warm it with a flint, and it will not disappear;
    "Massage it with divine salve and it will not lessen.
"With it, clever smiles give no happiness
    "And the music of strings and woodwinds only augments
        sadness.
"Even if the physician Ho put all his mind to it, he would not know
    how to set about curing it:
    "How could you, Master, hope to be able to diagnose it?"

The master colored and said: "I only remarked idly on your melancholy air; I did not then know for what reason you were melancholy, but [now] I can tell you how it came about.

"Today the great Way is hidden:
    "You live at the end of an era.
"You have succumbed to the prevailing vulgarity
    "And become infatuated by fame and rank.
"You have washed your hat strings and dusted your bonnet,
    "And tried to acquire glory and high position.
"You were unable to sit quietly in your seat
    "Or even finish a meal.
"Restless, agitated,
    "You became morose and withered.
"You sought after fame
    "Seized profit.
"Having long followed the primrose path,
    "You have wasted away your vital breath.
"I am going to give you the drug of Non-activity,
    "Make you a decoction of Tranquil Indifference,
"Prick you with acupuncture needles of Dark Emptiness,
    "Cauterize you with a prescription of Pure Simplicity,
"Place you in a room of Great Vastness,
    "Seat you on the couch of Silent Solitude,
"Have Wang-[tzu] Ch'iao take you by the hand and go off
        wandering,
    "Or the Yellow Duke take you walking and singing.
"Chuang-tzu will furnish you with food to nourish your spirit;
    "Lao Tan will give you a prescription that will enable you to
        preserve your nature.

"You will follow a long road and live hidden from the world,
"Mount the light clouds and soar on high."
His words left me
With my spirits jolted and my thoughts dispersed.
My mind and my aspirations had changed;
I wanted to take these perfect words to my heart
And revere these arcane rules.
Then suddenly all the melancholy that had beset me
Went away without taking leave.[128]

In the opening lines of this work the vocabulary shows that the author is thinking of Ch'ü Yüan in the brief piece in the *Ch'u-tz'u* called "The Fisherman," and like Ch'ü Yüan he is going to consult a Taoist to learn how to cope with his problems. Ch'ü Yüan was worried that he was unappreciated in a corrupt world; Ts'ao Chih is more introspective and tries to find a solution to his melancholy. The "physician Ho" was an ancient wise doctor who appears in the *Tso-chuan*.[129] The Master, whose name and whose remedies (capitalized in my translation) are all part of Taoist vocabulary, mainly culled from the *Lao-tzu*, analyzes his sickness and prescribes Taoist seclusion as a remedy. Wang-tzu Ch'iao, Chuang-tzu, and Lao-tzu are all well known. Chao Yu-wen suggest that the Yellow Duke could be the mysterious old man in the *Shih-chi* who gave Chang Liang a book called the *Great Duke's Art of War* and said he would appear as "a yellow stone" in thirteen years' time.[130]

If we took this piece at face value, it would prove that Ts'ao Chih had actually been converted to Taoism at some time, probably fairly late, in his life, since the sadness expressed in it certainly makes it seem to be from the period after he realized he would never achieve his ambitions. That one should not quite accept the piece at face value seems clear to me from the fragment of a *fu*, "Autumnal Thoughts" ("Ch'iu ssu" 秋思), which is written in the same elegiac vein, and in which Ts'ao Chih says: "It is difficult to emulate [Ch'ih]-sung-tzu and [Wang-tzu] Ch'iao: who could become an immortal?"[131] The conversion described in "Freedom from Melancholy"

[128] Like *TCCCC*, I have followed the version of the text in *I-wen lei-chü* 35, p. 622, in those rare cases of a variant reading.
[129] Chao 1; trans. James Legge, *The Ch'un Ts'ew with the Tso Chuen*, in *The Chinese Classics* 5 (London: Trübner & Co., 1872) pt. 1, p. 580.
[130] *SC* 55, p. 2035; trans. Burton Watson, *Records of the Grand Historian of China* (New York: Columbia U.P., 1961) 1, pp. 135–36. Wolfgang Bauer, "Der Herr von gelben Stein," *OE* 3 (1956), pp. 137–52, shows that the Yellow Duke is often associated with Taoist immortals.
[131] *TCCCC*, p. 471.

seems abrupt: the last six lines show Ts'ao Chih's receiving sudden en-
lightenment from the words of the Master, words that expressed ideas with
which Ts'ao Chih had surely been familiar since his youth, for they are a
combination of philosophical and religious Taoism every educated man had
studied. But here Ts'ao Chih is surely imitating the "Seven Stimuli" of Mei
Ch'eng 枚乘 (d. 140 B.C.), so that the abruptness is not a proof that he is
being satirical.[132] By its very existence the piece does show us that Ts'ao Chih
had really become interested in Taoism. Moreover, the way it is worded and
the appropriateness of the philosophy in relation to Ts'ao Chih's own life
should cause us to consider it seriously.

All of these texts, the "wandering immortal" poems, "Resolving
Doubts," and "Freedom from Melancholy," form a pattern and fit in so well
with what we know of Ts'ao Chih's last years that I find it hard not to believe
they show us a man seriously considering Taoism as an answer to his anguish
and sorrows. But there is perhaps one other possibility that we should
consider before ending: what if none of these texts were by Ts'ao Chih?

Hans H. Frankel in an important article[133] expresses skepticism about
the authenticity of many, perhaps even most of the works now going under
Ts'ao Chih's name, because Ch'en Shou 陳壽 (233–297), at the end of his
biography of Ts'ao Chih, says that Ts'ao's works "total a little more than one
hundred pieces,"[134] while some current editions contain close to 200 pieces
and others as many as 340. This is disturbing and would amply justify
Frankel's skepticism. But Chao Yu-wen in the preface to his edition (which
appeared two years after Frankel's article), shows that there must have been
at least two editions of Ts'ao Chih's works at the time of his death or shortly
thereafter, one actually a "selected works" chosen at the command of the
emperor, and another, a complete works, assembled by the poet himself.[135]

---

[132] See "Ch'i fa" 七發 (Wen-hsüan 34, pp. 1a–13b). This imitation does not mean that
"Freedom from Melancholy" is simply a conventional piece with no relation to Ts'ao Chih's
life; see Hans H. Frankel, The Flowering Plum and the Palace Lady (New Haven: Yale U.P., 1976),
pp. 186–211, and Knechtges, The Han Rhapsody, pp. 30–33, for illuminating remarks about Mei
Ch'eng's work, applicable also to Ts'ao Chih's piece.

[133] Hans Frankel, "The Problem of Authenticity in the Works of Ts'ao Chih," Essays in
Commemoration of the Golden Jubilee of the Fung Ping Shan Library (1932–1982) (Hong Kong: Hong
Kong U.P., 1982), pp. 183–201.

[134] SKC 19, p. 576.

[135] The fact that Ts'ao Chih himself speaks of including 78 fu alone in his works after weeding
out many more (TCCCC, p. 434), is already an indication that the figure of "over one hundred"
works is much too low. But in the anecdote told in Chin shu (mod. rpt.; Peking: Chung-hua shu-
chü, 1974), ch. 50, p. 1390, in which Ts'ao Chih 志, son of Ts'ao Chih by a concubine, is asked
by the Chin emperor to verify whether or not an essay was by his father, the young Ts'ao goes
home to look it up in an autograph table of contents prepared by his father and proves that the
edition in the palace was not complete.

III

It seems to me that all the works attributed to Ts'ao Chih that I have translated in this article are in fact genuine; they are of good quality and show, in their use of vocabulary and expressions, many similarities with his well-attested works. They have been highly praised. Chang P'u 張溥, at the beginning of his preface to Ts'ao Chih's works, singles out four of the "wandering immortal" poems for praise.[136] Cho Erh-k'an praises five of them and says, of "Immortals," that it makes later poems in the same tradition superfluous.[137] Sung Ch'ang-pai sees lines 7–8 of "The Immortals" as having inspired Tu Fu and Meng Chiao. Fang Tung-shu 方東樹 (1772–1851) places "Distant Voyage" above the poems by Kuo P'u 郭璞 (276–324) on the same theme and goes so far as to compare Ts'ao Chih's talent in it with that of the Duke of Chou and Ssu-ma Hsiang-ju.[138] Recent anthologists have included most of these ballads in their collections of Ts'ao Chih's works: Yü Kuan-ying includes six of them, Chao Fu-t'an seven, Itō Masafumi two; only "Flying Dragon," "East of P'ing-ling," and "I Speed in My Carriage" have been ignored.

The material we have read here seems to me to describe a real and meaningful, albeit hypothetical, evolution in Ts'ao Chih's thinking. Hostile to religious Taoism and to the charlatan immortality-seekers in his youth, his near incarceration and his despair of achieving some kind of merit in his maturity obliged this pure Confucianist to seek spiritual satisfaction in his life outside of Confucianism. The myth of the immortals, omnipresent in contemporary art and religion, represented a way to achieve a kind of imaginary freedom that real life denied him. Four of Ts'ao Chih's ballads on the theme of the immortals are allegorical complaints against his fate, but the six others contain almost no satire. It is hard to follow Chao Yu-wen all the way in his belief that in these poems Ts'ao Chih is expressing his ardent desire to achieve Taoist immortality, but I do believe, with him, that these poems are serious and that they show Ts'ao Chih more sympathetic to the immortals than he was in his youth. In these poems he is finding release from the frustrations of his everyday life, from what he must have considered the absolute failure of all his ambitions. He uses the tradition as myth, no longer only as allegory for his disappointment in politics, but also as a release in fantasy from the narrow confines of his fief and prison.[139]

---

[136] *San Ts'ao*, p. 144.　　[137] *San Ts'ao*, pp. 164–66.

[138] Sung Ch'ang-pai, quoted in *San Ts'ao*, p. 172. Fang Tung-shu, *Chao-mei chan-yen* 昭昧詹言 (Peking: Jen-min wen-hsüeh ch'u-pan-she, 1984) 2, p. 72. Fang also gives similar praise to "I Speed in My Carriage" on the next page. (These remarks are not contained in *San Ts'ao*.)

[139] Chu Kuang-ch'ien 朱光潛, "Yu-hsien shih" 遊仙詩, *Wen-hsüeh tsa-chih* 文學雜誌 3.4 (1948), p. 2, divides the "wandering immortals" genre into three categories and says Ts'ao Chih

TS'AO CHIH AND THE IMMORTALS

Is it too far-fetched to see his use of Taoist imagery as similar to Goethe's use of medieval Catholic imagery at the end of the second *Faust*? Goethe did not believe in the doctrine behind the imagery; Ts'ao Chih may not have believed in the doctrine behind the Taoist imagery he used, but it enabled him to escape in art, much as Catholic imagery enabled Goethe to give Faust his ultimate apotheosis. In both cases these great artists have made us "suspend our disbelief" and have ennobled their persona: Faust is exalted and Ts'ao Chih convinces us of his yearnings for some kind of immortality. These ballads, in any case, cannot be considered purely conventional works, variations on a theme dashed off to show Ts'ao Chih's virtuosity or simply to supply lyrics for a catchy tune. Anyone familiar with the high seriousness, not to say monomaniacal obsession with Confucian values characteristic of Ts'ao Chih's other works, will realize that such an interpretation of these ballads is simply unacceptable.

LIST OF ABBREVIATIONS

HHS	*Hou Han-shu* 後漢書
HS	*Han shu* 漢書
MH	*Les mémoires historiques de Se-ma Ts'ien* 司馬遷
SC	*Shih-chi* 史記
SKC	*San-kuo chih* 三國志
TCCCC	*Ts'ao Chih chi chiao-chu* 曹植集校注

---

fits into the second category of poets who, like Lu Chi, Pao Chao, and Yü Hsin, use the theme as an "artistic fiction" because of its intrinsic beauty. He then refines his definitions by saying Ts'ao Chih and Yü Hsin can also be placed in the first category of poets who express their frustration in allegories, without really believing in the immortals. When he discusses Ts'ao Chih in more detail, pp. 6–7, he says Ts'ao uses "the immortals as allegories to express his frustrations." Chu Kuang-ch'ien's article is full of sensitive insights and useful information, but I believe he errs in placing Ts'ao Chih, even partially, in his second category. Cheng Meng-t'ung 鄭孟彤 and Huang Chih-hui 黃志輝, "Shih-lun Ts'ao Chih ho t'a-te shih-ko" 試論曹植和他的詩歌, *Wen-hsüeh i-ch'an tseng-k'an* 文學遺產增刊 5 (1957), pp. 95–109, is a general introduction to Ts'ao's verse. In the good short paragraph, pp. 103–04, devoted to his "immortals" ballads, they, like the traditional critics, insist on the negative side. They are, according to them, "a form of forlorn consolation," "a cry of anguish against oppression." I believe this reading goes against the *tone* of these poems, which are not sad, but make us feel a kind of religious liberation.

IV

FROM SCEPTICISM TO BELIEF IN
THIRD-CENTURY CHINA

In the West, when we read tales of the supernatural or fairy tales by Grimm or Perrault, we think they are pure fantasy, fiction sprung from the fertile imagination of some story-teller. I think we are wrong to approach Chinese tales of the supernatural in the same way. The stories they tell are, in all probability, imaginary; it is difficult for us to believe in the immortals and demons that inhabit their pages. But the settings for these stories are historical: the dates are right, the places real and even the descriptions of what happened are most probably based on some kind of historical event that actually took place. I want to talk to you today about only one of these stories, but I think that I can prove that it is certainly historical and I believe it to be typical of a great number, perhaps the majority of Chinese tales of the supernatural. Once its historicity is shown, we will see what the tale can tell us of interest for the study of the evolution of Chinese thought.

The *Soushenji* 搜神記 [1] and the *Taiping guangji* 太平廣記 61[2] both contain accounts of a liaison between a yamen clerk and an immortal woman that seem, at first reading, to be commonplace tales of Taoist mirabilia typical of so many found in the Middle Ages. Closer investigation, however, shows them to be much more interesting: they throw light on the history of religious Taoism and on the evolution of medieval Chinese attitudes towards the supernatural in general.

There is in fact a third contemporary document describing this same liaison, and this third text proves that these tales are based upon a supposedly miraculous event that occured, or that was widely thought * to have occurred, in northern China around the middle of the third century A.D. The *Taiping guangji* version is taken from the *Jixianlu* 集仙錄 (also called the *Yongcheng jixianlu* 墉城集仙 , "An Account of the Assembled Immortals in Yongcheng", Xiwangmu's walled city in the Kunlun Mountains), by Du Guangting 杜光庭 (850-933)[3], and was thus published over six hundred years after the event. It is again as long as the *Soushenji* version, adding two sections to what is, except for a very small number of textual variants, a verbatim reproduction of the tale in *Soushenji*. It is well known that the *Soushenji* is a rifacimento. We thus have no assurance that all the stories in it were written down by Gan Bao 干寶 , the compiler, who was born around 285[4] and was thus a late contemporary of the events *

I would like to thank my friends J.R. Hightower and Michel Strickmann for their views on this paper, many of which I have incorporated in it. The former has supplied the title.

1. Peking: Zhonghua shuju, 1979, pp. 16-19. There are translations by Takeda Akira 竹田晃 , *Sōshinki* 搜神記 (Tôyô bunko 10), Tokyo: Heibonsha, 1964, pp. 32-35, and Yang Xianyi and Gladys Yang, *Poetry and Prose of the Han, Wei and Six Dynasties*, Beijing: Panda Books, 1986, pp. 95-97.

2. Peking: Zhonghua shuju, 1961, pp. 378-380.

3. This tale does not appear in the *Daozang* version of this work, *Daozang* 783, ce 冊 560-561.

4. Li Jianguo 李劍國 , *Tang qian zhiguai xiaoshuo shi* 唐前志怪小說史 , Tianjin: Nankai daxue chubanshe, 1984, p. 284.

described. But, since the story is also found (ascribed to the *Soushenji*) in the *Fayuan zhulin* 法苑珠林 ⁵ it must date, at the latest, from the mid seventh century when Daoshi 道世 (d. 683) compiled that work. The third document is a fu by Zhang Min 張敏 , an official who, as we shall see, had second-hand proof that convinced him of the veracity of the encounter between mortal and immortal[6].

I want first to present the most developed version of the tale, the one given by the Jixianlu and reproduced in the Taiping guangji, pointing out clearly the two passages that appear only in this version. The first of these two passages contains a glaring anachronism, but other elements in them coincide so well with what we find in the third document that I think we should at least give them a hearing. Ideally I would like to give a complete translation, but the text is about one thousand characters long and, since two thirds of it has already been translated into Japanese and English[7], I will give only an extended résumé, with important passages in complete translation.

The title of the story is the name of the immortal woman, Chenggong Zhiqiong 成公智瓊 . The story begins by presenting the hero, Xian Chao 弦超 , a lowly clerk (congshi yuan 從事掾) in the administrative center of what both versions of the story call the commandery, jun 郡 , of Jibei 濟北 , although Jibei was a principality, guo 國 , at the time the events took place. Jibei was to the northeast of Mt. Tai in what is now Shandong. During the Jiaping 嘉平 era (249-254) Xian Chao is said to have dreamt of a "divine woman", shennü 神女 , three or four times running. The Divine Woman introduces herself and tells Xian Chao she was born in Dong Commandery 東郡 which was about two hundred kilometers to the southwest of Jibei. Chenggong Sui 成公綏 (231-273), a poet whose work shows strong Taoist influence, was also from Dong Commandery and the famous reformer of religious Taoism, Kou Qianzhi 寇謙之 (d. 448), says he met an immortal (zhenren 眞人) named Chenggong Xing 興 early in his career[8], so that it may be that the family had close associations with the Taoist religion.

The immortal tells Xian Chao in his dream that she had been orphaned early and that the Emperor-on-High, Shangdi 上帝 (the *Soushenji* version says Tiandi 天地 , Heaven and Earth [?]), moved by her solitude and distress, sent her down to earth to marry. Xian Chao finds her extraordinary beauty irresistible when she actually comes to him in a covered carriage, attended by eight servants, wearing fine silk garments and looking like a flying immortal, feixian 飛仙 . She says she is seventy years old, but only looks fourteen or fifteen. She has prepared a banquet of rare dishes that they share. She says she is Jade Maiden, yunü 玉女 , from heaven and that they seem to be destined to marry (in the *Soushenji* only she adds that she has not come to recompense any favors he had done her (or perhaps merit on his part 不謂君德): he would gain nothing from the marriage, but no harm would come to him either. He would have a carriage at his disposal, delicate and exotic foods and all he needed of silk clothing. Being a divinity, she could not bear children, but she was not of a jealous nature and would not oppose his taking a mortal wife. And so they lived together.

The Divine Woman presents a poem to Xian Chao over two hundred lines long. Only eight lines are reproduced that resemble the verse the *Zhen gao* 眞誥 attributes to the immortals[9]. The lines are in

---

5. *Taishô shinshü daizôkyô* 大正新修大藏經 53 (No. 2122), pp. 304c-305a.

6. The fu is found in *Yiwen leiju* 79, Shanghai: Shanghai guji chubanshe, 1982, pp. 1352-1353.

7. Supra, Note 1. The *Taiping guangji* version is reproduced with annotation in *Taiping guangji xuan (xu)* 太平廣記選(續), Jinan: Qi Lu shushe, 1982, pp. 303-307. The annotation is by Wang Rutao 王汝濤 .

8. *Suishu* 35, p. 1093.

9. Studied by T.C. Russell, "*Songs of the Immortals: The Poetry of the Chen kao*", an unpublished Ph. D. thesis submitted to the Australian National University in 1985.

part obscure[10], but they end in a promise and a threat that are very easy to understand and again very similar to lines in the *Zhen gao*:

> If you accept me, I will make your entire family glorious:
> If you refuse me, I will cause calamities to appear.

She also wrote commentaries on the *Yijing* that enabled Xian Chao to predict the future. After seven or eight years his parents chose a wife for him and thereafter the Divine Woman visited Xian Chao only part-time, coming in the evening and leaving at dawn. Only he was able to see her, no one else.

Here the *Jixianlu* account expands six lines of the *Soushenji* into 33. The later simply says that ✱ suspicions were aroused when people heard talking in his room and saw signs of the Divine Woman's presence although no one actually saw her, and when questioned, Xian Chao divulged the secret. The *Jixianlu* adds much detail. During the revolt of Wen Qin 文欽 , which occurred early in 255[11] and the text anachronistically ascribes to the reign of the Emperor Ming who died in 240, the feudal princes were removed to the palace in Ye 鄴 , accompanied by their retinues[12]. Xian Chao found himself with three other clerks in the same small room. His roommates became suspicious, especially since the Divine Woman could hide her form, but not her voice, and her perfume filled the room. She also gave some remarkable bolts of silk and hemp mattresses to Xian Chao that he would not have found in Ye. Imprudent and naive, Xian Chao let out the secret which was reported to the Inspector of the Principality (jianguo 監國) sent from the central government to oversee the regional princes[13].

The *Soushenji* and *Jixianlu* accounts are then again identical and describe the Divine Woman's anger and sorrow when she decides to leave Xian Chao because she cannot allow her presence to be known. She gives him sumptuous presents of clothing and a poem and, weeping profusely, takes leave of him. Xian Chao is overcome with grief.

Five years later (260?) Xian Chao, on an official mission to Luoyang, came to the foot of Mt. Yu 魚山, fifty km to the southwest of Jibei, where he saw the Divine Woman's carriage at the bend of a road[14]. Overjoyed, they travel together to the capital where they continue to see one another until the Taikang 太康 era (280-290), but her visits are made only on festive occasions: the third day of the third month, the fifth of the fifth, the seventh of the seventh, the ninth of the ninth and on the first and the fifteenth days of each month. The Soushenji version ends with the statement that Zhang Maoxian 張茂先 (that ✱ is, Zhang Hua 華 , 232-300) used this tale as the theme for his fu, "The Divine Woman". This is obviously an error for Zhang Min whom we will introduce in a minute.

---

10. The translations given by Takeda Akira and the Yangs seem unsatisfactory to me (see Note 1, above); the suggestions given in Note 1, p. 304, by Wang Rutao (see Note 7 above) seem preferable, if not definitive.

11. *Sanguozhi* 3, pp. 132-133.

12. I have found no corroboration of this, but it is consonant with the mistrust of the feudal princes shown by the central government during the Wei dynasty.

13. On the term jianguo and the use of Inspectors to spy on the feudal princes during the Wei, see Lu Bi 盧弼 , *Sanguozhi jijie* 三國志集解 19, Peking: Guji chubanshe, 1957, p. 16a. The use of this term suggests that this part of the *Jixianlu* version is authentic or at least that its author was familiar with the *Shuzhengji* 述征記 by Guo Yuansheng 郭緣生 of the fourth or fifth centuries. This work, quoted by the *Taiping huanyuji* 太平寰宇記 13, p. 7b (edition whose preface is dated 1793), gives a résumé of the story in which Xian Chao tells all to the jianguo.

14. The goddess of Mt. Yu in Wang Wei's "*Song for the Temple of Mt. Yu*", "*Yushan shennü ci ge*" 魚山神女祠歌 , is thought ✱ to be Chenggong Zhiqiong; see *Wang Youcheng ji jianzhu* 王右丞集箋注 1, Peking: Zhonghua shuju, 1961, pp. 6-7, and *Yuefu shiji* 樂府詩集 47, Peking: Zhonghua shuju, 1979, pp. 687-688. ✱

✱ The Jixianlu version adds forty lines that purport to be the preface to this fu. Since the fu and its preface still exist in the Yiwan leiju, it is easy to see that Du Guangting (or the source he used) has in fact
✱ reproduced the first nine lines of the preface as it has come down to us in the Yiwen leiju[15], but he has also added 25 lines in between 11.5 and 6 that are not there. It is well known that the Yiwen leiju often abridges the texts it reproduces[16] and we will see that two lines at least of the fu proper seem to have been omitted[17]; has Du Guangting preserved the entire preface? Or has he reproduced or perhaps invented material that he either found useful for the propagation of the Taoist religion or simply interesting in itself? There is no way to know definitively today, but we have no a priori reason to reject the authenticity of the preface as he reproduces it.

✱ Here it is in translation, as the Jixianlu gives it:

One hears a great deal of talk here and there about immortals and yet no one has yet produced the slightest proof of their existence. But now, with the wife of Xian [Chao], we have something credible and near at hand, something that has been witnessed.
During the Ganlu 甘露 era [256-259] people who travelled to and from the capital from
✱ the area between the Ji and the Yellow River talked much about the affair. When I heard about it,
✱ I treated it as no more than supernatural hocuspocus 鬼魅之妖耳 . When I myself travelled in the east men were talking about nothing else, and everyone told the same story, but I still treated them all as men of little worth, ready to follow the latest fashion and tattle on about false frivolities. I said straight out that these were all unfounded rumors and did not take the trouble to verify them.
✱ In the meantime I met the Aide [zhangshi 長史] of Jibei, Mr. Liu 劉 , a man of discernment
✱ in whom I have complete confidence. He had seen Xian Chao [called by his zi, Yiqi 義起 , here and below] with his own eyes and heard what he had to say. He had read the poems [the Divine Woman] wrote, seen the clothing and objects she had presented. It is obvious that they were not the sort of things that a man as common and ignorant as Xian Chao would have got together. Moreover when he thoroughly interrogated those who knew Xian Chao, they said that, when the Divine Woman would come, they all smelled her perfume and heard the sound of her conversation. Thus it is clear that these things [her perfume and speech] were not the products of Xian Chao s erotic daydreams. There were also people who had seen that he was quite exceptional, that he could walk in a lake while it was raining without getting wet, which made him seem all the more bizarre.
Human beings who live in the presence of demons and spirits always fall ill and waste away. And yet Xian Chao remained safe and sound, in perfect health while he feasted and slept with a supernatural being, giving full vent to his passions, uniting his desires with hers. How extraordinary!

This last passage of the *Jixianlu* version is extremely interesting in that it shows the gradual conversion of a Confucian rationalist to the belief in the reality of the existence of Taoist immortals. It behooves us now to look into the identity of the author of this preface, and to see if what we can learn of his life will help us determine whether or not he could actually have been the author of the entire preface

---

15. Ch. 79, p. 1352. These lines are the first and last paragraphs of my translation below.
16. The preface by Ouyang Xun 歐陽詢 (557-641), p. 27 of the Shanghai edition, states in so many words that one of the aims of the collection was to "get rid of the unsubstantial and heterogeneous and excise the extraneous".
17. See below, Note 27.
18. Ch. 55, p. 1517.

as given here. Zhang Min appears only once in the Jinshu[18] where it is said that he was Regional Inspector (cishi 刺史) of Yizhou 益州 (Sichuan) around 280. Only one other work is preserved by him, a curious and ironic fu-like piece in which he makes fun of his brother-in-law (zifu 姊夫), Qin Ziyu 秦子羽 , too modest and honest to make his way in the world[19]. He dates this work to 265. Hong Mai 洪邁 (1123-1202), in the Fourth Series of his famous collection of memorabilia, Rongzhai suibi 容齋隨筆 [20], gives another version of this piece, accompanied by information on Zhang Min found nowhere else. According to a rare and incomplete volume called Jindai mingchen wenji 晉代明臣文集 that Hung Mai found in an old crate, Zhang Min came from Taiyuan 太原 (Shanxi) and occupied a number of official posts including, strangely enough, the post of Aide in Jibei, the same post that Zhang Min (as quoted in the Jixianlu) tells us was held by a certain Mr. Liu! (Hung Mai also tells us that he believes the Jixianlu version of this story to be by Zhang Min himself[21].) It is possible that Zhang Min's "travels in the east" were undertaken to join his new post and that his interest in the affair dates from that period in his life. Since he was Regional Inspector in Sichuan around 280, we should suspect his post as Aide (a lower graded post) dates from some years earlier, that is, after Xian Chao's departure for the capital, but when gossip about him had not yet ceased.

The title Zhang Min chose for his fu, "The Divine Woman", shows he was writing in a well-known tradition in which poets describe the erotic encounters between a bewitching supernatural woman and a mortal man (often the poet himself)[22]. The tradition was far from exhausted in the third century, for Chen Lin 陳琳 (d. 217), Wang Can 王粲 (177-217) and Yang Xiu 楊修 (175-219) all wrote works with this title, probably in 216 during Cao Cao's campaign in the south[23]. The poets' attitudes towards the eroticism in these fu vary considerably, although Confucian prudery usually prevails and puts a stop to proceedings before there is any sexual consummation. Zhang Ming's version is exceptional in this respect, although his debt to the tradition will be clear to those familiar with it. I will begin my translation with 1. 11 of the preface, since I have already translated 11. 1 to 10 as the first and last paragraphs of the Jixianlu version.

The Divine Woman

...I read the poems [the Divine Woman presented to Xian Chao] and found them so exceptional and fresh that I have written this fu about her.

"The August [Emperor-on-High] having seen that my virtue was immaculate,
"I advanced towards the towering Vermillion Gates.

19. Quoted in the Shishuo xinyu 世說新語 25, 7, translation by R. B. Mather, A New Account of Tales of the World, Minneapolis: University of Minnesota Press, 1976, pp. 402-406.
20. Ch. 4, pp. 851-853 of the Shanghai: Shanghai guji chubanshe, 1978 edition.
21. Ibid., p. 853; he calls this story the "Shennü zhuan" 傳, the title also used in Beitang shuchao 北堂書鈔 129, p. 8b (Taipei: Wenhai chubanshe, 1962 reprint).
22. This tradition is studied by J. R. Hightower in "The Fu of T'ao Ch'ien", Harvard Journal of Asiatic Studies 17 (1954), pp. 169-180. The earliest poem in the tradition, also called "The Divine Woman", attributed to Song Yu, is found in Wen xuan 19. There is a pioneering translation by Ed. Erkes, "Shen-nü fu, The Song of the Goddess", in T'oung Pao 25 (1927-1928), pp. 387-402.
23. Wu Wenzhi 吳文治 , Zhongguo wenxueshi dashi nianbiao 中國文學史大事年表 1, Hefei: Huangshan shushe, 1987, p. 233. Lu Kanru 陸侃如 , Zhonggu wenxue xinian 中古文學繫年 2, Peking: Renmin wenxue chubanshe, 1985, p. 37, dates Chen Lin's version to 208 for reasons that escape me. The works are gathered in Yiwen leiju 79, pp. 1351-1352. There is also a fragment on the same theme by Ying Yang 應瑒 (d. 217) in Quan shanggu sandai Qin Han sanguo liuchao wen, Quan Hou Han wen 42, p. 3ab (quoted from Taiping yulan 381).

IV

316

"Bowing low as I ascended the steep staircase, I entered the Privy Chamber,
"And stood in attendance before the grave purity of the Origin-of-All-Things.
5 "The Emperor took pity on me for the respectful diligence I had always shown,
"And wanted to send me to rest in the Middle Provinces,
"Having me in my celestial tranquility abide apart:
＊ "In truth I shall be a good consort of you, my husband."

Her [new] master [Xian Chao], bewildered, asked her:
10 "Are you not, perhaps
"The [fatal] Si 姒 of Bao 褒 who lived during the Zhou dynasty[24],
"Or [the incestuous] Wenjiang 文姜 of Qi 齊 [25],
"An evil woman or licentious demon
"Come to hide away here?
15 "Or are you a naiad from the Han River
"Or Ehuang 娥皇 from the Yangtse[26],
"Sated with the excesses of the True Men,
"Fatigued with serving the immortals?"

The Divine Woman, on hearing this, drew herself up with
ceremony and answered:
20 "I am in truth chaste and pure:
"How can you doubt it?
"I am, moreover, well-spoken and courteous;
"Respectful, I behave according to the ritual.
"My beauty is heaven-given;
25 "My abundant ornaments show forth my virtue.
"It is for these reasons that I have pleased the Sovereign:
"How could you suspect otherwise?"

Then they unrolled the bedding
And lowered the bed curtains.
30 When the good [viands] and heady [wines] were served,
They partook of their nuptial feast.
The subtle odors of her rich perfume
Caused their hearts to pound
As they gave full vent to their desires.
35 Then they sought the ultimate pleasures of the bedchamber,

---

24. A favorite of King You (reigned 781-771 B.C.) who brought about the fall of the Western Zhou and the deaths of the king and his son; see *Shiji* 4, translation by E. Chavannes, *Les Mémoires historiques de Se-ma Ts'ien* 1, Paris: Adrien Maisonneuve, 1967, pp. 284-285.

25. Wife of Duke Huan of Lu who had her brother kill the duke; see *Lienüzhuan* 7, translation by Albert O'Hara, S.J., *The Position of Woman in Early China*, Taipei: Mei Ya Publications, 1978, pp. 193-194.

26. The two widows of Shun said to have become naiads who haunted the Han and the Yangtse; see the *Liexianzhuan* 列仙傳, translation in Max Kaltenmark, *Le Lie-sien tchouan*, Paris: Collège de France-Institut des Hautes Etudes Chinoises, 1987, pp. 96-101.

To enjoy to the full the passions of the long night.
Their hearts were carried away and their vision blurred,
As they imagined echoes of voluptuous music of the past.

[And then, emptied of all desires in the mysterious silence,
40 Neither awake nor asleep, they were surprised [?][27]]

She sang the marvels of these hours
And made gifts of an abundance of fine clothing.
Lowering her head, with her hand on her heart, she announced her decision to depart;
Looking up, heaving a long sigh, she sobbed.
45 Rising into the cloudy vapors she transformed herself,
Leaving us behind: none know where she has gone.

Zhang Min has elegantly woven the elements of the story of Chenggong Zhiqiong and Xian Chao into a fu clearly inspired by the "*Shennü fu*" attributed to Song Yu: the reasons for visiting Xian Chao (11. ✱ l and 5), the gifts of clothing she gave him before she left him (1. 42), her sadness at her departure (11. 43-44), are all allusions to the story. To what point the *Soushenji* and *Jixianlu* include elements unknown to Zhang Min it is impossible to know today. I am inclined to believe that they are very close to the story as Zhang Min himself knew it. We are therefore in the presence of historical documents referring to a supposedly miraculous liaison lasting some thirty years, from A.D. 250 to 280.

What conclusions are we to draw? In the first place, Zhang Min's conversion shows us that, even among the literati of the ruling class, men were beginning to believe that religious Taoist mythology corresponded to reality. When we remember that a contemporary of these events, Ji Kang 嵇康 (223-262), who, moreover, was a deeply committed immortality-seeker and a firm believer in Taoist philosophy, said, in one of his most famous essays, that Taoist immortals "cannot be seen with our eyes"[28], we realize how fast immortals were coming to be accepted as everyday realities.

In the second place, Zhang Min's insistence upon the fact that the relations between Chenggong Zhiqiong and Xian Chao were sexual shows that, in popular belief at least, the Taoist religion was still quite uninhibited about sexuality in the third century[29]. Perhaps this tale can give us a further proof that the earliest Taoists, before the Maoshan revelations of 364-370 or the reforms of Kou Qianzhi fifty years or so later, viewed carnal, non-sublimated sexuality as an integral part of their religion[30].

In the third place, Zhang Min's fu and the events of his life show that this story, which seems, at first reading, to be pure fantasy, was based upon a happening of some sort that actually occurred. Perhaps we should look more closely at the stories in the Soushenji and the Taiping guangji and see what they ✱ can tell us about Chinese religious beliefs at different periods of history, however sceptical we may be about the miracles they relate.

---

27. These two lines are quoted from this fu in the commentary to the *Wen xuan* 30, Peking: Zhonghua shuji, 1974 reprint of the 1181 edition, pp. 29b-30a. I follow Yan Kejun 嚴可均 , *Quan shanggu ...wen, Quan Jin wen* 80, p. 1b, who places these two slightly obscure lines here.
28. "*Yangshenglun*" 養生論 , translated in D. Holzman, *La vie et la pensée de Hi K'ang*, Leiden: E.J. Brill, 1957, p. 83. ✱
29. Here below in any case. Chenggong Zhiqiong's exile in order to find sexual pleasure must mean that sexual relations among the immortals in heaven were not very satisfactory.
30. See Chapter 2 of Catherine Despeux, *Immortelles de la Chine ancienne: Taoisme et alchimie féminin*, 45390 Puiseaux: Pardes, 1990, pp. 27-42.

V

The Cold Food Festival in
Early Medieval China

MY aim in this paper is two-fold. First and foremost, I want to describe the Chinese festival called "cold food," or "eating cold food," *han-shih* 寒食, that appeared at the very beginning of the Christian era in the region around T'ai-yüan, Shansi, and slowly grew in importance until, just before the Sui dynasty, it was celebrated throughout China. Since under the Sui a new element was added to the festival that made it in fact a new festival during the T'ang and the Sung, I will be interested here only in the period I call the "early Middle Ages," from the Later Han until before the T'ang. My second aim is a negative one, to look into and negate the various theories previous scholars have put forward to explain the "origins" of this festival as they try to determine the basic impulse that made the Chinese want to celebrate just as they did when they did. As we will see, each scholar has put forth his own original idea, which often conflicts with or even cancels out those put forth by others. Their theories are usually based on some form of comparative anthropology, calling on parallels in other cultures to explain Chinese phenomena or, at best, on parallels from other periods of Chinese history to explain, anachronistically, early medieval phenomena. These authors seem, consciously or unconsciously, to consider the study of festivals to be a science, very much like a natural science, and to consider the festivals they study

52

to be like natural phenomena: Just as Chinese scientists can discover useful information about their laboratory mice from reports written about mice observed in a laboratory in New York (or anywhere else, at any time in history), so do these scholars feel that they can fill in information lacking in Chinese texts about a medieval spring festival, for example, with information gleaned from similar festivals in other parts of the world or from quite other periods in Chinese history. My intention is to show that this attitude is misguided and that festivals, like any other human social activity, cannot be interpreted correctly outside of their cultural and historical contexts. I would go so far as to say that any folkway or custom can only be interpreted in this manner. To use a homely example: the reason people today wash their hands differs to a very great extent from the reason people washed their hands in the past, before Pasteur. However similar folkways of different cultures or historical periods may seem at first glance, they are inextricably enmeshed in the culture and history of the people who practice them. And if this is true for such a mundane action, how much more is it true for actions concerned with religious or metaphysical phenomena, pure productions of man's imagination! I am afraid this attitude will leave many questions unanswered, but it has the merit, at least, of standing a good chance of getting right the few questions it does answer.

The earliest text to mention the cold food festival is a fragment from the *Hsin lun* 新論 by the philosopher Huan T'an 桓譚, a man whose exact dates are unknown but who probably died in the third

* of fourth decade of the first century A.D.: "The people in the commandery of T'ai-yüan at the height of winter abstain from using fire to prepare their food for five days. Even in cases of severe illness they do not dare to violate this proscription. They do this in honor of Chieh Chih-t'ui."[1] T'ai-yüan and Chieh Chih-t'ui 介之推 (later

---

[1] Quoted from *I-wen lei-chü* 藝文類聚 (Peking: Chung-hua shu-chü, 1959 facsimile reproduction of a Sung edition), 3.12a; *Pei-t'ang shu-ch'ao* 北堂書鈔 (Taipei: Wen-hai ch'u-pan-she, 1962 reprint of an 1889 edition), 143.8a; T. Pokora, *Hsin-lun (New Treatise) and Other Writings by Huan T'an (43 B.C.–28 A.D.)*, Michigan Papers in Chinese Studies, 20 (Ann Arbor: University of Michigan, 1975), pp. 122, 136–37; *Hsin lun* (Shanghai: Jen-min ch'u-pan-she, 1977), p. 47. The *T'ai-p'ing yü-lan* 太平御覽 (Peking: Chung-hua shu-chü, 1960 reproduction of a Sung edition), 27.5b says that the prohibition lasts five months; Pokora, p. 136, note 76, thinks we should read "in the fifth month," but this is strange, since the citation says it took place "at the height of winter."

called Chieh Tzu 子-t'ui) are the two constants around which the festival seems to have evolved. As far as I can see, the festival, or, more exactly, the observance of eating cold food, is not attested in any earlier source.

Chieh Tzu-t'ui is a very famous figure in China and there are many legends concerning him, many temples to his honor, and many literary works that mention him. But the first text in which he appears is the most important and contains the nucleus of all that follows. This text is the *Tso chuan* and I would like to paraphrase the most important parts of it because without this background much of what is to come would be meaningless. The passage occurs in the 25th year of Duke Hsi, that is in 635 B.C.[2] The Marquis of Chin (Ch'ung-erh 重耳), a famous hero, was chased out of his state by his unworthy brothers and wandered for close to twenty years in exile, accompanied only by a few trusted followers, until, in 635, he was finally able to regain his capital and take his rightful place as sovereign of his state. When he was back in Chin "he gave rewards to those who had followed him in exile. But Chieh Chih-t'ui asked for no emolument, and none was given to him." Chieh Chih-t'ui then makes a speech in the *Tso chuan* in which he says that he is not worthy of a reward for: "In truth it was Heaven that restored [the Marquis of Chin] to his place and it is wrong for [the others who received rewards] to think he regained his throne thanks to them." And he showers scorn on his fellow officers, calling them thieves "who consider Heaven's achievements to have been brought about by their own strength. He finds it impossible to associate with such ＊ persons and therefore decides to go into retirement. This he does in the company of his mother after she unsuccessfully attempts to persuade him to approach the sovereign in person to ask for his just rewards. His is rather strange behavior, and shows a proud and rather petulant character, but it earned him immortality as a loyal official who chose obscure retirement rather than sacrifice his principles. "After having sought for him without success, the Marquis of Chin then set aside lands in Mien-shang for him, saying, 'I do this in memory of my error [in neglecting Chieh Chih-t'ui] and to honor a good man.'" The lands set aside for Chieh Chih-t'ui were, as Legge translates, in all probability to "endow a sacrifice to him."

[2] *Tso chuan*, Hsi 24 (James Legge, *The Chinese Classics*, 5 vols. [Hong Kong: The Chinese University, 1960 reprint], 5:191–92).

54

This single reference to Chieh Chih-t'ui in the *Tso chuan* is dated
635 B.C. We hear of him again in a number of works in late antiquity and Han, always telling the same story, sometimes with
embellishments, saying, for example, that the Marquis of Chin
burned down the mountain where Chieh Chih-t'ui was hiding to
force him to come out (but burned him to death instead), or that
Chieh Chih-t'ui fed the Marquis during their exile with flesh from
his own thigh.[3] These sources praise him for various reasons: the
Ch'u tz'u songs extol him for his loyalty to the Marquis of Chin, and
as a paragon of the rebuked vassal in retreat; the *Lü-shih ch'un-ch'iu*
concentrates on his disinterestedness in material gain; and other
sources vary slightly the meanings they give to his flight from the
world.

His cult, in any case, seems to have been very strongly en-
trenched in his native region (near T'ai-yüan in the present province of Shansi), for in the references to it that I have been able to find
in the early medieval period, the central authorities have tried, time
and again, to do away with it, and always without avail. The earliest
reference to the cult, about a century after Huan T'an, occurs in the
biography of a man named Chou Chü 周舉 who died in 149. The
events described must have taken place around A.D. 130:

> After a short time Chou Chü was promoted governor of Ping-chou 并州 (Shansi). Ac-
> cording to ancient custom, in the commandery of T'ai-yüan, they observed the pro-
> hibition [called] the dragon taboo because Chieh Tzu-t'ui burned to death. All in
> the commandery said that during the month of his death his soul would be unhap-
> py if anyone made a fire and for that reason both the ruling class and the common
> people ate cold food during one month every winter. No one dared light his stove,
> which meant that the old and the very young found this hard to bear and many
> died every year.

---

[3] The *Shih chi* 史記 39.1660–62 account is the most complete and the least embellished. (All
references to the dynastic histories are to the Peking, Chung-hua shu-chü punctuated editions; cf. E. Chavannes, *Les Mémoires historiques de Se-ma Ts'ien*, 6 vols. [Paris: Adrien Maisonneuve, 1967 reprint], 4:291). Other accounts are in *Chuang-tzu* 29 (B. Watson, *The Complete
Works of Chuang Tzu* [New York: Columbia University Press, 1968], p. 329; *Ch'u tz'u* 楚辭,
"Chiu chang: Hsi wang-jih" (D. Hawkes, *Ch'u Tz'u: The Songs of the South* [Oxford: Clarendon Press, 1959], p. 75), "Chiu chang: Pei hui feng" (Hawkes, p. 80), "Ch'i chien: Yüan
ssu" (Hawkes, p. 128), "Chiu t'an: Hsi hsien" (Hawkes, p. 160); *Han Fei-tzu* 韓非子, 27
(W. K. Liao, *The Complete Works of Han Fei tzu*, 2 vols. [London: Probsthain, 1959], 1:272),
32 (Liao, 2:27); *Lü-shih ch'un-ch'iu chiao-shih* 呂氏春秋校釋 (Shanghai: Hsüeh-lin ch'u-pan-
she, 1984), 12.627–28.

Once installed in the province, Chou Chü wrote a funeral oration to be placed in Chieh Tzu-t'ui's temple. In it he said that to do away with fire in the height of winter harmed men's lives and was not what the sage [Chieh Tzu-t'ui] intended. He had the text circulated among the uneducated common people so they would go back to eating warm food. This helped clear up some of the popular superstitions and the local customs did, to a certain extent, evolve.[4]

The "dragon taboo" observed by the people in T'ai-yüan is explained by the T'ang commentary on this passage as referring to the fact that the eastern quarter of the sky in spring is called the "dragon" or the "green dragon," *ts'ang-lung* 蒼龍, and that when one of the most important stars in this part of the sky, the "heart," *hsin* 心, or "great fire," *ta-huo* 大火, appeared, people put out their fires fearing that its influence might cause great conflagrations. This idea, in its turn, seems to derive from a practice described in the *Tso chuan* according to which the people "took the fires out," *ch'u-huo* 出火, of their houses annually when the "heart" or "great fire" (Antares) culminated at sunset.[5] The T'ang commentary here is suggesting that the taboo on lighting fires was an ancient one based on the stars and not on the anniversary of Chieh Tzu-t'ui's incineration. (It says in so many words that this latter is only a "popular tradition.")

This T'ang interpretation is interesting but it is strange. Why should the appearance of a star in *spring* be singled out by the commentator as signaling the beginning of a festival in the middle of winter? It seems doubtful that the T'ang commentator had before him a text that differs from ours in which the word winter (and even "height of winter") appears twice.[6] He was most probably influenced by the festival as he knew it personally and that was in fact celebrated in the spring during the T'ang dynasty.

But if, as the passage in Chou Chü's biography implies, the

[4] *Hou Han-shu* 61.2024.

[5] *Tso chuan*, Hsiang 9 (Legge, 5:439). Cf. also D. W. Pankenier, "Astronomical Dates in Shang and Western Chou," *Early China* 7 (1981–82): 7. The close relation between the renewal of fires and the star Antares has recently been discussed by P'ang P'u 龐樸 in *Wen shih che* (Tsingtao), 1984.1:21–29.

[6] There are variants of this text, in particular the *I-wen lei-chü* 4.3b, which do say "spring" for "winter," but I believe they are erroneous. This has been proved, to my mind without appeal, by Nakamura Takashi 中村喬, "Kanshoku no kigen to sono denpa: Chūgoku no nenchū gyōji ni kansuru oboegaki" 寒食の起源とその伝播(中国の年中行事に関する覚え書き, *Ritsumeikan bungaku* 立命館文学 (Kyoto), 410–411 (1978): 692, note 8.

56

festival has nothing to do with spring or the "dragon" in the spring sky, how are we to interpret this "taboo"? The term appears in *Huai-nan-tzu*: "There is a dragon taboo for all of our decisions: to undertake something or push it aside, begin something or stop it."[7] Hsü Shen 許愼 (30–124) comments: "In China there are daily taboos to be observed in the service of the spirits; the northern and southern barbarians call these 'asking the dragon.'" Hsü Shen here, it seems to me, is equating "dragon taboos" with "daily taboos in the service of the spirits," one of which would be the taboo to use fire on the anniversary of Chieh Tzu-t'ui's death, and I believe this is the meaning we must give to the term "dragon taboo" here.

The *Hou Han-shu* passage shows us clearly that a festival was celebrated in honor of Chieh Tzu-t'ui for one month at the height of winter when Chou Chü came to office, and the use of modifiers at the end of the citation ("clear up *some of* the superstitions," "customs did, to a *certain extent* . . .") shows that if any changes actually occurred, they were relatively unimportant.

Less than a century after Chou Chü attempted to modify the festival and make it less lethal to the local population, we find Ts'ao Ts'ao 曹操 (155–220) trying to do the same thing. When he was in Shansi in 206, warring against Kao Kan 高幹, he issued the following edict:

Edict Which Makes Punishments Clear

I have heard it said that in T'ai-yüan, Shang-tang, Hsi-ho and Yen-men [that is, more or less, the present province of Shansi], 105 days after the winter solstice everyone puts out his fires and eats cold food. They say they do this in honor of Chieh Tzu-t'ui. Wu Tzu-hsü drowned in the River, but the men of Wu have not yet begun to stop using water. Why is only Chieh Tzu-t'ui favored by eating cold food?[8] Moreover, the north is a land of intense cold: the old and the very young, the emaciated and the weak will find unbearable hardship in observing this prohibition. When this edict arrives, it will be prohibited to eat cold food. If anyone violates this law the head of his family will be condemned to six months of hard labor, the chief civil servant to one hundred days of hard labor, and the magistrate will be docked one month's salary.[9]

---

[7] *Huai-nan-tzu* 淮南子 (*Chu-tzu chi-ch'eng* ed.), 21.370.

[8] This reference to Wu Tzu-hsü 伍子胥 appears only in *T'ai-p'ing yü-lan* 869.7b; it looks like a later, facetious addition to me.

[9] *I-wen lei-chü* 4.4a; *T'ai-p'ing yü-lan* 28.8a, 30.6a-b, 869.7b.

Things have changed since the time of Huan T'an and Chou Chü: The festival is observed throughout the province now, not only in T'ai-yüan commandery, and it takes place sometime around the end of the second or the beginning of the third lunar month, on the 105th day after the winter solstice (the 4th or 5th of April today), making it the only important popular festival to have a solar (and not a lunar) date. This is the date maintained throughout the centuries for the celebrating of this festival except that the Ch'in-ts'ao 琴操[10] by Ts'ai Yung 蔡邕 (133-192) or K'ung Yen 孔衍 (268-320) and the Yeh-chung chi 鄴中記 by Lu Hui 陸翽 (about 350)[11] tell us that it took place on the fifth day of the fifth month. Just what this aberrant date can signify, I do not know, although some explanations have been attempted.[12] It should be emphasized that both Chou Chü and Ts'ao Ts'ao did all they could to abolish the festival.

That neither of them had any success I believe can be seen in the following fragment by Sun Ch'u 孫楚 (ca. 220-282), a man from T'ai-yüan.

An Offering to Chieh Tzu-t'ui

In T'ai-yüan everyone makes offerings to Chieh Tzu-t'ui's soul. At ch'ing-ming [i.e., April 4 or 5] in the third lunar month they put out their fires and eat cold food, in extreme cases for a month in all, before and after this date. The governor of the province remained as a simple, outside spectator to all this.[13]

The meaning of this obscure last sentence is, I believe, that the festival was still not an official one: the provincial governor had no role to play, or perhaps was actually hostile to the whole idea.

In 317[14] some thirty or forty years after the death of Sun Ch'u we hear of the festival again, and again in the same region, and again

---

[10] Quoted in I-wen lei-chü 4.12b-13a.

[11] In the Wu-ying tien chü-chen-pan edition, p. 13b.

[12] J. J. M. de Groot, Les fêtes annuellement célébrées a Emoui (Amoy) (Annales du Musée Guimet; Paris: 1886), p. 213, rather weakly suggests the Ch'in-ts'ao (he, very uncharacteristically, mistakes this title for the name of the book's author) has given the date according to the Chou calendar which began in the eleventh lunar month, making the fifth month equivalent to the third in the Hsia calendar in use beginning with the Han. Nakamura Takashi, p. 710, note 13, thinks the characters 百有五日 could have been badly copied as 五月五日.

[13] There are two versions of this text: Pei-t'ang shu-ch'ao 143.8a (translated here), and T'ai-p'ing yü-lan 30.6a.

[14] According to the Chao shu 趙書 by T'ien Jung 田融 quoted in Pei-t'ang shu-ch'ao 143.8a.

of an attempt to abolish it. This time the opponent to the festival is Shih Le 石勒 (273–333), founder of the dynasty called the Later Chao. Shih Le was a Chieh 羯 from Shansi whose capital at this time was in Hsiang-kuo 襄國, that is the present Hsing-t'ai 邢台, Hopei. The text which tells of his opposition to "cold food' is long, but it is interesting and has bearing on the subsequent history of the festival.

There had been a tempest with torrential rains and lightning had struck the main gate of the Chien-te 建德 Hall and the western gate of the market in Hsiang-kuo and had killed five persons. The hail began on Mount Chieh 介山 in the principality of Hsi-ho 西河 (Fen-yang, Shansi, southwest of T'ai-yüan) and the hail stones were as big as hen's eggs. On the plains they lay three feet (72 cm.) deep, in the gullies more than ten (2m.42). There were innumerable deaths among those who were caught outdoors and among the animals. For over a thousand *li*, in T'ai-yüan, Le-p'ing (Hsi-yang), Kuang-p'ing (Chi-tse, Hopei), and Chü-lu (P'ing-hsiang, Hopei), trees were destroyed and the grain in the fields wiped out.

Shih Le was adjusting his ceremonial robes in the eastern lateral hall when he asked Hsü Kuang about this: "How many times during the preceding dynasties have there been catastrophes of this kind?" Hsü Kuang answered: "They have occurred in every dynasty, the Chou, the Han, the Wei and the Chin, but, although they are common occurrences, enlightened rulers have never failed to transform themselves because of them, showing that they "Fear the anger of Heaven" [*Shih ching*, no. 254]. Last year you prohibited "cold food." Chieh [Tzu]-t'ui is the spirit of the emperor's native place.[15] He has been venerated [there] throughout the ages and some think it was not proper to discontinue his worship. When only one man sighs, the royal Way is diminished: how much more so, when the spirits are dissatisfied, will the Emperor-on-high be moved! Even if you cannot let the whole empire join in this festival, it is fitting to permit the common people to worship him in the region around Mount Chieh, in the fief he received from the Marquis Wen of Chin."

Shih Le issued a document in which it was said: "Since 'cold food' is an old custom in Ping-chou, and since we were born partaking of these mores, we must conform to them. Previously we received counsel from without the court pretending that, since Chieh Tzu-t'ui was [only] a vassal of a feudal prince, a king [such as we are] should not observe a taboo because of him. We therefore followed this counsel. Is it possible that because we did we have brought about this catastrophe?

[15] Shih Le became "emperor" only in 330, a few years before his death and after the conquest of Former Chao. Before that, and since the end of 319, he was "king," *wang* 王. He was from Wu-hsiang, that is the present Yü-she 榆社, about a hundred kilometers to the east of Mount Chieh where Chieh Tzu-t'ui is said to have retired with his mother (to the south of the present Chieh-hsiu 介休). Hsü Kuang's use of the term "emperor," *ti* 帝, here means either that the *Chao shu* is wrong and this event is to be placed at the very end of Shih Le's career or that Hsü Kuang is anticipating and/or flattering.

Even though Tzu-t'ui is the spirit of our native place, it cannot be that improper eating [i.e., eating warm food?] would provoke these disorders. Let the royal secretariat hasten to consult the precedents in the old laws and let us hear them.''

An official presented a memorial in which he asked that, since Tzu-t'ui had been revered throughout the ages, "cold food" should be restored everywhere, that good trees should be replanted for him, a funerary temple erected and families designated to offer sacrifices to him.

Shih Le's Secretary of the Yellow Gate (*huang-men* [shih-] lang 黃門[侍]郎), Wei Hsiao 韋謏, opposed this counsel, saying: "In the *Ch'un ch'iu*[16] it is said that if ice is not stored according to the [natural] way, the *yin* breath will escape in the form of hailstones. Before Tzu-t'ui was born, what caused hailstones? These hailstones have been formed simply because the *yin* and the *yang* have been set askew. Tzu-t'ui, moreover, was a sage, how could he have provoked such terrible damage? You are certainly wrong to look for [the origin of these phenomena] in the realms of the occult. [The real origin?:] Although they now make ice houses, I fear the ice they have stored has not been put in places where the "*yin* is congealed and the cold-ness well enclosed" (*Tso chuan*, ibid.). Much of the ice is kept on the slopes of hills or on the banks of rivers and its vapors escape and form hailstones. Since Tzu-t'ui was loyal and wise, it is fitting that offerings be made to him in the region of the Mien River and Mount Chieh, but this should not be extended throughout the empire.''

Shih Le followed his advice. The ice houses were transferred to places heavy in *yin* and where the cold was intense, and in Ping-chou they observed "cold food" as in the past.[17]

Thus Shih Le failed where Chou Chü and Ts'ao Ts'ao had failed before him, and "cold food" was observed by the common people in Shansi in spite of governmental opposition. And yet the opposition continued. In 474 the Northern Wei prohibited the observance[18] and again in 496, but in the latter case they were obliged to backtrack a bit and "authorize 'cold food' in the localities on Mount Chieh; elsewhere it was prohibited.''[19]

---

[16] *Tso chuan*, Chao 4 (Legge, 5:595–96).

[17] *Chin shu* 105.2749–50.

[18] *Wei shu* 7A.140.

[19] *Wei shu* 7B.179. The *Ts'e-fu yüan-kuei* 62.19b, dates this prohibition to the "25th year of the T'ai-ho era," an era that lasted only 23 years. These two prohibitions seem to be independent of an edict of 492 mentioned in the *Tzu-chih t'ung-chien* 資治通鑑 (Peking: Ku-chi ch'u-pan-she, 1957), 137.4320: "The Wei ceased the sacrifices, *hsiang* 饗, at 'cold food'." As the commentary clearly shows, this refers to the fact that the Wei sacrificed to their ancestors on days chosen among the twenty-four solar periods, of which *ch'ing-ming*, the 105th day after the winter solstice, was the eighth. In 492, while they were busy adopting Chinese customs to replace those of their Toba ancestors, they decided to sacrifice as the Chinese did, choosing an auspicious day during the second lunar month of each season.

It seems clear that all the governments failed and that "cold food" spread to the entire country shortly after the promulgation of these two edicts, for we have two works both dating from the middle of the sixth century that tell us so. The first is the remarkable manual for agriculture and allied subjects called the *Ch'i-min yao-shu* 齊民要術 by Chia Ssu-hsieh 賈思勰, a book that dates from around 540.[20] After telling the story of Chieh Tzu-t'ui more or less as it was told in the *Tso chuan* with the later embellishments including his burning on Mount Chieh, the work continues:

Today when you look at the trees on Mount Chieh from afar, they all look black as if they had burned, and there is one [?] that looks as if a man were holding it in his arms. Generation after generation have worshiped here and there have been a certain number of miracles.

The common people took pity on Chieh Tzu-t'ui's destiny and on the anniversary of his death put out their fires, calling this "cold food." This fell on about the day before the solar period of *ch'ing-ming.* This practice has spread throughout China and become a well installed custom.[21]

The *Ch'i-min yao-shu* continues with an extremely detailed description of how to prepare a kind of congee called *li-lao* 醴酪 that was boiled in water that had been flavored with apricot pits and served with malt sugar. This account seems to mean that "cold food" was restricted to one day (the 104th day after the winter solstice), although the particle *kai* 蓋 that is used at the beginning of the sentence suggests that the author is not exactly sure. The word *Chung-kuo* 中國, that I have translated as China, may also mean "the Yellow River Basin,"[22] but the following text seems to me to prove that it means the whole of China.

This text is the *Ching Ch'u sui-shih chi* 荊楚歲時記 which is in effect a summation of what is known about early medieval festivals. The work as we have it is in very bad shape, the basic text by Tsung Lin 宗懍, who was born about 500 and died sixty-three years later, being often difficult to distinguish from a second text that has been added

[20] See the discussion by Shih Sheng-han 石聲漢, *Ts'ung Ch'i-min yao-shu k'an Chung-kuo ku-tai te nung-yeh te chih-shih* 從齊民要術看中國古代的農業的知識 (Peking: K'o-hsüeh ch'u-pan-she, 1957), p. 1.

[21] Miao Ch'i-yü 繆啟愉, ed., *Ch'i-min yao-shu* (Peking: Nung-yeh ch'u-pan-she, 1982), 9.521.

[22] As it is translated in the excellent version by Shih Sheng-han 石聲漢, *Ch'i-min yao-shu chin-shih*, 4 vols. (Peking: K'o-hsüeh ch'u-pan-she, 1958), 3:675.

to it as a commentary and that is by Tu Kung-chan 杜公瞻, who was probably born about the time of Tsung Lin's death. Although Tsung Lin, like most of the upper classes of the period, was from a family who claimed northern descent, he lived all his life in Chiang-ling 江陵 (Hupeh) and destined his book to be a description of the activities carried out there throughout the year; Tu Kung-chan, however, was from the north, and the addition of these two texts gives us a picture of Chinese festivals both in the north and in the south. It is precisely the text by Tsung Lin (and thus describing conditions in the south) that reads:

One hundred and five days after the winter solstice, a time of violent winds and rain, is called "cold food" when fires are forbidden for three days and sugared barley congee is prepared [beforehand.][23]

Tu Kung-chan in his commentary passes in review much of what we have already read about the festival, adding only a few details concerning the dishes that were eaten during it, and then indulges in a bit of historical theorizing as to the ultimate origin of the "cold food" festival:

Neither in the *Tso chuan* nor in the *Shih chi* do they say anything about Chieh [Tzu-] t'ui being burned to death. [But] in the *Chou li*, chapter "Ssu hsüan shih" 司烜氏, we read: "In the middle month of spring, using a bell with a wooden clapper, they announce the prohibition of fire in the capital of the state."[24] The commentary [of Cheng Hsüan] adds: "So that in the last month of spring the fires can be taken out." Nowadays "cold food" is dated according to the solar periods, and falls at the end of the second month of spring. *Ch'ing-ming* comes at the beginning of the third month: thus the prohibition of fire is probably an old Chou regulation.[25]

[23] The best edition of the *Ching Ch'u sui-shih chi* is the reconstruction by Moriya Mitsu 守屋 ✷ 美都雄, *Chūgoku ko saijiki no kenkyū* 中国古歳時記の研究 (Tokyo: Teikoku Shoin, 1963), pp. 320–92. This citation appears on p. 342. There is a good translation of the whole work by Helga Turban, *Das Ching-Ch'u sui-shih chi, ein chinesischer Festkalender* (Augsburg: Dissertationsdruck W. Blasaditsch, 1971); the Japanese translation by Moriya, Nunome Chōfū 布目 潮渢 and Nakamura Yūichi 中村裕一, *Kei So saijiki* 荊楚歳時記 (Tokyo: Heibonsha, 1978), contains important commentaries. The phrase "a time of violent winds and rain" seems out of place. Tu T'ai-ch'ing 杜台卿 in the *Yü-chu pao-tien* 玉燭寶典 thinks it so, and he attributes it to the *Ching Ch'u chi* 荊楚記, which is a proof this section is in fact by Tsung Lin and not by Tu Kung-chan, Tu T'ai-ch'ing's nephew. Nakamura Takashi, pp. 702–04, has a fairly good explanation for the phrase. He adds: "if they do not respect 'cold food,' there will be violent winds and rains" which would make good sense of the passage.

[24] *Chou li* 36 (E. Biot, *Le Tcheou-li ou Rites des Tcheou*, 3 vols. Taipei: Ch'eng-wen ch'u-pan-she, 1969, reprint of the 1851 ed., 2:381).

Tu Kung-chan implies that the *Chou li*'s prohibition of fire in the second month corresponds to the period of "cold food" and that the "taking out" of the fires in the third month corresponds to the relighting of the fires at *ch'ing-ming*. This is not as regular as he suggests since *ch'ing-ming* is a solar date (4th or 5th of April in our calendar; earlier according to the Julian calendar) and wanders about anywhere from the middle of the second lunar month to the middle of the third. "Cold food" could therefore take place in the third lunar month, or it could take place in the second; the parallels with the prescriptions of the *Chou li* in any case are at best impressionistic, because that text tells us nothing about how long the fires were extinguished or if they did indeed bring about a period of "cold food." In fact the Chou practices concerning the extinguishing and relighting of fires are far from clear.[26]

Tu Kung-chan's excursions into historical precedents for the festivals he describes are not always very serious. Sometimes (as in the case with "Easter eggs")[27] he seems to be looking for an early usage of the same words however improbable any real historical relation could be. Here, in the case of "cold food", it is hard to tell how serious he is. The *Chou li*, whatever its date, describes a society very different from the society at the beginning of the Christian era when we first encounter the "cold food" festival, and it is actually not concerned with "cold food" at all, but probably with a ritual relighting of fires. There is nothing in the more recent ritual texts, the *I-li, Li chi*, or in the dynastic histories, to allow us to see any kind of filiation or evolution from Chou times down to the beginnings of the Christian era concerning these practices. For all these reasons I feel it is wrong to seek for the origin of the "cold food" festival in early strictures against lighting fires that, as far as I can see, have nothing to do with it. We will soon see that the ritual relighting of fires described in the *Chou li* was actually resuscitated during Tu Kung-

---

[25] *Chūgoku ko saijiki no kenkyū*, p. 344.

[26] I take *ch'u-huo* 出火 to mean (as Biot, 2:381, "Comm. B," does) "to take the fire out of the houses" during the semi-annual migration from permanent dwellings to huts in the fields. This same term, in another context in *Chou li* 30, "Ssu kuan" 司爟, is translated by Honda Jirō 本田次郎, in *Shūrai tsūshaku* 周禮通釋, 2 vols. (Tokyo: Shūei Shuppan, 1979), 1:70-71, as "to use fire" and *nei-huo* 內火 as "to prohibit fire."

[27] Moriya, p. 345.

chan's lifetime and it is, I believe, this resuscitation that prompted
him to link "cold food" to the ancient practices.

We have now read all the existing historical texts on "cold food"
and seen that they all agree that the festival was held to celebrate the
memory of Chieh Tzu-t'ui. They disagree about the date, putting
forth "the height of winter," or 105 days after the winter solstice, or
the fifth day of the fifth lunar month as possibilities, but they show a
very clear geographical progression from the close vicinity of T'ai-
yüan, to the entire province of Shansi, and finally the whole of
China. The food actually eaten during the festival (described most
fully in the *Ch'i-min yao-shu* and not translated here) varies according to the texts and localities, but the object of the cult does not:
"cold food" was eaten in honor of a local hero, Chieh Tzu-t'ui,
from the earliest mention of the festival to the latest.

And yet it is not Chieh Tzu-t'ui but Tu Kung-chan's hypothesis
that has become a permanent fixture in the study of the "cold food"
festival. Everyone, in the East as in the West, has accepted it as fact
and based his theories as to the origin of the festival upon the
equivalence between Chou fire extinguishing and Han and post-
Han "cold food." The earliest study I could find in the West is in J.
J. de Groot (1854–1921), *Les fêtes annuellement célébrées a Emoui (Amoy).*[28]
De Groot's work in Amoy is of course well known and justly admired; he has given us first hand accounts of festivals that people
working in the field even today find invaluable. But his account of
the "cold food" festival is a case apart, because the festival as such
was not observed in Amoy (禁烟不到粤人國, as he himself quotes on
page 210 of his chapter), and he is interested in it only because this
festival "forme un parallèle trop frappant avec ce qui se faisait an-
ciennement en Europe et dans d'autres contrées, il se trouve trop
étroitement en rapport avec certaines coutumes populaires très
remarquables qui règnent à Emoui at aussi chez nous, pour que
nous ne nous y arrêtions pas un moment" (p. 210). De Groot thus
studies "cold food" as an exercise in comparative anthropology and
he begins by quoting a whole slew of ancient authorities,
Macrobius, Lucian, St. Epithanius, and especially Ovid, about the

---

[28] Annales du Musée Guimet (Paris, 1886), pp. 208-29.

extinguishing of fires in antiquity. He comes to the conclusion that these ritual observances are in celebration of the sun, and more particularly of the sun's victory over the powers of darkness at the spring equinox. He quotes Ovid (*Fasti* IV, 794) twice: "Sunt qui Phaëtonta referri credant" [There are those who believe these activities relate to Phaeton [i.e., the sun]] (pp. 209 and 214), the second time saying it can be applied as well to Chinese as to European antiquity: according to de Groot, the "cold food" festival, too, celebrates not Chieh Tzu-t'ui, but the rebirth of the sun in the spring. De Groot quotes only one Chinese source to prove this theory, the *K'an-wu* 刊誤, "Wiping out errors," by the late T'ang author Li Fu 李涪. This author, like Tu Kung-chan and de Groot, believes that the extinction of the fires in spring has nothing to do with Chieh Tzu-t'ui and is simply the distant inheritor of the customs described in the *Chou li*. De Groot quotes Li Fu as saying:

Le moment où l'on devait renouveler les feux était apres le temps du manger froid. Le soleil étant renouvelé alors, et on jetait ses vieux [feux] aussitôt après . . .

當改火之時是寒食節之後. 既日就新. 即去其舊.

I believe it is impossible to interpret the last two phrases as de Groot has. *Hsin* 新 and *chiu* 舊, I believe, must both refer to fire: "On the very day [after "cold food"] they renew [the fire], and immediately reject the old [fire]." The sentences that follow enforce this interpretation: "Nowadays people treat the new fire as something special, saying it should not see the old fire. . . ."[29]

It seems to me that de Groot, whose translations from the Chinese are usually unexceptionable, was carried away here by his theory:

---

[29] But actually de Groot's text is in all probability erroneous. The *Ssu-k'u ch'üan-shu chen-pen*, series 12, *K'an-wu* A.13a, version of this text has 既日就新, as do the other versions of this text I have been able to consult (e.g. Pai-ch'uan hsüeh-hai, *Li Fu k'an-wu* A.9b). De Groot quoted from an encyclopaedia which he calls "Miroir et source de toute recherche" and which may be the *Ko-chih ching-yuan* 格致鏡原. This encyclopaedia reading of "day" or "sun" is surely less good than *yüeh*. The passage should probably be read: "At the time of the changing of the fire, that is, after the festival of 'cold food,' having said that they were going towards the new [fire], they left the old. Today when people holding 持 [de Groot's text has 特 which he translates "specialement"] new fire say: 'Let it not see the old fire,' they are in fact acting according to this old usage."

A notre avis, [he says, p. 214], on ne saurait douter que l'usage d'éteindre les feux, puis de les rallumer après les trois jours où l'on mange froid, ne provienne de l'ancien culte du feu, spécialement du culte du soleil et donc du culte que tous les peuples connus de l'antiquité sans exception célébraient au printemps.

Not only does this theory cause de Groot to *perdre son latin* (so to speak), he also loses his sense of history, alleging in the last paragraph devoted to "cold food" (p. 229) that the observance "began to fall somewhat into disuse after the Han dynasty, and that, finally, in the fifth century A.D., emperor Wu of the Toba Wei dynasty prohibited it. . . ." We have just seen, on the contrary, that the festival begins in the Han dynasty and grows in importance from then on. It actually reaches its peak in the T'ang and Sung dynasties and begins to decline only a long time after the Sung.

But a disregard for anything like history seems to be the earmark of all the Western scholars interested in this festival. The most famous of them and by far the most influential, Sir James Frazer (1854–1941), the exact contemporary of de Groot, is surely a case in point. He looked upon himself as a scientist, the inheritor of Darwin who was to describe the evolution of our mental growth, from primitive magic, to religion, and, finally, to science, as Darwin had our physical growth, from amoebas to apes to men. The "primitive mind" for Frazer was something unique and undifferentiated, something completely different from civilized man, something so "simple" and "undeveloped" as to be lacking in any basically original characteristics. About the Hidatsa Indians, for example, he said:

In this simple worship of the mother-corn we may see as it were in miniature the origin of some of the great goddesses of classical antiquity, Isis, Demeter, and Ceres. The substantial difference between them being that whereas the corn-goddess of America was a personification of maize, the corn-goddesses of the old world were personifications of wheat or barley.[30]

One would think one was hearing de Groot talk of the "culte que tous les peuples connus de l'antiquité sans exception célébraient. . . ."

Since these "primitive" people were more or less all the same ("savages," "ignorant peasants") and since their evolution toward

---

[30] Letter by Frazer quoted in S. Hyman, *The Tangled Bank* (New York: Antheneum, 1962), p. 224.

a more civilized condition happened very late, he allows himself to study, pell-mell, civilizations centuries apart, on whatever continent they may have happened to appear. Listen to what he says about "cold food":

> In China every year, about the beginning of April, certain officials, called *Sz'hüen*, used of old to go about the country armed with wooden clappers. Their business was to summon the people and command them to put out every fire. This was the beginning of a season called *Han-shih-tsieh*, or "eating cold food." For three days all household fires remained extinguished as a preparation for the solemn renewal of the fire, which took place on the fifth or the sixth day of April, being the hundreth and fifth day after the winter solstice. . . .[31]

Frazer has telescoped the "cold food festival" into the prohibition of fires described in the *Chou li*, and incidentally, forgotten the word "bell" that went with the "wooden clappers" of the *Chou li* original; we will see what effect this has had on a later theory in a moment.

Frazer's telescoping of "cold food" back a thousand years is not inconsistent with de Groot's theories, or even Tu Kung-chan's, since the latter calls the festival "perhaps old Chou regulations," but of course Frazer is not going to worry about a discrepancy of a thousand years; his interest is the "primitive mind" and the reasons behind the festival. These he discusses at the end of the volume in a chapter entitled "The Interpretation of the Fire-festivals," where he asks (p. 329):

> In short, what theory underlay and prompted the practice of these customs? For that the institution of these festivals was the outcome of a definite train of reasoning may be taken for granted; the view that primitive man acted first and invented his reasons to suit his actions afterwards, is not borne out by what we know of his nearest living representations, the savage and the peasant.

To our surprise Frazer gives us not one, but two explanations of these fire festivals: they are either "sun-charms or magical ceremonies intended, on the principle of imitative magic to ensure a needful supply of sunshine for men, animals and plants by kindling fires which mimic on earth the great source of light and heat in the sky," or "simply purificatory in intention being designed to burn

---

[31] *The Golden Bough*, 3rd ed. (London, 1918), 7.1:136-37; the notes refer to G. Schlegel, *Uranographie chinoise* (1875), C. Puini (1887), and de Groot.

up and destroy all harmful influences. . . .'' Frazer originally opted for the former, but the work of Edward Westermarck in *Morocco* (where the supply of sunshine was, perhaps, more than needful) convinced him that he was wrong, or perhaps just slightly wrong.[32]

In any case, a disciple of Frazer's, R. Fleming Johnston (1874–1938), in the article in Hastings' *Encyclopaedia of Religion and Ethics*, vol. 10, devoted to "purification (Chinese)," on page 672, adopts his master's second thoughts about "cold food" and suggests that the term *ch'ing-ming* 清明 itself refers to "purification."[33]

The next scholar to have studied the festival is Wolfram Eberhard, certainly the best and most knowledgable specialist on Chinese festivals.

His two works on "Local Cultures in Ancient China" are absolutely essential reading for anyone concerned with the subject of festivals; they contain an extraordinary amount of references to historical materials—to dynastic histories, *pi-chi* accounts, stories in the *T'ai-p'ing kuang-chi* and elsewhere, encyclopaedias, T'ang poetry, specialized works on festivals. He has missed a lot (how could it be otherwise?) but I, for one, have never consulted him without finding new materials, things I have seen referred to nowhere else.

It is in *Lokalkulturen im alten China, 1, Die Lokalkulturen des Nordens und Westens*[34] that he takes up the problem of the "cold food" festival. As usual he gives us a superabundance of materials, and as usual I found new sources thanks to him that were unknown to me, even though I came to him after having studied the festival for a fairly long time (the volume is difficult to find and should be reprinted). Unlike his predecessors, he completely ignores the supposed Chou origins of the festival and concentrates on the realia of what actually went on, although he shares their propensity for ignoring history. But he is like them in that he cannot suppress a desire to know what

---

[32] On p. 330 and at the end of the chapter he attempts to combine the two views. There are severe criticisms of Frazer in L. Wittgenstein, *Remarques sur le Rameau d'or de Frazer* (Lausanne?, 1982), pp. 13–37.

[33] Johnston's article is intelligent, urbane, consistently interesting, but it also shows a certain disregard for history; on p. 472 he says: ". . . our Chou dynasty enthusiast . . . probably meant exactly what was in the mind of the 15th cent. [Thomas à Kempis]."

[34] Supplement to *TP* 37 (1942).

the *origin* of the festival is, and what he comes up with is, to say the least, surprising. On page 37, he remarks that the festival takes place 105 days after the winter solstice.

He rejects the idea that the festival could have taken place in the eleventh lunar month: "This would be in contradiction with the customs that make up the festival." For him "105 days are exactly three and a half months, by Chinese reckoning. In this case it is the half month that is noteworthy: the festival is clearly a spring festival. It must, according to the Chinese schematic calendar, be three months after the new year. That it is half a month later, means that there is another calendar system at work here, that is to say a calendar according to which the year does not start with a new moon . . . , but with a full moon." Earlier (p. 28), trying to make the Chinese festival calendar "meaningful," he posited a "spring full-moon calendar, a calendar that began at the spring equinox and at the full moon of the month." Thus he turns the "cold food" festival into a new year's festival, the primeval Chinese new year's festival. This seems very strange to me, and perfectly gratuitous.

Chieh Tzu-t'ui, as has been mentioned, appears in a number of early texts, aside from the *Tso chuan*, that all refer very exactly to his loyalty and to his exemplary death. But in one later text, the *Lieh-hsien chuan* 列仙傳, which dates from around 100 A.D.,[35] he has been metamorphosed into a Taoist immortal and doesn't die at all. Instead he disappears for thirty years and is then seen again on the shore of the Eastern Sea. The fact that in this tradition he does not die in the region of T'ai-yüan seems to me to show that the *Lieh-hsien chuan* version of the life of Chieh Tzu-t'ui has nothing to do with "cold food" and can be ignored. But Max Kaltenmark, in his remarkable translation of the book[36] provides a substantial note on Chieh Tzu-t'ui and gives a certain number of hints as to what he thinks the festival of "cold food" is all about, although he recognizes the fact that the *Lieh-hsien chuan* biography makes no allusion to it. Kaltenmark, too, believes it was a festival of "the renewal of fire," a festival "in any case in relation with the sun." He arrives

[35] Yü Chia-hsi 余嘉錫, *Ssu-k'u t'i-yao pien-cheng* 四庫提要辨證 (Peking: K'o-hsüeh ch'u-pan-she, 1958), p. 1201.

[36] *Le Lie-sien tchouan* (Peking: University of Paris, Centre d'études sinologique de Péking, 1953), pp. 88–90.

at this last conclusion after stating that the festival took place at the beginning of spring, at the winter solstice, or "even at the summer solstice." This seems a strange way to reckon solstices for the texts say "in the middle of winter for one month" and "the fifth day of the fifth lunar month" (which can fall anywhere from 28 May to 25 June). The 105th day after the winter solstice, moreover, is the end of spring for the Chinese and at least two weeks after the beginning of spring for us. Aside from that, I suppose you can say the festival was "in any case in relation with the sun," but then what annual festival isn't? Kaltenmark also puts the festival into relation with the springtime hunts during which the animals were flushed out by means of prairie fires[37] and mountains put on fire to provoke rain (a late source quoted in the *T'u-shu chi-ch'eng*).[38] But however interesting all these parallels are, they not only both refer to periods remote from the early Middle Ages—too early or too late—, but they are simply clever guesses and can hardly be considered proofs of what the festival was about at all. But, as in the case of Eberhard, the plethora of references to sources that mention Chieh Tzu-t'ui makes Kaltenmark's work precious indeed.

The last scholar to study or to comment on this festival is Claude Lévi-Strauss who, in the second volume of his "Mythologiques," takes up the question of "cold food" that he has found in Frazer.[39] Lévi-Strauss, I believe, is the direct descendant of Frazer. But where the latter declared himself the explorer of the "primitive mind," the former is the self-avowed analyst of the "human mind" *tout court*. They both pride themselves on being scientists, applying "scientific methods," learned from the natural and exact sciences to the study of social phenomena. It is in the comparison and "structural" analysis of materials culled from folklore throughout the world that Lévi-Strauss intends to discover universal constants that appear in all human thinking.

For him "cold food" is not interesting as "referring to the sun," or as "imitative magic" or as a "purificatory" service or as the start of a new year; for him it is a kind of Lent, a period of darkness

[37] *Li chi*, "Chiao-t'e-sheng" (Couvreur, *Li Ki* 1:588).

[38] *Ku-chin t'u-shu chi-ch'eng* 古今圖書集成 (Shanghai, 1884), "Chih-fang tien" 306; *T'ai-yüan fu pu wai-pien*, p. 16.

[39] Claude Lévi-Strauss, *Du miel aux cendres* (Paris: Plon, 1966), pp. 349-51, 397-99.

V

70

(*ténèbres*) during which the Chinese, like the Corsicans, men from the Pyrénées, the Béarn and the Labourd in France, the Sherente Indians, the English of the 16th century, South Americans, Melanesians, Australians, and Africans, make noise with instruments he calls *instruments des ténèbres* which in Europe at least replace the church bells that are silent (or have flown to Rome) for a period before Easter. The European example may seem to be an essentially Christian reaction, creating a period of silence in respect for the Passion. But Lévi-Strauss doesn't believe this because the makeshift *instruments des ténèbres* that replace them are universal. You are sceptical? The clinching argument is the Chinese: ''En Chine . . . vers le début du mois d'avril, certains fonctionnaires appelés Sz'hüen couraient jadis le pays armés de claquoirs de bois . . . pour rassembler la population et lui ordonner d'éteindre tous les foyers. Ce rite marquait le début d'une saison Han-shih-tsieh ou 'du manger froid' '' (p. 350). You have probably recognized that Lévi-Strauss is here translating Frazer, and that Frazer's error (or more probably, oversight), transforming the *Chou li*'s ''bell with a wooden clapper'' (Biot's and de Groot's ''cloche au battant de bois'') into a simple ''wooden clapper,'' has provided an enormous bi-lingual error, from French ''battant'' to English ''clapper'' and back to French ''claquoir'' (which means ''clapper'' all right, but not ''bell clapper''), thanks to the ambiguity of the English term ''clapper.'' And it is this error that has provided Lévi-Strauss with the missing link that makes the existence of ''instruments des ténèbres'' universal and allowed him to make pseudo-scientific formulae contrasting

$$\begin{cases} \text{feu absent} \\ \text{feu présent} \end{cases} \begin{cases} \text{disette} \\ \text{abondance} \end{cases} \begin{cases} \text{maigre} \\ \text{gras} \end{cases}$$

and on page 399: ''Les faits chinois semblent si proches de ceux que nous avons étudiés dans ce livre que leur rapide inventaire nous a permis de récapituler plusieurs thèmes: l'arbre creux . . . , enfin, l'opposition des cloches et des instruments des ténèbres symbolisant respectivement le paroxysme de l'abondance [i.e., the return of the bells from Rome and the end of Lent] et celui de la disette [i.e.,

Lent]." But the Chinese are not using "instruments des ténèbres," they are using "des cloches," that is instruments that, in his system, symbolize abundance, not dearth, and the whole argument falls to pieces.

I have rapidly passed in review the explanations of "cold food" festival by all the Western scholars who have touched on the subject.[40] There remain three articles by Japanese scholars who deal with the festival and whose work is on a much higher level of competence than most of those we have seen so far. The first (chronologically) is a very short note on Chieh Tzu-t'ui by Shigezawa Toshio 重澤俊郎,[41] interesting mainly because it insists that Chieh Tzu-t'ui was not the original inspiration for the festival (he quotes Tu Kung-chan's theory and the *Chou li*); this is confirmed, according to Shigezawa, by the fact that the festival spread far beyond the confines of his cult-domain, Shansi. Shigezawa's short article inspired Moriya Mitsuo 守屋美都雄 (1915–1966) to write a much longer and more important study[42] in which he, who was then the doyen of studies of Chinese festivals in Japan, presents much new material and many new theories. For the ultimate "origin" of the festival, however, he says he can find no explanation better than Frazer's (p. 756), although he admits (p. 754) that "strictly speaking there is not a single text that can be dated as pre-Ch'in" to confirm the solar origin theory.

Moriya's article in its turn inspired Nakamura Takashi 中村喬 to write another in which he builds on Moriya's theories, rejecting some and adding new ones of his own.[43] Nakamura's discussion contains more material and better analyses than any other I have read, but it would take too long for me to discuss them here. I have incor-

---

[40] Göran Aijmer, "Ancestors in the spring: The qingming festival in Central China," *Journal of the Hong Kong Branch of the Royal Asiatic Society* 18 (1978): 59–82, mentions "cold food" in passing, p. 65, but he makes so many mistakes (he has not understood, for example, that *ch'ing-ming* is the 105th day after the winter solstice. He says: "Approximately, it starts on the 5th of April and lasts until about the 20th of the same month" [p. 61]) that I have not thought it necessary to take his remarks into account.

[41] "Kai Shitai," in *Aoki Masaru hakase kanreki kinen: Chūka rokujū meika gengyō roku* 青木正兒博士還曆紀念：中華六十名家言行錄 (Tokyo, 1948), pp. 1–5.

[42] "Kanshoku kō" 寒食考, in *Wada hakase kanreki kinen tōyōshi ronsō* 和田博士還曆紀念東洋史論叢 (Tokyo, 1951), pp. 747–62.

[43] See above, note 6.

porated some of his ideas in my own discussion above (as can be seen in my footnotes); I would like only to mention here his theories about the origin of the festival, some of which I find purely speculative, some of which I find so interesting that, in spite of the fact that they are hypothetical, I feel I must at least mention them. Like almost all the scholars we have studied, Nakamura believes the fire changing spoken of in the *Chou li* and other ancient texts is in some way at the origin of the "cold food" festival, but his presentation of this theory (for theory it is, and he recognizes it as such) is at once more speculative and more sophisticated, taking into account the historical facts more concretely and flying off more wildly into the realms of completely unfounded hypothesis. He recognizes the fact that the festival called "cold food" dates only from the time of Huan T'an, but he believes it to have been made possible by or perhaps to have grown out of earlier practices. To do justice to his theories I would have to go through his article point by point and I just do not think it worthwhile here. In the main he follows Moriya's leads, finding a background or a "matrix" for the "cold food" festival in ancient ceremonies for changing fire, in rain seeking ceremonies, in the *fen-yeh* 分野 system, according to which Shansi was under the jurisdiction of the constellation Shen 參 (in Orion), a star (or stars) traditionally hostile to the Fire Star (Antares), which occasioned the extinction of "fires" when Orion appeared out of respect for this hostility to the "fire" star; and finally (and perhaps most interestingly) he identifies Chieh Tzu-t'ui with the witches who were burned in China in ceremonies designed to provoke rain. All of these ideas are based on actual Chinese texts, more or less well interpreted, and all of these texts are interesting in themselves, but none of them provides any factual, non-speculative basis for the existence of a "cold food" festival before the Later Han dynasty.[44] Nakamura himself recognizes the fact that the aim of "cold food" was *not* the changing or renewal of fire, but the interruption of fire, yet he cannot refrain from seeing the former as the descendant of

---

[44] His insistence on the date of the winter solstice for the "original" date of the fire changing ceremony seems the most unsatisfactory of his speculations. He lists the texts, the *Kuantzu*, the *Hou Han-shu* (quoted in a late secondary source), and even the Chü-yen bamboo slips (*Chü-yen Han-chien chia-pien* [Peking: K'o-hsüeh ch'u-pan-she, 1959], nos. 91–92; cf. D. Bodde, *Festivals in Classical China* (Princeton: Princeton University Press, 1975), pp. 296–98,

the latter. I find this pure speculation, idle speculation, unless and until some newly excavated material shows that there was a more direct relation between the two ceremonies.

Nakamura himself quotes a text that I believe clinches the matter and proves that the "cold food" festival in the early Middle Ages, or at least at the end of the early Middle Ages, when it reaches its height of popularity throughout China, had nothing to do with any ancient ceremony of the changing or renewal of fire. That text is in the *Sui shu* biography of Wang Shao 王劭 (d. *ca.* 610).[45] Wang Shao is known as a sycophantic official historian, much admired by the founder of the Sui dynasty. It was to the latter that he presented a memorial suggesting that his dynasty should renew the practice described in the *Chou li* which consisted in "changing the fire at each of the four seasons in order to prevent seasonal epidemics." I will not go into the arguments he uses, which seem to me to be made up in equal proportion of crass superstition and fallacious logic, but I would like to quote two sentences that seem important to our understanding of the "cold food" festival as it was observed at the time he was writing (in the last decade of the sixth century). At one point he says:

During the Chin dynasty, there were those who took Lo-yang fire when they crossed the Yangtze [in 317, to flee the northern invaders], and used it generation after generation, without ever letting it go out, until the fire's color became blue.

Whatever real events (if any) this nonsense is based on, it shows that Wang Shao believed the ancient custom of the renewal of fire was never observed, at least not strictly observed (as we know it was during the T'ang and Sung dynasties), during the Middle Ages at least as early as the Chin dynasty. He further underlines the fact that it was not observed by his contemporaries a few sentences later when, after emphasizing the usefulness of changing the fire, he adds:

---

which show, to my mind, that the fires were changed many times a year and not just once as he would have it. The historical examples he adduces for the burning of witches to provoke rain are not for "burning," *fen* 焚, but for "exposure," *p'u* 暴 (cf. E. H. Schafer, "Ritual exposure in ancient China," *HJAS* 14 (1951): 130-84). A better example for his theory would have been *Tso chuan*, Hsi 21 (Legge, 5:180), where it is actually suggested that a witch be burned, but which he does not quote.

[45] *Sui shu* 69.1601-02.

Even if the common people, because of long ingrained habits, cannot be made to conform immediately, these ancient models must be followed in the harem and imperial kitchens and in the kitchens of the imperial princes and princesses.

When we learn that Wang Shao was from T'ai-yüan, we realize the full importance of this memorial: the extinction of fires during the "cold food" festival, even in T'ai-yüan, was not looked upon by the common people or the official class, as being in any way related to the ancient *Chou li* practice of renewing the fires at the changes of the seasons.

If I may be allowed an hypothesis, I wonder if Wang Shao was not attempting to transform a popular cult into an official one by invoking an ancient authority, however tenuous that authority may have been. He did not succeed completely in his transformation of the cult, for Chieh Tzu-t'ui has remained associated with the festival down to today, but his reform seems to have dramatically altered its celebration, at least as it is described in official and literary texts, and may have been one of the elements that hastened the evolution that made the festival of "cold food" a general festival for the dead.

If anthropological theories about the origin of the festival are, as I have attempted to show, so flimsy, contradictory and, in the case of the Westerners, "un-Chinese," what can we say about the meaning of the festival without indulging in abstract speculation? It seems to me we can only repeat what the Chinese texts tell us, and I think that what they tell us is, actually, more interesting than all the solar, purificatory, calendrical, universal-human-spirit-vis-à-vis-Lent theories that have been heaped so generously and gratuitously on the festival.

We have already seen almost all the pre-T'ang references I could find to the festival. Eberhard mentions (p. 38) that there are some T'ang references to temples to Chieh Tzu-t'ui and he suspects there may have been some much earlier. There were, and they are mentioned three times in the *Shui-ching chu.*[46] Li Tao-yüan 酈道元, the author of the *Shui-ching chu* died in 527. This is what he tells us of a temple near T'ai-yüan:

---

[46] *Shui-ching chu* 水經注 (*Kuo-hsüeh chi-pen ts'ung-shu* ed.), 6.3, 4–5, 10.

The River Fen, flowing towards the [south-] west passes to the south of the city walls of Chin-yang 晉陽 [i.e., T'ai-yüan] where, formerly there was a temple to Chieh Tzu-t'ui. There is a stele in front of the temple. The temple hall is falling in; only a simple, solitary stele remains. The characters on it have been eroded and there is no way to make them out.

A little farther on we read:

Farther south the River Fen meets the River Shih-t'ung 石桐 which is the River Mien 綿. The river flows from Mount Mien in the sub-prefecture of Chieh-hsiu 界休 and flows toward the north to the west of the Shih-t'ung temple, which is the temple to Chieh Tzu-t'ui.

Formerly Chieh Tzu-t'ui fled the recompense Duke Wen of Chin wanted to give him and hid away on the mountain in [?] Mien-shang. When the duke was unsuccessful in his search for him he set aside Mien as fields to be enfeoffed to Chieh Tzu-t'ui saying, "I do this in memory of my mistake and to honor a good man." That is why they call this mountain Mount Chieh 介山. Thus Yüan Shan-sung 袁山松 [d.401] in his *Chün-kuo chih* 郡國志 says: "There is a temple to [Chieh] Tzu-t'ui in Mien-shang hamlet in the sub-prefecture of Chieh-hsiu."

There was, therefore, a temple to Chieh Tzu-t'ui on the mountain in the fourth century, since Yüan Shan-sung died at the beginning of the fifth. And in the long and curious passage that follows in the *Shui-ching chu* we see Wang Su 王肅 (195–256) imagine (or perhaps quote from an earlier source) a conversation between Confucius and Duke Ai of Lu in which a temple to Chieh Tzu-t'ui is quoted as an example for the type of trees that should be planted in front of a funerary temple. What should we conclude from such a quotation? Certainly that Wang Su, in the third century, was not unfamiliar with temples to Chieh Tzu-t'ui, and that he would not have been surprised if they existed at the time of Confucius. I am not suggesting that Wang Su (of all people) should be cited as proof of the existence of something almost a millennium before his time, but his use of this example, pushed back to the time of Confucius, seems to me to suggest, or even to prove, that at his time temples to Chieh Tzu-t'ui not only existed in the north of China, but probably that they had been there for a good long time.

And the last quotation from the *Shui-ching chu* suggests that at least as early as the Former Han farther south along the Fen there was another center of worship dedicated to our strong-minded hero. At the beginning of this passage Li Tao-yüan tries to prove that the mountain they call Chieh shan 介山 in the region of Fen-yin 汾陰 or P'i-shih 皮氏 was in fact another mountain, the Fen-shan 汾山, and he goes on:

There is a temple to a spirit on the mountain from the side of which flows a sacred spring. On the day sacrifices are made to it, it remains perfectly round, not losing a drop of water. They also call it the temple to Tzu-t'ui. Yang Hsiung 揚雄 (53 B.C.– A.D. 18) in the "Ho-tung fu" 河東賦 says:

> The sacred imperial carriage goes peacefully,
> Voyaging all over, at its ease.
> When [the emperor] looks at Mount Chieh
> He sighs for Duke Wen, has pity for [Chieh Tzu-] t'ui,
> Suffers for great Yü at Lung-men.[47]

The *Chin T'ai-k'ang chi* 晉太康記, *Ti-tao chi* 地道記 and *Yung-ch'u chi* 永初記[48] all say [Chieh] Tzu-t'ui hid away on this mountain, but in fact this is wrong. I believe Chieh [Tzu-] t'ui hid away on Mount Mien. When Duke Wen returned and enfeoffed him, putting aside land for Chieh [Tzu-] t'ui, he called the [Mien] mountain Mount Chieh 介. When Tu Yü 杜預 says it is in the sub-prefecture of Chieh-hsiu 界休 in Hsi-ho,[49] he is right.

Perhaps he is and perhaps he is not, but it seems clear that the "spirit" Li Tao-yüan says the temple was dedicated to was Chieh Tzu-t'ui (Yang Hsiung says as much during the Former Han). In 1929, in fact, Wei Chü-hsien 衛聚賢 argued that it was here, in southern Shansi rather than farther north near T'ai-yüan that Chieh Tzu-t'ui hid away; he also believes that the famous temple to the God of the Soil, Hou-t'u tz'u 后土祠, built by Emperor Wu of the Han in 113 B.C. near Fen-yin, was erected on the site of an old temple to Chieh Tzu-t'ui![50] "Cold food" was eaten in his honor in

[47] Translated in David Knechtges, *The Han Rhapsody* (Cambridge: Cambridge University Press, 1976), p. 60 and note 93.

[48] These texts are identified in Cheng Te-k'un 鄭德坤, *Shui-ching chu yin-shu k'ao* 水經注引書考 (Taipei, 1974; preface dated 1936), nos. 242, 245, 201.

[49] Hsi-ho 西河 is the present Fen-yang, Shansi. The allusion is to Tu Yü's commentary on *Tso chuan*, Hsi 24, *Ch'un-ch'iu ching-chuan chi-chieh* 春秋經傳集解 (*SPPY* ed.), 6.17b.

[50] "Han Fen-yin Hou-t'u tz'u i-chih te fa-hsien" 漢汾陰后土祠遺址的發現, *Tung-fang tsa-chih* (1929): 26.19:71–81. He mentions, p. 77, a Sung stele in the northern Chieh Tzu-t'ui temple (south of T'ai-yüan) which says that "Chieh Tzu-t'ui could provoke clouds and rain," *hsing yün-yü* 興雲雨. Max Kaltenmark, "Notes à-propos du Kao-mei," *Annuaire de l'Ecole Pratique des Hautes Etudes, Ve Section* 74 (1966–67): 20, mentions this in relation to the cult of the goddess Kao-mei, the "Supreme Go-between," playing on the sexual meaning of the words *yün-yü*. But he has made many mistakes in this short passage, taking the present

this region at least until the 1940s.[51] Whether or not there were temples erected to him in the seventh century B.C. after his enfeoffment by Duke Wen I do not know and to indulge in speculation on the subject would, I suppose, leave me open to the kind of criticism I have been using towards others.

My aim in this paper has been to present what we know about the "cold food" festival and attempt to discover what it meant for the early medieval Chinese. I have listed what earlier scholars have said about the festival and come to the conclusion that their ideas are actually not based upon what we know about the festival in historical times, but upon theories that attempt to discover the ultimate origin of the festival. Ovid, just before the passage quoted by de Groot from *Fasti* IV, takes up just this problem in reference to the origin of the Roman ceremonial of the Palilia, but he is impeded, he says, by the fact that there are so many causes alleged: He lists seven! Plutarch, in the second paragraph of his "Life of Coriolanus," lists three different reasons that would explain why the Romans used oak leaves to crown their heroes after a battle, and refuses to choose the ultimate reason among them. I believe he was wise and modest, he who lived so much closer to the invention of the customs he and Ovid discuss than we do to "cold food."

But what can we say with any certainty about the cult vowed to Chieh Tzu-t'ui in antiquity and in the early Middle Ages? If we are to believe the *Tso chuan*, land was set aside for the worship of Chieh Tzu-t'ui in 635 B.C., according to the Marquis of Chin, "in memory of my error and to honor a good man." Whether or not this actually happened in 635 B.C., it tells us something interesting: At the time the *Tso chuan* was written its readers would believe that such a reason was sufficient grounds for the establishment of a

---

place name, Ling-shih 靈石, to be a common noun, "pierre sacrée," and confusing this northern temple to Chieh Tzu-t'ui with the southern one, near Fen-yin, where Wei Chü-hsien would like to see the origin of the Han temple to the God of the Soil.

[51] Eberhard, p. 37, says the tradition is still a living one (1942), and Professor Ch'iao Hsiang-chung 喬象鐘 of the Academy of Social Sciences in Peking told me that she suffered as a young girl (in the 1920s?) when she lived in Lung-men, Shansi, when her family ate "cold food" during the festival in honor of Chieh Tzu-t'ui. She was somewhat put out to think that anyone could consider the festival to have a different origin.

religious cult. Can we go any further than this? Can we discover reasons for the worship of Chieh Tzu-t'ui that the *Tso chuan* account has ignored or deliberately obscured? Is the whole account a fabulation, the transformation of an earlier cult figure, the god of Mt. Chieh, for example, who was popular at the time of the writing of the *Tso chuan* and whom its author wanted to euhemerize? Or does Chieh Tzu-t'ui in fact belong to a class of divinized officials, together with Wu Tzu-hsü and Ch'ü Yüan? Or does his popularity among the peasantry come from the fact that he, feeling cheated by the existing powers as they must have felt, was a natural object of worship for a disgruntled lower class? Or was Chieh Tzu-t'ui's dissatisfaction feared by the peasantry (and the marquis) as having possible disastrous effects wrought on the region by his soul from beyond the grave? How can we even begin to hope to be able to answer questions like these? Only, it seems to me, when we know much more about ancient Chinese religious cults than we know today. Until we do, it seems foolhardy to attempt to use some sort of logic or reasoning power or even comparison with other cultures to reestablish the basic impulse behind religious worship that in all probability varied considerably according to the period, region and class of the worshipper involved.

That the early medieval Chinese who ate "cold food" at the risk of their lives had some imperative reasons for doing so I believe there can be no doubt. That they expected their worship to bring some kind of benefit (rain, good harvests, wealth, health, spiritual security of some sort?) certainly seems logical. But can we go any further? Can we say what was in their minds when they observed the festival? Can we be sure the god they worshipped as Chieh Tzu-t'ui was of some universal stereotype, a rain god, or a spirit of the mountain, or a stellar divinity? Has the name "Chieh Tzu-t'ui" been foisted on a popular deity by the official class eager to claim an outsider as one of their own (which seems almost diabolical, since they tried so hard to wipe out the festival altogether)? An affirmative answer to these last two questions would mean that, in the study of medieval popular religion, historical, textual tradition is meaningless and the religion will have to be reconstructed ahistorically from ideas that have filtered through the vigilance of the official historians eager to reconvert heterodox religion into orthodox Confucianism. I am less pessimistic and have more faith in the objectivity (and honesty) of the Chinese historians. Even if it would be simplistic to see the Chieh Tzu-t'ui worshipped during the "cold food" festival only as the loyal servant he is depicted as in the *Tso chuan*, we actually know almost nothing else about him. Even if it would be more "logical" or more in keeping with what we know of "primitive" religion in general to see him as some sort of symbol, we have no way of knowing just what sort he represents (the lack of unanimity among the theorists I have quoted proves this). Lévi-Strauss says that some of the elements we discover in the study of old legends and festivals are so strange that they beg explanation (*dont la bizarrerie lance un défi à la spéculation*),[52] but the strangeness of these elements is often, perhaps even usually, the strangeness of foreign ways that become familiar and "rational" when one becomes better acquainted with the culture that has given birth to them.

Perhaps archeology will one day reveal folklore elements in the worship of Chieh Tzu-t'ui that we know nothing of today. Until it does, I believe we will have to content ourselves with what the early medieval texts tell us.

---

[52] *Du miel aux cendres*, p. 399.

VI

Songs for the Gods: The Poetry of Popular Religion in Fifth-Century China

The forty-seventh chapter of *Yüeh-fu shih-chi* 樂府詩集, the great anthology of popular ballads compiled by Kuo Mao-ch'ien 郭茂倩 at the end of the eleventh century, contains a group of eighteen short poems. They are distributed under eleven titles, but as a group are called "Shen-hsien ko" 神弦歌, literally "Songs for the Gods Accompanied by String Instruments." It is my aim in this paper to introduce and translate these works, which, to my knowledge, have not been studied before in a Western language. The poems are very simple and straightforward, but they are often difficult to interpret because the popular religious cults they accompanied are so poorly known.[1]

Yüeh-fu shih-chi was compiled over five hundred years after the time when the poems are thought to have been written, but there is no reason to doubt their authenticity. Kuo Mao-ch'ien quotes *Ku-chin yüeh-lu* 古今樂錄 as his source, and this work, published in 568 by the monk Chih-chiang 智匠, is one of the earliest and best for the study of popular ballads.[2] The poems are placed by Kuo Mao-ch'ien at the end of the category called "Wu sheng" 吳聲 ("Music of Wu").[3] The other poems in this category, found in chapters 44–47, are charming quatrains in pentameter verse that describe the joys and sorrows of young people in love in the Wu area, that is, in the lower Yangtze basin around the capital of Nanking, then called Chien-k'ang 建康 (or Yang-chou 揚州). The "Songs for the Gods" are not all pentameter quatrains, but the place names mentioned in them show that they also

---

[1] I have based what follows mainly on the excellent chapter by Wang Yün-hsi 王運熙, "Shen-hsien ko k'ao" 神弦歌考, in his *Liu-ch'ao yüeh-fu yü min-ko* 六朝樂府與民歌 (Shanghai: Ku-chi wen-hsüeh ch'u-pan-she, 1955; 2d edn., 1957), pp. 167–81. Li Feng-mao 李豐楙, "Liu-ch'ao yüeh-fu yü hsien-tao ch'uan-shuo" 六朝樂府與仙道傳說, in *Ku-tien wen-hsüeh* 古典文學 (Taipei: Hsüeh-sheng shu-chü, 1968) 1, pp. 67–96, written without reference to Wang Yün-hsi's work, was helpful in my study.

[2] On this work see Wang Yün-hsi, *Yüeh-fu shih lun-ts'ung* 樂府詩論叢 (Shanghai: Ku-tien wen-hsüeh ch'u-pan-she, 1958), p. 148.

[3] Kuo, *Yüeh-fu shih-chi* (Peking: Chung-hua shu-chü, 1979; hereafter *YFSC*) 47, pp. 683–86. These poems may also be found in Lu Ch'in-li 逯欽立, *Hsien Ch'in Han Wei Nan-pei-ch'ao shih* 先秦漢魏南北朝詩 (Peking: Chung-hua, 1983), vol. 1, pp. 1057–60.   *

originated in the Nanking area. The *Ku-chin t'u-shu chi-ch'eng* 古今圖書集成 encyclopedia says that they were written during the Chin dynasty,[4] and it seems probable that they date from the last years of the dynasty, that is, from the early fifth century A.D. Ho Ch'eng-t'ien 何承天 (370–447) further confirms that "Songs for the Gods" are a kind of contemporary folk music.[5]

The lower Yangtze basin is traditionally associated with popular, unorthodox religion. The geographical monograph of the official history of Sui contains eight short phrases describing the "general character" of the region. Two of the phrases say, "the customs: belief in demons and spirits, a liking for excessive cults (*yin-ssu* 淫祠)."[6] Many tales found in *Hou Han-shu* speak of a superstitious peasantry of the region who ruined themselves in useless sacrifices and expensive ceremonies.[7] *Hou Han-shu* also tells us of a sorcerer, father of the famous filial paragon Ts'ao O 曹娥, who was "skilled in singing while accompanying himself on a string instrument," and who was drowned in 142 or 143 A.D. while apparently trying to pacify the god of the bore in the Ch'ien-t'ang River (Wu Tzu-hsü 吾子胥).[8]

The histories tell us of the constant war the authorities waged against these unofficial cults throughout China, but nowhere were they more unsuccessful than in Wu. A famous example is the cult rendered to Chiang Tzu-wen 蔣子文 on Mount Chung 鍾 near Nanking. Prohibited at the end of the Han, and prohibited and then tolerated by the kingdom of Wu, Chiang Tzu-wen received the posthumous title of "marquis."[9] Again prohibited by the Sung in 421, the temples were rebuilt around 454; and then, a dozen years later, prestigious titles were conferred on him and his followers.[10] When, a century later, the first ruler of the Ch'en dynasty visited Mount Chung (called Mount Chiang 蔣 since the Sung), he sacrificed at the temple of "Emperor" Chiang![11] Such was the reputation for religiosity and interest in popular cults in the kingdom of Wu (222–280), that in the fifth century

[4] *Ku-chin t'u-shu chi-ch'eng*, "Shen-i" *tien* 神異典 40, "*tsa kuei-shen*" pu 雜鬼神部, *i-wen* 藝文 2, p. 1a.
[5] *Sung shu* 宋書 (Peking: Chung-hua, 1974; hereafter *SS*) 19, p. 541.
[6] *Sui shu* 隋書 (Peking: Chung-hua, 1973) 31, p. 886.
[7] Wang, "Shen-hsien," pp. 167–68; R. A. Stein, "Religious Taoism and Popular Religion," in H. Welch and A. Seidel, eds., *Facets of Taoism* (New Haven: Yale U.P., 1979), pp. 53–81; *Hou Han-shu* 後漢書 (Peking: Chung-hua, 1965) 41, p. 1397; and 57, p. 1841.
[8] *Hou Han-shu* 84, p. 2794; cf. *Shih-shuo hsin-yü* 世說新語 (hereafter *SSHY*) 11; trans. Richard Mather, *Shih-shuo Hsin-yü: A New Account of Tales of the World* (Minneapolis: U. of Minnesota P., 1976), p. 293 (the dates given should be 142–143, not 107–125).
[9] *Sou-shen chi* 搜神記 (Peking: Chung-hua, 1979) 5, p. 57.   [10] *SS* 17, p. 488.
[11] *Nan shih* 南史 (Peking: Chung-hua, 1975) 9, p. 272; the visit took place November 17, 557, the day after his coronation.

men believed (wrongly) that the court in that kingdom had no formal ritual music and that professional singers were called upon to sing the third-century equivalent of "Songs for the Gods."[12]

The poems that we read below give us an inkling (but only an inkling) of what the popular cults actually comprised. The standard history (*Chin shu* 晉書), however, contains a few precious remarks that help us picture what went on. They are contained in the biography of one Hsia T'ung 夏統, a native of Yung-hsing 永興 (between Hang-chou and Shao-hsing in Chekiang) who lived around 280. His biography, in *chüan* 94, a chapter devoted to men who refused to serve in the government (*yin-i* 隱逸), can be divided clearly into three parts. First is a description of his poverty and his impassioned defense, against his relatives, of his life as a private citizen, refusing state service. Second, his cousins trick him into attending a popular religious ceremony, which is briefly described. Third, while in Loyang to buy medicine for his ailing mother, he meets the Defender-in-chief (*t'ai-wei* 太尉) Chia Ch'ung 賈充 (217–282), to whom he preaches a Confucian sermon on the moral purity of his native K'uai-chi and for whom he performs nautical tricks with his boat and sings, provoking mysterious meteorological phenomena. Chia Ch'ung attempts to attract him to his service with a brilliant military parade and beautiful singing girls. Hsia T'ung remains steadfast and returns to K'uai-chi. It is this last episode that provides the only date known in Hsia T'ung's life: Chia Ch'ung was Defender-in-chief from 276 to his death in 282.[13] Hsia T'ung's refusal to enter into Chia Ch'ung's service is of course an echo of his plea for a life far from politics in the first part of his biography, but it is the second part that interests us here.

Hsia T'ung was so angry with his relatives for having encouraged him to enter official service that he refused to see them anymore. It is at this point that the second part of his biography begins.

> At this time Hsia T'ung's mother fell ill and he took care of her and gave her medication. Because of her illness his relatives were able to see him again. His uncle Hsia Ching-ning 茍寧 was about to perform ✳

---

[12] *SS* 19, p. 541. They based their assumption in part on the fact that in January of 268 the king of Wu had female singers sing night and day during a ceremony for the re-entombment of his father; see *Chin shu* 晉書 (Peking: Chung-hua, 1974; hereafter CS) 59, p. 1371; and *Chien-k'ang shih-lu* 建康實錄 (Peking: Chung-hua, 1986), p. 99.

[13] Wan Ssu-t'ung 萬斯同, *Chin chiang-hsiang ta-ch'en nien-piao* 晉將相大臣年表 (Erh-shih-wu shih pu-pien edn., vol. 3), pp. 3d–5a.

a sacrifice to his ancestors.[14] He invited two sorceresses named Chang Tan 章丹 and Ch'en Chu 陳珠, both of them outstanding beauties. They wore splendid clothing and were excellent singers and dancers. They also knew how to vanish from sight and hide their shadows.

At the beginning of the first watch (seven P.M.) bells were struck and drums beaten with intermittent music from strings and wind instruments. Chang Tan and Ch'en Chu drew their knives and cut their tongues; they swallowed their knives and spit fire. From gloomy mists rays of light like lightning shot out. Hsia T'ung's cousins wanted to go to see them, but they feared he would raise difficulties, so they got together and tricked him, saying:

"Our uncle has just recovered from a serious illness and all of us, young and old, think it is an occasion for joy. We want to take advantage of the sacrifice he is going to perform to go and congratulate him. Will you come with us?" Hsia T'ung went along.

When they entered the gate, the first thing they saw was Chang Tan and Ch'en Chu in the central courtyard lightly dancing in a round. They chattered and smiled like otherworldly creatures as they performed a dance, as if they were flying, a dance during which they balanced goblets, nimbly passing them from one to the other. Hsia T'ung was so shocked and surprised that he fled not through the gate, but straight out crashing through the hedge.

Once back he upbraided the others.[15]

Hsia T'ung uses erudite allusions to *Shih ching*, Poems 51 and 54, to *Lun yü* (VIII/14 and VI/26), *Kuo yü* ("Chin yü" 7), and *Tso chuan* (Chao 28 and Huan 1) to revile his cousins and condemn with extraordinary violence what he calls dissolute behavior between men and women: "I have always regretted," he says, "not having been able to strike Shu-hsiang's head against the earth or gouge out Hua-fu's eyes," because the former married a woman for her beauty,[16] and the latter (both men of antiquity) ogled a married woman when she passed him.[17] That his cousins could carouse with

---

[14] Or perhaps to his father (and thus Hsia T'ung's paternal grandfather). There are parallel texts to this passage in *Ch'u-hsüeh chi* 初學記 (Peking: Chung-hua, 1962) 15, p. 373; *Pei-t'ang shu-ch'ao* 北堂書鈔 (Taipei: Wen-hai ch'u-pan-she, 1962) 112, pp. 3b–4a; and *T'ai-p'ing yü-lan* 太平御覽 (Peking: Chung-hua, 1960) 568, p. 9a, all quoting "Hsia Chung-yü pieh-chuan" 夏仲御別傳. *Pei-t'ang shu-ch'ao* clearly states he sacrificed to "his ancestors"; my quoted source, *CS* 94, p. 2428, is ambiguous: *hsien-jen* 先人 can mean either "father" or "ancestors."

[15] *CS* 94, p. 2428.

[16] *Tso chuan*, Chao 28; trans. James Legge, *The Ch'un Ts'ew with the Tso Chuen*, vol. 5 of *The Chinese Classics* (1872; rpt. Hong Kong: Hong Kong U.P., 1960), pp. 726–27.

[17] *Tso chuan*, Huan 1; trans. Legge, *Ch'un Ts'ew*, p. 36.

these base magicians was too much for him: he took to his bed and refused to talk to anyone.

Hsia T'ung's reaction to this form of popular religion, while probably compounded with monkish misogyny, was not unique. We have seen that the state tried (unsuccessfully) to combat the cult of Chiang Tzu-wen; it was hostile to all non-official cults throughout the empire. Not only was the Confucian state hostile to these unorthodox religious manifestations, but organized religion of all sorts (Taoist and Buddhist) combatted them and criticized in particular the kind of noisy floor shows that so offended Hsia T'ung: "loud noise, resounding drums, heard in the four directions."[18] Even what I suppose should be called religious Taoist "splinter groups" abominated these cults with their noisy music and blood sacrifices.[19] It is not surprising, then, that we have so little material on these despised cults, which makes our "Songs for the Gods" all the more precious to study.

SONGS FOR THE GODS

The problems in the translation of these eighteen short poems begin with the very first title. The words used, "Su-o" 宿阿, are unknown as a compound elsewhere, and neither Wang Yün-hsi nor Li Feng-mao have ventured a guess.

1. Spending the Night on the Hill

Su Lin opens the Gate of Heaven;
The Venerable Chao closes the Door of Earth.
Our Way is also the gods' Way:
Let the True Officials now descend!

Su Lin 蘇林 is a famous Taoist immortal. His hagiography appears in the collection *Yün-chi ch'i-ch'ien* 雲笈七籤,[20] and he has recently been studied for the role he plays in religious Taoism.[21] The Venerable Chao (Chao *tsun*

---

[18] Lu Hsiu-ching 陸修靜, *Lu hsien-sheng tao-men k'o-lüeh* 陸先生道門科略, in *Tao-tsang* no. 761, p. 9.

[19] Christine Mollier, *Une apocalypse taoïste: Etude du Dongyuan shenzhou jing* [洞淵神呪經] (Paris: Collège de France, Institut des Hautes Etudes Chinoises, 1990), chap. 2, part 2, p. 74.

[20] *Yün-chi ch'i-ch'ien* 雲笈七籤 104, pp. 1–5. Wang, "Shen-hsien," pp. 171–72, mentions other references. Hsiao Ti-fei 蕭滌非, *Han Wei Liu-ch'ao yüeh-fu wen-hsüeh shih* 漢魏六朝樂府文學史 (Peking: Jen-min wen-hsüeh ch'u-pan-she, 1984), p. 226, corrects the error he made in the identification of this figure in the original (1944) edition of his book.

[21] Isabelle Robinet, *La révélation du Shangqing dans l'histoire du taoïsme*, Publications de l'EFEO 137 (Paris: Ecole Française d'Extrême-Orient, 1984) 2, pp. 365–68; see also M. Porkert, *Biographie d'un taoïste légendaire: Tcheou Tseu-yang*, Mémoires de l'IHEC 10 (Paris: Collège de France, Institut des Hautes Etudes Chinoises, 1979), pp. 13–16, 29 ff.

趙尊) is more difficult to identify. Wang Yün-hsi suggests he is Chao Tao-yin 道隱, who is mentioned in the biography of K'ou Ch'ien-chih 寇謙之 (?–448) as the master of Li P'u 李譜 (the great-grandson of Lao-tzu and the saint who revealed the New Law to K'ou Ch'ien-chih). He is said to have obtained the Way during the Shang dynasty and to be the True Venerable, Chen-tsun 眞尊, of one of the thirty-six heavens between heaven and earth. If his heaven was a "grotto heaven," *tung-t'ien* 洞天, under the earth, the Venerable Chao may very well be Chao Tao-yin.[22]

This poem looks very much like an introductory prelude to a ceremony, asking the gods (here called True Men or Perfected)[23] to descend and the guardian of the earth to close his door so that earthly demons cannot appear and disturb the worship. The poem is very "Taoist" in every line and implies, in line 3, that the particular form of popular religion this poem accompanied was compatible with religious Taoism. Unless this first poem is actually a poem used by the religious Taoists themselves, this would set it apart from the others in the series.

The second poem, consisting only of two hexameters, bears a Taoist-sounding title: "Lord of the Way," *tao-chün* 道君. This was an official designation given to someone higher in rank than a True Man and is referred to at least as early as T'ao Hung-ching 陶弘景 (456–536).[24] But the title's relevance to the two hexameters is not clear, and the religious Taoist terminology disappears in these poems after the title of this second poem.

2. Lord of the Way

In the central court stands a tree that talks by itself,
A plane tree that spreads out its branches and covers them with
    leaves.

---

[22] See *Wei shu* 魏書 (Peking: Chung-hua, 1974) 114, p. 3052; J. R. Ware, "The *Wei Shu* and *Sui Shu* on Taoism," *JAOS* 53 (1933), p. 234. Wang, "Shen-hsien," pp. 171–72, believes that since Chao Tao-yin does not seem to appear elsewhere this poem must be dated long enough after the revelation to K'ou Ch'ien-chih (423) for him to have become a popular religious deity.

[23] The term used, *chen-kuan* 眞官, becomes common in T'ang times; see references in *Tz'u yüan* and *Dai Kan Wa jiten*. Is there perhaps an allusion in the poem's title to the "Nocturnal invocation," *su-ch'i* 宿啓, used to begin ceremonies in later Taoism? See Franciscus Verellen, *Du Guangting (850–933): Taoïste de cour à la fin de la Chine médiévale*, Mémoires de l'IHEC 30 (Paris: Collège de France, Institut des Hautes Etudes Chinoises, 1989), p. 90.

[24] In *Chen-ling wei-yeh t'u* 眞靈位業圖 (*Tao-tsang* no. 73) the highest divinities almost all contain the words "Tao-chün," "Lord of the Way," in their titles. The use of Taoist terminology in these first two poems is not surprising, since at its origins the Taoist religion was close to cults the common people practiced to keep away evil demons; see Ch'en Kuo-fu 陳國符, *Tao-tsang yüan-liu k'ao* 道藏源流考 (1949; Peking: Chung-hua, 1963), pp. 260–61.

6

There is no lack of magical trees in Chinese folklore and mythology, and this poem probably accompanied the worship of a local example. Wang Yün-hsi quotes a tale from the *Chih-kuai* 志怪 collection of fantastic tales that dates to the end of the Chin dynasty (around A.D. 400).[25] In it we discover a man dressed in yellow wearing a white hat who gets into bed with a woman sometime after midnight four or five nights running. When he has left on the morning of the last night, the woman in the bed admits to the hero of the tale that he is "The Youth of the Plane-tree Marquis" ("T'ung-hou lang" 桐侯郎), "the tree in the temple to the east of the road."[26] The hero captures him when he appears again the next night, but he has to let him go free when the plane-tree god provokes such high winds that the boat carrying him to the capital seems about to capsize. Perhaps these two (fragmentary?) lines refer to one of his breed, and the "Lord of the Way" is the usurpation of a Taoist title for a purely local cult of popular religion.

The following poem again most probably describes a popular cult. It is particularly difficult to translate because of the *impressifs* or "doublets" (*yang-yang* 佯佯 and *i-i* 翼翼) in the first two lines and (like most of the poems in the series) because of the lack of context: we actually know so little of what went on during these ceremonies.

3. The Saintly Youth

On the left (he dances) without affectation;
On the right (she dances) without stiffness:
The Immortal on one side of the Youth,
The Jade Maiden on the other.
The wine does not taste of crystal sugar
And brings forth the color in (the god's) cheeks.

Wang Yün-hsi quotes two examples of local goddesses called "saints" (*sheng* 聖, as in this poem),[27] and he suggests that the Immortal and the Jade Maiden are either goddesses who accompany the Saintly Youth or sorceresses who danced before the god to please him, just like those who had so

---

[25] See Li Chien-kuo 李劍國, *T'ang-ch'ien chih-kuai hsiao-shuo shih* 唐前志怪小說史 (Tientsin: Nan-k'ai ta-hsüeh ch'u-pan-she, 1984), p. 335.

[26] *I-wen lei-chü* 藝文類聚 (Shanghai: Ku-chi, 1982) 86, p. 1527. Wang, "Shen-hsien," pp. 172–73, quotes the *T'ai-p'ing yü-lan* 956, p. 5b, version; see also Lu Hsün 魯迅, *Ku hsiao-shuo kou-ch'en* 古小說鉤沈 (Peking: Jen-min wen-hsüeh, 1954), p. 189.

[27] Wang "Shen-hsien," p. 173, quoting *Nan shih* 51, p. 1264, and Liu Chih-lin's 劉之遴 *Shen-i lu* 神異錄, quoted in *T'ai-p'ing huan-yü chi* 太平寰宇記 92 (not 93 as he says), p. 14a, of an edition whose preface is dated 1793.

angered Hsia T'ung.[28] Chang Ya-hsin 張亞新 believes that these two are statues who flank the god.[29] I have translated as if it were these two figures who dance before the god, and I take them to be dancers who impersonate the immortal lads and jade lasses that appear so often in Taoist texts.[30]

* The methods for making "crystal sugar," *sha-t'ang* 沙糖, from sugar cane are said to have been imported from Central Asia into China only in the seventh century;[31] thus does the term here refer to some other form of sugar, or does this anachronism point towards a late date for our poem? Is this sugarless wine (*naturrein*, as the Germans say of their best white wine) of superior quality, suitable for libations to the Saintly Youth? Or is it, as Yü Kuan-ying 余冠英 suggests, of inferior quality, but good enough to brighten the *worshippers'* spirits and thus suitable for use in revering the god?[32] The concision and simplicity of this poem make it impossible to know who is correct.

The title of the following poem in two six-line stanzas bears the name of a goddess known as the Goddess of the Ears in early Taoist texts;[33] but it is highly probable that we are again in the presence of a local goddess, and not the Taoist Goddess of the Ears.

4. The Charming Girl

I

Wandering north near the rivers and lakes,
We look out upon water plants as far as the eye can see.
The lotus have burst into splendid flowers;
The limpid water is both pure and clear.
Strings accompany a rhythmic song,
Whose sounds seem to linger long in the air.

---

[28] Here he follows Hsiao, *Yüeh-fu wen-hsüeh*, p. 227.

[29] Chang, *Liu-ch'ao yüeh-fu shih hsüan* 六朝樂府詩選 (Honan: Chung-chou ku-chi ch'u-pan-she, 1986), p. 50.

[30] See, e.g., *Yün-chi ch'i-ch'ien* 55, p. 13a. There are many, many other references to Jade Lads and Jade Lasses and the like; see K. M. Schipper, *Index du Yunji qiqian*, Publications de l'EFEO 131 (Paris: Ecole Française d'Extrême-Orient, 1981), pp. 387–88, for further references. John Lagerwey of the Ecole Française de l'Extrême-Orient, Paris, informs me that today gods and goddesses in popular religious Taoist ceremonies are often flanked by Golden Lads, *chin-t'ung* 金童, and Jade Maidens.

[31] *Pen-ts'ao kang-mu* 本草綱目 (Peking: Jen-min wei-sheng ch'u-pan-she, 1978) 33, p. 1890; Edward Schafer, *The Golden Peaches of Samarkand* (Berkeley: U. of California P., 1963), p. 153.

[32] Yü Kuan-ying, *Yüeh-fu shih-hsüan* 樂府詩選 (Peking: Jen-min wen-hsüeh, 1954), pp. 93–94.

[33] *Lung-yü ho-t'u* 龍魚河圖, quoted in *T'ai-p'ing yü-lan* 881, p. 4b, and the commentary to *Huang-t'ing nei-ching* 黃庭內經 4, quoted in *Yün-chi ch'i-ch'ien* 11, p. 23, where the commentary cites *Chen kao* 眞誥.

II

As we stroll across the bridge
The water in the stream flows west.
On the bank is an immortal's residence,
Past which the fishes flow to the west.
They do not go away alone:
They go together in threes and twos.

The "songs accompanied by strings" in the penultimate line of the first stanza alert us to the fact that we are near a temple where "songs for the gods" are being played. The first two lines of the second stanza recall two lines of a ballad called "The Song of the White Hair" ("Pai-t'ou yin" 白頭吟): "Strolling near the imperial canal, / Whose waters flow to the west"[34] — or "to the east," because the line literally reads "east and west." But this is probably a case in which the poet has used two contrasting words to express the meaning of only one of them.[35] I have chosen "west" because of line 4.[36] The first line of the second poem may also be read "As we stroll on the bridge to Yüeh," the province southeast of Wu. The "immortal" of line 3 is, of course, the "Charming Girl," and her residence is the temple to her on the river bank. Like the goddess in Poem 6, the Charming Girl is probably a goddess to whom one prayed for marriage or for children. Do the fish symbolize her mate-making power or her power to give children? Fish symbolize fertility in China as in the West.[37]

We know nothing about the Charming Girl or her cult; we know a little more about the gods referred to in the two succeeding poems.

5. The Youth of the White Stone

I

The Youth of the White Stone
Lives near the River.
The Count of the River leads his procession
And the fish follow in the rear.

[34] *SS* 21, p. 622; *YFSC* 41, p. 600.

[35] Yü Kuan-ying, "Han Wei shih li te p'ien-i fu-tz'u" 漢魏詩裏的偏義複詞, in his *Han Wei Liu-ch'ao shih lun-ts'ung* 漢魏六朝詩論叢 (Shanghai: T'ang-li ch'u-pan-she, 1953), pp. 40–41.

[36] I follow Chang, *Yüeh-fu shih-hsüan*, p. 51; Yü, "P'ien-i fu-tz'u," p. 41, thinks there is an allusion here to the ballad "Ch'ien huan-sheng ko" 前緩聲歌: "In eastward flowing water there must be fish swimming westwards against the current"; he suggests the water in l. 2 is flowing east.

[37] Wen I-to 聞一多, "Shen-hua yü shih" 神話與詩, in *Wen I-to ch'üan-chi* 全集 (Peking: San-lien, 1982), pp. 134–36; see also Li, "Yüeh-fu yü hsien-tao," p. 74.

II

The stones piled up (before his temple) are (as beautiful as jade);
The pine trees planted in straight lines are kingfisher blue.
The beauty of the Youth is unique:
The world does not know his equal.

There are numerous White Stone Mountains in China. Wang Yün-hsi has identified the site described in this poem with the White Stone Fort, Pai-shih lei 白石壘, near the Yangtze north of Nanking and northeast of the Stone Citadel, Shih-t'ou ch'eng 石頭城, which played such an important role in medieval history.[38] He bases his identification on a story found in *chüan* 9 of *Sou-shen chi* 搜神記 about Yü Liang 庾亮 (289–340).[39] According to this story Yü Liang fell ill after having punched a red-eyed demon who had appeared before him in the latrine. He called a fortune-teller (*shu-shih* 術士) who explained:

> In the past, during the Su Chün 蘇峻 affair, your lordship prayed for good fortune at the shrine of the White Stone and promised to sacrifice an ox. Since you have not yet requited the god with your sacrifice (*chieh* 解),[40] this demon was sent to investigate. You cannot be saved.

The *Sou-shen chi* is made up of texts of unequal value, but this story is well attested elsewhere.[41] We know, moreover, that Yü Liang successfully held White Stone Fort against Su Chün who attacked it with vastly superior forces in 328,[42] and that he subsequently visited the spot.[43] We have a short text written by him in a temporary ancestral temple set up on the White Stone announcing the victory to the imperial ancestors.[44] There can be no doubt that a temple existed on this site in the fourth century and in all probability is the temple celebrated in this poem.

The Count of the River, Chiang-po 江伯, is probably the southern cousin of the redoubtable Count of the (Yellow) River, Ho-po 河伯, but he is not well known. The only references to him I have been able to find are

---

[38] Wang, "Shen-hsien," pp. 174–75; he quotes *Tu-shih fang-yü chi-yao* 讀史方輿紀要 (Peking: Chung-hua, 1957) 20, p. 914.

[39] No. 249, p. 120, of the edn. by Wang Shao-ying 汪紹楹 (Peking: Chung-hua, 1979).

[40] As in *Chuang-tzu* 4; trans. Burton Watson, *The Complete Works of Chuang-tzu* (New York: Columbia U.P., 1968), p. 65, and *Lun-heng* 25, "Chieh-ch'u" 解除.

[41] *SSHY* 17, no. 9; trans. Mather, *New Account*, p. 325; *CS* 95, p. 2475.

[42] *CS* 99, p. 2630.

[43] Probably at the end of his life; cf. *SSHY* 8, no. 107; trans. Mather, *New Account*, p. 237.

[44] *SS* 16, p. 448.

in a fragment from *Nan Yüeh chih* 南越志 by Shen Huai-yüan 沈懷遠, who lived in the first half of the fifth century,[45] and a line from a poem by Ch'u Kuang-hsi 儲光羲 (fl. 730).[46] We learn from the former simply that the count's underwater palace and style of living were not different from those of terrestrial counterparts.[47]

It is hard to know just who the White Stone Youth was. There were other gods with the same name who were probably totally unrelated to him.[48] I would think he was a purely local god, taking his name from the place of his worship, although it is possible that he was, at least partially, identified with the famous immortal called Master of the White Stones, Pai-shih hsien-sheng 白石先生, who appears in *Shen-hsien chuan* 神仙傳.[49] He seems to be a masculine counterpart of both the Charming Girl we have just met and the female deities we see in the next three sets of poems.

The goddess who is the subject of the following poem is often mentioned in medieval literature; she is the only god mentioned in the titles of these poems who is not completely unknown.

6. *The Young Damsel of the Blue Stream*

The gate opens on pure white water
Beside the bridge.
That is where the Young Damsel lives,
Alone, no young man with her.

The Blue Stream, Ch'ing-hsi 青溪 (sometimes called Pure 清 Stream), was in fact a canal built in 241–242.[50] Its water came from springs on Mount Chung (or Mount Chiang, or Mount Tzu-chin 紫金 as it is called today), and it entered the Ch'in-huai River almost due south of medieval Nanking. The temple was beside the dyke at the confluence of the canal and the

[45] *SS* 82, p. 2105.
[46] "T'ung chu-kung ch'iu-jih yu K'un-ming ch'ih ssu ku" 同諸公秋日遊昆明池思古, *Ch'üan T'ang-shih* 全唐詩 (Peking: Chung-hua, 1960) 138, p. 1398.
[47] *Nan Yüeh chih* quoted in *P'ei-wen yün-fu* 佩文韻府, under "Chiang-po."
[48] Rolf A. Stein, "Remarques sur les mouvements du taoïsme politico-religieux au IIe siècle ap. J.-C.," *TP* 50. 1–3 (1963), pp. 43–46, sees an analogy between our Yangtze White Stone Youth and a god with a similar name who appears on a stele dated 183 and who was the spirit of a mountain in Hopeh.
[49] See Sawada Mizuho 澤田瑞穗, trans., *Shinsen den* 神仙傳, vol. 8 of *Chūgoku koten bungaku taikei* 中国古典文学大系 (Tokyo: Heibonsha, 1969), pp. 355–56. Chang, *Yüeh-fu shih hsüan*, p. 52, is mistaken when he refers to the *Lieh-hsien chuan* as containing a possible model for the Youth of the White Stone.
[50] *Chien-k'ang shih-lu* 建康實錄 (Peking: Chung-hua, 1986) 2, p. 49. No mention of the temple is made in the work dated 756, which does list a multitude of Buddhist temples that lined the banks of the canal.

Ch'in-huai. It must have been very famous, for one source says the canal was named after it.[51]

The Young Damsel of the temple was, according to a fifth-century source, the third youngest sister of Chiang Tzu-wen,[52] which perhaps accounts for her celebrity and also for her power. According to the same source she was responsible for the death of the father of Hsieh Ling-yün 謝靈運 (385–433), who foolishly killed some fledglings nesting in her temple. Another source of the same period shows she was a music lover, eager to enroll the best players among mortals for her otherworldly concerts, after she has done them in.[53]

But the Young Damsel, as we see in the short poem devoted to her, seems to have been known especially as an amorous goddess. In an anecdote dated from the end of the fourth century she appears in a dream to a young Buddhist monk whom she had admired when he came to look at her temple. She informs him that he is to die and become her consort. Before his death he informs his brother monks of his misfortune and asks them to visit him in the Young Damsel's temple after his death. They do and are able to talk with him as in life. When, at his request, they chant the Buddhist liturgy for him for the last time, they all burst into tears.[54]

The most famous story about the goddess is found in *Hsü Ch'i Hsieh chi* 續齊諧記 by Wu Chün 吳均 (469–520), a writer highly renowned for his prose style. The story tells of one Chao Wen-shao 趙文韶 (unknown elsewhere), who lived near the central bridge on the Pure (that is, Blue) Stream. Homesick for his native K'uai-chi, he movingly sings a ballad while leaning on his front gate. A young servant girl appears and tells him her mistress enjoyed his singing. Chao invites her over and sings another song for her. She then shows virtuosity at the harp (*k'ung-hou* 箜篌) and accompanies her servant, who sings subtly suggestive songs that describe a lonely woman ready to give her heart to a lover. They pass the night together and exchange gifts. The next day, Chao Wen-shao happens to enter the Pure Stream

[51] Ku Yeh-wang 顧野王 (d. after 569), *Yü-ti chih* 輿地志, reproduced in Wang Mo 王謨, comp., *Han T'ang ti-li shu-ch'ao* 漢唐地理書鈔 (Peking: Chung-hua, 1961), pp. 23b–24a, where the stream is called "Pure," *ch'ing* 清.

[52] Liu Ching-shu 劉敬叔 (d. ca. 470), *I-yüan* 異苑 (Chin-tai pi-shu edn. [Shanghai: Po-ku-chai, 1922]) 5, pp. 3b–4a.

[53] Liu I-ch'ing 劉義慶 (403–444), *Yu-ming lu* 幽明錄, quoted in *Pei-t'ang shu-ch'ao* 109, p. 8b, and *T'ai-p'ing yü-lan* 577, p. 8b.

[54] In *Sou-shen hou-chi* 搜神後記 (Peking: Chung-hua, 1981), no. 50, pp. 31–32, this anecdote is said to take place at the end of the third century (during the T'ai-k'ang era); *T'ai-p'ing kuang-chi* 太平廣記 (Peking: Chung-hua, 1961) 294, p. 2343, gives the end of the fourth century (during the T'ai-yüan era), which is more appropriate.

Temple where he finds his presents and recognizes the Young Damsel and her attendant statues as the women he saw the night before. They never returned. The event is dated 428.[55]

Are these anecdotes and the four tetrameters of the ditty-like poem enough to say that the Young Damsel is a goddess of love, and that the bridge next to her temple is a bridge that brings lovers (like the Cowherd and the Weaver-girl) together?[56] It certainly seems as if we are in the presence here of an "excessive cult," one devoted to the union of lovers and marriage. But the character of the cult seems to have evolved, and in Ming times the Young Damsel was revered as a loyal wife who, during a period of disorders, drowned herself and her two daughters in the Blue Stream, in all likelihood to preserve her chastity.[57]

The following two poems also describe goddesses, but they are goddesses about whom we know nothing except what we learn from the poems themselves.

7. The Damsels of the Lake Shore

I

In the area surrounding the shores of Red Mount Lake
In the first three months of the year
The marshes filled with aquatic plants are covered in green.

II

The shores of the lake are the Red Mount's shingle beach;
The Great Damsel lives on the east of the lake,
The Second Damsel on the west.

The Red Mount Reservoir, Ch'ih-shan t'ang 赤山塘, was originally an artificial lake built during the Ch'ih-wu 赤烏 era (238–250). It was repaired continually during the centuries and still exists under the name Red Mount Lake 湖, east of Hu-shu 湖熟 and south of Chü-jung 句容, Kiangsu, which is southeast of Nanking.[58] The word chiu 就, which I have translated as

---

[55] This story is translated by Yang Xianyi and Gladys Yang in *Poetry and Prose of the Han Wei and Six Dynasties* (Peking: Panda Books, 1986), pp. 129–31; the Chinese text can be found in *Han Wei ts'ung-shu* 漢魏叢書 (1791 edn.), pp. 8b–9b.

[56] Li, "Yüeh-fu yü hsien-tao," pp. 74–75, suggests so.

[57] Hsiao, *Yüeh-fu wen-hsüeh*, pp. 227–28, quotes *Chiang-ning fu chih* 江寧府志, cited in *Ku-chin t'u-shu chi-ch'eng.*

[58] See *Tu-shih fang-yü chi-yao* 20, p. 945; *Chung-kuo hsin yü-t'u* 中國新輿圖, 3d edn. (Shanghai: Commercial Press, 1917), plate 10, still shows the lake.

"shore," nowhere has that meaning. Only the *Shuo-wen chieh-tzu* 說文解字 defines the character as meaning "heights, elevated."[59]

The third line of the first poem is found in various forms among the ballads of this and later periods.[60] The second line of the second poem reads: "The Great Damsel (is) to the east of the Great Lake." I follow a variant found in the *Ku-chin t'u-shu chi-ch'eng* encyclopedia.[61] The two poems resemble the poems concerning the Charming Girl (No. 4): first a description of the surrounding scenery, then of the shrine itself.

The following poem is the last in the series that is clearly related to popular religion. It again concerns an otherwise unknown goddess.

8. *The Damsel's Grace*

I

The Brilliant Damsel follows the Eight Winds
In the dense vapors between the clouds and the sun.
Animals of all kinds lead her procession;
The Scarlet Bird, the unicorn, and phoenix bring up the rear.

II

How high are the cypresses on the mountain's crest:
Winter and summer their needles do not wither!
They, above all, receive the grace of heaven
And flourish, branch and needle, luxuriantly.

The last two lines of the first stanza strongly resemble the first line of Poem No. 5, to the Youth of the White Stone. In both cases there is a suggestion of a ritual procession, aquatic in the case of Poem No. 5, airborne here. The Scarlet Bird, one of the twenty-eight stellar mansions as well as an auspicious omen, the unicorn, and the phoenix are all fabulous creatures that appear in order to welcome sage kings. It is very possible that in these two poems we see the description of religious processions,[62] of the kind we know took place in the Middle Ages in China.[63] The second stanza is again (as is the case with the first stanzas of Poems 4 and 7) a description, this time of a tree-clad mountain.

---

[59] *Shuo-wen chieh-tzu* (Peking: Chung-hua, 1963), 5 *hsia*, p. 11a.

[60] See, e.g., *Yüeh-fu shih-chi* 25, p. 364.   [61] As in n. 4, above, but p. 1b.

[62] Li, "Yüeh-fu yü hsien-tao," p. 75; he refers to an article by Piet van der Loon translated into Chinese that appears in *Chung-wai wen-hsüeh* 中外文學 5 (1979), presumably "Les origines rituelles du théâtre chinois," *JA* 265 (1977), pp. 141–68.

[63] Hama Kazue 濱一衞, "Gigaku genryū kō" 伎樂源流考, *Chūgoku bungaku hō* 中国文学报 9 (1958), pp. 1–16.

Is the Brilliant Damsel a sun goddess, as Wang Yün-hsi believes?[64] This would make her the only astral deity, as opposed to purely local, terrestrial gods, in our series. It would help explain the third line of the second stanza: the conifers on the mountain, close to the sun and the stars, receive greater benefit from their "effulgences," *ching* 景, than the plants and creatures of the plains.[65] But a "sun goddess" seems out of place among these homely local divinities.

The last three sets of poems also seem out of place in this series of "songs for the gods," for they have nothing religious about them.

9. The Young Lotus Pickers

I

From our boats we pick water chestnut leaves,
And, in passing, pluck lotus flowers.
We strike our oars and call our comrades
To unite their voices in the song of the lotus pickers!

II

In the east lake boys (sing) "Pulling Water-oats";
In the west lake, the songstresses (sing) "Picking Water-chestnuts."
We do not sing for pleasure,
But to dissipate our sadness.

These two quatrains are very much in the style of the southern popular ballads called Wu-sheng and Hsi-ch'ü, and it is hard to see how they would have been used in a religious ceremony. They seem to be modeled on popular "gathering songs" and to have been written by a fairly sophisticated poet.

The second stanza is very hard to understand without at least two textual emendations suggested first by Yü Kuan-ying,[66] and incorporated in the 1979 edition of *Yüeh-fu shih-chi*.[67] These emendations are based, in part, on the existence of two ballad titles among the southern popular ballads, "Pulling Rushes" ("Pa p'u" 拔蒲)[68] and "Gathering Water Chestnuts" ("Ts'ai ling" 採菱).[69] But, however one interprets these lines, the last

[64] Wang, "Shen-hsien," p. 178.
[65] See Michel Strickmann, "On the Alchemy of T'ao Hung-ching," in Welch and Seidel, eds., *Facets of Taoism*, pp. 177–78.
[66] Yü, *Yüeh-fu shih-hsüan*, p. 96.
[67] *YFSC* 47, p. 686.
[68] *YFSC* 49, pp. 718–19.
[69] *YFSC* 51, pp. 739 ff. The earliest known are by Pao Chao 鮑照 (405?–466). "Water-oats" translates *ku* 菰 (*zizania latifolia*).

two lines of the second quatrain are imbued with a form of melancholy that seems to take them out of the category of "popular" poetry and to make one feel the presence of a man of letters. There is a pun in the penultimate line: "We do not sing for pleasure." This can also mean "We do not sing to make music," a common pun throughout Chinese literature and not at all surprising in these southern ballads, where puns abound. Both the fact that this poem is so literary and that it has an emotional meaning in itself make it difficult for me to follow Li Feng-mao, who couples it with Poem 7 and sees them both as "possible expressions of sacrificial ceremonies concerned with agriculture."[70]

Aside from its enigmatic title, which may have religious overtones, the following poem again seems difficult to interpret as a "song for the gods."

10. The Boy under Brightness

I

He presses his horse up the slope before him,
The horse's hooves striking against the pebbles.
I don't care if they do strike the horse's hooves;
I only care for the lad on horseback!

II

Young Ch'en prancing about on his bay and white,
Young Lu mounted on his piebald steed,
Turning about the archery gallery,
They gaze at the gate, not wanting to return home.

Again we have here two quatrains very similar to southern popular ballads. The first looks like a love song, showing a young woman's solicitude for her young lover and her indifference to what he might be doing to his horse. The second is a vignette of young men's life, perhaps rich young men eager to prolong their sport and not go back to their families. If the two quatrains form a pair, the second could be put into the mouth of the lover of one of the young men, who is jealous of the attraction of the archery gallery over her own. I have accepted Wang Yün-hsi's suggestion and changed k'ung 孔, the second character of the first line of the second quatrain, to lang 郎, making it parallel with the second line.[71]

The last two quatrains are quoted almost word for word from other ballads, the first almost surely from Han times, the second a southern ballad

[70] Li, "Yüeh-fu yü hsien-tao," p. 75.   [71] Wang, "Shen-hsien," p. 179.

roughly contemporary with the "songs for the gods." The title is again obscure.

11. Of a Common Birth

I

Man's life lasts not one hundred years
And yet he holds within him one thousand years of woe!
Learn quickly how fast our span is run
And grasp a torch to wander forth in the night!

II

The years and months speed by
Already white autumn is upon us.
The crickets are singing in the empty hall:
Sadness comes, filling one with melancholy.

The first quatrain is a slightly modified version of four lines from "Hsi-men hsing" 西門行;[72] the second quatrain is even less modified from "Tzu-yeh pien-ko" 子夜變歌, No. 3.[73] The first quatrain is a carpe diem, the second, a lament for the passage of time. "White autumn" refers to the fact that in the system of correspondences of classical thought autumn is "white" or "colorless," *su* 素 (spring is green, summer red, and so forth). What these two have to do with the general title, "Of a Common Birth," is difficult to ascertain. Is it quasi-biblical: "As we are all born, (so shall we die . . .)?" The melancholy and sophistication of these two quatrains seem hard to reconcile with the rest of the series, as heterogeneous as this latter may seem. One is tempted to agree with Obi Kōichi: in the last two poems "of the series in particular we hardly feel any religious elements. Have everyday folksongs been diverted here and used just as they are as sacrificial texts?"[74]

CONCLUSION

The "Songs for the Gods" are a unique set of poems used in popular religion. In much reduced scale they represent for early medieval China what some of the poetry of the *Shih ching* and the *Ch'u tz'u* (the "Chiu ko"

[72] *YFSC* 37, p. 549; it also appears in no. 15 of the Nineteen Old Poems, *Wen hsüan* 文選 (Hu K'o-chia edn.) 29, p. 7a.
[73] *YFSC* 45, p. 655.
[74] Obi Kōichi 小尾郊一 and Okamura Sadao 岡村貞雄, *Ko gafu* 古樂府 (Tokyo: Tōkai daigaku, 1980), p. 306. Obi translates 10 of the 18 poems of the series (1–6, 9.1, 10.1, and 11.2).

in particular) represent for early and late ancient China. They were preserved in a collection made close to a century after their creation and thus
their authenticity need not be rejected out of hand. The gods they mention
and the ceremonies they allude to are, for the most part, unknown.

Are they a proper "series"? Are they given in the order they were sung
during a single ceremony? The first poem is a request for the gods to descend,
the very type of poem one would expect at the beginning of a ceremony. It
can be compared to a poem by Wang Wei, the first of two contained in the
same chapter of *Yüeh-fu shih-chi* as the "Songs for the Gods," which describes
a sacrifice to the goddess of Mount Yü 漁 (Hopeh), a poem entitled "Wel-
coming the God," "Ying-shen" 迎神.[75]

The succeeding six titles (eleven poems) are all to different divinities.
The White Stone Youth, the Young Damsel of the Blue Stream, and the
Damsels from the Lake Shore, the only divinities we can locate, all come
from the Nanking region, although the first and last are close to fifty
kilometers apart. Would a single ceremony include six different divinities
from localities so far apart? We know so little of these cults that it is
impossible to decide.

But the most difficult problem is to know how to account for the last
six poems (three titles). Are they just popular ballads from Wu that have
simply been added to these religious songs by mistake? They are the only
sets of poems in the series that correspond exactly in their prosody to the
Wu ballads, being pairs of pentametric quatrains. Are they really ceremonial songs vaguely concerned with agriculture or some sort of play or
sport that accompanied religious ceremonies much like the foot races that
accompanied Easter celebrations in the Middle Ages in Europe? Or are they
"everyday folksongs" that somehow were used as poems of separation? The
second poem by Wang Wei to the goddess of Mount Yü is called "Accompanying the Goddess," "Sung-shen" 送神, and the last quatrain of the
"Songs for the Gods" belongs to a category ("Tzu-yeh pien-ko") that was
sung as "accompanying" songs at the end of a set of ballads.[76] The problem
is complicated and perhaps insoluble, but these last six poems certainly
seem to be popular folksongs unrelated to the preceding twelve.

The literary quality of most of this poetry is not very high, which is
perhaps a confirmation of the fact that it was actually conceived as "utilitar-
ian" literature by unlettered authors. It is true that the poetic description
that makes up Poem I of "The Charming Girl" is lovely. The simplicity

[75] *YFSC* 47, p. 687.
[76] *YFSC* 45, p. 655; 30, p. 441. See also Wang, *Liu-ch'ao yüeh-fu yü min-ko*, pp. 63–70.

and awkwardness of many of the others, too, is striking (especially during this period of highly ornate verse), and the last poems compare favorably with many of the other popular ballads of the period.[77] It is these that have most interested anthologists. But the greatest value of these songs is the testimony they give to the existence of a popular religion about which we know so little.

[77] Lu K'an-ju 陸侃如 and Feng Yüan-chün 馮沅君, *Chung-kuo shih-shih* 中國詩史 (Peking: Tso-chia ch'u-pan-she, 1957), vol. 1, p. 232, think the opening poem to be "extremely clumsy," but consider the "love poetry" to be good, citing as examples nos. 5.2, 6, and 10.1. These poems make the authors think of the "Chiu ko" of the *Ch'u tz'u*, and they place these "popular sacrificial songs without any doubt far above the odes of the Chou (*Shih*, nos. 266–296) or (the Han ritual songs) 'Fang-chung tz'u-yüeh' 房中祠樂." The latter refers to "An-shih fang-chung ko" 安世房中歌, trans. E. Chavannes, *Les Mémoires historiques* (rpt. Paris: Maisonneuve, 1967) 3, pp. 605–11, from *Han shu* 22, pp. 1046–52.

LIST OF ABBREVIATIONS

CS   *Chin shu* 晋書
SS   *Sung shu* 宋書
SSHY   *Shih-shuo hsin-yü* 世說新語
YFSC   *Yüeh-fu shih-chi* 樂府詩集

VII

UNE FÊTE CHEZ SU SHIH
A HUANG CHOU EN 1082

SOMMAIRE

I. L'époque 1080-1082 dans la vie de Su Shih.
1. Les conditions de l'installation à Huang *chou* en 1080. 122
2. Le séjour au Ting-hui *yüan* et le poème sur le pommier sauvage. 122
3. Le thème du pommier sauvage, souvenir du Ssuch'uan natal. 125
4. L'installation au Lin-kao *t'ing* et la mise en culture du coteau Tung-p'o. 126

II. Les trois poèmes consacrés à la fête du « manger froid ».
1. Les fêtes du « manger froid » et du jour *ch'ing-ming*. 127
2. Le premier poème sur la pluie pendant la période du « manger froid » : sur le thème de la fuite du temps. 128
3. Le deuxième poème : sur la fête elle-même. 129
4. Le troisième poème : sur le rallumage du feu au jour *ch'ing-ming*. 132

*

ABRÉVIATIONS BIBLIOGRAPHIQUES

chi-ch'eng   Wang Wen-kao, *Su Wen-chung kung shih pien-chu chi-ch'eng* (éd. de 1819, reproduction T'ai-pei, 1967).
DKWJT   *Daikanwa-jiten*, dictionnaire en 12 volumes de Morohashi.
THGH   *Tōhōgakuhō*.
tsung-an   Wang Wen-kao, *Su Wen-chung kung shih pien-chu chi-ch'eng tsung-an* (formant les 45 premiers chapitres du *chi-ch'eng*).

Vers la fin de sa trop courte vie Étienne Balazs exprimait souvent le regret de n'avoir pas pu se pénétrer davantage de la poésie chinoise, poésie qu'il considérait comme une des gloires de la civilisation mondiale. Il l'avait pratiquée au début de sa carrière[1], mais avait dû la délaisser ensuite pour se consacrer à ses analyses passionnées et passionnantes de l'histoire chinoise. C'est en hommage à cet intérêt que j'offre cette courte note sur les poésies que le plus grand poète des Sung, Su Shih, écrivit en 1082, lors de la fête du « manger froid », *han-shih*, pendant son exil à Huang *chou*.

Il est bien connu que Su Shih fut l'adversaire constant et volubile des idées réformatrices de Wang An-shih et de son parti[2]. Ceux-ci prirent le pouvoir en 1069 et trois ans plus tard, par suite de son désaccord fondamental avec leurs réformes, Su Shih fut envoyé en province comme vice-préfet, *t'ung-p'an*, de la belle ville de Hang *chou*. Pendant huit ans il occupa des postes provinciaux dans l'est de la Chine. Mais il trouva les réformes de Wang An-shih tellement insupportables qu'il ne put s'empêcher de les critiquer dans des lettres et des poèmes, des écrits si merveilleux et souvent si spirituels que les réformateurs eurent vite fait de trouver Su Shih lui aussi insupportable. Un complot fut monté contre lui en 1079. Accusé de sédition contre l'empereur, il fut jeté en prison et obligé de se défendre en interprétant lui-même ses poésies. Il lui fallait prouver qu'elles restaient en deçà de la marge fine comme une lame de rasoir qui sépare, en Chine, la critique objective et bien intentionnée de la révolte séditieuse[3]. Il convainquit au moins l'empereur Shen-tsung qui l'amnistia le 23 janvier 1080, lui donnant le titre de *Chien-chiao shui-pu yüan-wai-lang Huang chou t'uan-lien fu-shih*, « vice-commissaire des milices de Huang *chou*, sous-directeur du bureau des eaux, sans charge », un titre nominal qui ne lui donnait ni charge... ni pécule. Il restait, de plus, en résidence surveillée dans les confins de la préfecture.

Il arriva le 24 février 1080, sans sa famille, à Huang *chou*[4]. Il résida d'abord dans un petit établissement religieux appelé le Ting-hui *yüan*, appartenant au monastère bouddhique An-kuo *ssu*. Ce monastère était

---

1. « Ts'ao Ts'ao, zwei Lieder », *Monumenta serica*, 2 (1937), pp. 410-420; traduction anglaise par H.M. Wright, in : É. Balazs, *Chinese Civilization and Bureaucracy*, New Haven, 1964, pp. 173-186.

2. *Cf.* J.T.C. Liu, *Reform in Sung China*, Cambridge (Mass.), 1959, p. 28 *et passim*.

3. Le *Wu-t'ai shih-an* prétend être le compte rendu de ce procès, compilé par un certain P'eng Chiu-wan des Sung. En fait, selon le *Ssu-k'u ch'üan-shu tsung-mu t'i-yao*, 64, il s'agirait d'une sélection de documents faite par Hu Tzu (*fl.* 1150) et reproduite dans son *T'iao-hsi yü-yin ts'ung-hua*, 1re série, ch. 42 (à partir de la p. 288 de l'édition de Pékin, 1962).

4. *Cf.* « Tao Huang-chou hsieh-piao », *Tung-p'o chi*, 25 /3b (éd. Ssu-pu pei-yao). Huang *chou* : act. Huang-kang, sur la rive nord du Yang-tzu (est du Hupei).

situé au sud des murailles de la petite ville et datait de 944, époque où il s'appelait le Hu-kuo *ssu*. En 1063, une vingtaine d'années avant l'arrivée de Su Shih, il avait reçu son nouveau nom et avait été reconstruit. Il se trouvait dans une épaisse forêt de grands bambous et, au dire même de Su Shih, « était si agréable qu'on oubliait d'en partir une fois qu'on s'y trouvait »[1]. Là, Su Shih pratiquait la méditation bouddhique, mangeait avec les bonzes, lisait exclusivement les écritures bouddhiques (et pas de « livres » *i.e.* de littérature séculière)[2] et se promenait solitaire en admirant les fleurs et les beautés du paysage méridional. Ses tout récents démêlés avec la justice, où il s'en était fallu de peu qu'il ne laissât sa peau, avaient été un choc sévère. Il répète souvent dans ses lettres datant de cette époque qu'il veut se réformer, se purifier de ses « fautes ». Une partie de ces remarques est sûrement écrite pour la galerie, pour convaincre les hommes au pouvoir qu'il s'est rangé, qu'ils n'auront plus à craindre sa langue un peu trop bien pendue. Mais il semble aussi que Su Shih se soit vraiment adonné à la méditation et ait eu ce qu'on peut appeler une « crise religieuse ». Les poèmes qui datent de cette époque témoignent d'une forte influence bouddhique[3]. Au moins cinq d'entre eux ont pour cadre le An-kuo *ssu* ou le Ting-hui *yüan*. Ils sont tous beaux, mais je ne veux en traduire qu'un parce qu'il jette une certaine lumière sur un des poèmes écrits pendant la fête qui forme le sujet principal de cet article :

Je loge temporairement au Ting-hui *yüan*. A l'est du temple, des fleurs de toutes sortes couvrent la colline, mais il y a un pommier sauvage que les gens du pays ne savent pas apprécier.

« Ville du Yang-tzu, terre pestilentielle où foisonnent plantes et arbres :
Une seule fleur célèbre y souffre, cachée et solitaire.
Elle sourit, si charmante, parmi les haies de bambous,
Tandis que pêchers et pruniers inondent la colline de toute leur vulgarité.
Mais je sais que la volonté du Créateur est profonde
D'avoir envoyé une telle beauté jusque dans cette vallée solitaire[4].

1. « Huang-chou An-kuo chi », *Ching-chin Tung-p'o wen-chi shih-lüeh*, ch. 54 p. 872 (éd. Pékin, 1957). Ce texte est une description du monastère, composée par Su Shih à la demande du supérieur juste avant son départ de Huang *chou*. On en trouvera des traductions partielles dans Lin Yutang, *The Gay Genius*, Londres, 1948, p. 184, et Andrew L. March, « Self and landscape in Su Shih », *Journal of the American Oriental Society*, LXXXVI (1966), p. 392.
2. *Cf.* « Yü Chang Tzu-hou shu », *Tung-p'o hsü-chi*, 11/26a.
3. *Cf.* Ogawa Tamaki, *So Shoku* (Chūgoku shijin senshū, 2e Série, 5, Tōkyō, 1962), p. 9 : l'auteur rappelle que le surnom de « Tung-p'o » (voir *infra*, p. 127) que Su Shih prit à cette époque était en fait celui de « laïc du Tung-p'o », Tung-p'o *chü-shih*, et avait donc des résonances bouddhiques. *Cf.* aussi Chikusa Masaaki, « So Shoku to bukkyō », *THGH* (Kyōto), 36 (1964), pp. 475-479.
4. Écho des deux premiers vers d'un poème de Tu Fu (*cf.* D. Hawkes, *A Tu Fu Primer*, Oxford, 1967, p. 78). La personnification de la Création (vers précédent) est fréquente chez Su Shih, comme le sont les personnifications de fleurs (dont ce poème est un exemple). Le « Créateur », *tsao-wu* ou *tsao-wu che*, est un synonyme du *tao* et

Sa supériorité naît spontanément de sa grâce naturelle ;
Elle n'a point besoin de plats d'or servis dans des salles luxueuses.
Son visage se colore légèrement quand le vin touche ses lèvres vermeilles ;
Quand elle relève ses manches bleu-vert sa chair émet une lumière rose.
La forêt est profonde, la brume sombre : les rayons de l'aube viennent tard ;
Le soleil est tiède, le vent léger : elle a assez de son sommeil printanier [1].
Dans la pluie il y a des larmes, et elle est mélancolique ;
Sous la lune, solitaire, elle est encore plus pure et chaste.
J'ai bien mangé et je suis tout à fait oisif ;
Je me promène à mon aise, la main sur le ventre.
Peu me chaut que ce soit une maison de laïcs ou la case de bonzes ;
Appuyé sur mon bâton, je frappe à la porte pour regarder les hauts bambous,
Quand subitement je rencontre une beauté sans pareille qui brille sur ma décrépitude.
Je soupire sans parler, frottant mes yeux malades [2].
Où ce vilain pays s'est-il procuré cette fleur ?
N'a-t-elle pas été transplantée du Shu occidental par quelque amateur ?
Mais il n'est pas facile de faire venir d'une si grande distance une racine si menue :
C'est sûrement quelque oiseau héroïque qui en a apporté ici, en volant, une graine
    dans son bec !
Il faut que nous pensions l'un à l'autre, réunis ici à la dérive au bout du monde :
C'est pourquoi je bois une grande coupe et chante cette chanson.
Demain matin, quand je serai sobre, je reviendrai encore seul ;
Comment supporterais-je de la toucher ? Sa neige tomberait en tourbillons. » (a) [3]

Ce beau poème est assez caractéristique de tous ceux que Su Shih écrivit à cette époque. Les remarques peu flatteuses pour le pays de son exil mises à part — ce sont les remarques traditionnelles d'un exilé chinois, où qu'il se trouve —, Su Shih se montre en train de jouir paisi-

---

apparaît déjà dans *Chuang-tzu*, 6. *Cf.* Ogawa Tamaki, *op. cit.*, pp. 15-16 (bref résumé dans Burton Watson, *Su Tung-p'o*, New York, 1965, p. 11).

1. Allusion à un épisode de la vie de la célèbre favorite de l'empereur Hsüan-tsung, Yang Kuei-fei. Convoquée chez l'empereur à un moment où elle ne s'était pas encore remise d'une beuverie matinale, elle dut paraître devant lui soutenue par deux esclaves. En la voyant, l'empereur sourit et dit : « Comment se pourrait-il qu'elle soit saoule? C'est simplement que la fleur du pommier sauvage n'a pas assez dormi ! » Le commentaire de Shih Yüan-chih (Sung du Sud) qui reproduit cette anecdote, renvoie au *Ming-huang tsa-lu* ; le *DKWJT* (sous *hai-t'ang*) renvoie au *T'ang shu*. Autant que je puisse voir, elle ne se trouve ni dans l'un, ni dans l'autre ; elle n'est pas racontée non plus dans Howard S. Levy, *Harem Favorites of an Illustrious Celestial* (T'ai-chung, 1958), où il est longuement question de Yang Kuei-fei. Je cite d'après le commentaire de Shih Yüan-chih (*op. cit.* ci-dessous, n.3).

2. Su shih a souffert toute sa vie de ses yeux et s'en plaint souvent ; *cf.*, par exemple, *Tung-p'o chih-lin*, ch. 1, p. 11 (éd. Ts'ung-shu chi-ch'eng).

3. Les lettres entre parenthèses et en italiques renvoient aux textes originaux chinois donnés à la fin de l'article. Le texte de ce poème et de ceux qui suivent est cité d'après le *Su Wen-chung kung shih pien-chu chi-ch'eng (infra: chi-ch'eng)*, éd. datée de 1819, reproduite à Taipei en 1967, 20 /11a-12a. Les 45 premiers chapitres du *chi-ch'eng* sont une biographie de Su Shih, par année, écrite par Wang Wen-kao (né en 1764) sous le titre de *Su Wen-chung kung shih pien-chu chi-ch'eng tsung-an (infra : tsung-an)*. Les poèmes de Su Shih arrangés par ordre chronologique et avec un commentaire compilé également par Wang Wen-kao, suivent la biographie, mais la numérotation des chapitres recommence à neuf.

blement des beautés naturelles de Huang *chou*. Le pommier sauvage (*pyrus spectabilis*, une espèce, dite « sibérienne », inconnu, autant que je sache, en Europe) est considéré par les connaisseurs comme un des plus beaux arbres à fleurs des jardins chinois. Il atteint plus de trois mètres de hauteur et ses jeunes feuilles sont teintées de rouge (*cf.* le vers 10). Les boutons sont d'un rouge vermeil, et les fleurs ouvertes rouges et blanches à l'extérieur et rose pâle à l'intérieur [1]. Cet arbre fleuri, que Su Shih découvre près de son premier gîte à Huang *chou*, est resté jusqu'à nos jours associé à sa patrie, le Ssuch'uan [2], où il est plus beau que dans le reste de la Chine. En découvrir dans son lieu d'exil, solitaire, caché au milieu des bambous sombres, c'était retrouver un vieil ami d'enfance en terre étrangère. Ces implications sont assez évidentes à la première lecture. Mais certaines allusions, au début du poème, suggèrent aussi que cette beauté cachée est, comme l'auteur, exilée de la Cour, et que, comme lui, elle ne s'en porte que mieux : le Créateur fait bien les choses ! La « beauté » de Tu Fu (vers 6) et surtout Yang Kueifei (vers 12), elle aussi originaire du Ssuch'uan, sont des dames de la Cour, mais ici, elles semblent plus belles, plus pures... et plus reposées ! Le poète ne s'introduit lui-même qu'au vers 15, comme un homme solitaire, oisif et simple, ne cherchant pas la compagnie des hommes, mais la vue des bambous. Sa rencontre soudaine avec la fleur est calculée avec art et très réussie dans le poème. Le dernier vers exprime toute la fragilité de la beauté de cette vie d'exilé solitaire : les pétales qui tombent éclairent d'une lumière rétrospective le poème entier et en révèlent la mélancolie sous-jacente.

Nous verrons que ce pommier sauvage réapparaît souvent dans les poèmes composés pendant son exil, mais celui que nous venons de citer semble être un de ses favoris. Il y fait allusion au début d'un poème écrit lors de la fête *ch'ing-ming* en 1084 :

« Une brume légère crachine, mais ne devient pas une vraie pluie ;
Appuyé sur mon bâton rustique, à l'aube, j'entre dans un jardin de fleurs innombrables.
J'ai un poème sur le pommier sauvage de la côte K'o,
Souriant seul dans la forêt profonde : qui oserait le mépriser ? » [4]

---

1. Ce pommier sauvage est décrit dans H.L. Li, *The Garden Flowers of China*, Chronica Botanica, No. 19, New York, 1959.

2. Kuo Mo-jo, dans la première phrase de son autobiographie, rappelle que son lieu d'origine (non loin de celui de Su Shih au pied du mont O-mei dans le Ssuch'uan) s'appelle « pays du parfum des pommiers sauvages » dans les monographies locales, bien que cette espèce de pommier sauvage odorant n'y fût plus plantée de son temps : Kuo Mo-jo, *Mo-jo tzu-chuan*, 1, *Shao-nien shih-tai*, Shanghai, 1953, p. 3.

3. Il se réfère souvent à cette fleur dans ses poésies. Un quatrain qui lui est entièrement consacré et qui semble dater de 1084 a été traduit par T.K. Tsai, *Chinese Poems in English Rhyme*, Chicago, 1932, p. 56.

4. *Chi-ch'eng*, 22 /19b. Ce poème se trouve aussi dans l'édition d'Ogawa, p. 162, et celle de Ch'en Erh-tung, *Su Shih shih-hsüan* Pékin, 1957, pp. 180-182.

Su Shih semble avoir été vraiment amoureux de ce pommier sauvage
(car il s'agit toujours du même), au point qu'il dit, dans un poème daté
de 1080 : « Je voudrais acheter la forêt du clan des K'o », c'est-à-dire
(d'après Wang Wen-kao) « la côte K'o » où l'arbre se trouvait [1]. L'auteur du *Shih-jen yü-hsieh*, Wei Ch'ing-chih, qui vécut à la fin des Sung
du Sud, nous dit, d'autre part : « Pendant toute sa vie Su Shih se plaisait
à faire des autographes de ce poème pour les donner. On dit qu'il fut
gravé sur pierre cinq ou six fois. C'est un poème qui lui donna satisfaction tout au long de sa vie. » [2]

Mais cette vie de célibataire courtisant les belles fleurs des forêts
était après tout assez artificielle pour un père de famille âgé de qua-
rante-trois ans. Son frère cadet bien-aimé, Su Ch'ê (ou Chê), arriva à
la fin du cinquième mois lunaire de l'année 1080, lui amenant femme et
enfants. Il n'est plus question de vivre avec les moines, et Su Shih démé-
nage dans un pavillon appartenant à un relais officiel sur le Yang-Tzu,
le Lin-kao *t'ing*. Ce relais se trouvait en dehors de la porte Chao-tsung [3]
de Huang *chou*, à quelques dizaines de pas au-dessus du fleuve [4], et
l'on y avait une vue splendide sur les collines environnantes. Su Shih
devait le privilège de s'y installer à la protection des magistrats locaux [5],
dont l'aide et l'amitié durent être d'une importance capitale pour lui
et sa famille. Mais le fait est qu'il est logé dans un bâtiment mis à sa
disposition par la bonne volonté de fonctionnaires, qu'il n'a pas de
traitement et très peu d'argent [6]. Le ton de ses poèmes et de ses lettres
— autant qu'on peut le discerner sous l'humour qui caractérise tant
de ses œuvres — s'assombrit. Au début du poème qu'il écrivit lors de
son déménagement, il dit :

« Je suis né entre ciel et terre,
Comme une fourmi sur une grande meule.
Dans sa petitesse, elle désire aller vers la droite ;
Mais elle n'empêche pas la Roue du Vent de tourner vers la gauche ! » [7]

---

1. « Hsiao chih Pa ho-k'ou ying Tzu-yu », *chi-ch'eng*, 20 /19b-20a. C'est d'après ce
poème qu'on peut dater l'arrivée de Su Ch'ê à Huang *chou* ; *tsung-an*, 20 /6a.

2. *Shih-jen yü-hsieh*, ch. 17, p. 384 (éd. Shanghai, 1958).

3. Le *Ming-sheng chih*, cité dans *chi-ch'eng*, 20 /20a.

4. « Yü Fan Tzu-feng shu », cité dans *tsung-an*, 20 /6b ; trad. Lin Yutang, p. 187.
Selon le *Tung-p'o chih-lin*, ch. 4, pp. 56-57 (éd. Ts'ung-shu chi-ch'eng), ce pavillon
était à 80 et quelques pas au-dessus du Yang-tzu ; c'est cette version qui est traduite
par March, *op. cit.*, pp. 378-379.

5. « Yü Chu K'ang-shu shu », *Tung-p'o hsü-chi*, 4 /12a.

6. Dans une lettre qui doit dater de la fin de 1080, Su Shih décrit d'une façon
humoristique ses difficultés pécuniaires. Des fragments de cette lettre ont été traduits
par Lin Yutang, *op. cit.*, p. 188 ; Ogawa, pamphlet annexe de son livre *So Shoku* ;
Watson, *op. cit.*, pp. 78-79. La lettre elle-même se trouve dans *Ching-chin Tung-p'o
wen-chi shih-lüeh*, ch. 45, pp. 770-773.

7. La « roue » ou « cercle du vent » est le plus bas des quatre cercles de la cosmo-

Un peu plus d'un an après son arrivée à Huang *chou*, les finances de Su Shih semblent avoir été à la dernière extrémité, et il se mit à travailler la terre. Un de ses amis lui procura plusieurs dizaines de *mu* de terre (un *mu* égalait à peu près 5,8 ares) sur un coteau appelé « Tung-p'o », « le coteau oriental », ancien site d'un campement militaire. La terre était remplie de gravats et de ronces et il s'épuisa à la travailler. Mais cette expérience du travail manuel l'a fortement marqué, et, après avoir fait construire un pavillon large de cinq travées sur le flanc du coteau, terminé dans un tourbillon de neige au début de 1082, il adopta le nom de son coteau comme surnom *(hao)*, appellation qu'il garda jusqu'à la fin de sa vie et sous laquelle il est familièrement connu aujourd'hui encore.

C'est au printemps de cette année 1082, donc quelques mois après l'adoption de sa nouvelle appellation, que Su Shih écrivit les trois poèmes qui forment le sujet principal de cet article. Ces poèmes ont pour arrière-plan une des fêtes les plus importantes du calendrier chinois, la fête des morts qui a été fixée, à l'encontre de toutes les autres fêtes du calendrier, selon l'année solaire, à 105 jours après le solstice d'hiver. Les origines de la fête sont obscures [1]. Sous les Sung, en tout cas, la fête, ou plus exactement, l'ensemble de fêtes qui avaient lieu avant et après le 5 ou 6 avril de notre calendrier (le 105e jour après le solstice d'hiver), a pris une grande importance. Les sources diffèrent beaucoup quant aux dates exactes des fêtes et même aux rites accomplis à chaque date, mais les grandes lignes des activités sont à peu près claires. Vers le 105e jour on éteignait tous les feux dans la maison après avoir fait une provision de plats cuisinés qu'on pouvait « manger froids » pendant les jours qui suivaient. Cette période de deux, trois ou même, à certains endroits campagnards, trente jours, s'appelait justement la fête du « manger froid », *han-shih*. On rallumait les feux à la fin de cette période, au jour

---

logie bouddhique et repose sur le vide (l'espace) ; *cf.* L. de La Vallée Poussin, *L'Abhidharmakośa*, 3 (Louvain, 1926), pp. 138-139. La monographie astronomique du *Chin-shu*, ch. 11 (trad. Ho Peng Yoke, *The Astronomical Chapters of the Chin shu*, Paris - La Haye, 1966, p. 5), d'autre part, décrit une théorie ancienne *(kai-t'ien)* selon laquelle « le ciel fait sa rotation vers la gauche comme une meule qui tourne, tandis que le soleil et la lune font leur rotation vers la droite... comme des fourmis qui marchent sur une meule. La meule tourne vers la gauche, tandis que les fourmis vont vers la droite, mais la meule va plus vite que les fourmis et les entraîne avec elle. »

1. D'après les sources citées dans les encyclopédies (*e.g.*, *T'ai-p'ing yü-lan*, 30 /6a-7a de la réédition de Pékin, 1960), la fête n'a pris la forme qu'elle avait sous les Sung que tardivement, vers le début des T'ang. Auparavant elle semble avoir été caractérisée par des jeux de football, polo et balançoire. Elle n'est bien attestée que vers la fin des Han, mais Liu Hsiang (*ca.* 79 — *ca.* 8 av. J.-C.) suggère une origine encore plus ancienne (cité dans *T'ai-p'ing yü-lan*, *op. cit.*). Sur cette fête, *cf.* aussi R. des Rotours, *Courtisanes chinoises à la fin des T'ang*, Paris, 1968, pp. 158, n. 1, et 159, n. 2, et les références auxquelles il renvoie, et *infra*, p. 128, n. 1.

ch'ing-ming du calendrier. A la capitale un feu rituel, produit par des moyens très archaïques au palais impérial, était distribué aux hauts fonctionnaires qui le rapportaient chez eux avec des flambeaux. Comme nous allons le voir à Huang *chou*, des distributions similaires ont dû avoir lieu aussi en province. Pendant toute cette période, on s'occupait des tombeaux des ancêtres qui se trouvaient dans les cimetières en dehors des villes ; mais le point culminant de la fête semble avoir été le jour même du *ch'ing-ming*, quand on sortait de la ville en masse, non seulement pour aller sur les tombes, mais aussi pour festoyer, goûter le printemps, les fleurs nouvelles et rares, boire du vin et s'amuser à la campagne, continuant ainsi, et sans doute inconsciemment, des rites très anciens du printemps accomplis dans la nature au bord de l'eau [1].

Le premier des deux poèmes écrits au moment du « manger froid » montre Su Shih en train de se lamenter sur le passage du temps, thème vénérable de la poésie chinoise. Le deuxième poème décrit plus en détail la fête même, et le troisième a pour arrière-plan le rallumage du feu au jour *ch'ing-ming*.

La pluie pendant la période du « manger froid »
Deux poèmes

« Depuis que je suis arrivé à Huang *chou*,
C'est ma troisième fête du manger froid.
Année après année je voulais regretter le passage du printemps,
Mais les printemps sont passés sans m'en laisser le temps !
Cette année, en plus, on souffre de la pluie :
Ces deux mois ont été comme un automne glacial [2].
Couché [3], j'entends parler des fleurs du pommier sauvage [4] :
La boue aurait sali leur neige fardée.
Dans le noir elles ont été subrepticement enlevées :

---

1. J. Gernet (*La vie quotidienne en Chine à la veille de l'invasion mongole, 1250-1276*, Paris, 1959, pp. 208-210) donne une bonne description de l'ensemble de ces fêtes à Hang *chou* à la fin des Sung. Sa description est fondée exclusivement sur le *Meng-liang lu*. Selon cette source, on sortait sur les tombeaux le jour *ch'ing-ming*, mais la chronologie de la fête, si l'on tient compte des sources parallèles, est bien moins claire. Selon le *Tung-ching meng-hua lu*, ch. 7, p. 39 (éd. Pékin, 1962), les sorties sur les tombeaux avaient lieu pendant toute la fête, et surtout le jour que le *Tung-ching meng-hua lu* appelle le « grand manger froid ». On trouvera plusieurs textes sur ce sujet, des Sung Méridionaux pour la plupart, dans *Tung-ching meng-hua lu chu*, ch. 7, pp. 187-188 (Pékin, 1959 ; rééd. T'ai-pei, 1963). J'insiste sur ces détails pour pouvoir déterminer aussi clairement que possible la chronologie des trois poèmes de Su Shih : les deux premiers parlent de la fête du « manger froid » et de la visite aux tombeaux ; le troisième du rallumage du feu le jour *ch'ing-ming*.
2. La fête du « manger froid » tombait, en général et en particulier en 1082, au début du troisième et dernier mois (lunaire) du printemps chinois.
3. Nous verrons plus loin qu'il était malade à cette époque.
4. Il s'agit évidemment du pommier sauvage qui forme le sujet du précédent poème, le seul dans la localité, et qui se trouvait assez loin du pavillon Lin-kao.

En vérité, il y a une force qui travaille au milieu de la nuit ! [1]
N'est-ce pas comme un jeune homme malade
Qui se relèverait de sa maladie la tête déjà blanchie ! » (b) [2]

Ce poème, comme celui sur le pommier sauvage, est un des plus admirés de Su Shih. Plus encore que le précédent il porte sur un thème traditionnel, celui de la fuite du temps. Les pétales du pommier sauvage ont été détachés par la pluie et trempés dans la boue [3], et leur disparition dans la nuit fait penser au passage où Chuang-tzu montre la relativité et donc l'impermanence de tout ce qui n'est pas Tout, tout ce qui se distingue du Tout, du *tao*. Chuang-tzu ne spécifie pas la nature de son voleur ; Su Shih nous fait penser qu'il est le Temps emportant les fleurs du printemps sans qu'on le voie opérer [4]. Le dernier couplet est particulièrement approprié par sa référence à la jeune saison du printemps et aux tendres fleurs du pommier sauvage. Il résume tout le poème, et, dans un certain sens, la vie de Su Shih : il a quarante-cinq ans ; il est exilé et malade ; il lui semble qu'il va se relever un vieillard oisif et inutile. La « neige fardée » des fleurs mortes dans leur prime jeunesse trouve un écho au dernier vers dans le thème des cheveux blanchis avant leur temps.

Le second poème, après une description pleine d'humour du temps humide, fait expressément allusion à la fête de la saison.

« Le Yang-tzu printanier veut entrer par ma porte :
Un temps de pluie qui ne veut pas en finir !
Ma petite maison est comme la barque d'un pêcheur,
Trempée de brume dans un nuage d'eau.
Dans la cuisine vide, on fait cuire des légumes grossiers ;

---

1. Allusion à *Chuang-tzu*, ch. 6, trad. Legge, p. 242 : « Vous pouvez cacher un bateau dans un ravin ou [même] une colline dans un marais et penser qu'ils sont en sécurité, mais un homme fort viendra au milieu de la nuit et les enlèvera. L'ignorant ne comprend pas que, même s'il y a un endroit qui convient pour cacher ce qui est grand et ce qui est petit, il y aura toujours un endroit où il pourra s'échapper. C'est seulement si vous cachez l'univers dans l'univers qu'il n'y aura pas d'endroit où il pourra s'échapper. »
2. Il y a des traductions de ce poème par Ogawa Tamaki, *op. cit.*, pp. 154-156, et B. Watson (trad.) : Yoshikawa Kōjirō, *An Introduction to Sung Poetry*, Cambridge (Mass.), 1967, p. 33. Le texte se trouve dans *chi-ch'eng*, 21 /17b-18a, et Ch'en Erh-tung, *op. cit.*, pp. 173-174.
3. *Cf.* les derniers vers du troisième des trois poèmes « Regardant les pivoines sous la pluie » (*chi-ch'eng*, 20 /14 b) : « Je ne supporterais pas qu'elles soient salies par la boue ; Je ferai cuire les fleurs tombées dans du beurre ! »
4. Selon le commentaire de Yoshikawa Kōjirō (*Sōshi gaisetsu*, Chūgoku shijin senshū, 2ᵉ série, 1, Tōkyō, 1962, p. 46) c'est pendant la nuit que la déchéance causée par le temps se manifeste le plus visiblement. Il se donne beaucoup de mal, d'autre part, pour expliquer comment Su Shih peut « entendre » la scène où les fleurs du pommier sauvage tombent dans la boue. B. Watson, dans sa traduction, supprime de telles explications sans doute parce que sa traduction (« I lie and listen to the cherry apple flowers ») les rend superflues.

Et dans le fourneau cassé, on brûle des roseaux mouillés.
Comment savoir que c'est la fête du manger froid ?
Je ne vois que le papier dans le bec des corbeaux.
La porte de mon souverain m'est neuf fois interdite ;
Les tombeaux [de mes ancêtres] sont à dix mille *li*.
Moi, je vais imiter celui qui a pleuré au bout de la route ;
Soufflez tant que vous pourrez : ces cendres mortes ne s'enflammeront plus ! » (c)[1]

Qu'il soit question dans les vers 5 et 6 de faire de la cuisine et du feu, donne à penser que ces poèmes se rapportent à une période indéterminée avant ou pendant la fête proprement dite ; dans les deux vers suivants, l'allusion semble d'ailleurs être aux corbeaux qui enlèvent les offrandes apportées sur les tombeaux. Mais le sens exact de ce huitième vers n'est pas tout à fait clair. Su Shih décrit une scène semblable dans un poème écrit à la fin de sa vie, en 1098, à Hai-nan pendant son dernier exil. Le poème a pour titre une longue préface qui commence en ces termes : « Les gens de Hai-nan ne fêtent pas le ' manger froid ' et vont sur les tombeaux le jour *shang-ssu* [le troisième jour du troisième mois lunaire][2]... » Et les deux premiers vers du poème sont les suivants :

« Le corbeau emporte la viande dans son bec, le papier s'envole en cendres :
Oh ! où est ma montagne familiale, éloignée de dix mille *li!* »[3]

Le sens des vers 7 et 8 semble donc être : « Le seul indice de la fête printanière du ' manger froid ' par ce temps automnal est que nous voyons les corbeaux enlever le papier gras sur lequel repose la viande apportée en offrande. » Ou est-ce des cendres du papier monnaie qu'on brûle devant les tombeaux qu'il s'agit ?[4]

L'année suivante (1083), à la même époque, Su Shih va pique-niquer avec des amis et, au cours de leur beuverie, il arrange les paroles d'une chanson de Po Chü-i pour accompagner leurs ripailles. Les deux premiers couplets, dans l'arrangement de Su Shih, sont :

« Les oiseaux crient, les pies jasent dans le grand arbre crépusculaire ;
C'est la fête de *ch'ing-ming* et du manger froid : (pour) quelle famille pleurent-ils ?
Le vent souffle sur la large plaine, le papier monnaie s'envole ;
Les tombeaux antiques se suivent sans interruption dans l'herbe verte du printemps. »[5]

Nous savons que Su Shih était fortement influencé par Po Chü-i à cette époque (son appellation, Tung-p'o, a été choisie en partie parce

---

1. *Chi-ch'eng*, 21/18a.
2. Littéralement « le premier jour marqué du caractère cyclique *ssu* [du troisième mois] ». Depuis les Wei, on fête le troisième jour du troisième mois. C'était à l'origine une fête de lustration qui avait pour but de chasser les impuretés de l'hiver.
3. *Chi-ch'eng*, 42/5a. La « montagne familiale » est le mont O-mei.
4. Comme le pense Ch'en Erh-tung, *op. cit.*, p. 174, n. 9.
5. La version de Su Shih, *tsung-an*, 22/1b ; original de Po Chü-i (très peu différent), *Pai-shih ch'ang-ch'ing chi*, 12 (2e fasc. ou *chih*)/55 b (éd. Pékin, 1960, pp. 4820-4821).

que Po Chü-i utilise l'expression à plusieurs reprises dans sa poésie)[1] ;
il est possible qu'il y ait un écho de ce poème dans celui de 1082. Mais
les corbeaux emportent-ils du papier dans leur bec ? Ils sont, en tout
cas, considérés en Chine comme des oiseaux funèbres, et même comme
des oiseaux de cimetières (car ils trouvent des offrandes alléchantes
devant les tombeaux [2]).

Les deux derniers couplets du poème de 1082 nous dévoilent les pensées de Su Shih, celles qui restaient sous-jacentes aux deux autres
poèmes : il se sent coupé de son souverain — qui est emmuré dans la
ville interdite et entouré de ministres hostiles au poète —, et se sent
loin de sa maison familiale au Ssuch'uan, les deux endroits où, bon
Chinois confucianiste, il pourrait donner toute sa mesure. L'avant-
dernier vers est une double allusion ; d'abord, et surtout, à Juan Chi
(210-264) qui avait l'habitude d'aller en voiture jusqu'au bout du chemin et d'y pleurer amèrement, exprimant ainsi son profond sentiment
de frustration dans un monde corrompu et déloyal [3] ; d'autre part,
ce vers rappelle un vers similaire de Tu Fu, lequel refuse, au contraire,
d'imiter Juan Chi pleurant au bout du chemin, pour l'imiter plutôt
lorsqu'il est saoul — autre thème lié à Juan Chi :

« Quand je suis sobre, je me saoulerai encore :
Je n'imiterai pas celui qui pleurait au bout de la route. » [4]

Le dernier vers, sur les cendres mortes, est lui aussi allusif. Selon le
Shih-chi (*ch.* 106), un jour où Han An-kuo, fonctionnaire éminent à
Liang au temps de l'empereur Ching (règne 156-141 av. J.-C.), se trouvait emprisonné, son geôlier l'humilia. Han An-kuo dit avec indignation : « Ne pense pas que des cendres mortes ne peuvent pas s'enflammer
encore ! » [5] Su Shih a été, lui-aussi, emprisonné ; il vit dans un monde
politique qui lui est hostile et qu'il juge déloyal — comme Juan Chi
considérait le sien : il pleurera, et n'essaiera pas de briller une fois encore
dans la carrière politique.

Ces deux poèmes sont donc des œuvres de découragement : le premier
se lamente sur le passage du temps ; le second sur l'exil et l'oisiveté
politique. Les images semblent choisies avec un grand naturel, mais en
fait révèlent un art suprême : les pétales blancs correspondent aux
cheveux blancs, les cendres mortes au papier monnaie qu'on brûle pen-

1. *Tsung-an*, 21 /2a.
2. *Cf.*, par exemple, la fin du conte de Lu-hsün, « Yao », dans la collection *Na-han*.
3. *Cf. Wei-shih ch'un-ch'iu* cité dans le *Shih-shuo hsin-yü*, C, p. 14a (éd. Sung,
rééd. Pékin, 1962). Su Shih, dans ses poèmes datant de cette époque d'exil à Huang
chou, fait au moins deux autres fois allusion à Juan Chi : *chi-ch'eng*, 20 /23a et 21 /12a.
4. *Tu-shih hsiang-chu*, 12 /22b. Le poème s'intitule : « P'ei Chang Liu-hou shih-yü
yen nan-lou ».
5. *Shih chi*, *ch.* 106, pp. 4-5 (éd. Takigawa, Pékin, 1955 ; trad. B. Watson, *Records
of the Grand Historian of China*, 2, New York, 1961, p. 132).

dant la fête ; et le tout est enveloppé dans une humidité glaciale qui semble faire obstacle à toute ambition, à toute idée de renouveau que le printemps, dans d'autres temps, aurait pu lui inspirer.

L'autographe de ces deux poèmes se trouve actuellement à Formose, dans la collection de l'ancien président de l'Academia Sinica, M. Wang Shih-chieh, et représente un des monuments de la calligraphie chinoise, le meilleur exemple connu de la calligraphie de Su Shih. Le rouleau n'est pas daté et il est impossible de savoir quand l'auteur transcrivit ces poèmes, mais on peut noter qu'il a tenu à les écrire ensemble et que son écriture s'affermit vers le milieu du second texte (« fourneau cassé » est écrit très gros) pour atteindre une sorte de fortissimo aux caractères « pleurer au bout de la route », se terminant sur un dernier vers mezzo-piano [1].

Le dernier des trois poèmes de cette année 1082 décrit le rallumage des feux à la fin du « manger froid ». Il est dédié à Hsü Ta-shou, préfet de Huang *chou*, qui a reçu Su Shih avec courtoisie dès son arrivée et n'a jamais cessé de le traiter avec égards pendant son séjour.

Le Préfet Hsü partage le feu nouveau [2]

« [Jusqu'à ce jour] je ne m'étais assis parfaitement droit dans le pavillon Lin-kao qu'une seule fois ;
Voici déjà le troisième changement du feu nouveau du *ch'ing-ming! [3]*
Le bois dans le fossé d'irrigation rit au nez des gens ;
Frottez [4] tant que vous pourrez — il est comme moi — il ne s'enflammera pas.
Le préfet de Huang *chou*, ayant pitié de ma longue maladie,
A partagé avec moi une corolle [de feu] rouge [qui éclaire] à travers toute la nuit.
Dans le passé un poisson du Fleuve sauta de la marmite cassée [5] ;

---

1. Le rouleau a été souvent reproduit ; *e.g.* dans le *Shodō zenshū*, XV (Tōkyō, 1961), reproduction en grandeur naturelle, sur dépliant en poche. Le magnifique colophon de Huang T'ing-chien est reproduit dans les planches 69-71 et il y a une brève histoire du manuscrit par Naitō Kenkichi, pp. 164-165.

2. Selon le *Chou li, ch.* 30, il fallait laisser mourir le feu à la fin de chacune des quatre saisons pour refaire du « feu nouveau » ; *cf.* H. Maspero, *La Chine antique*, Paris, 1955, p. 196. Sous les T'ang et les Sung, cette cérémonie était accomplie seulement à la fête *ch'ing-ming*, quand on distribuait du feu nouveau aux fonctionnaires. C'était sans doute par courtoisie que Hsü Ta-shou partageait son feu nouveau avec son hôte illustre et prisonnier.

3. La première année après son arrivée à Huang *chou*, Su Shih n'était en principe pas un résident de Lin-kao. Si nous suivions à la lettre l'indication du présent poème, nous devrions peut-être le reporter à 1083. Mais cette année-là, Su Shih est parti pique-niquer et, d'une façon générale, ses faits et gestes ne correspondent plus au ton du poème, dans lequel il se dit malade. Hsü Ta-shou a d'ailleurs quitté Huang *chou* en 1083 et est mort dans le courant de l'année ; *cf. tsung-an* 22 /3 a-b. Ce premier couplet est plutôt une façon hyperbolique de décrire le passage rapide des années à Huang *chou*.

4. Le feu rituel était produit par frottement du bois d'orme.

5. Allusion au fonctionnaire intègre des Han Postérieurs, Fan Jan (112-185) qui, après les désordres causés par les eunuques vers la fin de sa vie, habita une hutte de

Je n'ai qu'un poème pur qui se moque des grains de riz [1].
Je me lève, prends une bougie de cire et tourne autour de la chambre vide :
Je veux m'occuper à faire bouillir ou frire quelque chose [pour mon hôte], mais ne
peux ni l'un ni l'autre.
Je partagerai avec vous la lampe inépuisable [2],
Pour qu'elle éclaire l'obscurité et brise les chaînes de l'univers entier ! » (d) [3]

Ce poème redit ce que Su Shih exprimait à la fin du deuxième des
poèmes écrits pendant le « manger froid » : il n'a pas envie de s'engager
de nouveau dans le monde. Il souligne, avec humour comme toujours,
sa pauvreté — allusion qui est peut-être un peu plus que de pure forme
à ce moment, un an après avoir défriché son champ du « coteau oriental ».
La conclusion du poème, contenue dans le dernier couplet, et qui est
pour ainsi dire l'apothéose des flambeaux qui forment le sujet du poème,
nous rappelle l'intérêt que Su Shih montrait pour le bouddhisme à cette
époque. Pour remercier le magistrat du renouvellement de son feu, il
ne trouve rien de mieux que de lui offrir de partager son illumination
bouddhique : le flambeau-fleur et le flambeau-cire se métamorphosent
en un flambeau de la sagesse libératrice du Bouddha. La fête laïque et
même administrative du rallumage du feu se métamorphose en symbole religieux.

Dans sa pauvreté, Su Shih n'a pu remercier le préfet qu'avec ce beau
poème de circonstance ; que cet article soit de même une humble marque
de reconnaissance pour l'amitié qu'Étienne Balazs a bien voulu partager avec moi pendant les dernières années de sa vie.

---

chaume et dut, de temps en temps, se passer même de céréales. Les gens de son village
le brocardaient, non sans admiration, l'appelant par son *tzu* et par son ancien titre
pour décrire sa pauvreté : « La poussière s'amasse dans sa marmite de terre : c'est Fan
Shih-yün ; des poissons naissent dans sa marmite de métal : c'est Fan Lai-wu ! » *Cf.*
Hou Han-shu chi-chien, ch. 81 (= 111), p. 2954 (éd. Kuo-hsüeh chi-pen ts'ung-shu).
   1. Li Po se serait moqué de Tu Fu dans un poème qui est cité dans le *T'ang-shih
chi-shih, ch.* 18, p. 270 (éd. Pékin, 1965), mais qui n'est pas inclus dans son œuvre. Ce
poème commence par les mots : « Je rencontre Tu Fu sur la montagne d'un grain de
riz », et est en fait une critique moqueuse de la complexité des poèmes de son jeune ami ;
cf. W. Hung, *Tu Fu* (Cambridge, Mass., 1952), pp. 38-39. Les deux vers de Su Shih font
allusion à sa pauvreté et au motif de sa disgrâce : ses poèmes satiriques.
   2. « La lampe inépuisable », *aksayapradipa*, est l'illumination bouddhique laquelle,
transmise de croyant à croyant, « brillera » sans s'épuiser ; *cf. Vimalakīrtinirdeśasūtra,*
3 (trad. E. Lamotte, *L'enseignement de Vimalakīrti*, Louvain, 1962), p. 210.
   3. *Chi-ch'eng,* 21/18a-b.

CARACTÈRES CHINOIS

1. AUTEURS ET OUVRAGES CITÉS

Ch'en Erh-tung　陳邇冬：蘇軾詩選

Chi-ch'eng : voir Wang Wen-kao

Chikusa Masaaki　竺沙雅章：蘇軾と佛教

Hou Han-shu chi-chieh　後漢書集解

Hu Tzu　胡仔．苕溪漁隱叢話

Kuo Mo-jo　郭沫若：沫若自傳，少年時代

Lin Yutang　林語堂

Liu J.T.C.　劉子健

Lu-hsün　魯迅：吶喊

Meng-liang lu　夢梁錄

Ming-huang tsa-lu　明皇雜錄

Ming-sheng chih　明勝志

Ogawa Tamaki　小川環樹：蘇軾（中國詩人選集）

P'eng Chiu-wan (?)　朋九萬．烏臺詩案

Po Chü-i　白居易：白氏長慶集

Shih-shuo hsin-yü　世說新語

Shodō zenshū　書道全集

Su Shih　蘇軾．東坡集：到黃州謝表

　　東坡續集：與朱康叔書

　　東坡志林

　　經進東坡文集事略：黃州安國記

　　蘇文忠公詩編註集成：曉至巴河口迎子由詩，與章子
　　　　厚書，與范子豐書．

T'ang-shih chi-shih　唐詩紀事

Tsung-an : voir Wang Wen-kao

Tu-shih hsiang-chu 杜詩詳注 (倍章留後待御宴南樓)

Tung-ching meng-hua lu 東京夢華錄

Tung-ching meng-hua lu chu 東京夢華錄註

Wang Wen-kao 王文誥, 蘇文忠公詩編註集成

蘇文忠公詩編註集成總案

Wei Ch'ing-chih 魏慶之, 詩人玉屑

Wei-shih ch'un-ch'iu 魏氏春秋

Yoshikawa Kōjirō 吉川幸次郎, 宋詩概説

2. TERMES ET NOMS PROPRES

An-kuo *ssu* 安國寺

Chao-tsung *men* 朝宗門

chien-chiao shui-pu yüan-wai-lang

檢校水部員外郎

chih 帙

ch'ing-ming 清明

FAN JAN 范冉

FAN LAI-WU 范萊蕪

FAN SHIH-YÜN 范史雲

hai-t'ang 海棠

HAN AN-KUO 韓安國

han-shih 寒食

Hang *chou* 杭州

hao 号虎

HSÜ TA-SHOU 徐大受

HSÜAN-TSUNG 玄宗

Hu-kuo *ssu* 護國寺

Huang *chou* 黃州

Huang *chou t'uan-lien fu-shih*

黃州團練副使

Huang-kang 黃岡

HUANG T'ING-CHIEN 黃庭堅

JUAN CHI 阮籍

kai-t'ien 蓋天

K'o-shih 柯氏

Lin-kao *t'ing* 臨皋亭

LIU HSIANG 劉向

NAITŌ KENKICHI 内藤乾吉

O-mei *shan* 峨眉山

shang-ssu 上巳

SHIH YÜAN-CHIH 施元之

Shu 蜀

Su Ch'e	蘇轍		t'ung-p'an	通判
Su Shih	蘇軾		Tung-p'o	東坡
tao	道		Tung-p'o *chü-shih*	東坡居士
Ting-hui *yüan*	定惠院		Wang An-shih	王安石
tsao-wu	造物		Wang Shih-chieh	王世杰
tsao-wu che	造物者		Yang Kuei-fei	楊貴妃
Tu Fu	杜甫			

3. Citations

(a) 寓居定惠院.[院]之東雜花滿山.有海棠一株.土人不知貴也.

江城地瘴蕃草木   只有名花苦幽獨
嫣然一笑竹籬間   桃李滿山總麤俗
也知造物有深意   故遣佳人在空谷
自然富貴出天姿   不待金盤薦華屋
朱脣得酒暈生臉   翠袖卷紗紅映肉
林深霧暗曉光遲   日暖風輕春睡足
雨中有淚亦悽愴   月下無人更清淑

先生食飽無一事   散步逍遙自捫腹
不問人家與僧舍   拄杖敲門看修竹
忽逢絕豔照衰朽   歎息無言揩病目
陋邦何處得此花   無乃好事移西蜀
寸根千里不易致   銜子飛來定鴻鵠
天涯流落俱可念   為飲一樽歌此曲
明朝酒醒還獨來   雪落紛紛那忍觸

(b) 寒食雨　二首

自我来黄州　　已過三寒食
年年欲惜春　　春去不容惜
今年又苦雨　　兩月秋蕭瑟
臥聞海棠花　　泥污燕脂雪
暗中偷負去　　夜半真有力
何殊病少年　　病起頭已白

(c) 春江欲入户　雨勢來不已
小屋如魚舟　　濛濛水雲裏
空庖煮寒菜　　破竈燒溼葦
那知是寒食　　但見烏銜紙
君門深九重　　墳墓在萬里
也擬哭途窮　　死灰吹不起

(d) 徐使君分新火　臨皋亭中一老生
三見清明改新火　溝中枯木應笑人
鑽研不然誰似我　黄州使君憐久病
分我五更紅一朵　從來破釜躍江魚
只有清詩嘲飯顆　起攜蠟炬遠空室
欲事烹煎無一可　為公分作無盡燈
照破十方昏暗鎖

VIII

LA POÉSIE DE JI KANG

(première partie)

Abréviations bibliographiques

Couvreur: Séraphin Couvreur, *La chronique de la principauté de Lou*, 3 vol., réédition de Paris, 1951.

—, *Mémoires sur les bienséances et les cérémonies*, 4 vol., réédition de Paris, 1950.

Crump: J. I. Crump, Jr., *Chan-Kuo Ts'e*, Oxford, 1970.

Graham: A. C. Graham, *The Book of Lieh-tzu*, Londres, 1960.

Hawkes: David Hawkes, *Ch'u Tz'u: The Songs of the South*, Oxford, 1959.

Hervouet: Yves Hervouet, *Le chapitre 117 du Che-ki* (Bibliothèque de l'IHEC, vol. XXIII), Paris, 1972.

Hightower: James Robert Hightower, *Han shih wai chuan* (Harvard-Yenching Institute Monograph Series, vol. XI), Cambridge, Mass., 1952.

Jin shu jiaozhu: de Wu Shijian 吳士鑑 et Liu Chenggan 劉承幹, Pékin, 1928, réédition de Taiwan, sans date.

Kaltenmark: Max Kaltenmark, *Le Lie-sien tchouan*, Pékin, 1953.

Legge: James Legge, *The Chinese Classics 5, The Ch'un Ts'ew with the Tso Chuen*, Hongkong, 1872.

—, *The Yi king* (The Sacred Books of the East, vol. XVI), Oxford, 1899.

Mather: Richard B. Mather, *Shih-shuo hsin-yü: A new account of tales of the world*, Minneapolis, 1976.

Quan Jin wen: In *Quan shanggu Sandai Qin Han Sanguo Liuchao wen* de Yan Kejun 嚴可均 (1762-1843), réédition de Pékin, 1958.

Sanguo zhih jijie: De Lu Bi 盧弼 (préface datée 1936), Pékin, 1957.

Shanhai jing: Édition Sibu beiyao.

Shishuo xinyu: Édition Song dite du Kanazawa bunko, réédition de Pékin, 1962, 5 vol.

Shuijing zhu: Édition Guoxue jiben congshu, Shanghai, 1936.

Watson: Burton Watson, *The complete works of Chuang Tzu*, New York & Londres, 1968.

Wilhelm: Richard Wilhelm, *Kungfutse Schulgespräche (Gia Yü)*, Düsseldorf-Köln, 1961.

1

INTRODUCTION

J'ai déjà consacré un livre à la pensée de Ji Kang 嵇康 (223-262) dans lequel j'ai traduit quelques-uns de ses poèmes, principalement pour leur intérêt biographique[1]. J'aimerais reprendre ici le côté poétique de son œuvre, car, si Ji Kang est d'abord un penseur de premier ordre, il est aussi un poète important qui a sa place, modeste mais honorable, dans l'histoire de la poésie chinoise.

Les critiques

Les premiers critiques de son œuvre[2] le louent pour l'excellence de sa prose ou la rigueur de la logique de ses essais plutôt que pour la beauté de sa poésie. Son frère aîné, qui lui a survécu longtemps, dit dans sa biographie de Ji Kang que ce dernier «était doué pour la composition d'essais littéraires»[3] et l'auteur du *Sanguo zhi*, Chen Shou (233-297), dit plus simplement que «ses écrits étaient splendides»[4]. Et un auteur légèrement postérieur à Chen Shou, Li Chong 李充, qui a vécu au IVe siècle, met l'emphase aussi nettement sur les qualités de Ji Kang comme essayiste[5].

[1] *La vie et la pensée de Hi K'ang (223-262 ap. J.-C.)*, Leiden, 1957 (ci-après, *La vie et la pensée*). Dans la présente étude j'ai adopté la transcription officielle (*pinyin*) pour les mots chinois et en même temps la prononciation courante pour le nom de famille de Ji (et non pas Xi) Kang. À part le *Sanguo zhi jijie* et le *Jin shu jiaozhu*, les histoires dynastiques sont citées d'après la nouvelle édition ponctuée, publiée à Pékin à partir de 1959. Un index de la poésie de Ji Kang est paru à Kyoto en 1975: *Kei Kô shû «shi» sakuin* établi par Matsuura Takashi 松浦崇.

[2] Le *Ji Kang ji*, cité dans *Beitang shuchao* 100, p. 7ab (réédition Taipei, 1962), décrit l'admiration de Cao Rui, l'empereur Ming, pour la poésie de Ji Kang. Mais Dai Mingyang 戴明揚 *Ji Kang ji jiaozhu* (Pékin, 1962), pp. 328-329, montre facilement qu'il s'agit non pas de Ji Kang, mais de Li 李 Kang, un contemporain.

[3] *Sanguo zhi ji jie* 21, p. 23a (Pékin, 1957). Le terme *wenlun* 文論, que je traduis par «essais littéraires», comme presque tous les termes techniques se rapportant aux genres littéraires en chinois, n'est pas cristallin. À mon avis il ne s'agit pas d'«essais sur la littérature» comme l'usage du terme dans *Wenxin diaolong* 50, p. 128 (Wang Liqi 王利器, *Wenxin diaolong xinshu*, Pékin, 1951), pourrait le faire croire. Les autres usages du terme me font penser qu'il s'agit d'une description assez générale et que le mot «littérature» doit s'entendre dans un sens très large.

[4] *Ibid.*, p. 22b.

[5] «Hanlin lun» 翰林論, cité dans *Taiping yulan* 595, p. 1a (Pékin, 1960): «C'est

Il faut attendre un siècle et demi pour retrouver des remarques sur l'œuvre littéraire de Ji Kang. Liu Xie 劉勰 (465?-522?), l'auteur du *Wenxin diaolong*, parle de lui à plusieurs reprises. Dans son chapitre 47, «Vue d'ensemble sur le talent littéraire», Liu Xie aussi met l'accent sur ses qualités de prosateur : «C'est en se fiant à son esprit (*xin* 心)[6] que Ji Kang a rédigé ses essais, mais Ruan Ji 阮籍 s'est servi du souffle de sa vitalité même (*qi* 氣) pour faire ses poésies»[7]. Ces deux phrases sont strictement parallèles en chinois ; elles contiennent des rimes intérieures et des contrastes sonores très élégants ; elles sont, on le comprendra bien, très difficile à traduire. Peut-être que Liu Xie n'écrivait pas pour être compris tout à fait par la raison, mais plutôt pour être goûté par la sensibilité du lecteur raffiné. Quoiqu'il en soit, il est clair qu'ici il met l'emphase sur le côté rationnel et philosophique de l'œuvre de Ji Kang, qu'il contraste avec la fougue intuitive de la poésie de son ami Ruan Ji (210-263).

Mais Liu Xie ne dédaigne pas pour autant la poésie de Ji Kang — loin de là. Il dit encore que dans le monde des lettres,

pendant l'ère Zhengshi (240-249) les poètes faisaient des explications sur le *dao* et exprimaient, épars dans leur poésie, leur désir de devenir un immortel. He Yan 何晏 (190-249) et ses amis étaient, pour la plupart, superficiels. Il n'y avait, à l'époque, que deux hommes que nous pouvons prendre comme modèles : Ji Kang, grâce à sa volonté pure et altière, et Ruan Ji, grâce aux résonnances lointaines et profondes de ses idées[8].

Liu Xie ne fait que souligner un fait bien connu : Ji Kang et Ruan Ji sont les seuls poètes importants entre la très grande renaissance poétique qui a eu lieu pendant l'ère Jian'an (196-220) et la dynastie

quand on se met à débattre sérieusement des problèmes philosophiques que des contradictions s'élèvent. Ce qui est précieux dans l'essai, c'est de coller à la vérité sans se disperser. Les essais de Ji Kang atteignent la perfection». Les mots «les problèmes philosophiques» traduisent *mingli* 名理, un terme technique dont le sens est contesté ; cf. *Revue bibliographique de sinologie* 11 (1965), n° 517. Li Chong a écrit deux éloges de Ji Kang, un contenu dans *Beitang shuchao* 102, p. 11a, et *Taiping yulan* 596, p. 6ab, et un dans *Chuxue ji* 17, p. 412 (Pékin, 1962).

[6] Il y a peut-être ici une allusion à *Zhuangzi* 2 (Watson, p. 38) où il est question de «se fier à son esprit», ou, plus littéralement, de «prendre son esprit comme son maître».

[7] *Wenxin diaolong xinshu* 47, p. 123.

[8] *Ibid.* 6, p. 18.

des Jin fondée une cinquantaine d'années plus tard. Les références à la «volonté» de Ji Kang et aux «résonnances lointaines et profondes» chez Ruan Ji décrivent la qualité de la poésie des deux poètes: le premier, comme nous allons le voir, chante ses désirs de vivre loin du monde; le dernier s'exprime d'une manière «distante et abstraite» pour voiler sa satire politique. Un peu plus loin, dans le même chapitre, Liu Xie précise son jugement sur Ji Kang en le louant pour ses poèmes en tétramètres qui sont, selon lui, surtout très bien «ornés», *run* 潤, jugement assez contestable, et qui conviendrait mieux pour un poète de sa propre époque que pour Ji Kang.

Depuis les Han, quand les vers pentasyllabiques sont devenus le moyen d'expression le plus répandu dans la poésie en vers réguliers[9], Ji Kang est le seul poète à avoir excellé avant tout dans les poèmes en tétramètres. (Les sept poèmes de lui contenus dans le *Wen xuan* sont tous en tétramètres.) Et c'est peut-être à cause de cela que Zhong Rong 鍾嶸 (468/9-518), qui ne s'intéressait quasiment qu'aux poèmes en pentamètres[10], a relégué Ji Kang dans la deuxième des trois catégories qui compose son *Shi pin*. Son jugement sur Ji Kang est particulièrement difficile à comprendre parce qu'il le fait porter à la fois sur la poésie et sur le poète. Une traduction qui conserverait l'ambiguïté étant impossible, je ferai de mon mieux pour traduire comme s'il s'agissait uniquement de la poésie. Dans la première phrase il appelle Ji Kang par son titre et commet une erreur fréquente en le faisant vivre sous les Jin, alors qu'il est né et mort sous les Wei:

[La poésie du] Zhongsan [dafu] 中散大夫 des Jin ressemble en partie à celle de l'empereur Wen des Wei, [Cao Pi 曹丕], mais elle est encore plus sévère. Elle dévoile trop ouvertement les fautes d'autrui, et fait voir trop clairement le talent de l'auteur: tout cela nuit à l'extrême recueillement et raffinement de ces vers. Mais les métaphores sont si limpides, d'une telle portée, et sont employées avec tant de discernement, qu'on ne peut nier à cette poésie une place de haut rang[11].

---

[9] Cf. D. Holzman, «Les premiers vers pentasyllabiques datés dans la poésie chinoise», *Mélanges de sinologie offerts à M. P. Demiéville* (Bibliothèque de l'IHEC, Vol. XX, Paris, 1974), pp. 77-115.

[10] Voir le tout début de sa préface au *Shi pin*.

[11] Chen Yanjie 陳延傑, *Shi pin zhu* B (Hong Kong, 1959), p. 22.

Les difficultés d'interprétation de ce passage commencent au premier mot[12]. Zhong Rong commence presque toujours par situer le poète qu'il étudie dans une tradition poétique qui se réclame soit d'une des sections du *Shi jing*, soit d'un poète plus ancien, soit des poésies populaires et anonymes des Han (*gushi* 古詩). L'à-propos des ses choix n'est pas toujours évident. Tantôt il semble voir une parenté dans les thèmes traités, tantôt dans le style, voire même entre les personnalités des poètes. Et ici les mots choisis pour signaler cette parenté («ressemble en partie»), jamais utilisés ailleurs dans son livre, font croire que Zhong Rong n'était pas tout à fait sûr lui-même où résidait la parenté. Résidait-elle dans le langage direct, presque «vulgaire» des deux poètes (Kôzen Hiroshi)? Ou dans le fait qu'ils se ressemblaient dans leurs «désirs de se couper de la poussière du monde» en chantant les immortels taoïstes (Chen Yanjie)? Ou est-ce, plus simplement, des emprunts de vers et de vocabulaire, surtout sensibles dans le premier des poèmes intitulés «Aspirations» (cf. la 2ᵉ Partie de cette étude, ch. 5)? Ou est-ce une ressemblance entre les caractères entiers et indépendants de ces deux hommes? Ou est-ce tout cela ensemble? Sans doute ne faut-il pas trop s'attarder sur ces filiations de Zhong Rong qui sont, somme toute, assez imprécises.

Par ailleurs la difficulté de compréhension de ce court passage s'aggrave encore quand Zhong Rong dit que Ji Kang «dévoile trop ouvertement les fautes d'autrui»[13] et que ses «talents sont trop voyants»; parle-t-il ici de la poésie de Ji Kang ou de sa biographie? La coupure n'est pas du tout aussi nette en Chine que chez nous et il y a des fortes chances qu'il s'agisse des deux. Nous savons que l'exécution de Ji Kang en 262 a été due, en grande partie, au plaidoyer sévère fait par Zhong Hui 鍾會, un homme puissant que Ji Kang avait rudoyé en lui montrant ouvertement et clairement le peu d'estime qu'il avait pour lui. D'autre part, un ermite des montagnes, Sun

[12] Kôzen Hiroshi 興膳宏, «Kei Kô shi shôron», *Chûgoku bungaku hô* (Kyoto) 15 (1961), pp. 1-32, consacre huit pages (pp. 1-8) à une discussion de ce passage, ce qui montre au moins la complexité des problèmes d'interprétation.
[13] Ici Zhong Rong fait allusion au *Lun yu* 17, 24, mais les deux mots qu'il emploie, *jie zhi* 訐直, veulent dire aujourd'hui simplement «réprimander en face», sans note péjorative. Comme j'essaie de le montrer plus loin, l'allusion biographique me fait penser que Zhong Rong voulait rappeler le franc-parler de Ji Kang ici.

Deng 孫登, avait dit à Ji Kang que ses talents éminents lui nuiraient s'il persistait à les montrer dans le monde contemporain rempli de dangers[14]. On comprend donc plus facilement ces phrases comme commentaires sur la vie de Ji Kang que sur sa poésie. Peut-être même que la présence de l'ancêtre de Zhong Rong, Zhong Hui, l'a poussé a faire allusion à cet épisode si lourd de conséquences pour la vie de Ji Kang, en essayant de blanchir tant soit peu Zhong Hui.

Les dernières phrases du jugement nous ramènent à l'œuvre de Ji Kang elle-même, en rappelant les «discernements» philosophiques qu'il a montrés tant dans sa poésie que dans sa prose. Zhong Rong semble vouloir ici s'excuser d'avoir mis Ji Kang dans la deuxième catégorie de son livre et lui accorder, in extremis, une petite place tout de même de «haut rang».

Si les critiques semblent bouder un peu la poésie de Ji Kang en faveur de sa prose, il ne faut pas croire que ses vers n'étaient pas goûtés par ses contemporains ou pendant les siècles qui ont suivi sa mort. Nous verrons plus bas (p. 137) que Gu Kaizhi, le grand peintre du IVᵉ siècle, a été un admirateur de ses vers tétramétriques. Il a aussi imité le célèbre *fu* sur la cithare *qin*[15] de Ji Kang en en écrivant un sur la cithare *zheng* (dont des fragments sont réunis dans *Quan Jin wen* 135, p. 5b). Vers la même époque le grand général, héros de la bataille de la rivière Fei, Xie An, s'est montré grand amateur des vers de Ji Kang, à un moment très critique de sa vie (*infra*, pp. 134-135). Et, un siècle plus tôt, Xiahou Zhan 夏侯湛 (243-291) a incorporé des vers entiers du poème admiré plus tard par Gu Kaizhi dans son *fu* sur la chasse aux lièvres[16].

---

[14] Cf. *La vie et la pensée*, pp. 42-43.

[15] Ce *fu* a été bien traduit par R. H. van Gulik dans *Hsi K'ang and his poetical essay on the lute* (Tokyo, 1941), et j'ai décidé de ne pas le retraduire ici. Les Chinois classent les *fu* avec les écrits en prose et, en fait, je crois que ce *fu* de Ji Kang est assez différent des poèmes réguliers (*shi*) pour que je ne le replace pas ici dans l'étude de son œuvre poétique.

[16] Cf. *Yiwen leiju* 66, p. 5b (réédition de Pékin, 1959). Yang Shen 楊慎 (1488-1559) cite ces vers en se demandant s'ils sont de Ji Kang ou de Xiahou Zhan et semble donner la palme à ce dernier. Ye Weiqing 葉渭清 et Dai Mingyang (p. 15) n'ont pas de peine à montrer l'improbabilité de cette attribution, mais, étrangement, ni l'un ni l'autre ne font remarquer que Xiahou Zhan n'avait que 19 ans à la mort de Ji Kang, ce qui réduit sensiblement la probabilité que ce dernier aurait été influencé par lui.

L'œuvre et les éditions

Il ne reste plus aujourd'hui qu'à peu près deux tiers des soixante ou soixante dix mille mots de l'œuvre de Ji Kang qui existaient encore au IVᵉ siècle[17]. Les premières bibliographies appellent l'œuvre *Ji Kang ji* 嵇康集 [18] et disent qu'elle est divisée en quinze chapitres (sauf la monographie bibliographique du *Sui shu* qui ne donne que treize chapitres). Entre les Tang et les Song cinq chapitres ont dû se perdre, ne laissant ainsi que les deux tiers de l'œuvre primitive. Sous les Ming pour la première fois on voit apparaître le nom *Ji Zhongsan ji*, seul nom que les éditions courantes au début de ce siècle portaient encore. La meilleure de celles-ci est celle de Huang Xingzeng 黃省曾 dont la préface est datée du 18 octobre 1525 (reproduite dans les collections Sibu congkan et Wanyou wenku), mais il existait aussi, dans la Bibliothèque nationale à Pékin (alors appelée Jingshi tushu-guan), une copie manuscrite sortie du studio, le Congshu tang 叢書堂, d'un célèbre calligraphe des Ming, Wu Kuan 吳寬 (1435-1504). Cette copie porte encore le titre *Ji Kang ji* et semble, au dire des biblio-graphes des Qing cités par Luxun, être basée sur une édition Song[19]. La calligraphie de ce manuscrit est assez indifférente, et n'est certaine-ment pas de la main de Wu Kuan[20], mais ses leçons sont en général très supérieures à celles des éditions précédentes et elle a été largement utilisée dans les éditions de l'œuvre de Ji Kang faites par Luxun lui-même, le *Ji Kang ji* (préface datée de 1924), et le *Ji Kang ji jiaozhu* (Pékin, 1962) de Dai Mingyang (édition posthume)[21].

---

[17] Cf. Sun Sheng 孫盛 (307?-378?), *Weishi chunqiu*, cité dans *Sanguo zhi jijie* 21, p. 26b. Sun Sheng dit textuellement que «les soixante ou soixante-dix mille mots d'œuvres littéraires (*wenlun*) composés par Ji Kang étaient tous appréciés et chantés par tout le monde».

[18] Cette courte histoire du texte de l'œuvre de Ji Kang est·basée surtout sur un essai de Luxun 魯迅 (Zhou Zuoren 周作人) daté du 14 novembre 1926, le «Ji Kang ji kao», et publié dans *Lishi yanjiu* (Pékin) 1954, 2, pp. 97-103.

[19] Une bonne histoire de ce manuscrit est donnée par Obi Kôichi 小尾郊一. dans *Shinagaku kenkyû* (Hiroshima) 24/25 (1959), pp. 98-107 (résumée dans *Revue biblio-graphique de sinologie* 6, n° 596).

[20] Cf. Luxun, article cité, p. 99.

[21] Le manuscrit du Congshu tang, avec d'autres livres rares, a été envoyé à la Bibliothèque du Congrès américain à Washington avant l'avènement du régime actuel en Chine et j'y ai pu m'en procurer un microfilm. Ce manuscrit a été copié par Wang

114

Quelle proportion de l'œuvre poétique primitive nous a été préservée? Il n'y a, pour ainsi dire, pas de fragments d'œuvres poétiques perdues cités par d'autres poètes ou dans les encyclopédies[22], ce qui me fait penser que, ou bien nous n'en avons pas perdu beaucoup, ou bien les poèmes se sont perdus très tôt, avant la compilation des premières encyclopédies. Nous avons perdu, au maximum, huit poèmes depuis les Song, puisque Wang Mao 王楙 (1151-1213), dans son *Yeke congshu* 8, parle d'«avoir obtenu une belle copie manuscrite de l'œuvre de Ji Kang en dix chapitres qui contenait 68 poèmes»[23], et il reste 60 poèmes dans la version du Congshu tang (et 53 dans l'édition de Huang Xingzeng). Mais il est moins facile qu'il ne paraît à première vue de compter le nombre de poèmes dans son œuvre. Hong Yixuan 洪頤煊 (1765-1837), dans son *Dushu conglu*, déclare que dans sa version il y avait «66 poèmes, comme dans la version mentionnée par Wang Mao dans son *Yeke congshu*»[24]. C'est que dans l'œuvre de Ji Kang, qui compte plusieurs séries ou cycles de poèmes, il est souvent difficile de séparer les poèmes les uns des autres. Il se peut que Wang Mao ait mal compté; mais il est aussi fort possible que huit poèmes se soient perdus depuis son temps.

Il nous reste aujourd'hui 60 poèmes: 30 en tétramètres, 12 en pentamètres, 10 en hexamètres et 8 en mètres irréguliers. Dans les éditions actuelles, cette poésie ne semble pas arrangée dans un ordre quelconque. Je l'ai réarrangée assez arbitrairement selon le contenu

Yulou 王雨樓 et collationné par Wu Zhizhong 吳志忠, la copie faisant partie de la collection de Lu Xinyuan 陸心源, actuellement dans la bibliothèque du Seikadô, Tokyo (cf. Obi, art. cité, p. 106 et note 21). Cette copie n'est pas de la main de Wu Kuan comme je l'ai dit par erreur dans *La vie et la pensée*, p. 131, note 2.

[22] Cf. *Ji Kang ji jiaozhu*, pp. 327-330, où Dai Mingyang montre que les fragments de deux *fu* supposés par Yan Kejun d'être de Ji Kang sont en fait par d'autres (Xunzi et Ji Han 嵇含). Le «Baishou fu», attribué par Li Shan à Ji Kang (*Wen xuan* 23, p. 10b), a toutes les chances, il me semble, d'être aussi par Ji Han (cf. *Yiwen leiju* 17, pp. 7b-8a, et le «Jiu fu» attribué à Ji Kang dans de nombreux textes (e.g. *Quan Sanguo wen* 47, p. 4a, *Beitang shuchao* 148, p. 3a), pourrait aussi être par Ji Han (un «Jiu fu» par lui est cité dans *Beitang shuchao* 148, p. 3b). Dai Mingyang ne cite que deux vers passe-partout attribués à Ji Kang (et qui ne se trouvent pas dans son œuvre actuelle) par Wei Xun 韋絢 (début IXᵉ siècle) dans son *Liu Binke jiahua lu* et dans *Taiping guangji* 400, p. 3212 (Pékin, 1961).

[23] Cité par Luxun, p. 98; Kôzen Hiroshi, p. 29, note 1.

[24] Cité par Luxun, p. 99.

de chaque poème: poèmes écrits à son frère aîné, poèmes d'amitié, poèmes philosophiques, et, finalement, les poèmes autobiographiques écrits à la fin de sa vie.

2

POÈMES ÉCRITS À SON FRÈRE

Peu de poètes ont laissé une œuvre aussi monothématique que celle de Ji Kang. À quelques rares exceptions près, tous ses poèmes chantent la fuite du monde et ses dangers et la recherche d'un monde meilleur, le monde des immortels taoïstes. Aussi pourrait-on lire son œuvre poétique dans presque n'importe quel ordre. J'ai décidé de commencer par le long cycle de poèmes écrits à son frère aîné quand celui-ci est entré dans l'armée. J'ai déjà traduit six de ces 19 ou 18 poèmes[25], mais je les retraduirai ici pour pouvoir mieux faire ressortir la structure très savante du cycle entier. Mais est-ce un cycle véritable? Les opinions diffèrent, et les problèmes commencent avec le premier poème. Selon les éditions des œuvres de Ji Kang, ce poème est tantôt mis à part en dehors du cycle et intitulé «Poème à l'antique en pentamètres»[26], tantôt mis à la fin du cycle, comme le dix-neuvième poème[27], tantôt au début[28]. Le fait que le poème est écrit en pentamètres tandis que les autres sont en tétramètres n'est pas une preuve qu'il faille l'écarter du cycle. Il est vrai que le seul auteur à mélanger

[25] *La vie et la pensée*, pp. 19-21.

[26] Manuscrit du Congshu tang.

[27] Han Wei Liuchao baisan mingjia ji (édition Saoye shanfang, 1925), *Ji Zhongsan ji*, p. 33a; Han Wei shisheng, cité par Dai Mingyang, p. 3, mais ce dernier contient une note disant: «Ce poème est placé premier [des dix-neuf] dans l'œuvre complète de Ji Kang».

[28] Dans les éditions de Huang Xingzeng de 1525 (contenue dans le Sibu congkan et le Wanyou wenku) et de Xue Yingqi 薛應旂 de 1543 (*Liuchao shiji*, reproduit Taipei, 1972), et dans une note manuscrite du manuscrit du Congshu tang reproduite par Dai Mingyang, p. 2, il est dit que ce poème en pentamètres fait partie de la série pour son frère aîné. Dans son édition de 1924 Luxun met le poème à part, mais dans son article du *Lishi yanjiu* 1954, 2, il dit qu'il fait bel et bien partie du cycle. Kôzen Hiroshi, p. 10, remarque que Luxun dans son édition le considère comme un poème à part, et il ne s'en occupe pas dans sa longue discussion du cycle qu'il intitule, malgré cela, les «Dix-*neuf* poèmes écrits à son frère aîné…».

VIII

ainsi les mètres antérieur à Ji Kang est Cao Pi (celui justement que Zhong Rong appelle son modèle) dans ses «Trois poèmes écrits à Liyang» 黎陽作三首 où l'on trouve deux poèmes en tétramètres suivis d'un en pentamètres[29]; mais dans l'œuvre complète de Ji Kang nous trouvons deux autres exemples: les poèmes mis sous le titre «Partie à boire» (un poème en pentamètres suivi de six en tétramètres) et dans les cinq poèmes écrits à Ji Kang par Guo Xiashu (quatre en tétramètres suivis d'un en pentamètres)[30]. D'autre part, ce poème en pentamètres est cité dans deux encyclopédies des Tang: quatre vers sont cités dans le *Chuxue ji* 18, p. 448, sous le titre «Poème donné au bachelier[31] lors de son entrée dans l'armée», et six vers dans le *Yiwen leiju* 90, p. 4b, sous le titre «Poème donné par Ji Shuye au bachelier». Ces deux citations montrent que les auteurs de ces encyclopédies considéraient ce poème comme faisant partie du cycle. Plus important encore, le thème du poème s'apparente bien à celui du cycle en tétramètres. Mais il me semble impossible de trancher; je présenterai ce poème en pentamètres comme un genre de prélude au cycle sans l'y rattacher tout à fait.

Cependant, il reste à savoir si les dix-huit poèmes forment un véritable cycle ou s'ils ne sont qu'un ensemble de poèmes écrits autour d'un même thème, peut-être même écrits à des époques différentes. Dai Mingyang est de cet avis, et Chen Zuoming 陳祚明 (cité par Dai Mingyang, p. 3) essaie même de séparer les différentes parties en des ensembles plus cohérents. Je trouve que les dix-huit poèmes dans leur ordre actuel sont, à certains égards, difficiles à faire entrer

---

[29] Contenus dans Huang Jie 黃節, *Wei Wudi Wei Wendi shizhu* (Pékin, 1959), pp. 58-59. Zhang Pu dans son Han Wei Liuchao bai san mingjia chi, *Wei Wendi ji* 2, p. 4b, sépare les deux poèmes, intitulant les deux poèmes en tétramètres «Écrits à Liyang» et celui en pentamètres, «Liyang». Mais il n'est question de Liyang que dans le dernier poème (en pentamètres); le titre des deux premiers poèmes n'a de sens que s'il s'applique aux trois poèmes ensemble.

[30] Le poème «Partie à boire» est traduit *infra*, p. 172; les six poèmes qui le suivent, dans la 2ᵉ Partie, ch. 6.

[31] Le frère de Ji Kang portait le titre de *xiucai* 秀才, «talent éminent», qui était un des examens administrés depuis les Han aux candidats fonctionnaires choisis dans les provinces. Ma traduction de «bachelier» est un peu anachronique; ce n'est que plus tard que le titre devient le premier grade dans la hiérarchie des diplômes d'État. Sur le frère de Ji Kang, voir *La vie et la pensée*, pp. 18-19.

dans un véritable cycle de poèmes, mais qu'il y a trop de ressemblances entre eux, et qu'ils s'éclairent mutuellement trop bien pour qu'il n'y ait aucun lien entre eux. J'ai pris le parti d'essayer une interprétation cyclique, quitte à souligner les passages qui ne semblent pas en harmonie avec le tout[32].

Le titre du cycle varie quelque peu selon les éditions, mais elles sont presque toutes d'accord pour indiquer que ce sont des poèmes que Ji Kang envoie à son frère aîné lors de l'entrée de celui-ci dans l'armée. Les cinq (en fait six) poèmes qui sont cités dans le *Wen xuan* 24 portent le titre «Cinq poèmes donnés au bachelier qui entre dans l'armée» 贈秀才入軍五首. Li Shan identifie le «bachelier» comme le frère aîné de Ji Kang, Ji Xi 喜, dont le *zi* était Gongmu 公穆. Seul un des cinq commentateurs des Tang, Zhang Xian 張銑, croit qu'il s'agit d'un jeune cousin de Ji Kang dont on ne connaît pas le prénom. Nous ne savons pas quand le frère aîné de Ji Kang est entré dans l'armée et par conséquent nous ne savons pas non plus la date de ces poèmes. Il n'y a pas à s'étonner que Ji Xi soit rentré dans l'armée. Les guerres à la fois internes (contre les loyalistes révoltés) et externes (contre les royaumes de Wu et de Shu) n'ont pas cessé durant toute la vie de Ji Kang et les postes, même modestes, dans les bureaux des généraux menaient aux fonctions les plus importantes de l'État. Ne sachant ni la date, ni le service que Ji Xi a choisi, il est impossible de préciser le sens de son engagement. Tout ce que nous pouvons dire, et c'est important de le dire, c'est qu'en entrant dans une fonction publique Ji Xi a dû prendre parti dans la lutte politique qui déchirait le royaume de Wei.

Cette lutte opposait la famille régnante, les Cao, à un de leurs généraux les plus prestigieux, Sima Yi 司馬懿 (179-251), et à ses

---

[32] Kôzen Hiroshi accepte le caractère cyclique des dix-huit poèmes tétramétriques de cette série sans se poser de problèmes; il en fait même un des thèmes principaux de sa discussion. Il retarde sa discussion du poème en pentamètres pour *Chûgoku bungaku hô* 16 (1962), dans un article intitulé «Kei Kô no hishô» (désormais, Kôzen Hiroshi[2]), p. 4, où il le rattache hypothétiquement au cycle en disant que Ji Kang a voulu terminer en pentamètres pour pouvoir s'exprimer d'une façon plus «concrète» que ne le permettaient les tétramètres, forme, selon lui, qui porte à l'abstraction. Pour des raisons purement esthétiques, il me semble difficile d'admettre que ce poème puisse se trouver à la fin de la série.

descendants. Il est difficile de distinguer en détail aujourd'hui les raisons profondes qui divisaient ces deux adversaires, mais il semble assez clair que les Cao et leurs alliés représentaient une tendance novatrice, qu'ils s'efforçaient de s'opposer aux riches propriétaires héréditaires (dont était issu Sima Yi) pour rétablir un gouvernement central fort. La lutte était par trop inégale, car le mouvement de l'histoire allait dans le sens d'une «reféodalisation» de la Chine, où le gouvernement central devait de plus en plus partager son pouvoir avec les grandes familles régionales. En 249 une purge sanglante balayait les chefs de la clique des Cao et dès lors toute opposition aux Sima s'est trouvée vite écrasée. Et pourtant il y a eu des tentatives de rebellion contre les Sima à maintes reprises, en 251, 255, 259 et en 260, avant la prise de pouvoir formelle en 265. De quel côté Ji Xi allait-il s'engager? La famille Ji était alliée aux Cao par le mariage de Ji Kang à une princesse impériale; ils étaient aussi, comme les Cao, originaires du nord de l'Anhui actuel et les origines régionales jouaient (et jouent encore) un grand rôle dans le choix des alliances politiques en Chine. Ji Kang lui-même a pensé, pendant un court moment, venir en aide à un loyaliste, Guanqiu Jian 毌丘儉, qui a tenté une rebellion contre les Sima en 255[33]. Mais après la purge de 249, quand les Sima ont fortement affaibli les Cao, l'engagement dans la hiérarchie administrative était en fait un engagement chez les usurpateurs. Nous savons que Ji Xi a poursuivi une carrière politique sous les Sima après l'avènement de leur dynastie des Jin, devenant Impartial et Juste de la province de Yangzhou[34]. Nous savons même qu'il était un des officiers subordonnés, chargé d'affaires militaires, de Sima You 司馬攸, deuxième fils de Sima Zhao 昭, et que c'est lui qui a enfin pu persuader le filial Sima You de prendre de la nourriture après la mort de son père en novembre 265 — trois ans à peine après que ce père (Sima Zhao) ait fait exécuter Ji Kang[35]. D'autre

---

[33] *La vie et la pensée*, p. 28 (où le nom de Guanqiu Jian est incorrectement transcrit comme «Wou-k'ieou Kien»). Kôzen Hiroshi₂, pp. 14-15, décrit bien l'arrière-plan historique de cette période de la vie de Ji Kang.

[34] *Sanguo zhi jijie* 21, p. 22b (commentaire de Pei Songzhi); cf. aussi Dai Mingyang, p. 4.

[35] *Jin shu jiaozhu* 38, pp. 15b-16a. Le *Jin shu* de Zang Rongxu 臧榮緒 cité dans le

part, nous savons par des anecdotes racontées dans le *Shishuo xinyu* que Ji Xi était plutôt mal vu par les amis intimes de Ji Kang[36] et l'on voit bien dans les poèmes qu'il a écrit, en réponse à son cadet, que Ji Xi ne partageait pas du tout sa philosophie. Tout laisse croire que l'engagement de Ji Xi était du côté des Sima. Mais il est relativement peu important de savoir de quel côté il s'est engagé pour la compréhension de nos poèmes; ce qu'il faut savoir, c'est que son entrée dans l'armée signifie son entrée dans la vie active, dans les dangers de la vie politique. Le premier poème décrit cette entrée symboliquement: les deux frères sont présentés comme des oiseaux fabuleux, des phénix (c'est-à-dire, des êtres d'élite, qui se tiennent loin de la mêlée).

Dix-neuf poèmes donnés à mon frère aîné, bachelier,
lors de son entrée dans l'armée

[Prélude, en pentamètres]

Une paire de phénix cachaient leur éclat,
    Repliant leurs ailes sur la crête du mont Tai.
Ils levaient la tête pour sucer la rosée matinale
    Et se séchaient au soleil, secouant leurs plumes solennellement.
5 Ils chantaient longuement, et jouaient parmi les nuages,
    Descendant de temps en temps pour se reposer à l'étang des orchidées.
«Loin de nous la poussière de ce monde», disaient-ils,
    «Nous nous garderons intacts à tout jamais!»
Mais le monde est rempli de dangers insoupçonnés,
10   Et le garde-chasse est venu lier [la femelle].
Dans les nuages ses filets bouchaient les quatre horizons;
    Des rets se trouvaient éparpillés partout dans les hauteurs.
Il n'était pas facile [pour elle] de se mettre en mouvement;
    Il n'y avait pas de place pour étendre ses ailes.
15 Elle, qui vivait cachée, est allée vers une longue captivité,
    À été enfin domptée par le siècle.
Le mâle solitaire s'est envolé seul,
    Chantant sa douleur, cette séparation des vivants,
Errant çà et là d'amour pour sa compagne,

Taiping yulan 412, pp. 5ab, sans nommer Ji Xi, décrit un scénario semblable à la mort de la mère de Sima You, l'impératrice Wenming, née Wang, morte en 268.
[36] *La vie et la pensée*, pp. 26, 30.

VIII

20 Traînant son insatisfaction sur les versants des hautes montagnes.
On range les bons arcs quand il n'y a plus d'oiseaux;
  La vie d'un stratège sera sûrement en danger quand ses plans toucheront à
                                                            [leur fin.
Bien que ce soit nous-mêmes qui faisions notre propre destin,
  La route du monde est semée d'embûches.
25 Comment pouvons-nous retourner à notre état originel
  Pour garder en nous-mêmes le jade [de notre valeur], thésauriser en nous
                                                  [nos rares [stratagèmes]?
Promenons-nous tout à notre aise dans la Grande Pureté,
  L'un suivant l'autre, la main dans la main!

Les vingt premiers vers de ce poème sont inspirés d'une tradition
issue des ballades populaires (*yuefu*) qui décrit un couple d'oiseaux
qui doivent se séparer à cause de la maladie ou de la mort de la
femelle. Le prototype de ces poèmes semble être le poème intitulé
«Une paire de cygnes blancs» contenu dans le *Yutai xinyong* 1 ou
un poème très semblable contenu dans le *Yuefu shiji* 39, pp. 6ab[37].
Cao Pi et Cao Zhi ont tous deux écrit des poèmes sur le même
thème[38]. Cependant, le poème de Ji Kang introduit un élément
nouveau: la séparation du couple n'est plus due à la maladie ou à
la mort de la femelle, mais au fait qu'elle a été capturée par des
chasseurs et «domptée par le siècle». Ce nouvel élément ajoute une
note politique au poème, parce que «la capture» dans des filets est
une image fréquente qui dénote l'enrôlement d'un homme dans le
service d'un prince ou d'un haut fonctionnaire, ou plus simplement
dans le monde politique dangereux. Les derniers huit vers sont une
méditation sur les dangers de la vie publique qui débouche sur la
suggestion que le seul remède est un genre d'apothéose mystique
dans la «grande pureté».
  Le mot traduit par «phénix», *luan* 鸞, n'a, en fait, du phénix que
la qualité d'être un oiseau imaginaire. Pour les Chinois, il est surtout
un oiseau de bon augure qui apparaît pendant le règne d'un souverain
saint (Wang Yi 王逸, commentaire au *Chu ci*, «Jiu zhang», «She

---

[37] Cf. Yu Guanying 余冠英, *Han Wei Liuchao shi luncong* (Shanghai, 1963),
pp. 28-31.
[38] Le poème de Cao Pi se trouve dans Huang Jie, *Wei Wudi Wei Wendi shizhu*,
p. 51; celui de Cao Zhi dans *Yiwen leiju* 90, p. 9a.

jiang»: «Le *luan* et le *feng* 鳳 sont des oiseaux héroïques. Ils paraissent quand le souverain est saint et ils s'en vont quand il est sans vertu. Ils symbolisent le fait qu'un fonctionnaire sage avance avec difficulté, mais se retire aisément»). Ji Kang souligne le caractère faste de cet oiseau dans le vers 4 en employant deux mots qui rappellent une des remarques sibyllines contenues dans le *Yi jing* (Hexagramme 53) à propos d'un autre oiseau héroïque, le *hong* 鴻. On y trouve les deux mots que j'ai traduit «plumes solennellement», *yu yi* 羽儀, dans un contexte qui voudrait dire quelque chose comme «Le *hong* s'approche graduellement de la terre; ses plumes peuvent être utilisées dans des solennités», c'est-à-dire (d'après Wang Bi) que, grâce à son désengagement, à la hauteur de ses vues inébranlables, le *hong* (ou l'homme supérieur) devient un modèle d'action. Les cygnes blancs, époux fidèles du «vieux poème», sont devenus ici des symboles d'hommes éminents et désintéressés. Ils ne sont pas seulement désintéressés; ils se cachent du monde (vers 1-2) et se comportent (vers 3-6) un peu comme des ermites ou des immortels taoïstes. Leur symbolisme est donc riche et complexe, mais n'a rien d'obscur ou arcane pour le lecteur chinois de la poésie de cette époque.

Si Ji Kang s'était arrêté au vers 20 on pourrait peut-être, avec beaucoup de bonne volonté, imaginer qu'il s'était exercé à écrire un poème «à l'ancienne» (le manuscrit du Congshu tang l'appelle ainsi: «Wuyan guyi» 五言古意) qui décrit la séparation d'un couple d'oiseaux amoureux. Il faudrait, alors, ignorer le symbolisme traditionnel des phénix, les allusions au *Yi jing* et l'ambiance poétique et politique dans laquelle le poème a été écrit. Mais il ne s'est pas arrêté au vers 20, et les 8 derniers vers prouvent sans l'ombre d'un doute que ce poème est à lire comme une allégorie politique. Les vers 21 et 22 font allusion à un vieux dicton cité dans de nombreux textes anciens (e.g., *Han Feizi jishi* 10, ch. 31, p. 584, et à deux reprises dans *Shi ji* 41, p. 1746, et 92, p. 2625). Après la chasse, quand les oiseaux et les lièvres sont tous tués, on range les arcs et on fait bouillir les chiens de chasse pour les manger à leur tour (*more sinico*); de la même façon, selon le dicton, une fois un pays ennemi est conquis, on fait disparaître les stratèges qui ont assuré la victoire, par peur qu'ils n'essaient d'utiliser leurs talents contre leur propre pays. Il

n'y a, pour ainsi dire, pas de transition entre les 20 vers descriptifs du début du poème et les vers moralisateurs qui suivent. Mais l'image employée pour souligner les dangers qui attendent celui qui s'engage dans la vie de la stratégie politique reste une image tirée de la chasse : l'oiseau est capturé ; que celui qui l'a chassé fasse attention, car sa vie aussi est en danger.

Les deux vers suivants (23-24) soulignent les dangers de la vie dans le monde, insistant sur le fait que ces dangers sont si grands qu'ils annulent le stock de bonheur (ou malheur) dont nous sommes dotés par le destin. Les quatre derniers vers cherchent une solution à ces dangers très réels, prêts à s'abattre sur ceux qui se cachent (les phénix) aussi bien que sur ceux qui s'engagent librement (les stratèges). La solution est donnée dans la forme d'une question, et d'une apothéose mystique. Les mots dans le vers 25 traduits par « état originel » veulent dire littéralement « premiers vêtements » et font allusion aux vêtements de toile qu'un homme porte avant de s'engager dans la hiérarchie des fonctionnaires (quand il portera des vêtements de soie), à la période de sa vie où il était encore intouché par les compromissions et éclaboussures de la vie d'un courtisan (cf. *Chu ci*, « Li sao », Hawkes, p. 25, l. 57b). Son désir est de se garder intact, cachant en lui tout ce qui pourrait être considéré comme précieux (*Laozi* 70, *Han shu* 100B, p. 4248) et se perdre, dans une randonnée mystique, dans l'absolu, avec son ami. Le terme « grande pureté », *tai qing* 太清, est utilisé dans plusieurs textes (e.g. *Zhuangzi* 14, Watson, p. 156) pour décrire le *dao* ou le lieu de randonnée des Hommes Parfaits. Ji Kang semble rejeter toute possibilité de trouver la paix dans ce monde, soit en se cachant comme le font les phénix du début, soit en utilisant son savoir de « stratège ». Kôzen Hiroshi[2] (p. 12) cite le poème en prose de Baudelaire qui porte un titre en anglais : « Anywhere out of this world », pour décrire l'attitude de Ji Kang et, si nous pouvions extraire Baudelaire de « l'ennui » romantique dont il est le prisonnier pour le considérer comme un auteur religieux, son désir de fuir ce monde-ci pour une espèce de « là-bas » céleste ressemblerait bien au dénouement mystique de ce poème. La vie cachée, presque d'un immortel taoïste, décrite au début du poème ne semble pas suffire. Ji Kang cherche l'évasion complète, vraiment hors du monde.

Le poème, comme presque tous les poèmes de cette époque, est rempli de résonnances politiques, d'indices allégoriques ou symboliques. Peut-on les serrer de plus près pour découvrir les clés des allusions? Que représentent chacun des deux phénix du début du poème? Il est toujours difficile et souvent impossible de démêler ces allusions. Si ce poème fait effectivement partie de la série écrite à l'entrée de son frère dans l'armée nous avons sûrement le droit d'identifier les deux phénix aux deux frères. Mais peut-on préciser davantage? Selon Kôzen Hiroshi$_2$ (p. 5) «il va sans dire que» le vers 16, «à propos de l'oiseau 'qui a été dompté par le siècle', se réfère à Ji Xi qui entre dans une carrière de fonctionnaire, tandis que le vers 19... se réfère à Ji Kang lui-même». Mais un fin connaisseur des Qing, Zhang Qi 張琦 (1765-1833, frère de Zhang Huiyan 惠言), croit que dans les 16 premiers vers Ji Kang parle de lui-même. Le vers 10, traduit littéralement, se lirait: «Le garde-chasse est venu me lier», mais bien que le mot «moi» ou «me», *wo* 我, soit souvent utilisé dans les poèmes de cette époque pour indiquer un personnage principal, un peu comme on dit «notre héros» dans un roman, Zhang Qi semble vouloir le comprendre littéralement. Si ce poème était écrit après l'emprisonnement de Ji Kang (en 262), on pourrait le comprendre ainsi, et les derniers 12 vers, comme le dit Zhang Qi ([*Wanlin shuwu*] *Gushi lu* 4, p. 8b, réédition de Shanghai, 1927), seraient ses vœux de santé et sécurité pour son frère aîné, en espérant qu'ils pourront se retrouver ensemble un jour. Le poème, malheureusement, n'est pas daté, ce qui laisse ouverte la porte à toutes les théories. Mieux vaut ne pas essayer une explication allégorique trop rigoureuse: le poème décrit deux hommes supérieurs séparés par un mal non spécifié, et le poète semble désespérer de les voir réunis autrement que dans un genre d'extase mystique, une randonnée dans la Grande Pureté[39].

[39] Le terme «Grande Pureté» est souvent utilisé dans la poésie et n'a pas forcément un sens «mystique». Il apparaît dans un poème de He Yan (190-249) qui rappelle celui de Ji Kang, mais dans le poème de He Yan il semble symboliser quelque chose de très différent, les hautes sphères de la vie politique. Le poème est contenu dans le *Mingshi zhuan* cité dans le *Shishuo xinyu* 10 (Mather n° 6, p. 280). Le terme apparaît aussi dans le deuxième poème donné à Ji Kang par Guo Xiazhou (infra, p. 146) où il décrit un lieu idéal.

À la fin de sa préface du *Shi pin*, Zhong Rong donne une liste d'une vingtaine de poésies en pentamètres par des poètes différents, de Cao Zhi jusqu'au Vᵉ siècle, qu'il considère comme les chefs-d'œuvre[40] de la forme pentamétrique. Ce poème de Ji Kang est parmi eux. Il est digne d'être l'introduction à la série qui suit. Tous les éléments que nous verrons développés y sont : du bonheur original des deux personnages à l'apothéose mystique, en passant par leur triste séparation.

Les 18 poèmes en tétramètres qui suivent sont, avec les sept poèmes écrits par Cao Zhi à son demi-frère, le prince de Baima 白馬[41], les premiers cycles poétiques en Chine. Il est difficile de savoir à quel point la complexité du cycle de Ji Kang est due à la volonté de leur auteur et à quel point elle est due à des confusions textuelles, mais il ne peut y avoir de doute que ces poèmes suivent un ordre voulu, qu'ils représentent un véritable développement de la pensée de leur auteur et ne sont pas simplement des poèmes autour d'un thème mis bout à bout[42]. La série se compose de poèmes de longueurs différentes : dix poèmes de huit vers, cinq de douze, de nouveau deux de huit et enfin un poème de vingt vers. Comme tous les poèmes en tétramètres, ceux-ci baignent dans l'atmosphère du *Shi jing*, et sont farcis de citations mot à mot de ce livre canonique. Cette influence est surtout sensible dans les premiers poèmes, mais même

---

[40] Le terme employé par Zhong Rong pour décrire ces «chefs-d'œuvre» est *jingce* 警策, littéralement, «un bâton» ou «fouet d'admonition». Ce terme a été inventé par Lu Ji (261-303) dans son «Wen fu» (traduction A. Fang, *Harvard Journal of Asiatic Studies* 14 [1951], p. 538) où le sens est «un mot ou expression qui 'fouette' ou ravigote un morceau entier». Zhong Rong applique le terme à des poèmes entiers qu'il semble considérer comme «ravigotant» tous les autres poèmes en pentamètres par leur excellence ; ce sont, en somme, un genre de «pierres de touche».

[41] Traduits par H. H. Frankel, «Fifteen poems by Ts'ao Chih», *Journal of the American Oriental Society* 84, 1 (1964), pp. 1-14.

[42] Kôzen Hiroshi insiste sur l'interprétation de ce cycle comme une série de poèmes savamment structurée. Mais il ne souligne pas assez clairement toutes les difficultés que cette interprétation comporte et passe sous silence le fait que les critiques anciens ne sont pas du tout d'accord sur le caractère cyclique de l'œuvre. D'autre part, la «structure» strophique compliquée qu'il voit à la base de l'œuvre me semble artificielle. Mais j'ai beaucoup profité de sa discussion et j'ai fait miennes certaines de ses conclusions.

ici l'originalité de Ji Kang est apparente : il se sert du style canonique d'une façon personnelle.

Le cycle commence avec deux paires de poèmes. Chacune des deux paires de poèmes contient deux poèmes avec un certain nombre de vers identiques ou très semblables. L'imagerie de la première paire, basée sur des canards mandarins, fait penser au début du poème en pentamètres sur les phénix.

1

Les canards dans leur vol
  Font *susu* de leurs ailes.
Le matin ils se promènent sur les terres hautes,
  Et le soir ils se reposent sur l'îlot des orchidées.
5 Doucement ils caquètent, l'un après l'autre,
  Chacun regardant son compagnon du coin de l'œil.
Ils remuent leur tête d'une émotion à peine contenue,
  Se réjouissant, tout à fait à l'aise.

2

Les canards dans leur vol
  Sifflent et appellent leur compagnon.
Le matin ils se promènent sur les terres hautes,
  Et le soir se reposent au milieu de l'île.
5 Leurs cous entrelacés, ils agitent leurs ailes,
  Tout à fait à l'aise dans les flots purs.
Ils se délectent des orchidées odorantes ;
  Remuant la tête, ils se réjouissent ensemble.

Les canards mandarins sont bien connus comme symboles du bonheur conjugal, mais ils peuvent aussi symboliser l'amitié fraternelle (Dai Mingyang en cite des exemples). Les deux premiers vers sont cités mot à mot du *Shi jing* 216 et 181, et il y a des échos de ce livre et d'autres poèmes dans chaque vers. Le fait de répéter le même vers de strophe en strophe est aussi hérité du *Shi jing*, mais Ji Kang ne se limite pas à être imitateur. Il développe le procédé en faisant écho d'un poème à l'autre à un grand nombre d'expressions, les répétant dans le deuxième poème dans un endroit différent du premier (e.g., « tout à fait à l'aise » à la fin du vers 8 du premier poème est répété au début du vers 6 dans le deuxième poème) ou avec une légère modification («l'îlot des orchidées» à la fin du vers 4 du premier poème devient «le milieu de l'île» dans la même position exactement dans le deuxième poème). Les deux poèmes sont ainsi entremêlés comme les canards se sont entrelaçés leurs cous, et l'effet du poème, un effet quasi-musical, est très différent des poèmes du *Shi jing*, malgré les emprunts (comme le souligne Wang Fuzhi). La musicalité des vers provient aussi du fait qu'ils sont tous, sans exception, coupés en deux au milieu, après le deuxième mot. Cette régularité prosodique peut paraître ennuyeuse (c'est l'avis de Chen Zuoming). Mais en fait elle répond si bien au sens calme et harmonieux des vers qu'elle forme comme un arrière-plan de basse continue sur lequel les légères variations entre les deux strophes peuvent prendre leur relief. Non, le manque de variété rythmique est un des éléments qui ajoute aux charmes de ces vers.

On s'en rendra d'autant mieux compte que les vers qui suivent sont prosodiquement très différents, et l'effet produit l'est également.

3

Je nage dans la longue rivière
   Et me repose sur sa rive.
Je grimpe sur les hautes crêtes
   Pour y couper les épines.
5 Hélas! avançant ainsi
   Je marche solitaire, sans amis.
Je lève la tête vers le vent du sud
   Et mes larmes coulent comme la pluie.

4

Je nage[43] dans la longue rivière
   Et me repose sur son îlot.
Je grimpe sur les hautes crêtes
   Pour couper les lyciets.
5 Hélas! j'avance seul,
   Personne à honorer, personne pour me soutenir.
Je lève la tête vers le vent du sud,
   Tantôt assis, tantôt me tenant debout.

[43] Le manuscrit du Congshu tang écrit *mù* 沐, «se baigner», pour *yong* 泳, «nager», ici. Comme le dit Luxun, c'est une lecture possible, mais je suis de l'avis de Dai Mingyang qu'étant donné le souci de parallélisme dans ces «paires» de poèmes, cette lecture (inconnue des autres versions) est très improbable.

La calme monotonie du rythme symétrique des poèmes 1 et 2 est rompue dès le premier vers: la césure ne se trouve plus après le deuxième mot (c'est-à-dire en plein milieu du vers) mais après le premier dans la plupart des vers. Et à ce déséquilibre prosodique correspond le déséquilibre émotif du poète, ses larmes, son hésitation. Comme dans la première paire de poèmes, les vers dans les deux poèmes 3 et 4 sont entrelacés, mais d'une autre façon — un seul mot est substitué pour un autre (vers 2, 4, 5) ou des vers entiers sont répétés (vers 1, 3, 7); ce ne sont plus des paires de mots qui se déplacent ensemble. Les emprunts du *Shi jing* sont encore très sensibles, surtout dans le poème 3 où la moitié des vers sont mot à mot du livre canonique (vers 3 du *Shi jing* 3, vers 4 du *Shi jing* 9, vers 6 du *Shi jing* 119 et vers 8 du *Shi jing* 28), mais ce n'est pas une imitation laborieuse (Wang Fuzhi); Ji Kang a su introduire une note de tristesse, pour le moment non expliquée, et qui est renforcée par les irrégularités rythmiques.

Les raisons de cette tristesse sont dévoilées petit à petit dans les poèmes suivants. Les poèmes 5 à 8 sont encore deux paires de poèmes, mais ils sont liés entre eux par encore un autre procédé. Ji Kang emploie un procédé sans doute hérité de la poésie populaire mais qui apparaît déjà dans les poèmes (cités plus haut) que Cao Zhi a écrits à son demi-frère: les deux derniers mots du dernier vers du premier de la paire sont répétés comme premiers mots dans le deuxième poème de la paire[44].

5

Qu'il est doux ce vent bienfaisant
  Qui souffle sur la poussière légère,
Et qu'elle est pleine cette onde claire
  Qui fait tourner sur lui-même le poisson en promenade!
5 Mais dans ma peine
  Mon cœur est plein de celui qui est au loin.
Constamment éveillé en pensant à lui,
  Tout m'attire vers cet être cher.

[44] On trouve l'ébauche de ce procédé déjà dans le poème 247 du *Shi jing*.

128

6

Mais où est cet être cher,
  Qui m'a quitté pour un long voyage?
Il a rejeté ces plantes parfumées
  Pour revêtir l'armoise vile.
5 Il a beau se croire caché et lointain:
  La vie n'est que dangers!
Je pense à lui, cet homme supérieur:
  Le malheur n'est jamais loin!

Les beautés de la nature ne suffisent plus à réjouir le poète et nous apprenons la raison de sa tristesse: l'absence de «cet être cher», c'est-à-dire le départ de son frère pour l'armée. Les résonances du *Shi jing* deviennent plus atténuées: seul le dernier vers du sixième poème est une véritable citation d'un vers commun aux poèmes 39 et 44[45]. Les vers 3 et 4 du poème 6 emploient une terminologie inspirée des *Chu ci* («Li sao», Hawkes, p. 31, et ailleurs): les plantes parfumées, telle l'orchidée, sont des plantes pures qui poussent loin des hommes; les plantes viles, telle l'armoise, sont des plantes communes qu'on trouve partout. Les premières symbolisent l'homme qui reste loin des compromissions de la vie politique; les dernières, les opportunistes et les profiteurs. En quittant leur retraite le frère de Ji Kang se met du côté des gens du commun. Le vers 5 est cité mot à mot d'un poème de Zhang Heng 張衡 (dans la collection Han Wei Liuchao bai san mingjia ji, Shanghai, 1925, *Zhang Hejian ji* 2, p. 20b), mais l'inspiration commune des deux poètes est sans doute le *Yi jing*, «Xi ci» A (Legge, p. 369), où le terme «caché et lointain», *you shen* 幽深, fait référence aux choses cachées que l'adepte du *Yi jing* sait découvrir. En tout cas le poème se termine dans une atmosphère qui rappelle bien celle du *Yi jing*, une évocation des dangers inhérents à la vie politique.

Les deux poèmes suivants sont encore liés par leurs derniers mots («mon ami»), mais le premier des deux introduit des idées philosophiques que nous n'avons pas encore rencontrées.

---

[45] Avec le caractère 遐 pour le 瑕 du *Shi jing*. Le sens de ce vers est contesté; cf. B. Karlgren, *Glosses on the Book of Odes*, Stockholm, 1964, p. 126.

7

La vie de l'homme est de courte durée;
Le ciel et la terre sont éternels.
Une période de cent ans: ,
Qui l'appelerait une vie longue?
5 Je voudrais m'élever [au ciel] en immortel
Pour atteindre un état indestructible.
Je prends les rênes, mais j'hésite, perplexe:
Je lève la tête pour chercher mon ami.

8

Mon ami, où est-il allé,
Séparé de moi par les crêtes des montagnes?
Qui dit que le Fleuve est large?
On le traverserait sur un roseau!
5 Mais je déteste cette séparation sans fin,
Et qu'il ait parcouru la longueur de cette route!
Je regarde sans pouvoir l'atteindre,
Hésitant, errant çà et là.

Le septième poème nous dévoile, presque prématurément et d'une façon inattendue, ce qui sera le dénouement de la série et ce qui est le thème principal de l'œuvre de Ji Kang: la recherche de l'immortalité. La tonalité taoïste du poème est accentuée par une citation presque mot à mot du *Laozi* 7 dans le deuxième vers. Mais cette suggestion d'une solution taoïste, d'une ascension en immortel qui l'éloignerait de la tristesse de la séparation de son frère, n'est pas développée et le huitième poème reprend les lamentations. Avec de légères variantes de caractères, les vers 3 et 4 citent *Shi jing* 61 et le vers 7, *Shi jing* 28, tandis que le dernier vers est basé sur un vers d'un poème des *Chu ci*, le «Ai shi ming» (Hawkes, p. 136)[46].

À l'exception du poème 11, les poèmes 9 à 15 sont tous reproduits dans *Wen xuan* 24. Ils forment, en effet, une section légèrement distincte de ce qui précède et tout à fait distincte des trois poèmes

---

[46] Dans le vers 2 je suis les éditions imprimées pour le dernier caractère, *gang* 崗, plutôt que le manuscrit du Congshu tang qui lit *liang* 梁, «pont». Cette lecture donnerait la traduction, «Séparé de moi par les ponts suspendus des montagnes». Le copiste pensait peut-être au texte fort obscur du *Lun yu* 10, 18, où le terme «ponts des montagnes» apparaît.

qui suivent. Ce sont, comme les poèmes précédents, des poèmes qui chantent à la fois les beautés du paysage naturel et la tristesse d'être séparé de son frère. Mais leur ton est plus vigoureux, plus viril, et semble évoquer la vie militaire que mène son frère. La description de la nature, aussi, est plus détaillée, plus expansive. Ji Kang semble ici un précurseur des paysagistes poétiques (et picturaux) qui allaient fleurir bientôt en Chine, et c'est peut-être la raison pour laquelle le prince Xiao Tong a recueilli ces poèmes dans son anthologie.

Après l'hésitation qui marque la fin du huitième poème, dans les poèmes 9 et 10 Ji Kang semble vouloir atteindre son frère par son imagination en se peignant sous les traits d'un splendide guerrier galopant et chassant avec lui à travers monts et vallées. À partir du poème 9 Ji Kang renonce à présenter ces poèmes par paires. Mais les neuvième et dixième poèmes se suivent encore de très près, au point que le *Wen xuan* les présente comme un seul poème, malgré la différence de rimes.

9

Mes bons chevaux sont bien entraînés,
    Mes beaux vêtements étincelants.
Dans la main gauche je tiens [l'arc] Fanruo;
    Dans la main droite je garde [la flèche] Wanggui.
5 Galopant comme le vent ou l'éclair,
    Je poursuis de près les rayons du soleil, le vol des oiseaux!
Dominant le milieu de la plaine
    Je regarde en arrière débordant de vitalité.

10

J'amène mon bon ami par la main
    Pour le faire monter dans le char léger.
Nous gravissons la haute colline au sud
    Et traversons le cours d'eau claire au nord.
5 Nous levons la tête et faisons tomber les oies effrayées;
    Nous baissons la tête pour retirer les poissons des profondeurs.
Heureux dans notre promenade de chasse,
    Quelle est notre joie!

Les échos du *Shi jing* restent assez forts dans ces poèmes; il y a des citations partielles des poèmes 127, 252 et 80, et le dernier vers du dixième poème est mot à mot du poème 67. L'avant-dernier vers de ce poème est aussi une citation du *Shu jing*, ch. «Wu yi». Il y a quelques variantes textuelles qui ne changent pas grande chose à l'interprétation des vers. L'arc et la flèche mentionnés dans les vers 3 et 4 du neuvième poème apparaissent dans des textes anciens comme des armes célèbres de la haute antiquité. Fanruo est mentionné dans le *Zuo zhuan*, Ding 4 (Legge, p. 754), et les deux sont nommés ensemble dans le *Gongsun Longzi* 1 (Kou, *Deux sophistes chinois*, Paris, 1953, p. 22). Il y a d'autres échos des poètes de la génération précédant Ji Kang.

Ces deux poèmes sont placés au beau milieu de la série et semblent marquer un point d'arrêt (Wang Fuzhi), un moment de bonheur qui permettra au poète d'intensifier l'impression de tristesse dans les poèmes suivants. Mais ai-je eu raison de traduire ces poèmes à la première personne? S'agit-il plutôt de la description de Ji Xi en vaillant soldat (Chen Zuoming, Liu Lü) se promenant, dans le dixième poème, avec un camarade d'armes (Dai Mingyang)? Le chinois est ainsi fait qu'il permet ces ambiguïtés. Le «char léger» du deuxième vers du dixième poème semble bien être un char de guerre (*Zhou li*, trad. Biot 2, p. 132), mais la scène dépeinte est clairement une scène de chasse. On comprend mal, d'autre part, pourquoi Ji Kang voudrait embellir l'image de la vie militaire qu'il condamne ailleurs dans la série. J'aime mieux voir ces deux poèmes comme la description d'une rencontre idéalisée, imaginaire (Kôzen Hiroshi) entre les deux frères, rencontre qui servira à accentuer, par contraste, la tristesse de la solitude dans les poèmes qui suivent.

À partir du onzième et jusqu'au quinzième poème, les poèmes sont de douze vers, quatre vers de plus que les poèmes précédents. Dans ces cinq poèmes Ji Kang semble avoir besoin d'une forme plus ample pour développer ses idées. Ils sont tous des variations sur les mêmes thèmes, évoqués dans le même ordre dans chaque poème : la promenade dans la nature, la musique, et la solitude provoquée par l'absence de son frère. Seul le poème 14 introduit une note nouvelle, une allusion à la métaphysique taoïste qui ne sera reprise et développée que dans les trois derniers poèmes de la série.

11

Je monte sur les hauteurs et regarde au loin,
   Secouant la tête et soupirant.
Comme je me sens à l'étroit dans cette captivité!
   La chambre [de mon ami semble] si proche et la route est si loin!
5 Bien que ma musique soit belle,
   Qui m'accompagnera d'un chant clair?
Bien que mon visage rayonne de jeunesse,
   Qui s'épanouira avec moi?
Je lève la tête pour me confier aux nuages dans les hauteurs;
10   Je baisse la tête pour me livrer aux flots légers.
Je vais suivre le courant et m'enfuir au loin,
   Gardant mon chagrin dans les recoins des montagnes.

Ma traduction des difficiles vers 3 et 4 est basée sur le manuscrit du Congshu tang. Les autres versions donneraient:

Je déteste cette captivité;
   Au loin la route est longue.

La version traduite contient des échos du *Shi jing* 196 (vers 3) et 89 (vers 4). Ce dernier poème est la plainte d'une femme envers un amant peu assidu:

Sa chambre si proche,
   Sa personne si lointaine!

Ji Kang semble suggérer que l'absence de son frère est volontaire, mais le vers reste un peu obscur, ainsi que la suggestion dans le vers précédent qu'il est en «captivité»[47]. Il faut sans doute comprendre tout le poème comme la plainte d'un homme qui se sent privé de la seule liberté qu'il tient à cœur: la liberté de voir son ami. L'avant-

---

[47] Fukunaga Mitsuji 福永光司, «Kei Kô ni okeru jiga no mondai: Kei Kô no seikatsu to shisô», *Tôhô gakuhô* (Kyoto) 32 (1962), pp. 11-12, suggère qu'il y a une allusion politique ici à la retraite forcée de l'empereur déposé, Cao Fang, le prince de Qi. Selon le *Shuijing zhu* 9, p. 59 (de l'édition Guoxue jiben congshu), cette retraite se trouvait à Chongmen 重門, c'est-à-dire à une vingtaine de km à l'est de la maison de campagne de Ji Kang, dans le nord du Henan actuel, une quinzaine de km au nord de la ville actuelle de Huojia 獲嘉. Il est tout à fait possible que Ji Kang se trouvait à sa maison de campagne (ou s'y imaginait) quand il écrivait ces poèmes (cf. le poème 13 où il parle de «mon domaine»), mais une allusion politique me semble fort improbable ici, quelque soit la difficulté d'interprétation de ces vers.

dernier vers aussi appuie cette idée : le poète veut «fuir au loin» (ou «se cacher au loin») comme s'il était vraiment emprisonné.

Mais dans les poèmes suivants il oublie cette captivité tandis que les évocations de la nature deviennent de plus en plus frappantes.

12

Je cours vite dans mon char léger
    Et je me repose dans cette forêt dense.
Les arbres printaniers sont couverts de fleurs
    Et leurs feuilles tressées répandent de l'ombre.
5 Le vent de l'est murmure
    En sifflant sur ma cithare simple.
Les loriots disent *yaoyao*,
    Se tournant vers leur compagnon pour chanter leurs mélodies.
Ils me touchent et m'émeuvent,
10   Et me font penser à celui que j'estime.
O! la douleur de mon cœur
    Me fait siffler longuement et fredonner toujours des vers.

Les vers 3 à 6 de ce poème, selon Wang Fuzhi, «sont si beaux qu'ils ne semblent presque pas faits par un être humain». (Mais le vers 4 est en fait une citation de Zhang Heng, «Xi jing fu», non relevée par Dai Mingyang.) Même Chen Zuoming admet la beauté des vers 4 et 8, parce qu'ils ne sont pas des échos du *Shi jing*. Mais il y a encore des échos du livre canonique : le vers 5 est mot à mot du poème 35 et les vers 7 et 11-12 sont des variations de vers des poèmes 131 et 109 respectivement. Ji Kang lui-même cite le dernier vers de ce poème à la fin du dernier poème qu'il a écrit avant sa mort (2ᵉ Partie, ch. 5). Le poème 12 continue la méditation de Ji Kang sur la nature, une nature printanière qui semble, par sa beauté, lui apporter une consolation, mais qui en fait lui rappelle sa solitude. Le poème suivant continue la même méditation. Il est le seul de ces cinq poèmes à ne pas mentionner la musique.

13

Qu'ils sont immenses les cours d'eaux gonflés
    Qui entourent mon domaine!
Et le bois verdoyant et touffu
    Éclate de fleurs et de splendeur!

134

5 Les poissons et les dragons font clapoter l'eau;
  Les oiseaux des montagnes volent en bandes.
  Je vais atteler pour me promener
    Et à la tombée du jour j'oublie le retour.
  Je pense à mon bon ami,
10   Comme un assoiffé, comme un affamé!
  Que je le désire, sans pouvoir l'atteindre!
  Que ma tristesse est profonde!

Les commentateurs Liu Lü et He Zhuo soulignent le fait que les premiers six vers de ce poème (et surtout les vers 5 et 6) décrivent les unions printanières du monde animal et servent à rappeler au poète sa propre solitude. Le composé «poissons et dragons» du vers 5 semblent une invention de Ji Kang, repris plus tard par de nombreux poètes (dont Du Fu). On doit sans doute comprendre «les animaux aquatiques», mais le mot «dragon» ajoute une note magique et héroïque à cette description. Chen Zuoming et Dai Mingyang (p. 4 de son édition) insistent sur le fait que Ji Kang n'aurait jamais employé le terme «bon ami» pour se référer à son frère. Dai Mingyang déduit de ce fait que la série de 18 ou de 19 poèmes n'en est pas une et que ces poèmes ont été rassemblés par des éditeurs ultérieurs. Le terme «bon ami» provient du *Shi jing* 164 dans un contexte qui, en effet, compare le comportement de frères avec celui de «bons amis». Mais la critique me semble mal fondée (et est en effet passée sous silence par les autres commentateurs). À mon avis, rien ne nous empêche de croire que le frère aîné de Ji Kang était aussi son «bon ami».

Les poèmes de cette section sont de véritables poèmes paysagistes avant la lettre, l'école paysagiste n'apparaissant qu'une cinquantaine d'années plus tard[48]. Le fait que les numéros 10 et 13 à 14 sont inclus dans le *Wen xuan* montre qu'ils répondent au goût littéraire des successeurs médiévaux de Ji Kang. Une anecdote racontée dans le *Shishuo xinyu* 6 (Mather, n° 29) à propos du héros Xie An 謝安 (320-385) nous montre la célébrité de ce poème 13. Quand il s'est rendu compte, trop tard, que le banquet auquel il allait assister était

[48] Obi Kôichi, *Chûgoku bungaku ni arawareta shizen to shizen kan* (Tokyo, 1962), décrit les origines de cette école, parlant de Ji Kang et citant les poèmes 12 et 13 de cette série sur les pp. 135-138.

en fait un guet-apens qui pourrait lui coûter la vie, pour montrer son sang froid, Xie An s'est mis à psalmodier, «Qu'ils sont immenses les cours d'eau gonflés», tandis qu'il prenait calmement sa place au banquet. Son hôte et prétendu assassin, impressionné par son sang froid (et peut-être par son goût en poésie), a décommandé ses meurtriers.

Le poème suivant a été aimé par le grand peintre Gu Kaizhi 顧愷之 (*ca.* 344-405), autre amateur de la poésie de Ji Kang.

14

Je fais reposer mon équipage dans le jardin des orchidées
    Et je laisse paître mes chevaux sur le mont fleuri.
Mes flèches pleuvent sur les marais plats;
    Je jette mon fil dans le long fleuve.
5 Des yeux je suis le retour des oies sauvages;
    Ma main fait vibrer les cinq cordes [de ma cithare].
Où que je tourne mes regards je me sens parfaitement content,
    Et je laisse errer mon cœur dans le Grand Mystère.
Que j'admire ce vieux pêcheur
10   Qui, ayant attrapé le poisson, oubliait la nasse!
L'homme de Ying est parti:
    À qui pourrai-je dire tout ce que j'ai sur le cœur?

C'est avec la nature et la musique que le poète essaie d'assouvir sa tristesse et combler sa solitude. Les flèches qu'il fait pleuvoir (vers 3) sur les terrains de chasse, sont en fait des cailloux attachés à des fils eux-mêmes attachés aux flèches. Le chasseur tirait (à l'arbalète, vraisemblablement) ces flèches enfilées et espérait que les oiseaux s'attraperaient dans les fils. Le retour des oies sauvages au printemps est un événement riche en signification, symbolisant tout le jeu naturel qu'est le changement des saisons et le mouvement mystérieusement spontané de la nature. La cithare à cinq cordes que touche le poète passe pour être une invention de la plus haute antiquité, plus proche des sources «cosmiques» de la musique pentatonique que la cithare à sept cordes qui l'a graduellement remplacée dans la faveur des lettrés. Ji Kang se trouve ainsi, au vers 7 de ce poème, au comble du bonheur, tout à fait à l'aise dans l'univers, et son «accord universel» est comme symbolisé par son jeu musical: toucher les cinq cordes de la cithare, c'est jouer des Cinq Éléments de l'univers ; c'est être un genre de démiurge à l'image des saints immortels taoïstes. Le vers suivant (8) confirme cette interprétation ; il s'agit vraiment d'un genre de communion ou d'union mystique. Les deux vers suivants (9 et 10) soulignent l'impossibilité de décrire un tel état avec des paroles : le pêcheur, dont parle *Zhuangzi* 26 (Watson, p. 302), est un symbole de l'homme supérieur qui sait «oublier les paroles» une fois qu'une idée est saisie, qui sait se mouvoir dans les sphères mystiques au-dessus des paroles. Dans les derniers deux vers Ji Kang rappelle encore une fois sa solitude, cette fois-ci en faisant allusion à Zhuangzi et à son amitié pour Hui Shi. Dans *Zhuangzi* 24 (Watson, p. 269) nous voyons Zhuangzi raconter un apologue à ses disciples, apologue inspiré par la vue du tombeau de son ami et meilleur protagoniste philosophe, Hui Shi. Zhuangzi leur décrit la prouesse extraordinaire d'un artisan qui a su enlever un morceau de plâtre collé sur le nez d'un ami, appelé «l'homme de Ying», capitale de l'État de Chu. Le morceau de plâtre était aussi fin que l'aile d'une mouche, mais l'artisan, avec un mouvement de sa hache si rapide qu'elle soulevait le vent, l'a enlevé sans endommager le moins du monde le nez de son ami. Et celui-ci est resté calme et confiant pendant toute l'opération délicate. Mais quand le souverain de Song a fait appel à l'artisan pour pratiquer la même opération sur lui, l'artisan a refusé, disant que sa cible («l'homme de Ying») «était mort depuis longtemps», voulant dire, sans doute, que seule l'entente parfaite entre lui et l'opéré permettait la réussite de l'opération. Et Zhuangzi explique le sens de son apologue en disant que «depuis la mort du maître [Hui Shi], je n'ai pas de cible [ou partenaire valable] ; je n'ai plus personne à qui parler». (Ji Kang fait cette même allusion dans un autre poème, *infra*, pp. 162, 164.) Le dernier vers du poème est l'écho de ces mots de Zhuangzi, mais enrichi de résonnances philosophiques supplémentaires. Les deux derniers mots du poème, *jin yan* 盡言, ont deux sens : 1. «critiquer librement et sans crainte», et 2. un sens philosophique qu'ils retirent du *Yi jing*, «Xi ci» (Legge, pp. 376-377), où ils apparaissent dans la phrase «l'écriture n'exprime pas entièrement [le sens] des mots ; les mots n'expriment pas entièrement les idées». Du temps de Ji Kang ces phrases étaient le centre d'un débat philosophique: y a-t-il une réalité au-delà des mots, ou, au contraire, est-ce que réalité et langage sont identiques? Ji Kang lui-même (selon le *Yu hai*, cité par Dai Mingyang, p. 328) aurait écrit un essai selon lequel «les mots n'expriment pas entièrement les idées», «Yan bu jin yi» 言不盡意. Le sens de ce dernier vers serait donc double: le premier sens, «dire tout ce que j'ai sur le cœur», et un deuxième sens où Ji Kang reprend la pensée déjà exprimée dans les vers 9 et 10: il regrette le départ de l'homme avec qui il pouvait «aller jusqu'au bout des mots», c'est-à-dire, se passer de paroles—rejeter le côté purement formel du discours comme le vieux pêcheur rejette la nasse, parler en «oubliant les paroles» d'une réalité au-delà des mots[49].

Le *Jin shu* (*jiaozhu* 92, p. 47a) rapporte que le peintre Gu Kaizhi était un fervent admirateur des vers en tétramètres de Ji Kang et les illustrait en images. Il disait toujours: «Il est facile de faire 'sa main qui fait vibrer les cinq cordes', mais difficile de faire 'ses yeux qui suivent le retour des oies sauvages'». Ces deux vers (5 et 6) ont dû fournir un bon sujet au peintre, mais ils font aussi parti de l'atmosphère «mystique» de ce poème. Le *Jin shu* (*jiaozhu* 49, p. 18b) dit que Ji Kang avait des crises pendant lesquelles il «oubliait subitement de rentrer lors de ses randonnées dans les forêts en quête de simples» et que son ami Ruan Ji aussi avait des crises semblables en jouant de la cithare (*Jin shu jiaozhu* 49, p. 1b). Ce poème, après le poème 7, réintroduit le mysticisme dans la méditation du poète, et nous prépare pour le dénouement de la série à venir bientôt.

Bientôt, mais non tout de suite. Le poème suivant, le quinzième, est exclusivement consacré à la description de la solitude du poète dans sa belle retraite au sein de la nature.

15

La nuit silencieuse est calme et fraîche;
  La lune brillante luit sur ma fenêtre.
Une brise légère remue ma robe;
  Mes rideaux retenus par des cordons sont relevés haut.
5 Du bon vin remplit mes coupes,
  Mais il n'y a personne pour se réjouir avec moi.

---

[49] Le *Wen xuan* et d'autres éditions lisent *yu* 與 pour *ke* 可 dans le dernier vers, ce qui le rapprocherait encore davantage de la citation de Zhuangzi.

138

Les cithares grandes et petites sont de la fête,
   Mais qui les jouera avec moi?
Je désire ardemment celui dont je partage les goûts et que j'estime:
10   Son parfum est comme celui des orchidées.
Mais mon bel ami n'est pas là:
   Comment ne pas soupirer sans cesse?

Les scènes de chasse et de randonnées dans la nature sont terminées; la nuit est venue et le poète se trouve seul dans sa chambre, sans doute sur son lit à baldaquin qui servait de salon dans les maisons chinoises avant l'avènement des chaises vers l'an mil de notre ère. Le mysticisme du dernier poème est pour le moment oublié; le poète évoque pour la dernière fois la douleur causée par l'absence de son frère bien-aimé. La citation (vers 7) d'un vers du *Shi jing* 82 sera aussi la dernière allusion au livre canonique. Comme le dit Chen Zuoming, Ji Kang aurait pu s'arrêter là: il n'avait pas besoin des trois poèmes qui suivent. Mais tel n'était pas son dessein; ce poème 15, loin d'être la fin de la série, n'est qu'un intermède. La véritable fin, ce sont les trois poèmes qui suivent où les brèves suggestions de recherche de l'immortalité et du mysticisme apparues dans les poèmes 7 et 14 sont développées, et où la solitude du poète et l'absence de son frère sont presque oubliées. Il ne reste qu'un rappel très subtil à la fin du poème suivant.

16

Monté sur le vent, je m'en vais vers les hauteurs,
   Escaladant, au loin, les montagnes magiques.
Je me lie d'amitié avec Chisongzi et Wangzi Qiao,
   Me promenant avec eux, la main dans la main.
5 Le matin nous partons du mont Taihua
   Et le soir nous faisons étape à Shenzhou.
Pinçant de la cithare, entonnant des poèmes,
   Je peux, pendant un instant, oublier ma tristesse.

Ce poème fait allusion à de nombreux lieux communs dans la «poésie des immortels» de l'époque, puisés dans les *Chu ci*, le *Liexian zhuan* (les immortels Chisongzi et Wangzi Qiao sont étudiés sur les pp. 35-42 et 109-114 de la traduction de M. Kaltenmark) et le *Shanhai jing*. Ji Kang semble choisir un genre d'évasion pour se guérir de sa solitude qu'on trouve souvent chez les littérateurs de cette époque : la promenade dans des pays féeriques avec des immortels et, pour se consoler de ne plus faire partie de la vie active, une cure de cithare et de poésie dans une chaumière[50]. Mais le dernier vers nous apprend que cette retraite ne pouvait calmer ses angoisses que «pendant un instant». Le poème suivant, qui est assez étroitement lié au poème 16 sans qu'ils fassent tout à fait une paire (comme c'était le cas dans les poèmes au début de la série), reprend les éléments de cette évasion, mais sur un autre plan, sur un plan philosophique.

17

La cithare et la poésie peuvent nous réjouir ;
  Les randonnées lointaines sont précieuses.
Je garde le *dao* en moi et j'évolue seul,
  Rejetant toute connaissance, délaissant mon corps.
5 Solitaire et sans attaches,
  Que chercherais-je chez les autres ?
Pendant de longs séjours sur les pics magiques
  J'apporterai le calme à mes désirs et je nourrirai mon esprit.

Les deux premiers vers de ce poème rappellent vaguement les vers 7 et 2 du poème précédent ; Ji Kang continue ici, mais d'une façon très atténuée, de présenter ses poèmes par «paires». Mais autrement ces deux poèmes (et celui qui suit) ressemblent peu aux autres qui composent la série. Ce sont des petits précis de philosophie taoïste où le poète semble avoir oublié toute autre préoccupation. Le vers 3 (en adoptant la leçon 含 de la plupart des éditions contre la leçon 舍 du manuscrit du Congshu tang) rappelle *Laozi* 55, et le vers 4, *Laozi* 19 ; le poème entier prêche le détachement des choses de ce monde cher aux taoïstes et aux esprits religieux de tous temps et tous lieux. La tristesse provoquée par l'absence de son frère semble loin, complètement absorbée par la recherche de la paix de l'âme selon les prescriptions taoïstes.

Le dernier poème se distingue encore plus nettement des autres par sa forme, cinq quatrains, chacun basé sur une rime différente, mais il reste résolument philosophique, développant la pensée de détachement et de renonciation énoncée dans le poème 17.

---

[50] Dongfang Shuo 東方朔(154-93 av. J.-C.), «Feiyou xiansheng lun», *Han shu* 65, p. 2870, est sans doute le modèle pour l'avant-dernier vers.

18

Les gens vulgaires s'éveillent difficilement :
    Ils ne se détournent jamais de leur poursuite des choses matérielles.
Mais l'Homme Parfait regarde au loin :
    Il s'en remet à la spontanéité.
5 Les dix mille êtres sont un,
    Hébergés ensemble dans l'univers.
Si je le partage avec eux,
    Qu'aurais-je encore à regretter ?
La vie est comme un gîte flottant
10   Qui apparaît un moment et subitement s'en va.
Et les affaires du monde sont si embrouillées !
    Rejetons-les aux confins de la terre !
Même affamé, le faisan des marais
    Ne se tourne pas vers les bosquets des parcs.
15 Comment peut-on servir,
    Fatiguer son corps et peiner son cœur ?
Si nous estimons notre personne et méprisons notre renommée,
    Y aura-t-il «gloire» ou «honte» pour nous ?
Ce qui est estimable, c'est de pouvoir donner libre cours à notre volonté,
20   Et libérer notre cœur sans remords !

Ji Kang termine sa longue série de poèmes dans ces cinq quatrains
didactiques en faisant la leçon à son frère. Ayant surmonté sa propre
solitude en s'absorbant dans le *dao* et en partant pour des randonnées
mystiques, il essaie ici d'associer son frère à son mode de vie taoïste,
et surtout de le faire renoncer au monde. Il n'y a rien d'original
dans la philosophie décrite ; elle se trouve à peu près telle quelle
dans le *Zhuangzi*. Ji Kang demande à son frère de se détacher des
choses de ce monde pour qu'il puisse retrouver un état de nature,
de spontanéité, d'apprendre à voir le monde tel qu'il est, face à
l'éternité ou à l'absolu : un amas de quantités et de qualités relatives
que le taoïste sait assimiler à l'Un. Sa recherche de la spontanéité
le fait se détourner de la société des hommes et se concentrer sur
lui-même, sur sa personne, et il termine sa «leçon» en insistant sur
le fait que la liberté qu'on acquiert par son ascèse laisse «sans
remords», content de vivre dans l'anonymat et négligeant totalement
ses devoirs sociaux.

Ces dix-huit poèmes écrits à son frère aîné sont parmi les plus beaux poèmes en tétramètres écrits en Chine après le *Shi jing* et avant Tao Yuanming, peut-être même les plus beaux. Ji Kang a surtout su utiliser la langue du *Shi jing* à ses propres fins, incorporant, comme c'était l'habitude, de grands pans du livre canonique dans ses vers, mais toujours pour que ces citations participent vraiment au poème, pour qu'elles semblent sortir naturellement de la pensée de l'auteur. La variété des poèmes est telle et l'évolution des idées si savamment opérée que le lecteur suit le progrès spirituel comme s'il y participait. Les premiers poèmes sont presque de la musique dans leur réarrangement des vers du *Shi jing*, dans leur symétrie et dans les variations entre les paires de poèmes. L'absence du frère est décrite pour ainsi dire par petites touches placées dans des paysages idéalisés, des paysages «musicaux», tellement les vers semblent chanter. Le progrès du poète procède lentement, avec de nombreux arrêts et détours. Les poèmes les plus célèbres de la série, ceux compris dans le *Wen xuan* (poèmes 9 à 10 et 12 à 16), sont aussi les plus remplis de «beaux vers», du genre estimé par les littérateurs du Moyen Age. Dans tous ces poèmes la nature joue un très grand rôle, presque, mais pas tout à fait, le rôle principal. Le sujet de cette série n'est pas à proprement parler la nature en tant que telle; c'est la séparation de Ji Kang et de son frère. Mais la présence de la nature dans presque chacun des poèmes joue un rôle plus important que celui d'arrière-plan. Elle représente en fait la solution que Ji Kang offre à son frère, dans les trois derniers poèmes, pour se dégager de la vie poli-tique: la pratique de la mystique taoïste, le retour à la spontanéité naturelle (*ziran* 自然). Et la musique, qui joue un rôle à peine moins important dans les poèmes 11 à 15, fait partie intégrante de cette mystique[51]. C'est l'importance de la nature et dans les premiers poèmes et dans la mystique taoïste qui lie les premiers quinze poèmes aux trois derniers, mais il faut avouer que cette liaison n'empêche pas le lecteur de ressentir un petit choc entre le quinzième et le seizième poème et de trouver le dernier d'un didactisme qui jure avec le reste de la série. Ji Kang semble vouloir souligner, par le change-

---

[51] Cf. *La vie et la pensée*, pp. 71-72.

ment abrupt du style—d'un style fortement influencé par le *Shi jing* aux styles influencés par les *Chu ci* dans le poème 16 et par *Laozi* et *Zhuangzi* dans les deux derniers—qu'il décrit un véritable changement en profondeur de ses sentiments, une véritable conversion religieuse. La série ouvre ainsi des perspectives nouvelles, des prolongements religieux insoupçonnés dans les premiers poèmes. Aussi intéressants que ces prolongements puissent être sur le plan de la biographie de Ji Kang, je ne peux m'empêcher de sentir que ce changement subit de style et de ton dans les trois derniers poèmes nuisent considérablement à l'effet esthétique de l'ensemble. Le contraste entre l'art délicat du début de la série et la platitude didactique du dernier poème souligne, cependant, l'importance que Ji Kang attachait à ses recherches religieuses.

Le contraste entre ces trois derniers poèmes et les autres est si grand qu'on pourrait penser qu'ils n'appartiennent pas à cette série. La meilleure preuve du contraire sont les trois poèmes en pentamètres dans lesquels Ji Xi répond à son cadet[52]. Il commence, dans le premier poème, par brosser un paysage qui rappelle ceux des premiers poèmes de Ji Kang, mais son but, en fait, est de répondre à la philosophie décrite dans ces derniers poèmes[53]. Il s'oppose surtout à l'égoïsme qui sous-tend l'attitude de son cadet, à son mépris du monde et de ses valeurs sociales. Il défend les thèses d'une philosophie syncrétiste alors à la mode qui donne une métaphysique taoïste au confucianisme. Selon cette philosophie, qui doit aussi beaucoup au *Yi jing*, l'homme supérieur doit se partager entre sa vie spirituelle (et, à l'occasion, mystique) et sa vie sociale et politique de fonctionnaire impérial. Le tout dépend du «moment», de la «conjoncture»:

[52] Il y avait peut-être à l'origine quatre poèmes de Ji Xi à son frère, trois en pentamètres suivis d'un en tétramètres, mais le quatrième en tétramètres est composé de cinq vers d'un poème (par Ji Xi?) suivis de 15 vers sur une autre rime qui semblent être de Ji Kang lui-même. Luxun soupçonne une faute de copiste qui à la fin d'une page a recommencé deux pages plus tard avec un poème de Ji Kang. Ce poème décrit une randinnée mystique chez les immortels. Voir aussi 2e Partie, ch. 6.

[53] J'ai déjà traduit et commenté ces trois poèmes (*La vie et la pensée*, pp. 22-24. Par erreur le vers 6 du deuxième poème n'a pas été imprimé; il faut lire: «Prospérité et décadence ne sont que deux aspects complémentaires [d'une même réalité]».

On sort dans le monde ou l'on reste chez soi selon les ressources du moment :
Pour se montrer ou se cacher, il n'y a pas de principe fixe.
Il faut préserver son cœur en se maintenant dans le *dao*,
Scruter les transformations du monde, garder son calme tout en sachant
[évoluer[54].

À l'élan mystique et taoïste, Ji Xi répond par le bon sens confucianiste ; à l'émotivité et délicatesse des premiers poèmes de son cadet, par le raisonnement philosophique assez sec et froid. Son caractère, tel qu'il est dépeint dans des anecdotes du *Shishuo xinyu*, semble en effet l'avoir mis dans un autre monde social et intellectuel que celui de Ji Kang. Il a accompli une carrière honorable de fonctionnaire, montant les échelons jusqu'au grade de préfet, tandis que son cadet a toujours refusé de s'engager dans la politique, n'occupant jamais de poste supérieur à celui de Zhongsan dafu, poste honorifique qu'il a reçu lors de son mariage à une princesse impériale des Wei. Les deux frères représentent les deux pôles de l'esprit chinois, mais il faut dire que Ji Xi est bien plus typiquement lettré chinois que son cadet : les esprits aussi totalement, passionnement dévoués à leur salut spirituel que Ji Kang sont très rares.

3

POÈMES D'AMITIÉ

L'œuvre de Ji Kang contient deux autres échanges de poèmes avec des amis, et dans les deux cas nous remarquons le même désaccord dans la pensée des interlocuteurs que nous avons remarqué dans les poèmes de Ji Kang et ceux de son frère. Le premier groupe de poèmes que je traduirai comporte onze poèmes : trois de Guo Xiazhou 郭遐周, cinq de Guo Xiashu 郭遐叔 et trois poèmes de Ji Kang qui répond à ses deux amis. Les deux Guo, sans doute des frères, d'après leurs noms, sont inconnus par ailleurs, mais certains vers dans le premier poème de Ji Kang m'ont fait penser qu'on

---

[54] Il y a sans doute une allusion au *Li ji*, «Qu li», Couvreur 1, p. 2, dans ce dernier vers. Ma traduction de ce vers dans *La vie et la pensée*, p. 24, est erronée.

pouvait dater cet échange de poèmes de 258[55]. La date est discutable, mais elle aide à expliquer certaines allusions cryptiques dans le premier poème de Ji Kang et aussi la fin de son dernier poème. Si ces poèmes ont été écrits vers la fin de la vie de Ji Kang, 258 est presque la seule date possible; s'ils sont plus anciens, alors il est impossible de les dater. C'est vers 258 que Ji Kang est parti en voyage et c'est précisément le départ de Ji Kang, sans doute de sa maison de campagne dans le nord du Henan actuel, qui a été l'occasion pour les frères Guo de lui adresser des poèmes. C'est le troisième vers du premier poème de Guo Xiazhou qui nous apprend que les frères se sont retirés dans le nord.

Trois poèmes présentés par
Guo Xiazhou

1

Sans talents pour aider le monde,
 Et incapable de m'accorder aux mœurs de nos jours,
Je suis revenu dans ce recoin de mes montagnes du nord,
 Pour m'y promener tout à mon aise.
5 Les natures semblables se cherchent spontanément:
 Quand le tigre rugit, le vent de l'est devient frais.
Maître Ji et moi
 Avant même de nous connaître avions clairement les mêmes goûts.
Les anciens admiraient ceux qui se lient d'amitié à la première rencontre;
10 Quel mal y aurait-il à les imiter?
Rapprochant notre cithare *zheng*, prenant notre cithare *qin* mélodieuse,
 La main dans la main, nous nous divertissions dans la pièce vide.
Au repos dans une chaumière rustique,
 Quel besoin aurions-nous eu de belles princesses?
15 Dans notre cœur nous désirions prolonger nos années,
 Et, nos années prolongées, nous pensions au bonheur tranquille.
Mon ami ne finira pas ses jours ici;
 Il a changé ses plans pour s'en aller ailleurs.
La voiture est prête et nous sommes émus par le jour du départ,

---

[55] Voir *La vie et la pensée*, p. 42. Mon hypothèse a été reconnue comme probable par Kôzen Hiroshi₂, pp. 18-19. Dai Mingyang, p. 56, aussi met ces poèmes en rapport avec la fuite de Ji Kang vers le Hedong décrite dans le *Weishi chunqiu* cité dans le *Sanguo zhi jijie* 21, p. 25a.

20   Quand il va s'envoler au loin!
      La séparation aura lieu dans peu de temps:
      Déçu, j'ai de plus en plus de peine.

Dans les premiers quatre vers Guo Xiazhou se définit: c'est un homme qui a quitté le monde politique pour une raison ou une autre — désaccord avec les usurpateurs Sima? manque d'intérêt congénital pour la chose publique? Il appartient à une catégorie bien définie dans l'histoire chinoise: le retraité qui préfère vivre dans l'obscurité plutôt que de se compromettre dans l'arène des affaires politiques. Ces hommes s'expriment souvent dans des termes taoïstes; ils peuvent même être des taoïstes convaincus; mais la plupart du temps ils restent confucianistes bon teint, réalisant, en quelque sorte, la retraite forcée qui caractérise presque toute la vie de Confucius lui-même. Nous verrons, à la fin du troisième poème, que Guo Xiazhou appartient à cette dernière catégorie de confucianiste bon teint, mais dans les vers qui suivent (5-10) il semble vouloir se réclamer de la même chapelle que Ji Kang, ou au moins de se considérer en parfaite harmonie avec lui. Le mot que j'ai traduit par «natures» est en fait *qi*, «souffle, *pneuma, anima*». Guo Xiazhou donne à croire qu'il est de la même étoffe que Ji Kang et qu'ainsi ils ont tendance à s'unir. Le vers 5 est adapté du commentaire «Wen yan» du premier hexagramme du *Yi jing*: «Les notes semblables se répondent; les natures semblables se cherchent» (Legge, p. 411). Le vers 6 est adapté d'une phrase de *Huainanzi* 3, p. 36 (de l'édition Zhuzi jicheng, Pékin, 1954): «Quand le tigre rugit, le vent de l'est arrive», ce que le commentaire de Gao You explique par la théorie des influences réciproques entre les Cinq Éléments: «Le tigre est un être [de l'élément] terre, le vent de l'est, un vent [de l'élément] bois: le bois croît dans la terre. Ainsi, quand le tigre rugit, le vent de l'est arrive». L'idée n'est pas exactement la même que dans le vers précédent: la relation entre Ji Kang et Guo Xiazhou n'est plus considérée comme basée sur leur similitude foncière, mais sur un genre de réciprocité. Les amitiés «de ceux qui se lient à la première rencontre» qu'admiraient les anciens est une allusion à une anecdote qui décrit la première rencontre entre Confucius et un nommé Cheng Benzi de Qi (*Hanshi waizhuan*, Hightower, pp. 54-55). À leur première rencontre les deux hommes sont

VIII

restés dans leurs voitures respectives qu'ils ont rapprochées de façon que les ombrelles se touchent et se penchent, et ils ont bavardé ainsi ensemble toute la journée. Le vers 15 semble montrer que Guo Xiazhou, comme Ji Kang, était un chercheur d'immortalité, ce qui expliquerait, en partie au moins, les atomes crochus dont il fait état plus haut. La fin du poème nous montre que ce sont des poèmes d'adieu, et que Ji Kang, pour quelque raison inexprimée, a «changé ses plans pour s'en aller ailleurs». Comme j'ai suggéré plus haut, il s'agit peut-être de la fuite de Ji Kang vers le Hedong que j'ai datée hypothétiquement de 258.

Le deuxième poème est consacré entièrement aux lamentations sur le départ de Ji Kang.

2

Les poètes attachaient une grande importance aux séparations,
Et s'en allaient très lentement sur la route.
Song Yu était triste de monter sur la montagne
Pour regarder vers la rivière et prendre congé [d'un ami] qui retournait chez lui.
5 A! parler de ces hommes du passé
Ne fait qu'accroître ma douleur!
Je soupire: moi et le maître Ji
Dans un instant nous serons séparés pour longtemps.
En bas j'observe les poissons qui jouent dans les profondeurs;
10 Et en haut je regarde les oiseaux volant par paires.
[Ceux-ci] battent vite leurs ailes dans la Grande Pureté;
[Ceux-là] errent çà et là dans l'Étang de Cinabre.
Prenez respectueusement votre place,
Même si cela me contrarie dans mon cœur.
15 La séparation aura lieu dans un instant:
Je me sens affamé, comme si j'attendais mon repas du matin.

Il y a des échos des «poètes» dont il est question dans le premier vers dans tout le poème: le deuxième vers est adapté du *Shi jing* 35, les deux suivants le sont du début des «Jiu bian» attribués à Song Yu (*Chu ci*, Hawkes, p. 92), et le vers 14 rappelle encore le poème *Shi jing* 35 (deuxième vers de la deuxième strophe). Le dernier vers, enfin, est adapté du *Shi jing* 10. Ces souvenirs poétiques ne font qu'accroître la tristesse de Guo Xiazhou. Dans les vers 9 à 12 il se tourne vers la nature et admire la répartition spontanée des animaux, chacun à sa place. Les vers 11 et 12 exaltent cette répartition sur un plan idéal, la Grande Pureté (cf. *supra*, p. 123) et l'Étang de Cinabre (cf. Dan shui 丹水, *Shanhai jing* 2, p. 4a) étant des lieux mystiques ou mythiques. Le vers 13 fait apparaître la morale : face à ces répartitions naturelles du monde animal Guo Xiazhou demande, à Ji Kang de se soumettre lui aussi à l'ordre naturel et d'y «prendre sa place» s'il le faut. Mais cela ne l'empêchera pas de s'y opposer dans son cœur et de se lamenter de leur séparation.

Dans le troisième et dernier poème il fait appel à la morale confucianiste pour sécher ses larmes.

3

Les hommes se sont séparés depuis l'antiquité :
Ils ne sont pas des poissons jumeaux.
L'homme supérieur n'est pas attaché à son terroir :
Encore moins trouverait-il la paix dans sa demeure.
5 Tous en dedans les Quatre Mers sont frères :
Pourquoi craindre de manquer d'amis agréables?
Fu Yue s'est caché dans les grottes des précipices ;
Les poulains blancs sont entrés dans la vallée vide.
Les hommes se rassemblent selon leur mode de vie,
10 Et les autres êtres se différencient aussi selon leur espèce.
Là où l'on se trouve il y a des hommes sages et dignes :
Pourquoi s'inquiéter que ceux-là ne vaudront pas ceux-ci?
Ce qui importe, c'est que votre renom subsiste,
Que vos belles actions figurent dans les registres!
15 Les années passent si facilement ;
Les jours et les mois sont partis en un clin d'œil!
Courage, maître Ji!
Avec révérence et vertu, soyez prudent de votre personne!

Alors que dans son deuxième poème Guo Xiazhou sent sa douleur ravivée à la pensée des séparations décrites par les anciens, ici le fait que les hommes se sont séparés depuis l'antiquité semble le soulager. Les «poissons jumeaux» sont des poissons décrits dans le *Er ya* qui n'ont qu'un seul œil et qui doivent s'associer avec un compagnon pour pouvoir nager. Le troisième vers cite le *Lun yu* 4, 11, et le quatrième contredit *Laozi* 80. Le cinquième vers est encore une citation partielle du *Lun yu* 12, 5. Fu Yue 傅説, dans le vers 7, était

un saint de la haute antiquité qui vivait dans une grotte dans un
défilé où il travaillait comme cantonnier en servitude pénale. Le roi
des Yin, Wuding, qui l'avait vu en rêve, l'a pris comme premier
ministre (*Shi ji* 3, p. 102). Le vers 8 fait allusion à *Shi jing* 186,
interprété traditionnellement comme un poème satirique décrivant
des hommes sages, dédaignés par leur souverain, qui quittent la vie
publique et se retirent, montés sur des «poulains blancs». Les deux
vers suivants (9 et 10) sont presque mot à mot du *Yi jing*, «Xi ci» A
(Legge, p. 348). Ces vers, comme ceux qui suivent, essaient de montrer
le peu d'importance qu'il faut attacher au lieu où l'on se trouve:
tout ce qui importe vraiment (vers 13 et 14) c'est que nous nous
fassions un renom durable, que nos actions figurent sur les registres
(*jianshu* 簡書, «fiches de bambou», terme qui se trouve dans *Shi
jing* 168, et dont le sens exact n'est pas sûr: «rapports de service»
peut-être, ou «commandes impériales»?). Et Guo Xiazhou termine
en demandant à Ji Kang d'être prudent, pressentant peut-être que le
franc-parler de son ami allait lui valoir des ennuis.

Les vers 13 et 14 montrent que Guo Xiazhou est un vrai confucianiste, et ce sont ces vers que Ji Kang va mettre en question dans
les vers 15 et 16 de son dernier poème aux frères Guo. Il n'y a pas
de contradiction entre les désirs affichés par Guo Xiazhou de «prolonger ses années» (poème 1, vers 15) et ces sentiments confucianistes
exprimés ici: la recherche de la Longue Vie, avec toute l'hygiène
taoïste qui l'accompagne, est entrée profondément dans les mœurs
chinoises et même ceux qui ne croient pas à l'existence de cette
Longue Vie et sont hostiles au taoïsme en tant que tel ont adopté
bien des procédés des chercheurs de la Longue Vie taoïste pour
tâcher au moins de prolonger leur vie, sinon d'atteindre à l'immortalité.

Les cinq poèmes de Guo Xiashu sont bâtis sur le même plan que
ceux de son frère présumé: les quatre premiers, en tétramètres cette
fois-ci, chantent, avec un peu plus de chaleur, l'amour qu'il porte à
Ji Kang, et le dernier, en pentamètres, recherche une consolation
philosophique. L'avant-dernier vers des quatre premiers poèmes est
toujours le même: «La tristesse de mon cœur», et chacun des poèmes
contient le vers «Avec quelle rapidité».

Cinq poèmes présentés par
Guo Xiashu

1

Je pense constamment à vous rencontrer,
    Mais les journées sont trop courtes.
L'aube s'en va et le soir revient,
    Et je souffre toujours qu'ils passent si vite.
5 Le bonheur de nous voir était chaque fois renouvelé
    Comme les rivières qui se jettent dans la vallée.
Avec quelle rapidité
    Partez-vous pour d'autres contrées!
Le jour pour l'attelage est fixé,
10   La voiture parée, le groom commandé.
Je pense à vous,
    Parfait comme le jade,
Et la tristesse de mon cœur
    Me fait voir le rouge comme si c'était du vert!

La forme tétramétrique appelle naturellement la citation du *Shi jing*, comme nous l'avons déjà remarqué à propos des poèmes écrits au frère de Ji Kang. Ce poème de Guo Xiashu n'enfreint pas la règle: le deuxième vers vient du *Shi jing* 166; le neuvième vers rappelle *Shi jing* 39; et les vers 11 et 12 viennent de *Shi jing* 128 (la citation est mot à mot si l'on reconstitue le premier caractère d'après la forme primitive du manuscrit du Congshu tang). Le mot *wen* 溫, qui veut dire d'ordinaire «chaleureux, doux, aimable» est traduit «parfait» d'après la tradition exégétique pour ce passage du *Shi jing*. Selon Chen Zuoming, le dernier vers est très original; l'avant-dernier vers (vers 13), qui est répété dans les quatre poèmes en tétramètres, est textuellement du *Shi jing* 27.

Le deuxième poème, qui ne comporte que dix vers, alors que les trois autres poèmes en tétramètres comportent 14 et 16 vers, semble, selon Luxun et Dai Mingyang, être tronqué de quelques vers au début du poème.

2

Avec quelle rapidité
    Allez-vous nous quitter pour votre randonnée lointaine!

150

J'en éprouve de la crainte
  Et ne fais qu'y penser, de m'en attrister.
5 Je m'agite [dans mon sommeil], me tournant et me retournant,
  Veillant et dormant je vous cherche.
Mes pensées courent dans tous les sens;
  Mon esprit s'en va; mon corps reste ici.
La tristesse de mon cœur!
10 Comme mon affliction s'accroît!

Les vers 5 et 6 sont, à un caractère près, des citations exactes de *Shi jing* 1. Ces deux premiers poèmes ne font que réitérer avec chaleur la douleur du poète causée par le départ de son ami. Les deux qui suivent continuent dans cette voie, mais nous commençons à y voir poindre la philosophie consolatrice qui occupera le dernier poème tout entier.

3

Quand l'homme ne voit pas de choses désirables
  Son cœur n'est pas agité.
C'était ainsi dans la Création entière
  Qui ne comportait pas de bornes jusqu'à ses extrémités.
5 Mais une fois les fiefs départagés et les frontières fixées
  Les hommes se sont affairés après le gain et livrés aux contestations.
Vous et moi
  Ne sommes pas originaires du même pays,
Mais nous attachons grand prix à nos relations et sommes liés par nos sentiments,
10 Voulant nous revoir d'innombrables fois!
Avec quelle rapidité
  Vous partez vers une autre demeure!
Le jour point sans que je dorme,
  Éveillé jusqu'à l'aube.
15 La tristesse de mon cœur!
  Comme ma douleur et mes regrets s'accroissent!

Les six premiers vers de ce poème sont un peu déconcertants. Guo Xiashu semble vouloir décrire l'état d'unité primitive du cosmos, tant aimé par les taoïstes, pour minimiser ensuite le fait que Ji Kang et lui étaient d'origines provinciales différentes (vers 8). Les deux premiers vers sont presque mot à mot du *Laozi* 3 (Dai Mingyang croit qu'ils sont mot à mot et que le texte actuel du *Laozi*, qui ajoute le mot *min* 民 au deuxième vers, est tardif). Les vers qui suivent décrivent la destruction de l'unité primitive du monde par l'érection de frontières feudataires, la cible des désirs humains décriés dans les premiers vers. Ma traduction du huitième vers comprend le mot *guan* 貫 comme *xiangguan* 鄉貫, sens qui n'est attesté que sous les Tang, autant que je sache, alors que le binom *tongguan* 同貫 utilisé ici est courant au IIIᵉ siècle pour désigner des hommes «du même rang» ou «qualité». Peut-être que Guo Xiashu veut simplement souligner la spontanéité de ses relations avec Ji Kang, qui fait fi des différences superficielles ou mondaines qu'il peut y avoir entre les deux hommes: leur amitié est comme le monde à l'âge d'or, dépourvue de toute sophistication. Ils sont liés par la simple attirance de leurs sentiments, sans complications sociales. La fin de ce poème contient encore de nombreuses allusions au *Shi jing*: le vers 12 rappelle *Shi jing* 75; le vers 13 est mot à mot de *Shi jing* 196; et le vers 14 rappelle *Shi jing* 26[56].

Le quatrième poème commence encore avec des considérations philosophiques et se termine en lamentations passionnées[57].

4

Le ciel et la terre sont éternels,
    La vie de l'homme éphémère.
Si l'on ne connaît pas son destin,
    On ne peut se protéger, même l'espace d'un instant.
5 J'avais pensé qu'avec vous
    J'allais finir mes jours.
Nous nous serions divertis heureux,
    Par bonheur sans accidents.
Avec quelle rapidité
10   Allez-vous nous quitter pour votre voyage lointain!
Je sens mes sentiments se bloquer en moi,
    Mes paroles se figer dans ma bouche.

[56] Luxun et Dai Mingyang prétendent que le manuscrit du Congshu tang donne la leçon *tan* 歎 pour le dernier mot; le microfilm du manuscrit que je possède donne *yuan* 怨 comme toutes les éditions imprimées (à la p. 10b du manuscrit).

[57] Le neuvième vers est traduit en suivant la suggestion de Luxun; le texte dans toutes les versions donnerait: «Pourquoi [allez-]vous», sans doute une répétition automatique par un scribe du mot «vous» (*junzi* 君子) du vers 5. Les rimes de ce poème sont si étranges qu'il doit y avoir de nombreuses corruptions textuelles.

La tristesse de mon cœur!
 Comme je suis affligé!

Le cinquième et dernier poème est tout entier consacré à la philosophie. Le poète sublime sa douleur dans un rappel des convenances et des bonnes manières. La forme pentamétrique, venant à la suite de quatre poèmes tétramétriques, confère un caractère de conclusion définitive à ces vers.

5

Les hommes de bien dans leurs relations se plient aux convenances:
 Ils ne doivent pas se suivre constamment.
Il y a un ordre apparent dans l'univers
 Qui reste le même où que l'on soit.
5 Les Trois Vertueux [des Shang] n'alignèrent pas leurs traces:
 Ils sont estimables pour avoir égalé les exemples des Sages.
Les oiseaux qui volent en bande se poursuivent les uns les autres;
 L'oiseau de proie va seul, sans compagne.
Quel besoin avons-nous de nous humecter les uns les autres
10   Quand nous pouvons nous laisser aller tout à notre aise dans les fleuves et
                                                          [les mers?
Espérons que nous nous préserverons pendant de longues années
 Et, quand l'occasion se présentera, que vous reviendrez ici, à l'est.

Ce poème semble être divisé en deux parties, la première inspirée par Confucius et le confucianisme, la dernière par Zhuangzi et le taoïsme. L'unité morale dans la diversité du monde est illustrée dans la première partie du poème par l'allusion (vers 5) au *Lun yu* 18, 1, à propos des Trois Vertueux, trois parents du tyran Zhou 紂, le dernier empereur des Shang. L'un de ces parents est devenu son esclave, un autre a fui et le troisième a été tué par Zhou parce qu'il l'avait critiqué. Selon Confucius, «les trois hommes étaient vertueux». On peut accomplir le bien partout: quel besoin avons-nous de rester collés les uns aux autres? Et Guo Xiashu console son ami en invoquant un auteur qu'il savait que Ji Kang aimait par-dessus tous, Zhuangzi. Dans le sixième chapitre de son livre (Watson, p. 80) Zhuangzi, voulant montrer que nous devons être libres de toute entrave, et des autres, décrit les poissons qui «quand les sources se sèchent, se trouvent ensemble sur la terre et se mettent à s'humecter les uns les autres avec l'humidité qui les entoure, et à se mouiller avec leur bave. Il vaudrait mieux qu'ils s'oublient dans les fleuves et les lacs». Cet emploi des deux philosophies antiques, confucianisme et taoïsme côte à côte, est typique du milieu dans lequel Ji Kang a vécu. Il faut croire, aussi, que c'était une habitude, dans son milieu, de s'adresser des cycles de poèmes où s'exprimaient tour à tour l'amitié passionnée avec la tristesse des séparations, et la philosophie qui remet les choses en place. C'est ainsi que Ji Kang s'était adressé à son frère, que celui-ci lui a répondu, et que les deux Guo écrivent dans les poésies qu'on vient de lire.

Les trois poèmes dans lesquels Ji Kang répond aux deux Guo sont tous en pentamètres. Ils sont à la fois plus difficiles, plus obscurs que ceux des deux Guo, et plus instructifs. Ji Kang se livre à nous d'une façon plus personnelle, et c'est peut-être pourquoi ses poèmes sont tellement plus difficiles à lire. Les vers 11 à 16 en particulier sont presque incompréhensibles dans le contexte du poème, et des variantes très importantes dans les vers 2 et 11 montrent qu'une partie au moins de nos difficultés pourrait venir d'une corruption textuelle.

Trois poèmes en réponse
aux deux Guo

1

La masse des gens de l'empire
    Courent d'une capitale à l'autre,
Mais les deux Guo sentent bien qu'ils ne font pas partie de la foule
    Et s'en sont détachés pour venir dans le nord.
5 Ils prennent leur joie dans le *dao*, demeurant dans une humble chaumière;
    Aspirant vers un but supérieur, rien ne les trouble.
À un moment propice, répondant à leurs désirs,
    Nous nous sommes liés d'une joyeuse amitié.
L'homme de bien approuve cette fraternité,
10   Et fait en sorte que son affection résiste à l'épreuve toute la vie.
S'il manquait de volonté [dans son amitié], la catastrophe serait sûre de venir,
    Et amènerait de nombreuses brèches [dans ses relations].
Yuzi s'est caché à côté du pont;
    Nie Zheng a transformé son corps.

15 Réfléchir à leur exemple rend triste et craintif,
   Et fait penser à se tenir tranquille tant bien que mal.
   Maintenant je dois séjourner dans une autre région;
   Ma voiture préparée ne peut plus attendre.
   Mon plan initial était de jouir des charmes de votre compagnie jusqu'à la fin,
20 Mais maintenant nous ne pourrons plus nous réunir.
   Vous deux m'avez envoyé de beaux poèmes
   Dont le parfum est comme celui que l'orchidée cachée répand au loin.
   J'aime mon terroir et ceux qui me sont chers:
   Comment pourrai-je ne pas me laisser envahir par l'émotion?

Les difficultés commencent avec le premier vers. Le terme *youyou* 悠悠 provient à l'origine du *Lun yu* 18, 6 (dans la version de Lu le terme est écrit *taotao* 滔滔) et décrit l'activité désordonnée et confuse des gens ordinaires, du commun des mortels engagés dans la vie de tous les jours. Le terme est péjoratif. Le deuxième vers se lit, littéralement, «De la capitale inférieure, ils se précipitent vers la capitale supérieure». Mais on ne connaît pas d'usage sous les Wei des termes «capitales inférieure et supérieure». Une variante du manuscrit du Congshu tang donne «Ne se dirigent pas vers la capitale supérieure». Ce qui a encore moins de sens dans le contexte[58]. En suivant cette interprétation, les 10 premiers vers ne posent pas de problème: ils décrivent la communauté d'esprit établie entre Ji Kang et ses deux nouveaux amis. Mais que doit on faire des six vers suivants? Le vers 11 contient une variante importante: le mot «volonté», *zhi* 志, est écrit par un homophone, 智, qui veut dire «connaissances», dans le manuscrit du Congshu tang. Le mot «manquait», *gua* 寡, me semble aussi être écrit par un autre caractère dans la version originale du manuscrit (*xuan* 宣?, «promulguer, faire montre de»). J'ai choisi la leçon des textes imprimés parce que je crois que

---

[58] Kôzen Hiroshi₂, pp. 18-19, adopte cette leçon, mais lit *youyouzhe* comme un terme flatteur: «des hommes qui n'ont pas d'intérêt pour [les affaires vulgaires]». Il défend son interprétation en faisant allusion au «Yangsheng lun» de Ji Kang (*La vie et la pensée*, p. 90, où j'ai traduit «homme ordinaire»). Le terme apparaît encore dans le poème «Shu zhi» (Dai, p. 35) où il a aussi un sens péjoratif (2ᵉ Partie, ch. 5). Le terme *youyou tan* 悠悠談 a connu une certaine vogue sous les Jin. Tao Yuanming s'en sert dans le douzième de ses «Yinjiu shi» où J. R. Hightower traduit «pointless talk» (*The poetry of T'ao Ch'ien*, Oxford, 1970, p. 142), ce qui souligne assez le caractère péjoratif du terme.

Ji Kang ici met l'emphase sur l'importance de la volonté, comme il le fait au début de son «Jia jie» 家誡, «Préceptes familiaux» (édition Dai, p. 315): si l'on veut garder intact son amitié, il faut en avoir la volonté. C'est le sens des allusions dans les vers 13 et 14 à Yu Rang 豫讓 et à Nie Zheng 聶政, deux «spadassins» (ceke 刺客) *
dont les vies sont décrites dans *Shi ji* 86 et dans le *Zhanguo ce* (Crump, n°s 232 et 383). Ces deux héros ont perdu leur vie en essayant de venger leurs maîtres—des maîtres qui ont gagné leur affection parce qu'ils les ont traités en intimes. Yu Rang a été découvert alors qu'il se cachait sous un pont en attendant le passage de l'ennemi de son maître décédé; Nie Zheng, après avoir vengé son maître en tuant un grand nombre de personnes, s'est tailladé le visage et le corps avant de se donner la mort pour ne pas être reconnu et entraîner ainsi la mort de sa famille. Mais il faut avouer que ces allusions sont un peu violentes si le but de Ji Kang est simplement d'exprimer sa fidélité aux deux Guo. L'évocation de ces deux spadassins morts pour leurs maîtres ne peut que faire penser à une allusion politique, à l'attitude de Ji Kang lui-même face aux injustices que ses propres «maîtres» (les souverains des Wei, à qui il était allié par le mariage) subissaient de la main des usurpateurs Sima (Chen Zuoming). S'il s'agit en effet d'une allusion politique, elle est très, très rare dans l'œuvre poétique de Ji Kang. Son départ mystérieux de cette retraite nordiste s'expliquerait aussi pour des raisons politiques. Tout cela n'est qu'une hypothèse, mais une hypothèse très séduisante. L'avant-dernier vers contient un réponse à la fois à Guo Xiazhou (troisième poème, troisième vers) et une critique de Confucius (*Lun yu* 4, 11): Ji Kang est attaché à son terroir, et à ses amis, et répugne à les quitter.

Le deuxième poème reste très personnel et commence par des précisions autobiographiques que nous verrons développées dans d'autres poèmes.

2

Jadis j'ai reçu des bienfaits de mon père et frère aîné,
    Et, tout jeune, je n'ai pas eu de fardeaux à porter.
Épargné ainsi, je suis devenu tout à fait paresseux
    Et je suis venu me cacher dans un recoin de ces montagnes du nord.

VIII

156

5 Mon seul désir était de nourrir ma nature et mon destin
Et rester jusqu'à la fin de mes jours sans m'engager autrement.
Le temps ne m'a pas été favorable :
À la force de l'âge j'ai été exposé à la vie de luxe et de splendeur.
Timidement je me suis approché des usages du monde,
10   Constamment apeuré d'être embrouillé dans ses filets.
Fuxi et Shennong sont déjà loin de nous ;
Je m'en bats la poitrine de douleur et soupire seul.
Dongfang Shuo a conseillé [à son fils] d'attacher du prix [à un poste où] il
[pouvait se caser ;
Le vieux pêcheur aimait soulever les vagues [boueuses du monde].
15 Mais, se laisser aller [comme eux] a ses difficultés aussi,
Et mon cœur rejette de le faire.
Comme ce serait mieux de planer dans les airs en dehors des frontières,
De grignoter le beau jade et de rincer la bouche avec les vapeurs roses de
[l'aube !
Je laisserais derrière moi les choses matérielles, me débarrassant des liens vils,
20   Me promenant tout à mon aise dans la Grande Harmonie.
Nous nous rassemblerions entre amis sur les pics magiques
Pinçant de la cithare, chantant des chansons pures.
Les hommes qui savent vivre ainsi
Méritent mieux nos louanges que les Anciens !

Ji Kang attachait beaucoup d'importance au fait que son éducation enfantine avait été très libérale, et il lui attribuait ses penchants
taoïstes et ses désirs de mener une vie «naturelle» ou «spontanée»[59],
comme il le fait au début de ce poème. Les sentiments exprimés,
ses désirs de «nourrir sa nature» et de rester «sans s'engager», sont
tous bien taoïstes. Les vers 7 à 10 nous apprennent, pour la première
fois, je pense, dans son œuvre, que Ji Kang a été tenté par la vie
mondaine[60]. Il ne peut y avoir de doute qu'il y ait été exposé, étant
donné son rang dans la société et ses relations avec la famille régnante,
mais nulle part ailleurs ne parle-t-il de «s'être approché», même
«timidement», de la vie mondaine. Les vers 11 à 16, qui suivent
immédiatement cette confession, présentent une série d'alternatives

[59] Il développe les mêmes idées dans sa lettre à Shan Tao (Dai, p. 117 ; *La vie
et la pensée*, pp. 13-14) et dans son dernier poème (Dai, pp. 26-27, 2e Partie, ch. 5).
[60] He Qimin 何啓民, *Zhulin qixian yanjiu* (Taipei, 1966), pp. 72-73, cite ces vers
pour montrer les raisons qui, selon lui, ont fait que Ji Kang a changé sa pensée du
confucianisme au taoïsme.

à la vie mondaine. Fuxi et Shennong, tous les deux héros de l'âge d'or, semblent représenter cette période de bonheur idéal chantée à la fois par les confucianistes et les taoïstes. Ji Kang se lamente de ne plus vivre à cette période de simplicité naturelle dans le vers 12. Que faut-il faire, de nos jours, pour survivre dans une société corrompue? Dongfang Shuo, célèbre figure à la cour de l'empereur Wu des Han (157-87 av. J.-C.), avait perfectionné un mode de vie qui lui permettait de garder à la fois son franc-parler et sa tête en dissimulant ses paroles sous une forme de badinage rempli d'énigmes et de plaisanteries. Ses conseils à son fils sont préservés par Yang Xiong (*Fa yan* 11, p. 36, de l'édition Zhuzi jicheng; *Han shu* 65, p. 2874) et Ji Kang a consacré un poème entier à Dongfang Shuo (2ᵉ Partie, ch. 4). Le vieux pêcheur, dans le vers suivant (14), est le héros d'un petit opuscule dans les *Chu ci* (Hawkes, pp. 90-91). Il conseille à Qu Yuan, qui se plaint d'être souillé par un monde boueux, d'«évoluer avec le monde./ Si le monde est boueux, pourquoi ne pas l'aider à remuer la boue et à soulever les vagues?». Dongfang Shuo et le vieux pêcheur recommandent tous les deux un genre de modus vivendi dans la société où l'on peut se cacher en dissimulant ses vrais sentiments (Dongfang Shuo) ou participer soi-même à la corruption ambiante, sans trop s'en faire (le vieux pêcheur). Les vers 15 et 16 rejettent la solution de ces deux figures, non seulement parce qu'elle «a ses difficultés aussi», mais parce que Ji Kang la considère (vers 17 et suivant) comme d'un autre ordre que la retraite spirituelle et mystique qu'il prône dans presque tous ses poèmes. Il ne faut pas croire que Ji Kang est ici en train d'évoquer des exemples antiques pour le plaisir d'allonger un peu son poème. Les exemples qu'il cite, les alternatives qu'il pose sont autant de problèmes vitaux qui se présentaient à lui dans sa vie réelle, et à tant de ses contemporains. Son ami Ruan Ji, par exemple, a joué un peu le rôle de Dongfang Shuo dans ses rapports avec les usurpateurs Sima, et les deux Guo semblent avoir opté pour l'abandon pur et simple de la société. Ji Kang a posé le même genre de problèmes dans un autre écrit, le «Divination pour résoudre des doutes», «Bu yi» 卜疑 (Dai, pp. 134-142), où il passe en revue toutes les possibilités qui s'offraient à l'homme de la classe dirigeante de son époque (la nostalgie pour les héros de l'antiquité

Fuxi et Shennong y est aussi évoquée; Dai, p. 138). Comme dans cet écrit, dans ce poème Ji Kang ne choisit pas, ou plutôt il choisit en s'élevant, par un saut mystique qui nous est devenue familier, vers un domaine spirituel décrit dans des termes empruntés des *Chu ci* et du *Zhuangzi*. À quel point est-ce une véritable prise de position religieuse? À quel point est-ce, comme le soutient Chen Zuoming, une façon de «fausser ses vrais sentiments» (qui seraient de servir la dynastie légitime) pour exprimer son mécontentement par allégorie? Ignorons ce problème pour le moment, et constatons encore que Ji Kang déclare, ostensiblement au moins, qu'une vie de contemplation mystique est préférable à l'engagement politique ou social. Les deux derniers vers vont même plus loin, et placent les adeptes du mysticisme taoïste au-dessus même des grands saints de l'antiquité, une prise de position qui choquerait chez un auteur moins non-conformiste que Ji Kang.

Dans le troisième et dernier poème Ji Kang décrit le monde décadent dans lequel nous vivons, en insistant, comme il le fait si souvent, sur les dangers qui le remplissent.

3

Regardez de près les affaires de ce monde en décadence:
   Difficultés, dangers; tristesse et anxiété partout.
Les hommes agissent donnant-donnant, par marchandages toujours renouvelés:
   Le grand *dao* se cache et ne se montre plus.
5 La route plate est plantée de ronces:
   Comment pourrait-on s'y promener en sécurité?
Les stratèges rivalisent entre eux:
   Renommée et position ne sont pas durables.
Le phénix évite les filets
10   Et perche au loin sur les monts Kunlun.
Zhuang Zhou compatissait avec la tortue divine;
   Sou de Yue craignait la voiture royale.
L'Homme Parfait préserve ce qu'il y a en lui-même;
   Il cache sa nature foncière et jouit du Vide Mystérieux.
15 Mérite et renommée ne valent pas la peine que nous nous sacrifions pour eux,
   Pour nous voir inscrits sur les registres!
Ainsi nos goûts sont clairs:
   Il y a de quoi faire soupirer Yang Zhu aux croisements des chemins!
Allez, allez! suivons chacun notre ambition!
20   J'ose vous quitter: nos voies ne sont pas les mêmes!

Les premiers six vers de ce poème nous décrivent le monde après l'âge d'or, un monde où l'innocence primordiale a été remplacée par l'esprit de compétition, de gain et de perte, de «réciprocité», qui est restée une des pierres de touche de l'activité sociale chinoise[61]. Les hommes de l'âge d'or connaissaient intuitivement «le grand *dao*» parce qu'ils regardaient le monde à travers un genre de stupeur unificatrice, ne voyant plus les contingences; ils vivaient «dans le *dao*». Mais toutes les distinctions, tous les marchandages entre ce qui est à moi et ce qui est à toi, ont caché le *dao*. Tout ce qui reste, c'est une route, une route plate, peut-être, mais sur laquelle nous trouvons mille embûches, des piquants pour arrêter notre progrès paisible, des ruses et des complots pour rendre toute véritable réussite sociale durable impossible. Le phénix, oiseau noble, sert encore de symbole à Ji Kang pour l'homme supérieur qui sait se cacher d'un monde rempli de dangers, et trois citations de Zhuangzi viennent renforcer ses idées. Zhuangzi plaignait la tortue divine, dont la carapace servait à la divination et faisait partie du trésor de Chu pendant trois mille ans. Il savait que cette gloire posthume ne lui servait à rien et que la tortue aurait été bien plus héureuse loin de la cour, «traînant sa queue dans la boue» (*Zhuangzi* 17, Watson, p. 188). Le prince de Yue, Sou (substituant, avec Dai Mingyang et d'autres, 搜 pour le 稷 du texte), s'est caché dans la grotte de cinabre plutôt que de monter sur le trône où ses trois prédécesseurs sont morts assassinés. Retrouvé par ses sujets, avant de monter dans la voiture royale envoyée pour le ramener, «il a regardé vers le ciel en criant: 'Un souverain? Un souverain? N'y a-t-il que moi qu'on ne puisse laisser de côté?'» (*Zhuangzi* 28, Watson, p. 311). Le prince de Yue savait, comme les Hommes Parfaits dont parle Zhuangzi, qu'il faut «d'abord préserver ce qu'il y a en soi-même avant de le préserver chez les autres» (*Zhuangzi* 4, Watson, p. 54). Dans toutes ces citations Zhuangzi nous apprend l'importance primordiale que nous devons à nous-mêmes: non seulement pour éviter les dangers du monde extérieur, mais pour cultiver ce que nous appellerions notre «vie spirituelle» (vers 14).

[61] Cf. Yang Lien-sheng, «The concept of *'pao'* as a basis for social relations in China», in J. K. Fairbank, ed., *Chinese thought and institutions*, Chicago, 1957, pp. 291-309.

VIII

Ji Kang rejette la recommandation de Guo Xiazhou (poème 3, vers 14, *supra*, p. 147) dans son vers 16 et puis constate que ses goûts diffèrent de ceux des deux Guo. Il fait allusion au célèbre soupir de Yang Zhu qui s'afflige de voir le nombre infini de voies qu'un homme peut prendre dans la vie—pour se perdre, car le Vrai Chemin est unique (*Liezi* 8, traduction Graham, pp. 173-174). Et dans les deux derniers vers Ji Kang congédie ses amis de naguère d'une façon qu'on ne peut qualifier que de brutale. Est-ce un cas aigu de ce phénomène de dénouement philosophique sec et froid que nous avons constaté à la fin des autres poèmes entre Ji Kang et ses amis? Ou est-ce une véritable rupture que Ji Kang essaie de provoquer? Les deux Guo se sont révélés, à la fin de leurs séries de poèmes, de vrais confucianistes, désireux de se faire un renom, malgré leur «fuite» de la vie politique, et c'est, ostensiblement au moins, ce désir foncier que Ji Kang condamne dans ces derniers vers. Mais nous avons vu que, dans son premier poème, Ji Kang suggère, d'une façon voilée, et dans des vers qui montrent malheureusement des signes de corruption textuelle, qu'il reste fidèle à la maison des Wei, qu'il pense avec effroi aux exemples sanglants d'hommes qui ont donné leur vie pour venger leur maître. Peut-être qu'il faut voir, dans la rupture abrupte à la fin de ce dernier poème, un essai fait par Ji Kang pour dissocier ses amis de ses propres plans séditieux, comme sa lettre rompant les relations avec Shan Tao semble être écrite pour blanchir ce dernier qui est, en fait, resté son intime jusqu'à la mort, et même au-delà de la mort puisque c'est à Shan Tao que Ji Kang a confié son jeune fils lors de son exécution. Mais ce ne sont là que des hypothèses. La rupture d'amitié pour des différends philosophiques ou même scientifiques n'est que trop fréquente dans l'histoire et dans le monde où nous vivons. Peut-être Ji Kang trouve-t-il vraiment qu'il est impossible de s'associer avec des hommes aussi bien pensants que les deux Guo. Mais la suggestion d'un engagement politique par Ji Kang dans le premier poème est à souligner, même si elle est hypothétique: ce serait la seule fois dans toute son œuvre poétique qu'il ferait montre d'un quelconque intérêt aux querelles dynastiques qui secouaient son époque.

Le troisième échange de poèmes dans l'œuvre de Ji Kang nous montre un personnage un peu mieux connu (mais à peine) que les deux Guo. Il s'agit de Ruan Kan 阮侃, *zi* Deru 德如, un membre du clan Ruan dont est issu le grand poète Ruan Ji, autre ami de Ji Kang. Il était connu comme «un homme de talent, habile dans la conversation philosophique (*mingli*), raffiné et cultivé. Ami de Ji Kang, son poste officiel le plus élevé a été celui de préfet du Henei [la partie du Henan actuel au nord du fleuve Jaune, où se trouvait la maison de campagne de Ji Kang]»[62]. Il est dit aussi que «le 20 juillet 281, un moineau blanc ayant été vu deux fois dans le Henei, à Nanyang, Ruan Kan l'a fait attraper pour le présenter à l'empereur»[63]. Mais l'œuvre la plus importante de Ruan Kan qui reste aujourd'hui est composée de deux essais qui font partie d'un débat philosophique avec Ji Kang[64]. Ruan Kan a commencé la discussion par un essai contre la géomancie appelé «Le choix d'une habitation n'a aucun effet, heureux ou néfaste, sur l'entretien de la vie». Cet essai est suivi d'une critique de Ji Kang, d'une contre critique de Ruan Kan et d'une dernière réponse de Ji Kang. Ostensiblement, Ruan Kan semble être un rationaliste en lutte contre les superstitions vulgaires et, en fait, ses attaques sont très pertinentes, très «modernes». Mais très vite on s'aperçoit qu'il ne s'agit pas, au fond, d'être pour ou contre la géomancie ou les superstitions populaires: Ruan Kan et Ji Kang en fait s'opposent sur le problème du fatalisme et du libre arbitre. Pour Ruan Kan la géomancie n'a pas d'effet sur notre vie parce que celle-ci est réglée étroitement par le destin (*ming* 命) que

[62] Le *Chenliu zhiming* cité dans *Shishuo xinyu* 19, p. 20a.
[63] *Song shu* 29, p. 841; le «Nanyang» du *Song shu* doit être une erreur pour Heyang ou Shanyang, ce dernier étant le lieu où se trouvait la maison de campagne de Ji Kang (cf. *Song shu* 29, p. 876).
[64] J'ai parlé de cet échange dans *La vie et la pensée*, pp. 60-67 (voir aussi Hou Wailu et al., *Zhongguo sixiang tongshi* 3 [Pékin, 1962], pp. 172-174). J'y ai mis en doute l'identité de Ruan Kan comme auteur des essais parce que je croyais que le seul indice de ce fait était la table des matières du manuscrit du Congshu tang (*La vie et la pensée*, p. 61, n. 1). Mais la monographie bibliographique du *Sui shu* 34, p. 1002, attribue un «Essai sur l'entretien de la vie» («Shesheng lun» 攝生論, les trois derniers mots du titre de l'échange d'essais) à «Ruan Kan, préfet du Henei», ce qui rend l'attribution tout à fait vraisemblable. Voir la discussion de Dai Mingyang, pp. 265-266.

162

nous avons reçu du ciel à notre naissance; tout ce que nous pouvons faire, c'est de vivre sobrement en se conformant aux préscriptions de la morale confucianiste traditionnelle[65]. Ji Kang s'oppose au rationalisme étroit de Ruan Kan pour prôner un genre d'intuitionisme mystique qui permettrait à l'homme de s'élever au-dessus du déterminisme ou du fatalisme prêché par les confucianistes. Les deux amis s'opposent ainsi sur des problèmes de base et nous verrons le reflet de cette opposition dans leur échange de poésies.

Cette fois c'est Ruan Kan qui part et Ji Kang qui lui adresse le premier poème.

Poème donné à
Ruan Deru

Rempli de tristesse je retournais à ma vieille case,
    Blessé dans les tréfonds par une émotion intense.
C'est au bon moment que je vous ai rencontré:
    Vos paroles consolatrices étaient parfumées comme l'orchidée.
5 Nous regrettions, alors, [de ne pas nous être connus] plus tôt,
    Mais, dès que nous nous sommes vus, notre joie a été égale à celle de vieux
                                   [amis!
Nous ne savions pas qu'enfin nous nous séparerions pendant longtemps:
    Y penser m'attriste et augmente mes soupirs.
Il y a toujours de l'imprévu:
10   La séparation est facile, la rencontre si difficile!
Quand l'homme de Ying est parti subitement
    Le maçon de pierres a cessé de parler.
Le faisan des marais finira ses jours parmi les mauvaises herbes;
    La tortue divine est toute joyeuse de s'enfoncer dans la boue.
15 Un nom glorieux salit la personne;
    Un rang élevé attire toutes sortes de calamités.
Il vaut mieux rejeter les liens extérieurs,
    Et laisser aller sa volonté en développant au plus haut degré son souffle vital.
Yan Hui était l'émule de Shun;
20   Xizi admirait Huang Xuan.
Mais quel genre d'homme étaient Quanzi et Pengzu,

---

[65] C'est sur l'aspect rationaliste et «matérialiste» de la pensée de Ruan Kan qu'insiste Rong Zhaozu 容肇祖 dans un article intéressant paru dans le *Guangming ribao* (Pékin) le 26 janvier 1962 intitulé «Wei Jin zhi ji Ruan Deru de weiwu zhuyi sixiang». Néanmoins il a soin de souligner le fatalisme de Ruan Kan dans les derniers paragraphes de son article.

Eux qui mettaient toute leur volonté à rechercher la tranquillité?
Petit à petit, insensiblement, nous nous adonnons tout entier à nos désirs
[immédiats,
Et, une fois le temps écoulé, nous ne pouvons plus le rattraper.
25 Pour s'engager dans le cycle reproductif de la vie il faut prévoir et accumuler;
Il ne faut plus être tenté de se laisser aller à son aise.
Dans le midi il fait sec et chaud:
Vous devez en finir vite avec vos projets personnels.
Vous êtes d'une nature à aimer la vertu:
30 Pendant votre voyage, attention aux rhumes!
Je m'efforce de vous dire ce que j'ai dans mon cœur;
Que je me sens triste en vous écrivant!

Dans l'ensemble on suit assez bien la pensée de ce long poème
fait d'aveux d'amitié et d'un sermon taoïste, mais un certain nombre
de vers restent obscurs. Les deux premiers nous décrivent le poète
accablé de tristesse. Est-ce la preuve que ce poème a été écrit au
moment de la mort de sa mère, vers 260[66]? Sans aucun autre indice,
une telle hypothèse semble hasardeuse. Nous verrons, quand nous
lirons le poème qu'il a écrit lors de la mort de sa mère (et d'un frère
aîné), à quel point extrême il a été affecté, mais existe-t-il au monde
un homme qui n'ait été «rempli de tristesse» et «blessé dans les
tréfonds» qu'une seule fois dans sa vie? Ces deux vers nous montrent
simplement que la rencontre avec Ruan Kan[67] a eu lieu à point
nommé, lors d'un gros chagrin. Mais il est possible aussi d'interpréter ces vers comme s'ils exprimaient le chagrin de Ji Kang après
le départ de son ami Ruan Kan. Nous verrons, en effet, en lisant
le dernier vers du deuxième poème de Ruan Kan que celui-ci a reçu
le poème de Ji Kang alors qu'il avait déjà accompli au moins une
journée de son voyage. Ji Kang l'a sans doute écrit en rentrant chez
lui après avoir dit adieu à son ami et l'a expédié par messager pour
qu'il le reçoive à sa première étape. Rien de plus naturel pour Ji
Kang que de se décrire au début de son poème rentrant tristement
chez lui après la scène d'adieu. Les dix vers qui suivent décrivent

---

[66] Telle est la théorie des auteurs du *Zhongguo sixiang tongshi* 3, p. 163.
[67] J'adopte la leçon du ms du Congshu tang: 吾 pour 數 pour le quatrième
caractère du troisième vers. L'autre leçon indiquerait que Ji Kang avait rencontré
plusieurs amis en même temps que Ruan Kan.

VIII

son amitié et se terminent avec la même allusion à «l'homme de Ying»
de *Zhuangzi* 24 qu'il a employée dans le quatorzième poème écrit à
son frère (*supra*, pp. 135-136).

Mais à partir du vers 12 Ji Kang change de ton et se lance une
fois encore dans une prédication contre les dangers de la vie publique,
ce qui fait croire que Ruan Kan est parti s'engager dans le monde
politique. Le faisan et la tortue, symboles de la vie naturelle tirés
de *Zhuangzi* 3 et 17, nous sont déjà familiers (*supra*, pp. 140 et 158).
Le «développement au plus haut degré du souffle vital» est un écho
de *Mencius* 2A, 2, un passage très discuté, où Mencius semble sous
l'influence de la pensée taoïste. Ici Ji Kang va plus loin que de prêcher
le renoncement aux choses de ce monde; dans les vers 18 à 24 il
entre dans le vif de sa philosophie religieuse. Le vers 18, avec son
rappel de Mencius, montre qu'il préconise un développement psychi-
que, le «souffle vital» (*qi*) dont parle Mencius étant un des composants
de l'âme (ou de l'esprit). Les deux vers suivants (19-20) font allusion
à deux personnages historiques qui ont su transcender le monde des
contingences quotidiennes pour essayer de se hisser jusqu'au niveau
des très grands saints de l'antiquité mythique. Yan Hui était le disciple
préféré de Confucius; c'est Mencius (3A, 1) qui parle de son admiration pour Shun: «Yan Yuan [= Hui] dit: 'Quel genre d'homme était
Shun? Quel genre d'homme suis-je? Un homme qui fait des efforts
peut aussi devenir comme lui!'». L'admiration de Xizi, c'est-à-dire
Xi Peng 隰朋, pour Huang Xuan, c'est-à-dire Huangdi, l'empereur
Jaune, est décrite dans *Zhuangzi* 24 (Watson, p. 270)[68]. En se faisant
les émules de ces deux saints de la haute antiquité, Yan Hui et Xi
Peng se sont élevés au-dessus des hommes plongés dans la poursuite
du quotidien; mais que dire des saints «immortels» Quanzi et Pengzu
(*Liexian zhuan*, Kaltenmark, pp. 68-71 et 82-84) qui se sont élevés
au-dessus du monde des contingences non pas en vouant un culte
aux saints d'antan, mais en forgeant eux-mêmes leur propre sainteté

[68] Selon Zhou Ying 周嬰, *Zhi lin* 厄林 3, pp. 51-52 (éd. Congshu jicheng), ces
deux vers de Ji Kang sont inspirés par le commentaire de Zhao Qi 趙岐 (mort en
201) à *Mencius* 7A, 7, reproduit dans le sous commentaire de Sun Shi 孫奭 (962-
1033). En effet, ces deux admirateurs de saints mythiques y sont évoqués ensemble,
comme le fait Ji Kang dans ce vers.

par la recherche de la «tranquillité» (il y a une allusion subtile au *Lun yu* 2, 10, où Confucius souligne l'importance de l'endroit où l'homme trouve sa «tranquillité» dans le jugement de son caractère)? Ji Kang ici, comme dans sa lettre à Shan Tao, prend ses distances avec la tradition confucianiste pour prôner la recherche de l'immortalité taoïste. Il reconnaît l'importance d'élever ses vues vers un idéal (vers 19-20), mais voudrait changer l'idéal de la sainteté confucianiste en salut personnel. Les vers 23-26 insistent sur le fait qu'il ne faut pas se perdre dans les contingences[69], dans les changements sans fin de la vie (allusion au *Yi jing*, «Xi ci» A, Legge, p. 356). Ces quatre vers montrent combien Ji Kang transforme le taoïsme ancien. En préconisant l'accumulation graduelle d'un stock d'énergie vitale ou de «sainteté», il montre sa dette envers le confucianisme[70]. Dans les derniers six vers Ji Kang prend congé de son ami, mais plusieurs vers restent obscurs (on voit mal le lien entre les vers 29 et 30 par exemple). Le grand nombre de variantes montrent que cette obscurité peut venir de corruptions textuelles. Il se peut aussi, comme souvent dans des «poèmes-lettres» de cette époque, qu'il s'agisse d'allusions personnelles que nous ne pouvons plus comprendre.

Ji Kang parle (dans le vers 27) du «midi» que Ruan Kan va visiter, et, dans le premier des deux poèmes de sa réponse, celui-ci nous montre qu'il se dirige vers le sud (je suppose que les deux amis se trouvaient dans le nord du Henan, dans la propriété de campagne de Ji Kang). Son poème suit, grosso modo, le mouvement du poème de Ji Kang; mais sa réponse au sermon taoïste est franchement confucianiste dans ce premier poème.

1

Deux poèmes de réponse
par Ruan Deru

Je suis parti tôt de la case aux sources chaudes
　Pour faire étape, le soir, dans les murs de Xuanyang.

---

[69] Idée reprise dans l'essai «Yang sheng lun»; cf. *La vie et la pensée*, pp. 89-90, et Hou Wailu, *op. cit.*, pp. 175-176.
[70] Cf. *La vie et la pensée*, p. 76.

VIII

Je me retourne pour regarder tristement en arrière,
    Pensant à mon ami.
5 Quelle chance que nous nous soyons rencontrés :
    Avec vous j'ai trouvé le bonheur,
Et, bien que nous ne nous fréquentions pas depuis longtemps,
    Notre affection surgit de cœurs sincères.
Le bon jade a besoin d'être poli :
10   C'est ainsi que Yufan a reçu sa forme.
Bien sûr que la perle de Sui brille :
    Mais c'est en la frottant qu'on fait ressortir son éclat.
Être avec vous, c'est être avec des orchidées et des pierres :
    Vous avez en votre personne la solidité des unes, le parfum des autres.
15 Vous arrivez presque à élargir la Voie des anciens,
    En coupant du bois de santal et en attendant que le Fleuve devienne clair.
Qui aurait pensé que nous nous séparerions,
    Et que je voyagerais au loin, comme emporté par le vent ?
Près de la voiture j'ai tenu votre main pour vous dire adieu ;
20   Comme vos bons conseils me semblent perspicaces !
Vos belles paroles remplissent mes oreilles
    Et je prends ma ceinture pour les y inscrire à mon propre usage.
Tang et Yu sont éloignés de nous par mille années ;
    Nous ne sommes pas contemporains des Trois Dynasties.
25 [Les cours donnés par Confucius entre] le Zhu et le Si sont terminés depuis
                                      [longtemps ;
    Il n'y a plus personne pour écouter ses paroles subtiles.
Zeng Sheng a changé sa natte avant de mourir ;
    Zhong You a lié les cordons de son bonnet.
Comment pourrait-on aimer [les richesses] de Jin et de Chu ?
30   Restez plutôt sans rien pour pouvoir garder votre intégrité,
    Comme le dragon retiré qui préfère s'enrouler dans la boue,
    Ou la tortue divine qui cache ses pouvoirs magiques.
J'espère observer vos paroles,
    Nourrir mon intégrité pour garder ma vie intacte.
35 Les dangers abondent dans les landes orientales ;
    J'y vais pour un court séjour, non pas pour y rester longtemps.
J'espère que vous ne vous ferez pas de soucis pour moi
    Et que vos promenades heureuses vous amèneront la tranquillité.

Les deux premiers vers décrivent, sans doute, la première étape du voyage de Ruan Kan, de la «case» de Ji Kang (le même mot est utilisé dans le premier vers de son poème) à «Xuanyang». Dai Ming-yang dit qu'il n'y a pas de ville ancienne de ce nom et suggère

«Yiyang» 宜陽, le caractère *yi* 宜 étant facilement corrompu en *xuan* 宜. Mais Yiyang se trouvait à 150 km au sud-ouest de la maison de campagne de Ji Kang, beaucoup trop loin pour une étape à cheval, avec le Fleuve Jaune à traverser en route par surcroît. Dai Mingyang cite aussi la monographie locale de la région de la maison de Ji Kang, le *Xiuwu xian zhi* de 1840 qui parle d'une commanderie de Yiyang sous les Wei Postérieurs dans cette région, et les auteurs de la monographie, sur le témoignage de ce deuxième vers du poème de Ruan Kan, disent que *yi* doit être une faute pour *xuan*, et qu'il existe des restes de vieilles murailles à Xuanyang yi 驛 («Relais de Xuanyang»), 18 *li* au sud-est de la ville de Xiuwu. Il existait un Xuanyang à cet endroit en 1917 quand un atlas de la Chine a été publié par la Commercial Press de Shanghai (première édition, 1913) et je me demande s'il ne s'agit pas de cette localité, à une trentaine de km au sud-est de la maison de Ji Kang, dans une région qui abondait en sources. Un indice supplémentaire, aussi cité par Dai Mingyang, est l'*Ancheng ji* 安城記 de Wang Fu 王孚 (cité dans le *Taiping yulan* 71, p. 2b) qui décrit des sources chaudes au sud de la ville de Yiyang dans lesquelles on pouvait faire cuire des œufs. Or, ce que Dai Mingyang néglige de dire, c'est que Ancheng se trouvait dans cette région, au sud de l'actuel Yuanwu 原武, à une trentaine de km au sud-est du relais de Xuanyang. Le Yiyang de Wang Fu serait donc dans cette région et non le Yiyang bien connu à 150 km de là au sud du Fleuve Jaune.

Ruan Kan, comme Ji Kang, commence son poème en faisant l'éloge de cette amitié que les deux hommes ont ressentie si subitement. Dans les vers 9 à 12 il insiste sur la nécessité de parachever cette amitié comme on polit le jade (*Shi jing* 55; Yufan était une belle pierre de Lu mentionnée dans *Zuo zhuan*, Ding 5, Couvreur 3, p. 520) ou comme on fait briller une perle (la perle Sui ou du marquis de Sui, est mentionnée dans *Zhuangzi* 28, Watson, p. 313, et *Huainanzi* 6, p. 91). Les orchidées et les pierres, dans les deux vers suivants, sont devenues un thème fréquent dans la peinture chinoise. Ruan Kan arrive au plus haut point de ses louanges de Ji Kang dans les vers 15 et 16: «Élargir la Voie» est une allusion au *Lun yu* 15, 28: «L'homme peut élargir la Voie; ce n'est pas la Voie qui puisse élargir l'homme». Et le vers 16 est une allusion au *Shi jing* 112, un poème qui contraste un bûcheron vaillant et actif aux fainéants de la cour. «Attendre que le Fleuve devienne clair» veut dire «attendre l'avènement de l'âge d'or» ou d'un souverain exemplaire. Ainsi Ruan Kan décrit Ji Kang en train de cultiver son jardin en attendant des jours meilleurs pour sortir dans la vie active.

Le vers 17 fait écho au vers 7 du poème de Ji Kang et décrit la séparation inattendue des deux amis. Dans les vers qui suivent Ruan Kan semble faire allusion à ce que j'ai appelé le «sermon taoïste» dans le poème de Ji Kang (vers 13-26). Mais les termes qu'il emploie pour décrire ce «sermon» sont tout à fait confucianistes! Il y a des échos du *Lun yu* dans les vers 21 et 22 (*Lun yu* 8, 15, dans le vers 21, et *Lun yu* 15, 5, dans le vers 22). Tang et Yu (dans le vers 23) sont les parangons du confucianisme, les anciens rois Yao et Shun. Zengzi dit (*Li ji*, Couvreur 1, p. 138) que lui et Zi Xia «ont servi le Maître [Confucius] entre le Zhu et le Si», deux rivières dans l'ancien pays de Lu (Shandong). Les «paroles subtiles» (vers 26) sont dites «interrompues» après la mort de Confucius au début de la monographie bibliographiques du *Han shu* 30. Les quatre vers suivants réfèrent tous à des disciples de Confucius. Ruan Kan semble répondre aux idées taoïstes exprimées par Ji Kang dans son «sermon» par des exemples de vertus confucianistes extraordinaires. Ji Kang avait fait l'éloge (vers 21-22) des taoïstes qui «mettaient toute leur volonté à rechercher la tranquillité» pour se procurer la Longue Vie des immortels. Ruan Kan rétorque en invoquant des exemples d'hommes qui se sont couverts de gloire en respectant strictement les règles du rituel traditionnel (et donc confucianiste) lors de leur mort. Zeng Shen, le disciple confucéen Zengzi, a demandé, quand il se savait mourant, qu'on change la natte sur laquelle il était couché parce que cette natte (reçue en cadeau d'un usurpateur) était en principe réservée à l'usage des fonctionnaires bien au-dessus de son rang (*Li ji*, Couvreur 1, pp. 125-126). Zhong You, le disciple confucéen Zi Lu, a été mortellement blessé lors d'une escarmouche et les cordons de son bonnet ont été rompus. Selon le *Zuo zhuan*, Ai 15 (Couvreur 3, p. 715): «Il dit, 'Un homme de bien qui meurt n'enlève pas son bonnet'. Et Zhong You est mort en liant les cordons de son bonnet». Les vers 29 et 32 qui suivent semblent répondre aussi, avec des allusions au canon confucianiste, aux vers dans le poème de Ji Kang qui chantent le renoncement des choses de ce monde (les vers 15-16). Le même disciple Zengzi est cité dans *Mencius* 2B, 2 (Legge, p. 213): «Les richesses de Jin et de Chu sont inégalables. Qu'ils gardent leurs richesses: je garderai ma vertu!». Et une citation célèbre de Confucius à propos du disciple Yan Hui nommé (un peu péjorativement) par Ji Kang dans le vers 19 de son poème inspire le vers 30 du poème de Ruan Kan: «Le Maître [Confucius] dit: '[Yan] Hui arrive presque [à la vertu parfaite]. Il reste souvent sans rien.'» (*Lun yu* 11, 18). Le renoncement taoïste est ainsi réinterprété en renoncement confucianiste. Et les deux vers suivants (31-32), en reprenant quatre de ses mots, répondent au vers 14 du poème de Ji Kang: «*La tortue divine* est toute joyeuse de *s'enfoncer* dans *la boue*». Mais, venant à la fin de toutes ces citations du canon confucianiste, ces mots perdent une bonne partie des résonnances taoïstes qu'ils ont dans le poème de Ji Kang.

Ruan Kan a si bien rendu confucéens les sentiments taoïstes de Ji Kang que son vers 33 semble presque ironique. Le terme choisi pour le mot que j'ai traduit «intégrité», *zhen* 貞, est même plutôt mal vu par les taoïstes (cf. *Zhuangzi* 14, Watson, p. 156, qui traduit «honneur»). Ruan Kan, comme tous les interlocuteurs de Ji Kang que nous avons lus, passe des idées taoïstes aux idées confucianistes avec grande aisance; dans ce premier poème, cependant, les attitudes taoïstes sont mises au service d'une philosophie de base confucianiste.

Je ne sais pas le sens exact de l'expression «landes orientales» du vers 35. Dai Mingyang la traite comme un nom de lieu, Dongye, qu'il situe (se basant, à tort à mon avis, sur le *Hou Han shu* 57, p. 1848) dans le Henan central (l'actuel Xuchang 許昌). Mais l'expression apparaît assez souvent dans les textes anciens et médiévaux sans avoir le sens d'un nom de lieu bien défini (y compris la citation du *Hou Han shu*). Ji Kang lui-même s'en sert comme sobriquet dans son essai sur la musique[71] et dans le poème traduit plus bas, p. 172, comme le nom d'un saint taoïste. Peut-être même que le fait de ne

[71] *La vie et la pensée*, p. 68 et note 1.

pas déterminer le lieu exact où «les dangers abondent» rend ceux-ci d'autant plus effrayants.

Le premier poème de Ruan Kan est d'inspiration surtout confucianiste; dans les vers 15 à 20 du deuxième il fait un petit effort pour se mettre au diapason de la pensée du poème de Ji Kang, mais son «taoïsme» est plutôt timide, et banal.

2

Il n'est pas facile de faire résider ensemble deux hommes de belle nature :
   Une bonne conjoncture est vraiment difficile à préserver longtemps.
Venu ici pour me reposer,
   J'ai trouvé, chez vous, comme un parfum d'orchidées.
5 Tous mes désirs me poussaient à me divertir avec vous pour toujours,
   Comme une paire d'oiseaux qui battent leurs ailes et voltigent ensemble.
Nous ne savions pas qu'à la fin nous nous séparerions pendant longtemps,
   Une séparation qui nous enverrait dans des régions différentes.
Comme mes quatre étalons courent vite!
10   Le voyageur annonce que la route sera longue.
J'avance en regardant en arrière, évoquant votre image dans ma pensée,
   Laissant errer mes yeux, m'arrêtant souvent.
Je m'appuie sur la traverse de la voiture et redouble mes soupirs,
   Pensant à vous: comment pourrais-je vous oublier?
15 C'est la tranquillité qui est à la base de la Voie :
   Laozi détestait la violence.
Quand le malheur arrive, la personne subit de graves dommages;
   Rongzi savait ce qui amène la paix.
Nous devons, en vérité, nous réjouir de la tortue sainte :
20   Il y a un avertissement clair dans ses boyaux arrachés.
Que ce poème neuf [que vous m'envoyez] est chaleureux!
   Plus je le chante, et plus j'en suis ému.
Je sors votre lettre pour réciter vos belles paroles :
   Je ne me lasserai pas de les garder à tout jamais.
25 Jamais je ne manquerai à ma promesse de revenir,
   Jusqu'à ce que nous soyons encore ensemble dans la maison des bois.
Chassez loin de vous vos pensées tristes;
   Ne vous laissez pas blesser à cause de vos sentiments [d'amitié pour moi].
À force de guetter la route [pour vous voir?] j'oublie l'étape,
30   Et réponds, en attendant, à la lettre qui est venue.

J'ai adopté la suggestion textuelle de Dai Mingyang dans le vers 12 (不 pour 太 ou 大). Les seules allusions qui demandent un commentaire sont toutes dans les vers «taoïstes», 15 à 20. L'allusion à Laozi est au chapitre 42: «Les hommes violents ne meurent pas de leur belle mort». «Rongzi», dans le vers 18, est sans doute Rong Qiqi 榮啓期, un ermite «taoïste» qui apparaît dans *Liezi* 1 et dans divers livres plus ou moins contemporains de Ji Kang (dont son propre *Gaoshi zhuan*, cité dans le *Taiping yulan* 509, p. 4a). Sa formule pour atteindre la paix était de rester pauvre et attendre la fin de sa vie. Les vers 19 et 20 font allusion à *Zhuangzi* 26 (Watson, pp. 298-299) où il est question d'une tortue dont la carapace donne 72 réponses justes quand on l'utilise pour la divination. Elle était assez sage pour donner des réponses justes, mais pas assez pour empêcher sa mort. La sagesse suprême, c'est de préserver notre vie, notre bien suprême. Ruan Kan semble prévoir que la «sagesse» de Ji Kang est d'un genre qui lui apportera plutôt malheur qu'autre chose, et il emploie ces allusions taoïstes, comme il a employé des allusions confucianistes dans son premier poème (vers 16, 29-30), pour conseiller la retraite et la vie obscure à son ami.

Alors que Ji Kang s'est montré presque méprisant aux deux Guo à cause de leur attitude confucianiste bon teint, la tiédeur des sentiments taoïstes de Ruan Kan ne semble pas avoir raffraîchi l'ardeur réciproque des deux amis le moins du monde. Les trois poèmes sont remplis de sentiments d'amitié, de cette amitié de tête et de cœur qui a joué un si grand rôle dans la poésie chinoise. Est-ce que Ji Kang a passé outre ses appartenances philosophiques cette fois-ci, ou est-ce que Ruan Ji pratiquait, comme tant de confucianistes bon ✱ teint de tous les temps, des recettes taoïstes pour «nourrir sa vie», ce qui aurait donné aux deux hommes un terrain d'entente? La partie la plus intéressante du «sermon taoïste» de Ji Kang (vers 19 à 26 de son poème) semble adressée à un pratiquant qu'il essaie d'encourager.

Quoiqu'il en soit, Ji Kang semble avoir été, malgré ses tendances mystiques et son désir si souvent réitéré de fuir le monde, un bon camarade, un homme qui attachait du prix à ses amitiés. Il nous reste deux poèmes où il décrit des réunions amicales dans des termes qui montrent combien il y était attaché. Le premier que je citerai, en pentamètres, est suivi, dans la plupart des éditions, par six poèmes en tétramètres. Mais ces poèmes en tétramètres ne semblent pas du tout apparentés au premier en pentamètres et je les traduirai plus bas (2ᵉ Partie, ch. 6). Ces deux poèmes sur des réunions amicales restent assez près de leurs modèles écrits par les poètes de l'ère Jian'an et dont les plus beaux sont rassemblés dans le *Wen xuan* 20. Mais Ji Kang est trop original pour suivre aveuglément ses devanciers et, dans les deux poèmes, il termine sur une note tout à fait nouvelle. Voici le premier poème :

Partie à boire

Quel plaisir de se promener dans le parc,
   De regarder partout sans jamais s'arrêter !
Toutes les plantes regorgent de fleurs parfumées ;
   Au loin se dresse bien haut une terrasse élevée.
5 Les arbres de la forêt se mêlent confusément ;
   Dans l'étang sombre jouent les carpes.
Avec des boules légères nous tirons sur les oiseaux en vol ;
   Avec des lignes fines nous pêchons la brême.
Un tir qui fait mouche soulève de belles louanges,
10   Et nos souffles divers s'unissent dans nos chants [d'éloges].
Près du ruisseau nous offrons un vin pur ;
   Une chanson murmurée sort d'entre les dents blanches.
Sur une cithare simple on joue une pièce raffinée :
   Et nos voix pures s'élèvent, portée par le vent.
15 Comment cette réunion ne me ferait-elle pas plaisir ?
   Mais je regrette l'absence de Dongyezi,
   Et, au milieu de la fête, je pense à cet homme caché
   Qui a su garder un mode de vie primitif, soignant sa vie à sa fin comme à
                                   [son début.
Il ne me reste plus qu'à m'adonner tout entier aux cordes de ma cithare
20   Et confier ainsi mon cœur à mes amis intimes.

Les quatorze premiers vers de ce poème doivent beaucoup aux poètes de l'ère Jian'an ; la promenade dans le parc, la pêche, la chasse, le vin, la musique, tous ces éléments s'y trouvent déjà, souvent dans des vers très ressemblants. Le caractère conventionnel de ces vers est accentué par les mots que Ji Kang choisit pour les poissons qu'on pêche à la ligne. Si l'on traduit directement, ce seraient des esturgeons et des thons — drôle de pêche pour les environs de Luoyang ! Mais les deux caractères paraissent ensemble dans *Shi jing* 57 et je pense que Ji Kang les emploie ici simplement pour rappeler ce passage, donnant ainsi un écho canonique à sa description. Ma traduction («brême») est de la plus haute fantaisie; j'ai préféré respecter la réalité ichtyologique puisque l'allusion au *Shi jing* serait perdue en français de toute façon.

Le tir aux oiseaux dans le vers 7, si l'on croit les dictionnaires, a lieu au moyen d'arbalètes. Les «boules légères» sont sans doute, comme nous l'avons vu ci-dessus (p. 135), des cailloux attachés aux fils, eux-mêmes attachés aux flèches d'arbalète. Les vers 9 et 10 semblent rappeler deux vers d'un poème par Liu Zhen 劉楨 intitulé «Tir au milan», «She yuan»: «Les hommes louent d'une seule voix:/ 'Que votre tir était expert!'» (voir aussi les quinzième et seizième vers du poème «Ming du pian» de Cao Zhi). Je suis la leçon du manuscrit du Congshu tang pour le premier caractère du neuvième vers (*yan* 研, «expert», pour le *zuo* 坐 des autres versions). En gardant la leçon des autres versions, on peut traduire: «Pendant la séance nous chantons de beaux éloges», mais il me semble que des vers en rapport avec la chasse sont plus appropriés ici que de beaux éloges venus d'on ne sait où. Le chant et la musique ne commencent que dans les vers 12 et suivants. Le chant du vers suivant vient tout naturellement après le vin. Il est donné sans doute par une chanteuse (sinon Ji Kang n'aurait pas attiré l'attention sur la blancheur de ses dents) et accompagné par la cithare, instrument de prédilection du poète. Comme les parties à boire de ses prédécesseurs, celle de Ji Kang est idéalisée, un hâvre de bonheur, de sport, d'art et d'amitié dans la vie de ces guerriers et courtisans.

L'originalité du poème de Ji Kang réside principalement dans les derniers six vers. Malgré l'idéalisation de cette réunion, elle ne satisfait pas le poète; les joies de la pêche et de la chasse, de la camaraderie et de la musique ne lui suffisent pas. Qu'est-ce qui lui manque? Qui est ce Dongyezi 東野子 dont il est question dans le vers 16? Dai Mingyang croit qu'il s'agit de Ruan Kan qui, comme nous venons de voir dans le premier poème qu'il a adressé à Ji Kang (*supra*, p. 166 et p. 169), est parti à Dongye («les landes orientales») pour un court séjour. Mais il serait étrange que Ji Kang l'appelle ici le «sage de Dongye» ou «maître Dongye» simplement parce qu'il y est parti en voyage. Ji Kang emploie aussi ces mots pour se donner un sobriquet («maître de Dongye», Dongye zhuren 主人) dans son essai sur la musique (*La vie et la pensée*, p. 68 et note 1). Je crois qu'on peut difficilement admettre une allusion à Ruan Kan ici; la tristesse de Ji Kang n'est pas simplement le regret de l'absence d'un ami cher parmi les convives. Il me semble que le Dongyezi à qui il fait allusion ici est plutôt un ermite antique, Dongye Huo 獲, qui a appris de son maître Guiguzi 鬼谷子 «l'art de protéger sa vie». La seule difficulté, c'est que cette figure, qui aurait vécu pendant la période des Royaumes combattants, n'est mentionnée que par un livre très tardif, le *Shandong tongzhi* (cité par Morohashi Tetsuji, *Dai Kan Wa jiten* 6, p. 197b). C'est pourtant de lui que je crois qu'il s'agit ici, et sa présence dans ce poème nous apprend beaucoup sur les aspirations fondamentales de Ji Kang. Dans un moment qui devait être un moment de satisfaction totale, Ji Kang pense au sage antique, «l'homme caché» décrit dans le *Yi jing* (Hexagramme «Lü», Legge, p. 79), et qui savait garder intact en lui-même toute la puissance primitive dont est doté l'homme «naturel», non diminué par la civilisation. L'absence de ce sage à la réunion plonge Ji Kang dans un tel état de mélancolie qu'il n'a qu'un recours: essayer de s'exprimer dans la musique, essayer de la faire dire ce que les paroles sont incapables de dire[72].

Le deuxième poème sur le thème d'une réunion amicale est en tétramètres. Il est précédé, dans le *Wen xuan* 29 et dans la plupart des éditions, par les mots «Za shi» 雜詩, que les commentateurs comprennent comme «Poème n'appartenant pas à une catégorie fixe», ou «Poème à thème mélangé», ou «Poème sans titre»[73]. Quelque soit le sens du titre, il s'agit ici d'un poème d'amitié et de réunion amicale, assez proche du poème «Partie à boire» que nous venons de lire. Dans le manuscrit du Congshu tang ce poème ne porte pas

[72] Ce poème a été traduit dans *La vie et la pensée*, pp. 37-38, et par H. Maspero, *Le taoïsme et les religions chinoises* (Paris, 1971), p. 338.

[73] C'est dire qu'ils ne comprennent plus le sens de ces mots. Li Shan (*Wen xuan* 29, p. 13a) croit que le terme indique que le poète écrit «en dehors des genres établis, en s'exprimant directement au contact avec son sujet»; Li Zhouhan (*Liuchen wen xuan* 29, p. 18a) croit que le terme indique que «l'inspiration pour le poème est multiple»; alors que le *Monkyô bifu ron* 文鏡祕府論 du moine japonais Kûkai 空海 croit qu'il s'agit seulement du fait que le titre d'origine était perdu quand le poème a été inclus dans le *Wen xuan*.

de titre et se trouve en effet à la fin des poèmes en tétramètres mis à la suite du poème «Parti à boire», mais à mon avis il est le seul de ces poèmes en tétramètres qui mérite vraiment de porter ce titre. Le poème est un des plus beaux des poèmes de Ji Kang et ressemble beaucoup aux autres du même genre, riches en descriptions des plaisirs de la vie des jeunes seigneurs. Ces deux faits expliquent sans doute pourquoi il a été inclus dans le *Wen xuan*.

Poème sans titre

Une brise légère amène la fraicheur
    Et chasse les brumes tout à l'alentour.
La lune, éclatante de clarté,
    Est pendue à l'angle haut du mur.
5 Ému, j'invite mon noble ami
    Et, la main dans la main, nous montons dans la même voiture.
Nos coursiers magnifiques sont bien entraînés :
    Élevant leurs mors, ils marquent le pas.
Et puis, rapidement nous voyageons dans la nuit
10   Pour atteindre la chaumière de notre ami.
Les lanternes brillantes déversent leur éclat ;
    Les tentures fleuries sont étendues de toute leur longueur.
Des coupes [en forme] de phénix on verse un vin doux ;
    Dans des chaudrons divins on fait cuire du poisson.
15 La musique des cordes dépasse celle de Ziye ;
    Les chants surpassent ceux de Mianju.
Notre hymne de la Grande Simplicité se répand au loin,
    Et, baissant la tête, nous louons le Vide Mystérieux.
Où sont les hommes supérieurs [dignes de ces amis]?
20   C'est avec eux que je veux m'allier!

Ziye, dans le vers 15, est le *zi* du Maître Kuang 師曠, célèbre musicien et connaisseur de musique de l'antiquité souvent mentionné dans les textes anciens (e.g. *Zuo zhuan*, Xiang 18, Legge, p. 479), et Mianju 綿駒 dans le vers suivant, un chanteur de grand renom (*Mencius* 6B, 6, 5). Le poème, comme le précédent, fait clairement partie de ces poèmes qui célèbrent les réunions amicales dont nous trouvons tant d'exemples à cette époque. Ému par la beauté du paysage nocturne, le poète invite un ami (vers 5) à monter dans sa voiture (vers 6, du *Shi jing* 41) pour aller (vers 7 est inspiré du *Shi jing* 167; vers 9 est du *Shi jing* 21) à une réunion chez un ami commun. La description de l'opulence du décor et des mets et de l'excellence de la musique est de rigueur dans ces poèmes. Les «coupes [en forme] de phénix» (vers 13) sont peut-être, comme le dit Zhang Xian, des coupes décorées d'images de phénix. Elles ne se réfèrent pas plus à un ustensile réel que les «chaudrons divins» du vers suivant qui, selon ce même commentateur, était fait de fer et se remplissaient sans qu'on y verse quoique ce soit et faisaient bouillir leur contenu sans être chauffés. Ji Kang marque son poème de son originalité dans les derniers quatre vers seulement. Les chants entonnés à cette réunion ont tout à fait l'air d'être des chants taoïstes. La Grande Simplicité, *taisu* 太素, du vers 17, se réfère soit à la nature humaine dépouillée de ce qui n'est pas directement appris spontanément (*Huainanzi* 2, p. 22), soit à une des hypostases dans le développement du cosmos (*Liezi jishi* 1, p. 4); le Vide Mystérieux, *xuanxu* 玄虛 (terme utilisé dans le troisième poème aux frères Guo, vers 14, *supra*, p. 158) est une description du *dao* (*Han Feizi jishi* 20, p. 369). Les amis de Ji Kang sont donc des taoïstes, ou au moins s'intéressent au taoïsme. À mon avis, c'est à ces amis que le poète pense dans le dernier couplet, comme je l'indique dans ma traduction. Mais les commentateurs ne sont pas tous d'accord. Li Shan, dans son commentaire du *Wen xuan* 29, p. 17b, identifie le modèle pour le dernier vers comme une phrase du *Han shu* 100 B, p. 4268 : «Les Han à leur avènement traitaient les peuples au loin avec douceur, et *s'allièrent avec eux*» (ou, «les acceptèrent comme vassaux»). Mais il ajoute que Ji Kang ici veut *servir*, *shi* 仕, ces «hommes supérieurs». He Zhuo 何焯 et Dai Mingyang s'opposent à cette interprétation, et disent que les mots que j'ai traduits par «m'allier», *poufu* 剖符 (littéralement, «partager une taille»), ne veulent pas dire «servir», mais simplement «s'associer avec», «partager les joies de»[74]. C'est aussi mon avis. Ce poème, comme la «Partie à boire», est un poème d'amitié sans relents politiques, mais

[74] Je ne peux accepter les traductions de von Zach («Wer könnte in Vortrefflichkeit wohl mit Dir verglichen werden?») ou de Shiba Rokurô 斯波六郎 et Hanafusa Hideki 花房英樹 (*Monzen*, dans Sekai bungaku taikei 70, Tokyo, 1963, p. 99) qui traduisent le mot *er* 爾 (que je traduis par «eux») par «des hommes vulgaires»: «Qui, parmi des hommes de talents éminents, s'allierait avec des hommes vulgaires pour servir comme fonctionnaire?».

même si, avec Li Shan, nous gardons à l'expression «partager une taille» des résonnances politiques qu'elle avait assurément à ses origines, le contexte montre que Ji Kang cherche des «hommes supérieurs» d'un genre un peu spécial—non pas des grands administrateurs, mais des musiciens versés dans les hymnes taoïstes avec qui il veut «s'allier».

Ainsi, comme dans les poèmes écrits à son frère et aux amis, dans ces poèmes décrivant des réunions amicales, Ji Kang ne peut s'empêcher de terminer sur une note taoïste. Est-ce une formule poétique vide de sens réel? Une façon détournée de s'opposer au régime, comme le veut la tradition? Quelle que soit l'interprétation qu'on donne à ces poèmes, l'omniprésence du taoïsme est un fait indéniable, frappant.

(à suivre)

VIII

(deuxième partie)

4

POÉSIE PHILOSOPHIQUE

Dix poèmes en hexamètres

Comme nous l'avons vu, la philosophie occupe une grande place dans les poèmes de Ji Kang écrits à son frère et à ses amis. Si j'ai consacré ce chapitre à la «poésie philosophique», c'est qu'il y a un certain nombre de poèmes qui sont entièrement dévoués à l'exposé d'une philosophie taoïste ou tout au moins teintée de taoïsme. Le premier cycle de poèmes que je présenterai ici est une série de dix poèmes très courts qui sont en effet des stances ou sentences gnomiques arrangées très savamment, et d'une façon très originale, en quatre vers de six pieds précédés d'un vers de cinq pieds. Les hexamètres sont très peu usités en chinois, et il est possible que les premiers exemples sont à peu près contemporains de Ji Kang. Il est vrai que le *Wenzhang yuanqi* 文章緣起, attribué à Ren Fang 任昉 (460-508) et d'authenticité douteuse, déclare que les premiers vers de six pieds sont de Gu Yong 谷永 (mort vers 10 av. J.-C.), mais la première trace de vers encore existants sont de Kong Rong 孔融 (153-208) et, surtout, de Cao Pi, premier empereur des Wei[75]. Quelque soit

[75] Zhao Yi 趙翼, *Gaiyu congkao* 23, p. 452 (de l'édition de Shanghai, 1957), donne une histoire de la forme, et déclare que les vers de Gu Yong et de Kong Rong n'existent plus. Trois poèmes en hexamètres sont attribués à Kong Rong dans l'anthologie dite des Tang mais d'authenticité douteuse, *Guwen yuan* 8, pp. 9b-10a (éd. Sibu

leur authenticité, les poèmes de Kong Rong et de Cao Pi ressemblent prosodiquement beaucoup à ceux de Ji Kang. Ces trois poètes utilisent deux césures, coupant le vers en trois parties égales de deux syllabes. Le résultat est un vers statique, un peu hâché, mieux fait pour déclamer des sentences que pour exprimer des sentiments lyriques. La raideur de ces vers est encore accentuée par le fait qu'ils sont tous rimés, comme c'est souvent le cas dans la poésie populaire, alors que dans la poésie savante les vers pairs seulement sont rimés. Ji Kang fait précéder chacun des dix quatrains en hexamètres qui composent cette série par un vers de cinq pieds, rimé lui aussi, mais avec une seule césure après la troisième syllabe, ce qui est très inhabituel et ajoute à la très grande originalité formelle de ces poèmes.

Les premiers deux poèmes mettent en scène les deux empereurs légendaires de l'antiquité dont les règnes ont été vantés comme l'âge d'or.

1

Dans la haute antiquité, il y avait Yao et Shun :
Ces deux hommes étaient de vertu et de mérite égaux.
Ils n'ont pas favorisé leurs parents en leur transmettant le trône de l'empire.
Nobles, simples et indulgents,
5 Ils ont pacifié et aidé tous les hommes entre les Quatre Mers.

Le vers 3 fait allusion au fait que ni Yao, ni Shun n'ont laissé le trône à leurs enfants, comme c'était la règle à partir de Yu, successeur de Shun et fondateur de la dynastie des Xia. Cette impartialité, *gong* 公, est une vertu très estimée aussi bien par les confucianistes que par les taoïstes, et exaltée par Ji Kang lui-même dans son essai

congkan). Fan Wenlan (*Wenxin diaolong zhu* 7 (section 34), p. 584 (note 8)) considère les poèmes des faux, tandis que Suzuki Shûji 鈴木修次, *Kan Gi shi no kenkyû* (Tokyo, 1967), p. 480, les accepte, un peu à contre cœur, comme authentiques, ce qui est étonnant, étant donné que le commentateur du *Guwen yuan* lui-même, Zhang Qiao 章樵 (début XIIIᵉ siècle) les tient pour des faux de l'époque de Cao Pi. Je ne vois pas de raison de ne pas accepter les poèmes hexamétriques de Cao Pi comme authentiques. Il y en a un de cinq vers (tous rimés) reproduit dans le *Xiandi zhuan* cité dans le commentaire du *Sanguo zhi* 2, p. 65, et le poème «Fait à Liyang» en hexamètres se trouve dans le *Yiwen leiju* 59, p. 6a. Les historiens de la forme hexamétrique semblent tous ignorer ces vers de Ji Kang.

325

«Se délivrer des sentiments personnels» (*La vie et la pensée*, pp. 122-130).

Le deuxième poème continue la glorification des deux souverains de l'âge d'or, mais ici ils sont appelés par ce que certains commentateurs considèrent les noms des fiefs qu'ils ont occupés avant d'accéder au trône.

2

Au temps de [Yao de] Tang et [Shun de] Yu, on gouvernait par le *dao*.
 Tous les nombreux états vassaux vivaient en harmonie familière, sans litiges.
 Les sages et les sots réalisaient tous leurs ambitions.
 Ils étaient paisibles et joyeux, s'oubliant intérieurement.
5 Qu'elle était belle, cette époque, et digne de nous réjouir!

«Gouverner par le *dao*» était l'idéal des confucianistes comme des taoïstes, et, telle est l'ambiguïté du syncrétisme chinois que ce poème, comme le premier, pourrait passer indifféremment comme «taoïste» ou «confucianiste». Seul le vers 4 semble faire pencher pour le taoïsme: «s'oublier intérieurement», *neiwang* 內忘, fait penser à l'oubli mystique de soi qui joue un si grand rôle dans la philosophie taoïste. Mais il se peut aussi qu'il y ait une corruption textuelle ici. Le mot que je traduis «s'oubliant», *wang* 忘, à l'encontre des autres fins de vers, ne rime pas. On pourrait imaginer qu'il serait une erreur pour le mot *mei* 美, «beau», et qu'il faudrait lire «beaux intérieurement», le composé *neimei*, qui rimerait, apparaissant au début du «Li sao», alors que *neiwang* semble inconnu ailleurs.

Ce n'est qu'à cause de la rime que je cherche une variante pour le mot «s'oubliant», pas du tout pour essayer d'épurer ce poème de ses relents taoïstes. Le troisième poème, en effet, n'est qu'un amalgame de citations de Laozi.

3

L'utilisation de l'intelligence donne lieu à des contrefaçons.
 Plus les lois et les ordonnances sont claires, plus il naîtra des brigands:
 Une chose appelle l'autre automatiquement et sans cesse.
 Le Grand Homme, mystérieux et tranquille, ne fait pas de bruit.
5 Il contrôle [le peuple] avec quiétude, et [le peuple] se corrige tout seul.

Le premier vers de ce poème est presque mot à mot la deuxième phrase du chapitre 18 du *Laozi*, et les vers 2 et 6 des remaniements de phrases du chapitre 57. Le cinquième vers, par surcroît, est inspiré de *Huainanzi* 20, p. 349. Le tout forme une petite homélie de philosophie taoïste sur les méfaits de l'intelligence et de ce qui atteint à la spontanéité irrationnelle de l'homme primitif.

Le quatrième poème ne contient qu'une seule citation du *Laozi*, mais n'est pas moins une explication de la philosophie taoïste pour autant.

4

La renommée ou la personne, laquelle est la plus chère ?
Hélas ! les gens du monde se sacrifient à la gloire,
Et, dans leur course effrénée, épuisent leurs forces et perdent leur essence vitale.
　Leurs gains et leurs pertes s'embrouillent ; ils restent tristes et épouvantés,
5 Et puis, accablés de travail, ils ne connaissent pas de repos.

Le premier vers est mot à mot le début du *Laozi* 44, et la suite, sans qu'il y ait de citation directe, développe la philosophie taoïste antique d'une façon à la fois traditionnelle et originale. Le portrait psychologique de l'«homme du monde» qui, dans sa course à la gloire, confond ce qui est véritablement profitable pour son bien-être et se trouve coincé dans un cycle inextricable et accablant, semble plus près de nous que les descriptions un peu abstraites de Laozi. La leçon du manuscrit du Congshu tang du deuxième mot du dernier vers, *tan* 貪, ajouterait encore à ce portrait en suggérant (si je comprends bien) que l'homme du monde «se rendait lui-même avide» de ce travail accablant, qu'il recherchait gloutonnement à s'accabler. Mais le terme *zitan* 自貪 ne me semble pas très idiomatique en chinois, et je crois qu'il faut le rejeter.

Le poème suivant, encore inspiré du *Laozi*, suggère une façon de remplacer cette vie consacrée à la recherche du gain par autre chose.

5

Entretenir sa vie trop grassement attire le malheur.
　Quand or et jades remplissent les maisons, celles-ci ne peuvent être gardées.
Les hommes antiques trouvaient leur paix dans ce qui est grossier et méprisé,
　Ayant le *dao* et sa vertu comme seuls amis.
5 C'est pour cela qu'ils ont pu prolonger leur vie et ne pas dépérir.

327

Les deux premiers vers sont inspirés du *Laozi* 50 et 9 respectivement. Les mots «entretenir sa vie», *shengsheng* 生生, qui apparaissent aussi dans le poème donné à Ruan Kan (*supra*, p. 163, vers 25), posent des problèmes. Ils apparaissent aussi dans le *Yi jing* et dans *Zhuangzi* 6 (Watson, p. 83), mais chaque fois avec des sens différents. Il s'agit ici sans doute à la fois de l'entretien concret de la vie physique et de la façon de s'attacher trop étroitement à la vie en tant que telle. Les taoïstes demandent le détachement de tout, sauf du *dao*, qui est tout et qu'il est ainsi impossible d'aimer d'une façon personnelle. Le dernier vers nous rappelle que la recherche de l'immortalité faisait partie du taoïsme de tous temps, et qu'elle joue un rôle très important dans la vie et la pensée de Ji Kang. Ici l'immortalité semble venir par surcroît à ceux qui vivent détachés des biens matériels.

Dans le poème suivant les méfaits de la gloire et de la haute position sont accompagnés des méfaits dus aux passions sexuelles et gastronomiques.

6

Quand la renommée et la conduite sont très en vue les calamités augmentent;
Quand le rang est élevé, le pouvoir important, les malheurs trouvent une
[fondation.
Les beautés charnelles attaquent notre être sans que nous nous en doutions;
Les saveurs fortes sont extrêmement toxiques, difficiles à digérer:
5 Comment se fait-il que les hommes avides de ces choses n'y réfléchissent pas?

Les deux premiers vers décrivent les dangers dus à la renommée; les deux suivants, ceux dus à la luxure. Le lien sous-entendu entre ces deux est sans doute que le premier entraîne le second: le haut rang était naturellement accompagné de luxure, et l'indulgence des sens, tout comme le dérèglement de l'esprit, détruisait l'équilibre psychosomatique et empêchait l'accession à l'immortalité ou à la Longue Vie.

Les quatre derniers poèmes de ce cycle sont des portraits des hommes du passé qui étaient, d'une façon ou d'une autre, exemplaires. Ce qui est intéressant, c'est qu'à part Dongfang Shuo, aucun n'est à proprement parler un héros du taoïsme, mais tous montrent des vertus «taoïstes». Le premier est un courtisan de l'empereur Wu des Han.

7

Dongfang Shuo était parfaitement pur.
De l'extérieur, il paraissait vénal, mais au fond de lui-même, il était vertueux.
Il salissait sa personne et faisait le clown, cachant son nom;
Il ne s'est pas laissé ligoter par les entraves du monde.
5 Insatisfait dans ses désirs, il ne s'est pas engagé.

Dongfang Shuo (154?-93? av. J.-C.) est un personnage complexe, paradoxal même, et dans ce petit poème Ji Kang est conscient de cette complexité. Dongfang Shuo est surtout connu comme un bouffon, un genre de fou du roi à la cour de l'empereur Wu des Han. Il s'est formé autour de lui une légende peut-être même de son vivant et en tout cas peu de temps après sa mort[76], et il est entré sans doute assez tôt dans le panthéon taoïste[77]. Mais on peut interpréter le poème de Ji Kang simplement en se référant à la biographie de Dongfang Shuo par Ban Gu 班固 (32-92) dans *Han shu* 65. Dans cette biographie nous voyons Dongfang Shuo faire le clown en pissant dans le palais impérial ou en montant des mises en scène assez extravagantes destinées à attirer l'attention de l'empereur. Mais nous le voyons aussi présenter à l'empereur, avec un courage tout à fait remarquable, des réprimandes cinglantes, réprimandes qui auraient pu très facilement lui coûter la vie. Ban Gu lui-même, suivant Yang Xiong 揚雄 (53 av.-18 ap. J.-C.)[78], tous les deux confucianistes collet monté, condamne assez sévèrement Dongfang Shuo dans la biographie qu'il lui a consacrée, mais à la fin de son *Han shu* (100 B, p. 4258)[79] il prend soin

[76] Liu Xiang disait que quand il était jeune et qu'il questionnait des vieux du temps de Dongfang Shuo (qui est mort une quinzaine d'années avant la naissance de Liu Xiang), ils lui disaient que Dongfang Shuo aimait raconter des histoires pour épater les gens vulgaires, et que c'est ainsi que des légendes sont nées à son égard (*Han shu* 65, p. 2873). Sur Huan Tan et Dongfang Shuo, voir T. Pokora, *Hsin-lun (New treatise) and other writings by Huan T'an (43 B.C.-28 A.D.)* (Michigan Papers in Chinese Studies No. 20), Ann Arbor, 1975, pp. 37, 125, et note 97 (pp. 141-142). Pokora va jusqu'à mettre en doute l'existence historique de Dongfang Shuo, ce qui me semble abusif.
[77] La légende se trouve dans le *Liexian zhuan*, n° 42, Kaltenmark, pp. 137-138. Dongfang Shuo, dans la religion populaire, est devenu dieu des orfèvres; cf. H. Maspero, *Le taoïsme et les religions chinoises* (Paris, 1971), p. 167.
[78] *Fa yan* 11, p. 36.
[79] Traduit par B. Watson, *Courtier and commoner in ancient China* (New York et Londres, 1974), p. 79.

de signaler, parmi ses clowneries, deux des réprimandes. Yang Xiong et Ban Gu reprochent surtout à Dongfang Shuo ce qui semble être sa philosophie défaitiste de la vie de fonctionnaire. En effet, Dongfang Shuo conseille à son fils d'essayer surtout de «se caser» (Ji Kang y fait allusion plus haut, pp. 156-7), d'éviter le martyre, de se remplir le ventre, de se cacher et de se moquer du monde. Mais ces recommandations sont en complet désaccord avec non seulement ses réprimandes héroïques et désintéressées contre l'empereur Wu, mais aussi avec les deux écrits (des proto-*fu*) contenus dans sa biographie et qui font sa renommée littéraire. Ces œuvres se présentent comme des apologies d'un fonctionnaire qui n'a pas fait une brillante carrière parce qu'il est né dans un monde trop bien gouverné, qui n'avait pas besoin de grands héros (comme il aurait su l'être), mais en fait ce sont des œuvres satiriques contre l'Establishment qui ne laisse pas percer les talents méritoires (c'est-à-dire, lui-même).

Ces deux aspects de sa vie, ses clowneries et sa philosophie défaitiste, d'un côté, son courage et son désir de percer dans le monde actif de l'autre, sont parfaitement contradictoires et Ji Kang a bien raison de le souligner dans ce petit poème. Il était «parfaitement pur» et «paraissait» seulement «de l'extérieur, vénal». Ji Kang le loue de se cacher en faisant le clown et d'éviter ainsi les «liens du monde». Le dernier vers est obscur et, exceptionnellement, j'adopte le texte courant plutôt que celui du Congshu tang. Ce dernier donne 所以知足無營 où les deux premiers caractères représentent une locution de la langue parlée moderne inconnue au temps de Ji Kang. Une traduction donnerait: «Aussi a-t-il su se contenter sans s'engager», où «savoir se contenter» réfère à *Laozi* (chapitres 33, 44 et 46). La leçon que j'ai suivie, quoiqu'un peu gauche, résume bien la vie de Dongfang Shuo: frustré dans sa carrière, il a néanmoins refusé de manœuvrer pour arriver à une haute position.

Le taoïsme chez Dongfang Shuo est assez superficiel. Les quatre personnages qui sont sujets des trois derniers poèmes de la série ne sont pas taoïstes du tout et me font penser que nous avons tort de chercher quoique ce soit d'exclusivement «taoïste» chez Dongfang Shuo pour expliquer sa présence dans cette série de poèmes. Le huitième poème met en scène deux héros confucianistes sortis tout droit du *Lun yu*.

8

Ziwen de Chu a occupé habilement son emploi publique.
Trois fois il est devenu grand ministre sans s'en réjouir.
[Hui] de Liuxia s'est abaissé et a bravé la honte :
   Il n'a pas considéré son rang et son traitement comme des biens personnels.
5 Calmes, déférents : dans l'antiquité il n'y avait que ces deux !

Ziwen 子文 était une des appellations de Duo Guwutu 鬭榖於菟,
«Duo allaité par une vieille tigresse», qui est mentionné dans le *Zuo
zhuan*, Zhuang 30 (l'année 633 av. J.-C.). Là on dit qu'il est devenu
grand ministre et qu'il a dépouillé sa maison pour venir en aide à
l'État de Chu pendant une période de difficultés. Il a secouru son
pays à plusieurs reprises (*Zuo zhuan*, Xi 5 et 20) et est mort en 604
(Xuan 4). C'est dans le *Lun yu* 5, 18, que nous apprenons que «Le
grand ministre Ziwen a été employé trois fois comme grand ministre
sans montrer de joie sur son visage; et trois fois il a été destitué de
cette fonction sans montrer de mécontentement. Et chaque fois sans
faute il a informé son remplaçant des affaires courantes».

Hui 惠 de Liuxia 柳下 était l'appellation de Zhan Qin 展禽 qui
est mentionné dans le *Zuo zhuan*, à l'année 724 (Wen 2) dans un
passage qui cite Confucius (cf. aussi *Lun yu* 15, 13), mais c'est sans
doute au *Lun yu* 18, 2, que Ji Kang fait allusion ici : «Quand Hui
de Liuxia était juge (*shishi* 士師), il a été trois fois démis de ses fonctions. Quelqu'un lui dit : 'Ne feriez-vous pas mieux de vous en aller?'.
Il répondit : 'Quand on sert honnêtement, on sera démis trois fois
où qu'on aille; et si je voulais servir d'une façon malhonnête [et ne
pas être démis], quel besoin aurais-je de quitter le pays de mes
parents?'». Le terme «braver la honte», *mengchi* 蒙恥, semble être
tiré de l'éloge de Hui de Liuxia fait par sa veuve rapporté dans le
Lienü zhuan.

Comme dans les deux premiers poèmes de cette série, Ji Kang ici
loue le désintéressement de ces deux héros antiques, un désintéressement qui leur permet de ne pas être atteints psychologiquement par
leur destitution officielle. Leurs vertus sont tout à fait «confucianistes»,
les vertus d'hommes engagés dans la vie active. Dans le poème suivant,
nous voyons la louange de la retraite qu'on aurait de la peine à
qualifier de «confucianiste» ou «taoïste».

9

La femme de Laolai[zi] était sage et intelligente.
Elle n'a pas voulu que son mari soit ministre de Chu.
Elle a su fuir les traitements officiels et cultiver la terre dans la retraite.
Prenant sa joie du *dao*, sans emploi, cueillant des plantes aquatiques,
5 Jusqu'à la fin elle a perfectionné sa moralité altière sans fléchir.

Laolaizi 老萊子 est une figure encore plus obscure que Dongfang
Shuo et, comme ce dernier, il est quelquefois présenté comme un
«taoïste», bien que plus souvent il soit décrit comme un parangon de
piété filiale. Quoiqu'il en soit du Laolaizi historique (s'il y en a jamais
eu[80]), Ji Kang ici s'inspire de sa biographie telle qu'elle apparaît dans
le *Lienü zhuan* et le *Gaoshi zhuan*. Dans ces textes on voit Laolaizi
vivant en hermite au sud du mont Meng 蒙 (au sud de Mengyin,
Shandong), invité par le roi de Chu à gérer le gouvernement. Laolaizi
accepte, mais sa femme s'y oppose, craignant qu'ils perdent leur
liberté. Laolaizi se ravise et suit sa femme au sud du Yangzi où ils
vivent tout proche de la nature. Il est assez rare dans la Chine
ancienne de voir un homme suivre l'avis de sa femme, mais, pour le
reste, cette fuite de l'engagement politique est très répandue, et le
vocabulaire que Ji Kang emploie dans le quatrième vers, avec des
échos du *Lun yu* 1, 15 (cf. *Shi ji* 67, p. 2196), *Xunzi* 15 (section 21),
p. 268 (éd. Zhuzi jicheng) et *Shi jing* 15, montre que fuir le monde
peut être «taoïste» ou «confucianiste» (ou les deux à la fois).

Le dernier poème décrit un pur confucéen, disciple direct du
Maître.

10

Ah! ce sage antique qu'était Yuan Xian!
Il a rejeté les mets riches et les visages roses.
Il était heureux d'être souvent démuni de tout, d'avoir faim et froid.
D'aspect humble, mais de corps libre, de cœur large,
5 Il a réalisé ses ambitions, restant sans malheur toute sa vie.

---

[80] La monographie bibliographique du *Han shu* 30, p. 1730, donne 16 *pian* 篇
d'œuvres de Laolaizi, dans la catégorie des taoïstes. Sima Qian (*Shi ji* 63, p. 2141)
présente Laolaizi dans la biographie de Laozi comme s'ils étaient le même homme.

Yuan Xian 原憲, dont le *zi* était Si 思, est cité deux fois dans le *Lun yu*. Dans le chapitre 6, 3, il renonce à son salaire de neuf cents mesures de grain, mais est encouragé à les accepter par Confucius qui lui suggère de les distribuer parmi ses futurs administrés. Le chapitre 14 commence par le prénom de Yuan Xian et porte son nom comme titre; il est quelquefois considéré comme écrit par lui. Le premier paragraphe de ce chapitre concerne aussi le salaire d'un fonctionnaire qui trouve honteux d'accepter un salaire dans un état qui n'est pas gouverné selon le *dao*. Dans le *Shi ji* 67, p. 2208, et dans le *Zhuangzi* 28 (Watson, pp. 315-316), Yuan Xian, vêtu de haillons et logé dans une chaumière, se moque de l'opulence de Zigong, autre disciple de Confucius, disant qu'il préfère sa pauvreté aux richesses gagnées grâce à une conduite en désaccord avec le *dao*. Yan Hui, autre disciple de Confucius, est loué par le Maître (*Lun yu* 11, 18) parce qu'il est «souvent démuni de tout».

Il est difficile de distinguer un seul thème commun qui lierait ensemble ces dix poèmes. Ils baignent tous dans une même atmosphère de renoncement aux sentiments personnels, de la fuite de la célébrité et des richesses et la recherche de l'équanimité face aux vicissitudes de la vie. La tendance générale des poèmes (surtout les poèmes 3 à 6) est taoïste, mais les deux premiers poèmes et les quatre derniers sont plutôt d'inspiration complexe, louant des traits de caractère communs aux deux philosophies chez des personnages qu'on doit qualifier de héros confucianistes. Le tout fait penser à une œuvre de propagande taoïste un peu subversive: on glisse d'un parangon confucianiste à un autre tout en développant la philosophie de Laozi. Les hexamètres statiques, un peu cahotants et gauches, bon enfant et rimés, semblent choisis pour faire passer le tout sans que le lecteur puisse opposer un raisonnement contraire. Sur le plan esthétique, ou sur le plan du pouvoir d'émouvoir, on ne peut pas appeler cette série de poèmes une réussite; mais sur le plan de la rhétorique, du pouvoir de convaincre le lecteur de la vérité du message religieux prêché par Ji Kang, on ne peut pas nier l'efficacité de cette remarquable série de petits sermons versifiés.

Sept poèmes en tétramètres sur le chant Qiu Hu

La série de sept poèmes en forme de *yuefu* est à la fois plus réussie sur le plan esthétique et mieux organisée. Les quatre premiers poèmes prêchent une philosophie de renoncement aux richesses, honneurs et aux désirs semblable à celle de la série précédente et les trois derniers tirent en quelque sorte la conclusion de ce renoncement en chantant les joies de la vie libre et exaltée des immortels taoïstes. La forme utilisée ressemble beaucoup à une, ou peut-être deux, séries de *yuefu* par Cao Cao qui vont sous la rubrique du «Chant de Qiu hu», ce qui est une référence à une histoire d'infidélité conjugale masculine et fidélité féminine qui n'a aucun rapport (comme c'est souvent le cas) avec les poèmes de Cao Cao et de Ji Kang. Cette rubrique concerne, sans doute, un poème ou une chanson qui portait ce titre et qui a donné le modèle musical ou prosodique à ces poèmes. Les poèmes de Cao Cao[81] sont assez obscurs. Ils semblent à première vue être des chants à la gloire de la vie des immortels dans les hautes montagnes de l'ouest. Mais à deux reprises au moins, Cao Cao se détourne du monde des immortels pour rentrer dans le monde des hommes et reprendre sa place de facto comme chef de l'État.

Les poèmes de Ji Kang imitent d'assez près la forme des poèmes de Cao Cao : les deux premiers vers sont répétés ; une courte phrase («Je le dis en chantant», chez Ji Kang et «Je dis mon ambition en chantant», chez Cao Cao) apparaît comme l'avant-dernier vers ; et le dernier vers, chez Cao Cao, répète le premier de chaque poème, et, chez Ji Kang, en général, le dernier vers répète le deuxième vers ou un vers composé des mots choisis dans les deux premiers vers. Chez Ji Kang seuls les deuxième et dernier vers sont des pentamètres ; tous les autres sont des tétramètres. La prosodie est, on peut le voir, assez compliquée, mais le résultat est de donner l'apparence de poèmes à chanter et de cacher ainsi le caractère didactique du contenu. Les deux premiers poèmes, avec leur dénonciation des richesses et hon-

---

[81] Ces deux poèmes sont traduits par E. Balazs, *Chinese civilization and bureaucracy* (trad. H. M. Wright), New Haven et Londres, 1964, pp. 173-186, et D. von den Steinen, «Poems of Ts'ao Ts'ao», *Monumenta serica* (Peiping) 4, 1 (1939), pp. 177-179.

neurs, semblent continuer le message des poèmes en hexamètres que nous venons de lire.

1

Richesses et honneurs, noblesse et gloire
   N'apportent, en vérité, que tristesse et calamités en abondance.
Richesses et honneurs, noblesse et gloire
   N'apportent, en vérité, que tristesse et calamités en abondance.
5 Ce que les anciens craignaient,
   C'était d'agrandir la maison pour cacher la famille.
Les hommes nuisent à leurs supérieurs,
   [Comme] les, animaux détestent le filet.
Il n'y a que la pauvreté et la condition basse
10   Qui permettent de vivre sans histoires.
Je le dis en chantant :
   Richesses et honneurs attirent tristesse et calamités en grand nombre!

L'allusion dans le sixième vers est au 55e hexagramme du *Yi jing* (Legge, p. 186) où il s'agit du Texte de la sixième ligne (la plus haute). Cette ligne décrit une condition de grande abondance et de grand malheur, l'accroissement des biens ne pouvant mener qu'au malheur. Les vers 7 et 8 sont presque mot à mot d'un adage rapporté dans le *Guo yu*, «Zhou yu» B, p. 84 (de l'édition de Shanghai, 1978), et, avec des variations, dans le *Zuo zhuan*, Cheng 15, et le *Shuo yuan* 10, p. 13a (édition Han Wei congshu, Shanghai, 1925). Le poème entier est une déclaration des dangers des richesses dans un monde, si l'on peut croire les vers 7 et 8, menacé par la lutte des classes.

Le deuxième poème poursuit ce même sujet, mais met l'emphase sur les aléas de la vie politique, où, il faut dire, sous les régimes autocratiques, les dangers des positions élevées étaient (et sont) considérables.

2

Il est facile d'être pauvre et de condition basse ;
   L'art de vivre noble et prospère est difficile.
Il est facile d'être pauvre et de condition basse ;
   L'art de vivre noble et prospère est difficile.
5 Flatterie éhontée ou parole franche
   Mènent au désastre [toutes les deux].

Les accidents ont une infinité de causes
   Et changent le bonheur en malheur:
   Si vous voulez emmener votre chien jaune [à la chasse],
10   Vous ne pourrez pas réaliser votre désir.
   Je le dis en chantant:
     L'art de vivre noble et prospère est difficile.

Les deux premiers vers montrent que Ji Kang voyait très bien ce que sa philosophie avait d'arbitraire et de provocant parce qu'ils sont en fait la transformation de deux phrases d'un auteur des Han qui voulaient dire exactement le contraire de ce qui Ji Kang leur fait dire ici. Il s'agit de deux phrases de Feng Yan 馮衍 (né vers le début de notre ère): «Il est facile d'être bon quand on est riche et noble, difficile de savoir vivre pauvre et de condition basse» (citées dans le *Hou Han shu* 28 B, p. 984). Ji Kang reconnaît implicitement, en utilisant ces deux phrases presque telles quelles, qu'il est volontairement paradoxal, qu'il dit le contraire de ce qui se dit d'ordinaire. Le cinquième vers contient une variante, le ms du Congshu tang donnant 接 pour le 佞 des éditions imprimées. Il faudrait lire: «Ils [les riches?] ont honte de recevoir des paroles franches». C'est la solution que suggère Ma Xulun, mais elle ne me satisfait pas. Il me semble plutôt que Ji Kang est ici en train de gronder les riches et puissants d'une façon générale et de dire que leurs paroles, qu'elles soient fausses ou vraies, ne feront que les impliquer dans les affaires de l'État et les mener à la catastrophe. Les vers 9 et 10 sont comme la preuve de cette philosophie et sont une allusion aux dernières paroles du ministre du Premier Empereur des Qin, Li Si. Celui-ci, après la mort de son souverain, a été exécuté avec toute sa famille. Selon sa biographie dans *Shi ji* 87, p. 2562, il se serait tourné vers son deuxième fils lorsqu'ils s'approchaient de l'échafaud pour lui dire combien il regrettait de ne pas pouvoir partir à la chasse aux lièvres avec lui en emmenant leur chien jaune. La chute du pouvoir de Li Si et son exécution sont souvent évoqués comme symboles des «accidents» (vers 7) et vicissitudes de la vie politique.

Le troisième poème évoque la philosophie du *Yi jing* (15ᵉ hexagramme) et de Laozi tout en poursuivant la recherche d'une vie paisible commencée dans les deux premiers poèmes.

3

Soyez modeste dans vos mérites et vous serez sans remords;
Soyez sincère et honnête et vous resterez longtemps en paix.
Soyez modeste dans vos mérites et vous serez sans remords;
Soyez sincère et honnête et vous resterez longtemps en paix.
5 La Voie du Ciel nuit à ce qui est plein;
Ceux qui aiment la victoire seront détruits.
La violence amène la catastrophe;
S'occuper trop d'affaires invite les calamités.
Si l'on veut atteindre au bonheur paisible
10   Il n'y a qu'un seul moyen: être sans excès.
Je le dis en chantant:
Soyez sincère et honnête et vous resterez longtemps en paix.

Le premier et le cinquième vers font allusion au quinzième hexagramme du *Yi jing*, «Modestie». La troisième ligne de l'hexagramme
parle de «mérite et modestie: l'homme supérieur aura le bonheur
jusqu'à la fin». Le remords est un sentiment souvent évoqué dans le
Yi jing, mais, si l'on suit la variante 寡 pour 無: «avoir peu de
remords», il y a un écho du *Lun yu* 2, 18. Le *tuan* du quinzième
hexagramme dit que «la Voie du Ciel réduit ce qui est plein et
ajoute à ce qui est modeste». «Sincère et honnête» pourrait être
aussi un écho du *Lun yu* où ces mots apparaissent ensemble six ou
sept fois. Ils apparaissent aussi dans le *Zhuangzi*, mais presque toujours dans des contextes où ces vertus sont considérées défavorable-
ment. Le vers 7 rappelle *Laozi* 42 et le vers suivant au moins trois
auteurs des Han. Le poème entier, malgré le rappel de Laozi, semble
plus «confucianiste» que «taoïste», comme d'ailleurs, les deux précédents poèmes de la série. Il y a un grand terrain d'entente entre les
deux tendances philosophiques et ces trois premiers poèmes, comme
la série hexamétrique, peuvent être rattachés aussi bien à l'une qu'à
l'autre.

C'est avec le quatrième poème que nous commençons à voir un
changement vers le taoïsme qui caractérise les écrits en prose de Ji
Kang.

4

Ceux qui surmènent leur esprit s'abîment;
Donner libre cours à ses désirs dessèche l'homme.

337

Ceux qui surmènent leur esprit, s'abîment;
    Donner libre cours à ses désirs, dessèche l'homme.
5 Yan Hui est mort jeune,
    Comme, plus tard, Tongwu.
Laissez aller votre corps à une licence excessive
    Et vous serez sûr d'aller tôt à votre mort.
Quelles choses sont vin et luxure
10 Que nous les innocentions?
Je le dis en chantant:
    Le vin et la luxure dessèchent l'homme.

La philosophie taoïste de ce poème est assez facile à suivre: le travail intellectuel et la vie débauchée sont tous les deux nocifs. Mais les vers 6 et 10, tous les deux présentant des variantes textuelles, sont difficiles à comprendre et peut-être corrompus. Je lis le deuxième vers aussi dans la version du Congshu tang (極欲令人枯; Dai Mingyang fait erreur quand il écrit 疾 pour le premier caractère de ce vers). Yan Hui était le disciple préféré de Confucius. *Lun yu* 6, 3, et 11, 6, disent: «Yan Hui était un homme qui aimait les études, mais, hélas, son destin a été court et il est mort [jeune]». Il me semble clair que Ji Kang veut nous faire croire ici que c'est parce qu'il «aimait les études» que Yan Hui est mort jeune. Tongwu 童烏 était le sobriquet du fils de Yang Xiong. Lui aussi était extrêmement intelligent (il parlait de la métaphysique, *xuan* 玄, avec son père à l'âge de neuf *sui*), et il est mort très jeune (*Fa yan* 5, pp. 14-15). La leçon des éditions imprimées du vers 6 (不 pour 下) donnerait: «Il [c'est-à-dire Yan Hui] n'a pas atteint Tongwu». Chen Zuoming et Huang Jie essaient d'expliquer cette leçon, le premier disant que Yan Hui a suscité sa mort en se laissant aller à ses passions, le second, qu'il n'a pas suivi le régime préconisé par Ji Kang dans son essai «Nourrir la vie». Les deux auteurs sont d'accord que Tongwu est mort à cause de son destin, ce qui le rend moins coupable que Yan Hui. Ma Xulun suit la leçon du ms en préconisant que Yan Hui est mort à 18 *sui* (*Hou Han shu* 30B, p. 1070), et que, malgré son jeune âge, il bat encore Tongwu, mort deux fois plus jeune. Quelque soit l'interprétation de ce vers, je crois que Ma Xulun a raison quand il dit que Yan Hui et Tongwu sont cités parce qu'ils sont morts jeunes après s'être distingués par leur intelligence et, sous-entendu, à cause d'une trop grande activité intellectuelle précoce. Les vers 7 à 10 commentent la deuxième partie du refrain initial. Les deux premiers mots du vers 10 se lisent 自令 dans le ms et 今自 dans les éditions imprimées. Dans l'un ou l'autre cas, je crois, avec Huang Jie, qu'il y a un écho, dans le mot 宰 à la fin du vers, du *Shang shu*, «Jiu kao»: «C'était toujours le vin qui était coupable». Dans ce quatrième poème Ji Kang se révèle taoïste, avec l'emphase sur le taoïsme religieux et les régimes de la Longue Vie.

Le cinquième poème, sans doute le plus beau de la série, s'appuie fortement sur la pensée de Laozi et de Zhuangzi.

5

Je renonce à la sagesse, je rejette les études
  Et je laisse errer mon cœur dans le Silence Obscur.
Je renonce à la sagesse, je rejette les études
  Et je laisse errer mon cœur dans le Silence Obscur.
5 Si je faute, je n'ai pas de remords,
  Et quand j'atteins mon but, je n'en retire pas de satisfaction.
Je jette ma ligne dans un seul torrent,
  Mais ma joie est celle d'un roi dans son royaume.
Je dénoue mes cheveux et je m'en vais chantant,
10 Tandis que les souffles harmonieux remplissent les frontières.
Je le dis en chantant:
  ╴Je laisse errer mon cœur dans le Silence Obscur.

Le premier vers contient des allusions au *Laozi* 19 et 20: «Je renonce à la sainteté, je rejette la sagesse» et «Renoncez aux études et vous serez sans tristesse». Le terme «Silence Obscur» apparaît dans un *fu* de Yang Xiong (*Wen xuan* 9, p. 3a). Les vers 5 et 6 sont une allusion à *Zhuangzi* 6 (Watson, p. 75), dans la leçon du ms du Congshu tang, mais il faut corriger cette leçon et pour *fu* 復, lire l'homonyme 弗, comme le texte de *Zhuangzi*, presque mot à mot le même que le texte du poème de Ji Kang. Le terme *zide* 自得, que je traduis par «satisfaction», veut dire aussi «bonheur» ou même «satisfaction de soi», «vantardise».·Les vers 7 et 8 font allusion peut-être à des remarques contenues dans une lettre que le père de Ban Gu, Ban Si 班嗣, a écrit à Huan Tan 桓譚. Ban Si décrit Zhuangzi (appelé Yanzi 嚴子 pour éviter le tabou du nom de l'empereur Ming) dans les phrases suivantes: «Il pêche dans un seul torrent, et les dix-mille êtres ne s'opposent pas à son ambition; il prend sa retraite sur un seul coteau, et ne changera pas son bonheur pour tout l'empire» (*Han shu* 100A, p. 4205). Ji Kang cite cette lettre dans son *Shengxian gaoshi zhuanzan* (Dai, p. 415). Je traduis la variante du Congshu tang pour le vers 10 (氣 pour 者). La leçon des éditions imprimées donnerait (comme traduit A. Waley, *Chinese poems*, Londres, 1948, p. 83): «Aux quatre frontières on s'harmonise avec moi». Dans les deux versions le poète décrit une harmonie universelle provoquée peut-être par la présence d'un Homme Parfait, *zhenren* 眞人, tel qu'il apparaît dans le passage cité du *Zhuangzi*. Dans la version du manuscrit, cette harmonie se manifeste dans les souffles du *yin* et du *yang*; dans la version des éditions imprimées (moins bonne, à mon avis), l'harmonie est humaine, celle d'une fraternité entre les hommes.

Le rejet de la culture et de la sagesse des poèmes 4 et 5 prépare aux voyages mystiques chez les immortels des deux derniers poèmes.

6

Je pense avec Wang Qiao
  Monter sur les nuages et voyager aux Huit Pôles.
Je pense avec Wang Qiao
  Monter sur les nuages et voyager aux Huit Pôles.
5 Nous survolerons les Cinq Pics,
  Traversant en un instant des distances infinies.
Il me donnera des herbes divines
  Qui feront pousser toutes seules des ailes couvertes de plumes.
Expirant et inspirant la Grande Harmonie,
10 Affinant ma forme physique, je transformerai mon teint.
Je le dis en chantant:
  Je pense m'en aller me promener aux Huit Pôles.

Nous avons déjà rencontré Wang Qiao, ou Wangzi Qiao (*supra*, p. 138); les Cinq Pics sont les monts Tai (Shandong), Heng (Shanxi), Hua (Shaanxi), Heng (Hunan) et Song (Henan), aux quatre directions et au centre; et les Huit Pôles sont les extrémités du monde aux huit directions. Le poème entier est une description un peu stéréotypée d'une randonnée avec un immortel. Il n'y a que l'expression «transformer mon teint», *yise* 易色, qui semble originale; elle veut dire «regagner un teint d'enfant» (Dai Mingyang).

Le dernier poème est aussi très peu original.

7

J'erre çà et là sur le mont Zhong
Et j'arrête ma voiture à la Muraille Étagée.
J'erre çà et là sur le mont Zhong
Et j'arrête ma voiture à la Muraille Étagée.
5 [Le ciel] en haut est couvert par le Dais Multicolore;
[La terre] en bas est diaprée par les fleurs de l'Arbre Ruo.
Je reçois le *dao* de la Reine Mère,
Et la suis pour monter à la Cour Pourpre.
Je m'abandonne sur la Grande Route céleste
10 Pendant mille années de Longue Vie!
Je le dis en chantant:
J'erre çà et là à la Muraille Étagée.

Le mont Zhong 鍾 du premier vers est glosé dans le commentaire du *Huainanzi* 2, p. 22, comme étant un autre nom des Kunlun, les montagnes des immortels à l'ouest. La Muraille Étagée, Zengcheng 增城, selon le même livre (4, p. 56), se trouve dans les Kunlun, et, selon le *Shuijing zhu* 1, p. 1, Cengcheng 層城 (même orthographe que dans ce poème), est le point culminant des Kunlun, le séjour du Grand Empereur, Taidi 太帝. Le Dais Multicolore, Huagai 華蓋, a plusieurs sens mais semble indiquer un constellation ici, celle composée de neuf étoiles qui couvre le trône du Grand Empereur (cf. *Jin shu* 11, p. 289; Ho Peng Yoke, *The astronomical chapters of the Chin shu*, Paris et La Haye, 1966, p. 69). L'Arbre Ruo se trouve à l'extrême ouest, à l'endroit où se couchent les dix soleils (*Shanhai jing* 17, p. 7a; les références données par Huang Jie ne sont pas à propos ici). La Reine Mère est la Reine Mère de l'Ouest, Xi wang mu 西王母, importante divinité taoïste qui réside dans les monts Kunlun (cf. *Mu tianzi zhuan* 3, trad. R. Mathieu, Paris, 1978, pp. 44 et suiv.). La Cour Pourpre, Zi ting 紫庭, indique la cour de l'Empereur Céleste, mais, autant que j'aie pu voir, le terme n'apparaît pas avant Ji Kang.

Ces deux derniers poèmes dans cette série de sept ressemblent beaucoup à des *yuefu* sur le même thème des immortels par Cao Cao et son fils Cao Zhi. Dans tous ces poèmes nous retrouvons quelques épisodes semblables: la promenade en montagne ou dans les nuages, la rencontre avec un immortel, le don d'une drogue ou d'une recette, ou d'un livre saint, la réalisation de la Longue Vie des adeptes taoïstes[82]. Le *yuefu* de Cao Pi, «Zhe yangliu xing», appartient à cette catégorie, et a peut-être fourni un modèle pour les vers 7 et 8 du sixième poème de Ji Kang. Mais dans les dernières strophes de son poème Cao Pi nie l'existence des immortels et se proclame partisan de la «Voie des Saints» (confucianistes). L'existence d'un assez grand nombre de ces poèmes par des poètes différents, dont certains (tels Cao Zhi et Cao Pi) ont déclaré par ailleurs qu'ils ne croient pas aux immortels, nous oblige à nous demander quel sens il faut leur donner. Est-ce que ce sont des écrits de circonstance, des élucubrations formelles, faites pour chanter à table et pour souhaiter une vie longue à un convive? Des écrits satiriques dans lesquels le poète annonce son désir de quitter le monde corrompu? Ou faut-il accepter le sens premier, et croire le poète quand il dit qu'il désire «prolonger sa vie» et «se promener avec Wangzi Qiao» dans une randonnée mystique sur les cimes sacrées? Il n'y a pas de solution passe-partout à ce problème. Les premiers poèmes dans cette tradition, et sans doute la plupart de ceux qui les ont suivis, sont ambigus. Le «Li sao» de Qu Yuan, un poème qui décrit une ascension chamaniste et qui se termine par ce qui semble être une décision de suivre la vie d'un adepte taoïste, baigne tout entier dans un contexte politique et satirique, et les autres poèmes du *Chu ci* sont également ambigus[83]. Dans les autres poèmes des *Chu ci* et dans les *yuefu* qui traitent du thème des immortels, la fuite du monde politique corrompu semble partout présente. Il me semble que nous devons admettre sinon la primauté de la politique sur le religieux, au moins un lien important entre les deux, un lien que rien dans nos propres traditions ne permet d'apprécier.

Mais revenons aux poèmes de Ji Kang. Les deux derniers sont si stéréotypés et rappellent tant ceux des poètes «incroyants» qu'on doit se demander le sens qu'ils peuvent avoir dans cette série. On ne peut s'empêcher de les considérer autrement que comme symboliques.

[82] Cf. Funatsu Tomihiko 船津富彦, «Sô Shoku no yûsen shi ron», *Tôyô bungaku kenkyû* (Tokyo) 13 (1965), pp. 49-65 (*Revue bibliographique de sinologie* 11, n° 505).

[83] L'ambiguïté de ce thème commence au tout début de la tradition: cf. D. Hawkes, *Chu ci*, p. 21, et «The supernatural in Chinese poetry», *University of Toronto Quarterly* 30, 3 (1961), pp. 311-324.

Et pourtant, leur position à la fin de cette série de poèmes taoïstes qui prêchent le rejet de tout ce qui peut nuire à une vie mystique — les richesses et les honneurs, les désirs charnels, et jusqu'à la vie de l'intellect — nous oblige à les accepter comme des descriptions au premier degré de l'exaltation mystique. Chen Zuoming, prisonnier de la tradition allégorique ou satirique de ces poèmes, interprète le sixième comme le désir de Ji Kang de «se séparer du monde, parce qu'il n'arrivait pas, au fond, à s'entendre avec les gens du commun sans se compromettre» (cité par Dai Mingyang). Je ne peux pas me rallier à son avis. Cette série de poèmes est consacrée toute entière à la description d'un dépouillement religieux qui mène à une randonnée mystique dans la meilleure tradition taoïste, et s'apparente ainsi à la série de poèmes écrits à son frère aîné.

Un autre poème sur le même thème, et qui ressemble beaucoup aux deux derniers que nous venons de lire, contient peut-être un élément allégorique. Il s'agit d'un poème en pentamètres réguliers intitulé : *Immortels en promenade*.

Immortels en promenade

Au loin je regarde le pin sur la montagne :
   Au plus fort de l'hiver il reste foisonnant de verdure.
Comme il se trouve placé haut,
   Se tenant seul, sans son pareil jusqu'au loin !
5 Je voudrais me promener à sa base,
   Mais les sentiers sont coupés et ne l'atteignent pas.
Wang Qiao s'en va en me soulevant,
   Monté sur un nuage, conduisant six dragons.
Tournoyant dans les airs, nous jouons dans le Jardin Mystérieux,
10   Et rencontrons Huang Lao sur la route.
Il m'enseigne la Voie de la Spontanéité,
   Et je rayonne comme un enfant dont on dissiperait l'ignorance.
Je cherche des simples dans les recoins du mont Zhong
   Que je consomme pour changer de mine.
15 Je mue comme la cigale, en rejetant tout attachement impur,
   Me liant d'amitié [avec ces immortels] et prenant logis à Bantong.
On joue la musique «les Neuf Shao» pour accompagner nos parties à boire :
   Comme ces chants élégants sont harmonieux !
Je quitterai à tout jamais les hommes vulgaires,
20   Et personne ne pourra plus suivre mes traces.

Le mot traduit par «hiver» dans le deuxième vers se lit «vallée», *gu* 谷, dans tous les textes. Je suis Dai Mingyang qui justifie sa correction en citant une imitation d'un poème de Ji Kang écrite par la femme, née Xie 謝, de Wang Ningzhi 王凝之 (celui-ci mort en 399). Son poème commence par les vers: «Je regarde, au loin, le pin sur la montagne;/ Au plus fort de l'hiver il ne perd pas ses aiguilles» (cité dans *Yiwen leiju* 88, p. 6a). Dans tous les textes le vers 7 doit se lire: «Wang Qiao s'en va en me rejetant», ce qui ne donne pas de sens dans le contexte. Luxun suggère de substituer 异, caractère que le *Shuowen* glose comme voulant dire «soulever». Cette partie du poème (du vers 6 à la fin), la véritable «promenade des immortels», ne présente pas de très grandes originalités. Les allusions sont au monde des immortels: pour Wang Qiao, ou Wangzi Qiao, voir *supra*, p. 138 et p. 339; le Jardin Mystérieux, appelé «Jardin suspendu», *xuan* 懸 dans *Huainanzi* 4, p. 56, et «mystérieux» dans *Shuijing zhu* 1, p. 1, et mont Zhong (voir p. 340) sont tous les deux dans les Kunlun, les monts des immortels. Huang Lao est un dieu qui joue un rôle important dans le taoïsme religieux sous les Han[84]. Bantong 板桐, selon le *Huainanzi* 4, p. 56, où l'on écrit *fan* 樊, se trouve aussi dans les Kunlun. Les Neuf Shao sont une musique très ancienne attribuée à l'empereur Shun (*Huainanzi* 13, p. 212).

Les épisodes de cette deuxième partie du poème se rencontrent dans d'autres poèmes de cette époque, comme nous l'avons déjà vu. Ce qui est intéressant surtout dans ce poème de Ji Kang, c'est la juxtaposition des deux parties qui le composent. C'est seulement après avoir observé le magnifique pin solitaire haut sur la montagne et compris qu'il ne pouvait s'y approcher (vers 5-6) que Ji Kang s'élève dans les airs pour se promener avec les immortels. Il semble clair que ce pin sur la montagne joue le rôle d'un symbole, mais il me semble aussi que nous aurions tort de vouloir serrer de trop près le sens de ce symbole. Le pin dans la poésie ancienne est en général un symbole de courage, constance et loyauté, étant un arbre qui reste toujours vert, même pendant les périodes de grand froid. C'est aussi un arbre qu'on trouve souvent solitaire, et c'est un des rares qui

---

[84] Cf. H. Maspero, *Le taoïsme et les religions chinoises*, pp. 403-404, 464-465, 527.

pousse sur les hauteurs des massifs montagneux. Je crois qu'il faut voir tous ces éléments dans ces vers de Ji Kang : le pin représente un idéal de constance et de fermeté, mais un idéal inapprochable. Pourquoi est-ce inapprochable? Ji Kang ne nous le dit pas. Faut-il voir dans l'inabilité de s'approcher de cet idéal de fermeté et de loyauté une image de l'inabilité de Ji Kang de rester fidèle à son souverain? L'explication est tentante, les données historiques concordantes (l'usurpation des Sima a été effectuée d'une telle façon que la famille impériale est restée inapprochable pendant les dix dernières années de leur règne) et le fait que Ji Kang était marié à une princesse impériale l'a certainement attaché fortement aux Cao. La juxtaposition de ces deux parties du poème demande une explication et celle d'une déception dans la vie active qui mène à une vie de recherche de l'immortalité est satisfaisante parce qu'elle est traditionnelle dans ce genre de poèmes, elle correspond aux données de la vie de Ji Kang et, surtout, elle ressort des vers du poème eux-mêmes. Mais faut-il conclure que Ji Kang «ne recherche pas vraiment les immortels : il veut simplement 'quitter à tout jamais les hommes vulgaires'», comme le dit Chen Zuoming, en citant le dernier vers de ce poème? Je ne pense pas. Au mieux, on pourrait dire que, dans ce poème, la recherche de l'immortalité semble être un pis-aller.

Dans ces poèmes philosophiques Ji Kang nous montre encore une fois ses aspirations taoïstes qui paraissent ici plus complexes que dans sa prose. Il y a une exploitation de la tradition confucianiste et aussi, dans le poème que nous venons de lire, la suggestion d'une nostalgie de la vie politique assez rares dans son œuvre. Ces poèmes nous montrent à la fois un homme influencé par le syncrétisme philosophique ambiant, mais aussi et surtout un penseur et un esprit religieux profondément épris des valeurs de la philosophie taoïste.

5

LES POÈMES AUTOBIOGRAPHIQUES

En 260 et puis en 262, la dernière année de sa vie, Ji Kang a écrit les seuls poèmes qu'on puisse, avec plus ou moins d'assurance, dater. Ce sont tous des poèmes d'une très grande originalité et le dernier est un testament d'une très grande importance, peut-être son chef d'œuvre poétique.

La première poésie doit dater d'environ 260 ou 261, c'est-à-dire un ou deux ans avant sa mort et avant ses derniers testaments poétiques dont les traductions termineront mon étude. Il s'agit d'un long poème intitulé «Pensant à mes parents», «Siqin shi» 思親詩, écrit en vers appelés «chanson de Chu», *Chu ge* 楚歌, vers qu'on trouve dans les *Chu ci* (dans les «Jiu si» de Wang Yi notamment), et qui sont composés de six syllabes séparées au milieu par une césure (marquée par un caractère purement phonétique, *xi* 兮). Les rimes sont par couplets, et changent avec chaque couplet.

Le poème, une lamentation très tendue, un cri douloureux et presque sans répit, décrit la peine de Ji Kang à la mort de sa mère et d'un de ses frères aînés. Il parle de cet événement (ou de ces événements) dans sa «Lettre à Shan Tao»: «Je viens de perdre la joie d'avoir ma mère et mon frère aîné» (édition Dai, p. 126). On peut dater cette lettre de 261[85], donc ce poème doit dater à peu près du même moment. Le frère aîné qu'il pleure dans ce poème n'est pas celui à qui il a écrit les dix-neuf poèmes traduits plus haut; ce frère-là, Ji Xi, lui a survécu et est devenu un fonctionnaire important sous les Jin. Le père de Ji Kang est mort quand celui-ci était très jeune (Dai, p. 117, et *infra*, p. 354) et il a été élevé par sa mère et son frère aîné.

---

[85] Ji Kang a écrit cette lettre pour refuser à Shan Tao d'occuper le poste que ce dernier venait de quitter. Or, nous savons que Shan Tao a quitté ce poste en 261 (Pei Songzhi cite le [*Shan*] *Tao xingzhuang* 山濤行狀, in *Sanguo zhi* 21, p. 607). Mais Ji Kang dit aussi, dans la lettre (Dai, p. 126), que son fils a sept ans, et le *Jin shu* de Wang Yin, cité dans le *Wen xuan* 43, p. 6b (commentaire à ce passage de la lettre), dit que ce fils avait neuf ans à la mort de son père. Si Ji Kang est en effet mort en 262, il y a une contradiction ici. Il se peut que Ji Kang soit mort une année plus tard, en 263 (telle est l'hypothèse d'Achilles Fang, *The chronicle of the Three Kingdoms* 2, Cambridge, Mass., 1965, pp. 398-9). Ou y aurait-il une faute de texte? Hou Wailu et al. (p. 163) datent la lettre de 260; je l'ai datée de 261 (*La vie et la pensée*, p. 44), mais j'ai donné la date de naissance du fils de Ji Kang comme 254, ce qui est une erreur, et j'ai mal interprété un passage tiré de Hu Kejia (il faut supprimer les dernières trois lignes et demie de ma note 3 de la p. 49). C'est quand Zhong Hui occupait le poste de Sili xiaowei qu'il a plaidé pour l'exécution de Ji Kang; or il a quitté ce poste vers la fin de 262, ce qui me semble confirmer la date traditionnelle de 262 pour la mort de Ji Kang (cf. A. Fang, *loc. cit.*).

Pensant à mes parents

Que faire de cette tristesse, tristesse sans recours?
Ma douleur est continuelle, mon cœur brisé.
Cette tristesse, que faire d'elle? J'ai tant de pensées affligées.
Mes émotions sont bloquées en moi, et ne peuvent se dissiper.
5 Soudain je suis sans appui, orphelin et seul au monde;
   Je ressens une douleur en moi; je pleure à en perdre la voix.
Je pensais rendre vos bienfaits, mais vous êtes loin, inaccessibles.
Je suis ému [au souvenir] de l'éducation que vous m'avez donnée; mes senti-
                                     [ments me déchirent.
Hélas! ma mère et mon frère aîné! Vous êtes pour toujours ensevelis!
10 Quand je me rappelle votre apparence, je sens tout se briser en moi.
Je m'émeus au printemps, pensant à mes parents affectueux;
   Je veux les voir une fois encore, mais je n'ai pas le moyen de trouver leur
                                          [route.
Je regarde vers le mont du Sud, et pousse des soupirs de douleur;
   Je m'émeus en voyant leur accoudoir et leur canne, et je pleure à chaudes
                                        [larmes.
15 Je me souviens du passé, quand ma mère et mon frère étaient là;
Mon cœur était tout joyeux, pensant qu'il vivraient aussi longtemps que les
                                     [Quatre Mers.
Mais ils sont déjà partis et je ne peux pas les suivre;
Mon cœur est angoissé, rempli seulement de chagrin.
Je monte dans la salle vide: elle est déserte, sans refuge;
20 Quand je vois les choses qu'ils ont laissées, mon cœur se brise.
Mon chagrin au milieu de la nuit, à qui puis-je le raconter?
J'essuie seul mes larmes, gardant ma douleur dans mon sein.
Tous les jours mes parents sont plus loin de moi, et tous les jours je pense
                                    [plus profondément à eux;
J'aime celle qui m'a donné la vie, et mes larmes coulent sur mon sein.
25 Ma tendre mère n'est plus: qui me gâtera?
Je m'apitoie sur moi-même, mon cœur plein de tristesse.
Je me plains au ciel azuré, mais le ciel ne m'entend pas.
Mes larmes tombent comme la pluie; mes soupirs atteignent les nuages.
Je voudrais rejeter cette tristesse, mais elle revient toujours;
30 Ma douleur est intense, et je ne peux l'extirper.

Cette forme, le chant de Chu, particulièrement bien adaptée à ce
genre d'explosion émotive, a sans doute aussi suggéré un certain
nombre de citations des *Chu ci* (le premier vers rappelle le «Jiu ge»,
Hawkes, p. 40, 1. 25; le 4ᵉ, «Jiu zhang», Hawkes, p. 63, 1. 40b; le 26ᵉ,
«Jiu bian», Hawkes, p. 93, 1. 10), et le sujet même entraîne des cita-

tions du *Shi jing* 202 (les vers 5 et 7-8 du poème de Ji Kang), un poème qui décrit la douleur d'un fils privé de ses parents. L'évocation du printemps dans le vers 11 est peut-être une allusion au *Li ji*, «Ji yi» (Couvreur 2, pp. 271-272): «Au printemps, lorsque la rosée avait humecté la terre, en la foulant du pied, il [l'orphelin pieux] éprouvait un sentiment de crainte respectueuse, comme s'il avait été sur le point de voir les âmes de ses ancêtres défunts». Le mont du Sud (vers 13) est peut-être encore une allusion au *Shi jing* 202 qui, dans ses deux dernières strophes, décrit le désarroi du poète orphelin quand il regarde «le mont du Sud», symbole de longévité (dans *Shi jing* 166). L'évocation de l'accoudoir et de la canne dans le vers suivant (14) rappelle le début d'un poème, «Duange xing», de Cao Pi, écrit vraisemblablement à la mort de son père, Cao Cao, en 220: «En haut je regarde ses rideaux et le ciel de son lit; / En bas, son accoudoir et sa natte. / Ces choses restent comme elles l'ont toujours été, / Mais l'homme [qui s'en servait] n'est plus là». Il y a d'autres échos de poèmes et (surtout) de *fu* des Han postérieurs et (comme toujours) du *Shi jing*, mais ce poème contient plutôt moins d'allusions que la plupart des poèmes chinois de cette époque.

Ce qui le caractérise, en fait, c'est son originalité. Il semble être une cascade de sanglots jetée sur le papier. Wang Fuzhi (cité par Dai Mingyang, p. 40) reproche à ces vers d'être «prolixes et superficiels» comparés aux vers structurés d'«Immortels en promenade». Mais le poème est émouvant et, aussi étrange que cela puisse paraître dans un pays comme la Chine où la piété filiale joue, et a sans doute toujours joué, un rôle énorme dans la vie du peuple, le «Duange xing» de Cao Pi, un poème en tétramètres portant aussi le titre «Siqin shi» de Wang Can (177-217), et ce poème de Ji Kang sont les seuls, depuis le *Shi jing* 202, à décrire la douleur d'un fils pieux à la mort de ses parents. Le poème de Ji Kang reste unique dans la violence de l'expression des sentiments. Il est un autre exemple de la naissance de la subjectivité, d'un intérêt nouveau dans les émotions de l'individu et dont Ji Kang est un précurseur notoire[86].

[86] Ce poème est contenu dans le *Yuefu guangxu* 樂府廣序 de Zhu Jiazheng 朱嘉徵 (1602-1684) qui dit qu'il doit accompagner un morceau de musique joué sur la cithare. Professeur Jao Tsung-i 饒宗頤 me dit qu'il doute de l'authenticité de ce poème. Les

Le deuxième des trois titres que je traduirai est composé de deux poèmes. Ils ont été écrits sans doute en 262. Le titre donné, «Aspirations», «Shu zhi shi» 述志詩, montre que ces poèmes appartiennent à une catégorie traditionnelle, et que Ji Kang va nous dévoiler les raisons pour lesquelles il ne s'est pas engagé dans la vie politique. Le premier des deux poèmes est écrit tout en symboles et en allusions; les deux sont en pentamètres réguliers.

Aspirations

1

Le dragon caché nourrit son corps divin;
    Il lave ses écailles et joue dans l'étang des orchidées.
Il tend le cou, pour admirer [l'antique empereur] Dating,
    Et piétine, attendant [le retour] de [Fu]xi, l'Auguste.
5 Le nuage de bon augure n'étant pas encore apparu,
    Il erre çà et là sur le versant est de la montagne.

Je ne suis pas comme la masse des gens
    Qui s'en vont à petits pas pour faire comme tout le monde.
Les espèces rares se répandent difficilement partout:
10   Ce sont les paroles viles qui abondent en tous lieux.
Un échec cause des remords,
    Et fait qu'une aspiration élevée ne peut plus se déployer.
Le dur travail de la terre a stimulé Ning Yue;
    Le tapis de selle [ignominieusement offert à] Zhang Yi l'a encouragé [à
                                      devenir ministre].

15 Je vais m'en aller, quittant mes compagnons,
    Et, me servant de mon fouet comme d'une canne, chercher maître Vaste Rive.
Quand le phénix *jiaoming* bat ses ailes,
    Comment l'oiseleur pourrait-il le dompter?
Je m'ébattrai dans la Grande Pureté
20   Et y chercherai de nouveaux amis.
Nous joindrons nos ailes pour planer dans la Voie lactée,
    Buvant la rosée, mangeant l'Arbre de Jade.

Je pense souvent aux gens du monde
    Qui attellent tôt leurs voitures pour courir tous à toute allure.

encyclopédies des Tang et des Song ne le citent pas, alors qu'ils citent le poème du même titre de Wang Can.

25 Ce sont le vide et la tranquillité qui nous permettent d'être nous-mêmes :
La gloire n'en vaut pas la chandelle!

Le dragon caché du premier vers apparaît fréquemment dans le *Yi jing* où il symbolise le Grand Homme qui se retire pendant une période défavorable. Dans le vers suivant, le manuscrit du Congshu tang donne la variante «sauter», *yao* 曜, pour le «laver», *zhuo* 濯, des textes imprimés. Cette variante donnerait : «Les écailles (c'est-à-dire, le dragon) sautantes jouent dans l'étang des orchidées». Dating et Fuxi sont mentionnés dans *Zhuangzi* 10 (Watson, p. 112) comme des souverains légendaires de l'âge d'or. Le nuage de bon augure multicolore apparaît pour annoncer une période faste (*Shi ji* 27, Chavannes 3, p. 396) qui accompagne l'arrivée d'un souverain sage. «La masse des gens» traduit un doublet du *Lun yu* 18, 6, que nous avons déjà vu dans le premier des poèmes aux deux Guo (*supra*, p. 153 et note 58). Je suis le manuscrit du Congshu tang et la suggestion de Dai Mingyang pour la reconstitution du premier caractère du huitième vers. Les vers 13 et 14 contiennent des allusions à deux personnages qui, ayant rencontré des échecs (comme dans le vers 11), réagissent d'une façon positive et réussissent leurs carrières. Ning Yue, pour s'échapper à la vie de paysan, s'adonne aux études pendant ses périodes de repos et devient, après quinze ans, le maître du duc Wei des Zhou (*Lüshi chunqiu* 24, p. 314); Su Qin a incité Zhang Yi à devenir ministre de Qin (d'un passage attribué au *Shi ji* qui ne s'y trouve plus, mais est cité dans le *Yiwen leiju* 69, p. 5a). Le vers 16 contient une allusion au *Zhuangzi* 28 (Watson, pp. 310-311) où un roi pacificiste préfère quitter son royaume, «se servant de son fouet comme d'une canne», plutôt que de plonger son peuple dans la guerre. Vaste Rive (Hongya 洪崖) est un immortel antique qui aurait déjà trois mille ans d'âge au temps du légendaire Empereur Jaune, d'après des sources tardives (cf. *Shenxian zhuan*, trad. Sawada Mizuho, Chûgoku koten bungaku taikei 8, p. 418). Le phénix *jiaoming* 焦明 (on écrit aussi *jiaopeng* 鵬) apparaît dans le «Shanglin fu» de Sima Xiangru (Hervouet, p. 120; l'allusion à l'oiseleur, *ibid.*, p. 173). La Grande Pureté apparaît dans de nombreux textes comme un synonyme pour le *dao* ou le Ciel (voir plus haut, p. 122 et note 39). Il y a trois variantes dans les vers 23 et 24 dans le manuscrit du Congshu tang, mais deux d'entre elles sont malheureusement illisibles. Les vers 21, 18, 25 et 26 sont cités tels quels d'une ballade nommée «Shanzai xing» attribuée à Cao Pi[87].

Les idées ne sont pas toujours faciles à suivre, surtout dans les vers 11 à 14. Un grand homme (= un dragon) reste caché pour attendre des jours meilleurs. Le «je» du vers 7 est dans le texte, mais en fait peut se référer au dragon: l'identification du héros au dragon est totale dans le poème. Un être supérieur ne peut pas faire comme tout le monde, surtout en cas d'échec; mais il peut rebondir, comme Ning Yue et Zhang Yi, et réussir malgré tout. Ji Kang ne nous décrit pas son échec. S'agit-il de sa maladresse vis-à-vis de Zhong Hui qui a été à l'origine de son incarcération et de sa mort? Les «paroles viles» du vers 10 font penser à la déposition de Zhong Hui, et nous verrons dans le deuxième poème qu'on doit dater ces deux poèmes à la fin de la vie de Ji Kang quand ces événements ont eu lieu. En tout cas, la stimulation reçue de cet échec a eu un effet très différent chez Ji Kang que chez Ning Yue et Zhang Yi: il décide de quitter le monde pour se consacrer aux joies de la vie des immortels.

Le deuxième poème développe certaines de ces mêmes idées, mais d'une façon beaucoup plus personnelle, introduisant des éléments autobiographiques d'un très grand intérêt.

2

La petite caille agit en seul maître dans sa parcelle d'armoise,
    Et rit quand elle voit survoler le phénix.
Un puits effondré sert de maison à la grenouille,
    Mais comment la tortue divine pourrait-elle y habiter?
5 Je regrette d'avoir été maladroit dans ma vie:
    J'ai agi arbitrairement, et j'y pense sans cesse.
J'ai été loin des réalités, séparé du monde:
    Je n'ai pas espéré des louanges selon les idées reçues.
Les affaires du passé ont été une erreur,
10   Mais je peux encore sauver ce qui va venir.

[87] Le texte du poème de Cao Pi se trouve dans le *Song shu* 21, p. 613. Sur l'usage à cette époque de vers empruntés à d'autres poèmes, voir H. H. Frankel, «The formulaic language of the Chinese ballad 'Southeast fly the peacocks'», *Zhongyang yanjiu yuan lishi yuyan yanjiu so ji kan* (Taibei) 39 (1969), pp. 219-244.

Pourquoi me mêlerais-je des affaires des hommes,
    Pour me rendre le cœur triste?
De toutes mes forces je pense aux anciens,
    Et dans mes rêves je divine leurs traits glorieux.
15 Je voudrais rencontrer quelqu'un qui me comprenne,
    À qui je pourrais ouvrir mon cœur insatisfait et en dévoiler les subtilités cachées.
Dans les grottes des précipices il y a beaucoup d'ermites;
    Je m'élèverai jusqu'à eux pour chercher un maître.
Le matin je monterai au col du mont Ji,
20   Et à la tombée du jour je ne connaîtrai pas la faim.
Je vivrai caché en nourrissant mon âme,
    Et pendant mille ans je resterai toujours en paix avec moi-même.

Les quatre premiers vers font allusion à deux passages du *Zhuangzi*.
Les deux premiers au premier chapitre du *Zhuangzi* (Watson, p. 31)
qui décrit une petite caille qui se moque d'un oiseau immense parce
qu'elle est incapable d'en apprécier les qualités héroïques; les deux
suivants au chapitre 17 (Watson, pp. 186-197) qui décrit le désarroi
d'une petite grenouille quand elle entend la description de la mer
Orientale faite par une tortue qui y habite. Il n'y a pas de lien direct
entre ces quatre vers et les vers qui suivent; leur rôle est de souligner
le contraste entre le poète, qui aspire à la grandeur taoïste, et les
gens du commun.

Les vers 5 à 10 sont tout à fait étonnants. Ji Kang y bat sa coulpe
comme presqu'aucun poète chinois ne l'a fait avant lui (mais voir
infra, note 90). Les poètes antérieurs, ceux du *Chu ci* par exemple,
regrettent beaucoup de choses dans leurs poèmes, mais jamais leur
propre comportement qui, à leurs yeux, reste toujours «pur comme
l'orchidée cachée»; leurs regrets se dirigent toujours vers les autres,
les méchants, les vulgaires incapables de les comprendre. Il est vrai
que Ji Kang s'identifie, tacitement au moins, à ces héros taoïstes
qu'il cite en exorde, mais il reconnaît explicitement ses maladresses
ici, se plaint d'avoir été «loin des réalités» (allusion au commentaire
Xiang du quatrième hexagramme du *Yi jing*), et, si faisant, montre
un genre d'introspection inconnue dans la poésie chinoise avant lui.
Son désir de se corriger (vers 9-10) est une citation presque mot à mot
d'un proto-taoïste qui chante devant Confucius (*Lun yu* 18, 5). Ce
personnage, appelé «le fou de Chu», chante pour persuader Confucius
de quitter le monde de la politique:

O! phénix, phénix!
  Que ta vertu s'est affaiblie!
Inutile de te gronder pour le passé,
  Mais tu pourras te rattraper à l'avenir.
Arrête! Arrête!
Ceux qui nous gouvernent aujourd'hui sont en danger!

Il est toujours hasardeux de vouloir identifier avec trop d'exactitude les origines autobiographiques des remarques faites par des poètes dans leurs vers, mais il est difficile ici de ne pas penser que Ji Kang se refère à ses démêlés avec Zhong Hui et la malheureuse affaire de Lü An qui lui a coûté la vie[88]. Dans le contexte du poème, et en se rappelant de cette chanson tirée du *Lun yu*, nous ne devons pas être très loin de la vérité si nous voyons des allusions à des erreurs commises par Ji Kang dans la vie publique.

Les vers qui suivent, d'ailleurs, en sont une confirmation, parce que Ji Kang y dit clairement qu'il veut quitter «les affaires des hommes». Dans ces vers il y a des échos des *Chu ci*, de *Zhuangzi* 28 (Watson, p. 318) et de *Laozi* 10, et le vers 14 est cité tel quel du poème 16 des «Dix-neuf poèmes anciens». La fin du poème en général donne l'impression d'une fin stéréotypée, encore une apothéose lyrique sur le thème des immortels. Le mont Ji 箕, du vers 19, est associé (au moins depuis les Han: *Han shu* 72, pp. 3095-3096) aux ermites Xuyou 許由 («Laissez-aller») et Chaofu 巢父 («Le nicheur»), deux hommes qui auraient refusé de servir le sage empereur Yao pour ne pas se laisser «polluer» par la vie politique. Chen Zuoming dit que les vers 19-20 montrent «on ne pourrait plus clairement» le désir de Ji Kang d'imiter les frères Boyi et Shuqi et de ne pas servir les usurpateurs Sima. Il semble croire, lorsque Ji Kang dit qu'il «ne connaîtra pas la faim», qu'il pense aux deux frères qui sont morts, justement, de faim sur le mont Shouyang, ayant refusé de toucher le salaire offert par les conquérants Zhou. Mais un des buts du régime des adeptes de la

---

[88] Voir *La vie et la pensée*, pp. 45-48, et *infra*, pp. 356-357. Hou Wailu et al., p. 162, citent ces vers de ce poème pour le dater de la dernière année de la vie de Ji Kang, 262.

VIII

Longue Vie était de pouvoir se passer des «cinq grains», et trouver à se nourrir uniquement en faisant la cueillette des plantes sauvages (*La vie et la pensée*, pp. 53-54) : si Ji Kang pense à Boyi et Shuqi (et celui qui le nierait serait bien hardi) il pense aussi à les dépasser et à donner un sens nouveau à la retraite du monde politique en «nourrissant son âme». Et c'est ainsi qu'il s'identifie aux figures héroïques, le dragon caché, le phénix et la tortue divine, en réalisant sa Longue Vie.

Un, ou peut-être deux ans après avoir perdu sa mère et son frère aîné et sans doute à l'époque où il a écrit les deux poèmes que nous venons de lire, Ji Kang a été mis en prison. J'ai déjà parlé des raisons de cette incarcération et de sa mise à mort (*La vie et la pensée*, pp. 45-49) : Ji Kang a été exécuté surtout à cause de son indifférence au service publique, sacro-saint aux yeux des confucianistes partisans de la Doctrine des Noms (*mingjiao* 名教). Ce poème écrit pendant son incarcération est à la fois une autobiographie, une apologie et une autocritique. Les deux mots qui composent le titre font sans doute allusion à la description que Ban Gu a faite (*Han shu* 62, p. 2738, 100, p. 4257) de l'œuvre de l'historien Sima Qian, son prédécesseur. Celui-ci, comme Ji Kang plus tard, a été faussement accusé, emprisonné et, non pas mis à mort, mais châtré ; Ban Gu dit : «Dans sa *captivité* il a exprimé son *angoisse* 幽而發憤». Le mot difficile dans cette citation est le mot *fen* 憤, que je traduis par «angoisse». Ce mot a plusieurs sens allant du «vif désir» ou «ardeur» de *Lun yu* 7, 8, à «indignation» ou «colère» qui est le sens le plus usuel (mais non pas le plus ancien). Comme nous le verrons en lisant le poème, Ji Kang n'exprime ici ni «indignation», ni «colère», mais un genre d'angoisse ou d'insatisfaction et je crois que ces traductions plus larges du mot conviennent mieux ici, et sans doute aussi dans d'autres textes où la traduction «indignation» est plus fréquente (e.g., *Shi ji* 130, p. 3300). Voici la traduction littérale de ce dernier poème de Ji Kang, poème où il retourne à sa prosodie favorite, les tétramètres. Certains passages, qui font sans doute allusion aux circonstances qui ont mené à son incarcération (e.g., les vers 17-28), sont obscurs et allusifs. J'en parlerai plus longuement à la fin de la traduction.

Angoisse au cachot

Hélas! j'ai peu de chance!
Encore jeune, j'ai perdu mon père.
Triste et seul sans le savoir,
Quand j'étais encore dans les langes.
5 Ma mère et mon frère aîné m'ont élevé
Avec affection et sans sévérité.
Confiant dans leur amour, je me laissais aller orgueilleusement,
Sans discipline, sans maître.
Alors, arrivé à l'âge adulte,
10 Fort de leur gâterie, je n'en faisais qu'à ma tête.
J'ai élevé mon cœur, admirant les hommes antiques,
Et je me suis abandonné à ce goût.
J'ai confié mes amours à Laozi et à Zhuangzi,
Méprisant les choses extérieures pour estimer la personne privée.
15 J'ai mis tout mon cœur à garder ma simplicité primitive,
Maintenant ma nature comme elle était à son origine, gardant intacte mon
[intégrité.
Mais je n'ai pas été intelligent:
Amant du bien, j'ai mal compris les autres hommes.
La défaite de Ziyu
20 A fait soulever couche sur couche de poussières.
Le Grand Homme doit tout contenir en lui-même:
Il doit pouvoir cacher les impuretés et avaler les hontes.
Quand les hommes ont beaucoup de vices,
On ne peut plus faire valoir ses propres idées au gouvernement.
25 Et seul un esprit borné, comme moi-même,
Ferait apparaître clairement, alors, ceux qui sont bons et ceux qui sont
[mauvais.
Mes yeux se sont ouverts et je pense à mes fautes:
J'en souffre comme d'une blessure.
Je voudrais réduire mes fautes,
30 Mais des calomnies s'élèvent de toute part.
Ce n'est pas dans mon tempérament de nuire aux autres êtres,
Et [pourtant] à plusieurs reprises j'ai attiré leur haine.
J'ai honte devant Liuxia [Hui] qui, dans le passé, [faisait fi des calomnies];
Et je rougis, aujourd'hui, devant Sun Deng [qui m'a prédit que je ne saurais
pas vivre dans le monde].
35 J'ai trahi, en moi, mes premières ambitions;
Et, vis-à-vis des autres, j'ai honte devant mes bons amis.
Je lève mon regard en admiration vers Yan [Junping] et Zheng [Zizhen]:
Ils ont pris leur plaisir dans le *dao* et ont vécu oisifs,

VIII

355

Sans s'engager dans les affaires du monde,
40   Gardant paisibles leur esprit et leur souffle.

Hélas! Je n'ai pas été bon:
    En me laissant embrouiller dans les affaires, j'ai trouvé beaucoup de soucis.
Mais tout cela n'est pas tombé du ciel:
    En fait, c'est le résultat de ma bêtise et de ma négligence.
45 La vérité a été cachée, le malheur s'est noué,
    Et à la fin j'ai été mis en prison.
J'ai répondu à l'interrogatoire méprisable,
    Prisonnier dans ce cachot isolé.
En vérité j'aurais honte de plaider pour qu'on me fasse grâce:
50   Le moment ne m'est pas favorable.
Bien que je dise que j'ai fait mon devoir, que j'ai été droit,
    J'ai été humilié dans mon esprit, blessé dans ma volonté.
J'aimerais me laver le corps dans le Canglang:
    Mais comment cela pourrait-il réparer le mal?

55 Les oies sauvages chantantes cacardent harmonieusement,
    Et déploient leurs ailes pour se promener vers le nord.
Elles se mettent en route au bon moment,
    Contentes d'elles et sans mélancolie.
Hélas, je soupire angoissé:
60   Je ne peux pas être des leurs!
Les affaires sont allées contre mes désirs,
    Et je me trouve retenu si longtemps ici [dans cette prison].
La faillite et la réussite sont réglées par le destin:
    Que peut-on chercher à faire encore?
65 L'homme antique a dit:
    Si tu fais du bien, tiens-toi loin de la renommée!
Il faut suivre son temps respectueusement et silencieusement,
    Et alors on n'engendrera ni fautes ni remords.
[Le fils du seigneur] Wanshi était parfaitement prudent;
70   Il a donné la sécurité à ses parents et préservé la gloire [familiale].
Les affaires de ce monde sont embrouillées, confuses,
    Et ne font qu'agiter mes sentiments.
Il faut rester sur ses gardes quand on jouit de la paix et du bonheur,
    Et alors on peut finir ses jours bienheureux et vertueux.

75 Ils rayonnent, les champignons magiques
    Qui fleurissent trois fois en une seule année!
Moi seul, je serais quel genre d'homme?
    J'ai un but, sans pouvoir l'accomplir.
Tirant la leçon de mes malheurs, je pense rebrousser chemin,
80   Mais je sens, dans mon cœur, une douleur tenace.
Je veux m'efforcer dans le futur

D'être sans [renommée] parfumée ni [notoriété] malodorante.
Je cueillerai des fougères dans les replis des montagnes,
    Laissant mes cheveux dénoués dans les grottes rocheuses,
85 Sifflant longuement et fredonnant toujours des vers,
    Entretenant ma nature foncière, nourissant ma longévité !

Comme c'est toujours le cas quand il écrit en tétramètres, Ji Kang dans ce poème fait un usage abondant de citations de vers entiers du *Shi jing* et d'allusions ou d'emplois grammaticaux ou de vocabulaire archaïsants imitant ce livre canonique. Je ne signalerai que les citations de vers entiers. Le frère aîné auquel il fait allusion dans le vers 5 est sans doute le frère qui est mort avant lui, et dont il parle dans le poème «Pensant à mes parents», et non pas Ji Xi à qui il a écrit le cycle de poèmes en tétramètres que j'ai choisi pour commencer cette étude. Les premiers seize vers sont faciles à comprendre. Les difficultés commencent avec les vers 17-40. Je marque un paragraphe au vers 17 en dépit du fait que la rime ne change qu'au vers 20. Il y a peut-être dans le vers 18 une allusion au *Zuo zhuan* (Xiang 29, Legge, p. 549) : un homme dit à un autre : «Vous ne mourrez pas d'une mort naturelle. Vous aimez le bien, mais vous ne savez pas choisir les hommes». Allusion ou non, Ji Kang ici est en train de se lamenter de ne pas savoir choisir ses amis, et il faut décrire ici les événements qui l'ont conduit au cachot si nous voulons arriver à comprendre ce passage extrêmement allusif et difficile.

Ji Kang avait un ami nommé Lü An 呂安. Le frère aîné de Lü An, Lü Xun 巽 (ou 遜) a eu des relations illicites avec sa belle-sœur, après l'avoir saoulée. Lü An a voulu porter plainte, mais Ji Kang, ami des deux frères, désirant éviter un scandale public et un procès fracassant, l'en a dissuadé. Lü Xun, inquiet et voulant se couvrir en prenant les devants, a accusé son cadet d'avoir battu leur mère, un crime contre la piété filiale punissable de mort. Lü Xun, en faveur auprès du généralissime Sima Zhao, l'usurpateur, et auprès de Zhong Hui, un de ses puissants généraux, a eu gain de cause, et Lü An a été déporté à la frontière. Lü An, naturellement, s'est plaint, et dans sa plainte, naturellement aussi, a cité Ji Kang qui, après tout, l'avait empêché de poursuivre son frère dès le début de l'affaire. Or, Ji Kang, quelques années auparavant, quand Zhong Hui était allé lui rendre visite, l'avait reçu si froidement que ce dernier lui en voulait à mort. C'était justement Zhong Hui qui était en ce moment Sili xiaowei 司隸校尉, post puissant qui faisait de lui un genre de gardien des mœurs dans la province autour de la capitale. C'est sa déposition, dans laquelle il s'en prend directement à la vie détachée de la cour et du service public que mène Ji Kang, qui a été la cause directe de l'exécution de celui-ci (cf. *La vie et la pensée*, pp. 45-48).

Les commentateurs ne semblent pas être très familiers avec ces faits de la biographie de Ji Kang (qui sont pourtant facilement accessibles dans le *Zizhi tongjian* 72, pp. 2464-2465, trad. A. Fang 2, pp. 381, 396-399), car la quasi totalité d'entre eux croient que Ji Kang fait allusion à Lü An quand il dit «j'ai mal compris les autres hommes», alors qu'il est beaucoup plus vraisemblable d'y voir une allusion à Lü Xun qui est le grand traître dans cette affaire et que Ji Kang avait accepté comme ami (voir la lettre qu'il lui a écrite, traduit dans *La vie et la pensée*, p. 46). Le célèbre penseur iconoclaste Li Zhi 李贄 (1527-1602) dans son *Fen shu*, «Livre incendiaire» (ou, plus exactement, «à incendier») 5, p. 207 (édition de Pékin, 1961), croit que le texte tel que nous l'avons de ce poème ne peut faire allusion qu'à Lü An, et à cause de cela il croit que le texte est corrompu, contenant des vers ajoutés ultérieurement par des «amateurs d'histoires». Chen Zuolong et Chen Jin 陳僅, tous les deux cités par Dai Mingyang, p. 27, croient aussi qu'il s'agit de Lü An et acceptent cette identification sans se plaindre de corruption textuelle. Mais Li Zhi a certainement raison de dire que cette identification rend Ji Kang un personnage incompréhensible, ou pire. Selon le *Wenshi zhuan* (cité dans *Shishuo xinyu* 6, Mather, n° 2, mais sa traduction est erronée ici), «Quand cette affaire malheureuse est arrivée à Lü An, Ji Kang est allé à la prison pour témoigner en sa faveur». S'il s'agissait effectivement de Lü An dans le poème, Ji Kang serait un homme qui se plaint parce que sa défense d'un ami faussement accusé (en partie par sa faute) l'avait amené au cachot. Il ne s'agit évidemment pas de Lü An, mais de son frère Lü Xun, et le premier commentateur du *Wen xuan*, Li Shan, l'a bien compris et l'a signalé à deux reprises, après le vers 18 et après le vers 20. Les versions de son édition, cependant, sont presque toutes erronées: quelque «amateur d'histoires» a dû corriger son texte, parce que les versions les plus répandues (la version de Hu Kejia et ses imitations) portent le mot «An» là où l'on doit lire «Xun». Même Dai Mingyang, qui croit pourtant que l'allusion est à Xun, reproduit cette erreur. Et je l'aurais reproduite moi-même si je ne possédais pas la réédition de la meilleure version de la plus ancienne édition de ce commentaire, l'édition de You Mao 尤袤 (1127-1194) de 1181 reproduite à Pékin en 1974[89]. Dans cette version Li Shan dit très clairement, et à deux reprises, que Ji Kang fait allusion à Lü Xun.

Plus exactement Ji Kang se plaint, dans le vers 18, d'être un mauvais juge d'hommes en général, mais les vers qui suivent montrent, je crois, qu'il pense à Lü Xun ici en particulier. Ziyu, dans le vers 19, apparaît dans le *Zuo zhuan* (Xi 27, Legge, p. 201). Général cruel envers ses propres soldats, qu'il fait fouetter et dont il fait percer les oreilles, il a perdu une bataille, mais le vrai coupable de la perte de la bataille, ce n'est pas Ziyu, d'après l'anecdote racontée dans le *Zuo zhuan*, mais l'homme qui lui a passé le commandement des troupes. Il s'agit donc d'une anecdote qui condamne un mauvais choix d'hommes, interprétation qui est renforcée par le vers suivant qui est une allusion au *Shi jing* 206 : «Ne poussez pas la grande voiture ; la poussière vous aveuglera». Ces vers sont choisis pour gloser, dans le *Xunzi* 27, p. 338 (de l'édition Zhuzi jicheng), les phrases suivantes : «Il faut être prudent et choisir ses amis parmi les hommes de bien : c'est cela le fondement de la vertu». Et ces mêmes vers «illustrent» un passage du *Hanshi waizhuan* 7, 20 (Hightower, p. 244), sur l'importance de bien choisir les hommes qu'on emploie. «La défaite de Ziyu» et la «poussière» du vers 20 concernent donc le choix de bons amis et le désastre qui résulte quand on choisit mal. Ji Kang se critique lui-même d'avoir provoqué la catastrophe en choisissant Lü Xun comme un homme

[89] L'édition de 1181 a servi de base à l'édition de Hu Kejia en 1809, l'édition la plus répandue aujourd'hui. Mais les planches en bois de l'édition de 1181 ont subi de nombreuses corrections au cours des siècles, et la réédition de Pékin est basée sur une version appartenante à la Bibliothèque de Pékin qui contient beaucoup moins de corrections : seules la table des matières et la table des variantes entre les éditions de Li Shan et des Cinq Fonctionnaires en fin de volume contiennent des regravures (plus la p. 21 du *juan* 45 qui a été remplacée par une autre édition de la Bibliothèque de Pékin). Ces regravures sont indiquées dans le repli des pages et permettent de montrer que les récentes rééditions de ce texte à Taibei sont très inférieures à la réédition de Pékin de 1974.

de bien et en lui faisant confiance. Les commentateurs et traducteurs donnent des explications variées de ces vers obscurs. Seul Dai Mingyang donne ce qui est, à mon avis, la bonne explication, mais il faut admettre que ces deux vers et les vers 23-24 ne sont compréhensibles qu'après référence aux sources des allusions qu'ils contiennent.

Les vers 21-22, bien qu'ils contiennent des allusions au deuxième hexagramme du *Yi jing* et au *Zuo zhuan*, Xuan 15, se comprennent sans référence à ces sources. Ji Kang continue son autocritique et se condamne de ne pas s'être comporté en «Grand Homme», et de ne pas avoir su fermer les yeux aux crimes qu'il voyait autour de lui. Une telle attitude peut paraître très peu digne d'un «Grand Homme», mais il y a des occasions où il faut savoir se taire, et les deux vers suivants, 23-24, décrivent une telle occasion. Le vers 23 cite textuellement le *Shi jing* 254, strophe 6: «Quand les hommes ont beaucoup de vices, / Ne dressez pas devant eux vos propres vices». Mais l'allusion ne s'arrête pas là. Ces vers, comme les vers du *Shi jing* auxquels Ji Kang fait allusion dans le vers 20, ont été cités pour gloser un texte du *Zuo zhuan*, Xuan 9 (Legge, p. 305), dans le *Zuo zhuan* lui-même et ensuite dans le *Kongzi jiayu* 19 (trad. Wilhelm, pp. 103-104). Ce texte du *Zuo zhuan* décrit un prince et deux de ses conseillers qui partagent la même maîtresse et qui, pour s'amuser, portent sur eux des articles de ses sous-vêtements à la cour. Un homme intègre les dénonce. Confucius cite ces vers du *Shi jing* pour condamner (étrangement) l'homme intègre qui les a dénoncés: il y a des moments où il vaut mieux se taire, où la moralité ambiante est si basse que, de toute façon, la critique ne sert à rien, où «on ne peut plus faire valoir ses propres idées au gouvernement». L'allusion de Ji Kang à sa propre situation, mis au cachot pour avoir dénoncé l'immortalité de Lü Xun, est évidente. Mais il y a aussi une critique très virulente de la moralité ambiante, ce qui explique peut-être le fait que Ji Kang a choisi une forme aussi allusive dans ces vers.

Le vers 25 est presque mot à mot du *Shi jing* 107 et le vers 29 du *Lun yu* 14, 26. Dans ces vers Ji Kang semble considérer ce qui n'est, en fait, qu'un trait de caractère, sa franchisse, comme une «faute». Il s'agit sans doute de son ingérence dans l'affaire de son ami Lü An, mais peut-être aussi son rudoiement de Zhong Hui, par lequel il montrait à ce jeune dandy puissant et orgueilleux exactement ce qu'il pensait de lui. Les vers 30-32 aussi visent sans doute Zhong Hui et les autres partisans de la Doctrine des Noms qui l'avaient pris en grippe. Les vers 33 et 34 sont souvent cités (dans les biographies de Ji Kang dans le *Sanguo zhi* 21 et le *Jin shu* 49, par exemple), mais les commentateurs ou traducteurs ne sont pas toujours d'accord sur le sens qu'il faut leur donner. Hui 惠 de Liuxia 柳下 («dessous le saule») est un personnage mentionné dans le *Lun yu* 15, 13 et 18, 2. Je crois que Ji Kang le cite ici parce que Hui de Liuxia était indifférent aux calomnies : trois fois dégradé, il est resté fidèle à son pays et à son poste. Ji Kang l'avait déjà cité dans sa «Réponse à la critique de son essai 'Nourrir la vie'» (*La vie et la pensée*, pp. 99-100) pour louer son indifférence superbe aux richesses et aux honneurs, à la gloire comme à la honte. Dans le contexte de ce poème je crois que Ji Kang aussi pense à cette indifférence aux réactions du monde, indifférence qu'il n'a pas su imiter dans, par exemple, sa réaction à Zhong Hui. Li Zhouhan, des Cinq Fonctionnaires, semble d'accord avec cette interprétation, mais Shiba Rokurô croit que Ji Kang a honte devant le fait que, bien que trois fois dégradé, Hui de Liuxia a bien voulu resservir l'État(?). Von Zach dit que Ji Kang loue Hui de Liuxia et Sun Deng parce qu'ils ne critiquent pas les autres. Mais Sun Deng a critiqué Ji Kang, et je crois que c'est précisément à cause de sa critique qu'il est cité ici. Sun Deng était un ermite que Ji Kang a rencontré dans les montagnes et avec qui il a vécu pendant trois ans (*La vie et la pensée*, pp. 42-43). Avant de le quitter, Sun Deng a critiqué Ji Kang d'être trop doué, et de trop mal connaître les hommes. Les vers 35 et 36 réitèrent les deux vers précédents d'une façon plus abstraite.

On peut trouver que la «honte» que ressent Ji Kang semble excessive : il est, après tout, en prison parce qu'il a voulu aider son ami et rétablir la justice. Mais Ji Kang toute sa vie a essayé de vivre selon les préceptes taoïstes; il a essayé de se détacher du monde; et il a honte de son échec. Les deux personnages qu'il cite dans le vers 37 sont précisément deux exemples assez anciens (entre les deux Han) d'hommes qui ont su vivre en ermite, détachés du monde et s'adonnant à leur culture personnelle (*Han shu* 72, p. 3056). Et Ji Kang continue de s'accuser jusqu'au vers 54, avec une telle insistance, et d'une façon qui n'a, pour ainsi dire, pas de précédents dans la poésie chinoise[90], que nous ne pouvons pas ne pas nous étonner et nous demander pourquoi. S'agit-il, comme le dit Li Zhi, d'une interpolation? Est-ce que Ji Kang essaie de faire amende honorable, d'acheter bassement ses geôliers en s'humiliant devant eux (la clique des Sima)? Je crois que, au terme de cette étude de sa poésie, et même sans avoir besoin de se référer à ses œuvres philosophiques en prose, nous pouvons répondre à ces questions. Ji Kang se sent coupable de ne pas avoir suivi les préceptes des saints taoïstes qu'il révère et il bat sa coulpe pour essayer de calmer son insatisfaction et sa frustration dans sa prison.

Le vers 43 est cité du *Shi jing* 193 et en le citant Ji Kang semble s'accabler de sa propre culpabilité. Les vers 45-50 décrivent l'emprisonnement. «L'interrogatoire méprisable» du vers 47 est sans doute une forme d'interrogatoire légale, *xun* 訊 (voir A. F. P. Hulsewé, *Remnants of Han law*, p. 79). Un commentateur du *Han shu* contemporain de Ji Kang, Zhang Yan 張晏, est cité par Li Shan sur ce terme. D'après lui il s'agit de redemander la même question au détenu trois jours plus tard pour savoir si la réponse correspond à la première. De toute façon, nous pouvons être sûr que l'interrogation n'était pas une chose douce. Le vers 48 implique qu'il est au secret, réclusion rigoureuse. Le vers 50 est une citation du *Lun yu* 17, 1: «Les jours et les mois passent; les années ne nous attendent pas». Mais ici, comme le dit Li Shan, le sens est différent: Ji Kang se lamente d'être à contre-courant, en désaccord avec son temps. Les derniers quatre vers (51-54) soulignent le sentiment de culpabilité qui remplit le poème. Il a certainement le droit de dire (vers 51) qu'il a «fait son devoir» vis-à-vis de Lü An, et (vers 52) qu'il a été «blessé» ou peut-être «bloqué dans sa volonté». Le vers 53 est inspiré d'un chant d'enfant qu'on trouve à la fois chez *Mencius* 4A, 8, et à la fin du poème «Yufu» des *Chu ci* (Hawkes, p. 91):

Quand les eaux du Canglang sont claires,
 J'y lave les cordons de mon bonnet;

---

[90] Une exception notable est le poème intitulé «Ze gong» 責躬, «Réprimande à moi-même» (*Wen xuan* 20, pp. 4a-6b), où Cao Zhi s'humilie devant son frère, l'empereur Wen, en s'accusant de toutes sortes de péchés.

Quand les eaux du Canglang sont boueuses,
J'y lave mes pieds.

Mencius utilise ce chant pour dire que la condition de l'eau du Canglang est responsable de l'usage qu'on en fait, et c'est ainsi des hommes qui provoquent l'usage qu'on fait d'eux par leur propre attitude vis-à-vis d'eux-mêmes: un homme qui se méprise, sera méprisé par d'autres. Dans le *Chu ci*, et d'une façon générale, on interprète ce poème comme une incitation à renoncer à servir un pays mal gouverné, à se retirer de la politique quand le moment n'est pas propice. Il me semble que Ji Kang pense surtout à Mencius ici, et que ses ablutions dans le Canglang ne peuvent servir à rien, puisqu'il se tient lui-même pour coupable; mais il se peut aussi qu'il pense à l'allusion plus courante et qu'il continue à se lamenter de ne pas avoir su se garder loin du monde politique, de ne pas s'être lavé les pieds dans la rivière plutôt que les cordons de son bonnet de fonctionnaire.

Le vers 55 (cité du *Shi jing* 34) marque un changement de sentiment, ainsi qu'une nouvelle rime (dans le vers 56): Ji Kang une fois encore tourne son regard vers les oiseaux du ciel pour chanter la vie libre et naturelle, loin des dangers politiques. Dans le vers 59 il utilise le mot du titre, *fen*. Morohashi Tetsuji (*Dai Kan Wa jiten* 4, p. 1187d, n° 34) traduit le mot par *ikari*, «colère, indignation»; Shiba Rokurô, p. 105b, par *urami*, «amertume, rancune»; von Zach, «sehr beklage ich». Il est, bien sûr, possible que Ji Kang utilise le mot dans un autre sens ici que dans le titre, mais le contexte me semble exclure la possibilité de l'idée de «colère» ou de «rancune» dans ce vers. Ces vers semblent décrire un genre de résignation qui devient tout à fait fataliste dans les vers 63-64. Suzuki Shûji signale ce vers comme un exemple du genre d'émotion contradictoire qu'un poète exprime dans sa poésie alors qu'un philosophe la rejetterait. Il dit que ce vers est en contradiction avec les vers 42-43 («Mais tout cela [= mon malheur] n'est pas tombé du ciel:/En fait il est le résultat de ma bêtise et de ma négligence»), comme l'est le vers 50 («Le moment ne m'est pas favorable»)[91]. Ils le sont aussi avec l'anti-fatalisme

[91] «Kei Kô Gen Seki kara Tô Emmei e», *Chûgoku bungaku hô* (Kyoto) 18 (1963), pp. 25-29.

VIII

soutenu par Ji Kang dans ses essais philosophiques (*La vie et la pensée*, pp. 61-67). L'évocation du destin ici, en tout cas, semble libérer Ji Kang en partie de ses sentiments de culpabilité et la fin du poème est moins angoissée que le reste. Les dix vers 65-74, qui partagent une rime nouvelle, prêchent une philosophie répandue à l'époque composée d'éléments cueillis dans Zhuangzi et dans le *Yi jing* et qui enseigne la prudence, la modération, surtout dans les moments de paix et de prospérité. Le vers 66 cite *Zhuangzi* 3 (Watson, p. 50): «Si tu fais le bien, tiens-toi loin de la renommée; si tu fais le mal, tiens-toi loin du châtiment». Le vers 67 est un amalgame de mots du *Shi jing* 127 et du *Shu jing* («Yue ming», Legge, p. 250). Wan Shi, dans le vers 69, a sa biographie dans *Shi ji* 103 et *Han shu* 46. Lui et ses fils se sont comportés d'une façon si respectueuse des convenances et du rituel traditionnel qu'il sont devenus de hauts fonctionnaires. Il est ironique que ce soit le dernier personnage historique cité par Ji Kang, lui qui a consacré un ouvrage entier (*Shengxian gaoshi zhuanzan*, «Les biographies et éloges des saints, sages et hommes éminents») aux hommes très différents de ces confucianistes bon teint. Le vers 72 est presque mot à mot de *Shi jing* 199 et le vers 73 cite le *Kongzi jiayu* (Wilhelm, p. 64). «Bienheureux et vertueux» traduit deux termes assez énigmatiques du premier hexagramme du *Yi jing*.

Dans les derniers dix vers Ji Kang retrouve partiellement la voix que nous avons entendue dans ses poèmes qui chantent les immortels. Les champignons magiques, nourriture de prédilection des chercheurs d'immortalité, contiennent des espèces capables de fleurir trois fois en une année: Ji Kang se compare à eux, lui qui est incapable de réussir sa vie une seule fois. Le vers 82 est inspiré du *Shi jing* 235, 7. Le vers 83 rappelle à la fois les frères Boyi et Shuqi qui sont morts de faim en mangeant des fougères plutôt que de servir la nouvelle dynastie des Zhou, et l'immortel des «Jiu ge» des *Chu ci* (Hawkes, p. 43) caché «dans les replis des montagnes». Ji Kang se cite lui-même dans le vers 85 qui est le même que le dernier vers du douzième poème écrit à son frère (*supra*, p. 133). Dans le contexte de ce poème antérieur («Ô! la douleur de mon cœur / Me fait siffler longuement et fredonner toujours des vers») ce vers a une tonalité mélancolique à laquelle on ne s'attendrait pas ici (Shiba Rokurô traduit: «Je siffle à cœur joie, chantant aussi tranquillement des vers...»). Cela nous rappelle que le sifflement, *xiao* 嘯, en chinois joue un rôle très particulier, surtout dans des contextes taoïstes ou de recherche de l'immortalité, comme c'est le cas ici. Le sifflement est une méthode pour communiquer avec les esprits et pour atteindre l'immortalité, et, d'une façon générale, il a des résonnances très différentes de ce que nous pourrions imaginer en occident[92]. Ce poème ne se termine donc pas aussi gaiement que ce «sifflement» pourrait nous le faire croire. La «douleur tenace» du vers 80 le poursuit et dans ces derniers vers il chante la vie qu'il aurait aimé mener, mais qu'il sait qu'il ne réalisera jamais.

Dans les trois derniers poèmes écrits par Ji Kang à la fin de sa vie nous voyons bien les éléments nouveaux qu'il a apportés à la poésie chinoise: l'émotivité exaltée du poème écrit en souvenir de sa mère et de son frère aîné et le rigoureux examen de sa propre conscience auquel il procède dans les deux derniers poèmes. C'est en rendant sa poésie plus intérieure et en y montrant les divisions de sa propre âme que Ji Kang innove le plus et qu'il a laissé sa marque sur la poésie écrite en Chine après lui.

6

POÈMES DIVERS

Il y a un certain nombre d'anomalies dans l'œuvre de Ji Kang qui montrent que le texte que nous avons aujourd'hui ne doit pas être arrangé de la même façon qu'à l'origine. Ceci est surtout vrai pour le premier chapitre de l'œuvre (contenant la poésie). En particulier, le manuscrit du Congshu tang, d'une part, et l'arrangement des poèmes dans les éditions imprimées, d'autre part, montrent des différences importantes. Ce sont ces différences qui ont incité l'excellent spécialiste de la poésie médiévale, Lu Qinli 逯欽立, à consacrer un article à l'établissement d'un *ur*-texte, paru dans le *Guoli zhongyang tushuguan guankan* (Nankin) 1, 3 (1947), pp. 25-27 (cet article m'a été

---

[92] Le mot *xiao* a un assez large éventail de sens, allant de «gémir» au «sifflement»; cf. D. Holzman, *Poetry and politics*, pp. 151-152.

aimablement signalé par Monsieur Jao Tsung-i). Malheureusement, Lu Qinli n'a pas pu voir le manuscrit lui-même et ne le cite que d'après l'édition de Luxun et les articles de Ye Weiqing, «Ji Kang jiaoji», *Guoli Beiping tushuguan guankan* 4, 2 et 5; 5, 2-4; 9, 6. Le résultat, c'est qu'il n'a pas pu se rendre compte de l'incohérence irréparable d'une bonne partie de ce manuscrit et qu'il s'est embarqué un peu à la légère dans une reconstruction qui est à mon avis impossible. Je mentionne cet article parce qu'il s'attaque à un problème réel, qui est l'existence d'un certain nombre de poèmes en tétramètres dans l'œuvre de Ji Kang qu'on n'arrive pas à arranger dans un ordre quelconque. Les idées de Lu Qinli sur l'attribution de certains poèmes qui forment l'échange entre Ji Kang et son frère aîné me semblent tout à fait erronées, et je ne crois pas utile de les réfuter ici une à une. Mais il est clair que le quatrième poème en tétramètres, alors que les trois premiers sont en pentamètres, que Ji Xi aurait écrit à Ji Kang, est fait d'un très court fragment (quatre vers) d'un poème qui est peut-être de Ji Xi (mais le fragment est trop court pour pouvoir identifier son auteur) suivi de seize vers qui sont sans doute de Ji Kang. Je traduirai ces seize vers à la fin de ce chapitre. Mais d'abord je voudrais traduire six poèmes similaires qui semblent aussi être mal placés dans son œuvre.

Ces six poèmes en tétramètres se trouvent, dans les éditions imprimées aussi bien que dans le manuscrit du Congshu tang, rangés après le poème intitulé «Partie à boire» et dont la traduction se trouve plus haut, p. 172. Si je ne les ai pas traduits à la suite de ce poème, c'est que, à mon avis (partagé par Wang Fuzhi et Chen Zuoming), il n'y a aucun rapport entre eux. Le poème «Partie à boire» décrivait une véritable réunion amicale; les six poèmes en tétramètres ressemblent plutôt aux poèmes paysagistes de la série écrite à son frère. Il est possible qu'ils suivent «Partie à boire» en montrant Ji Kang seul en train de se promener après avoir quitté ses amis. Mais ils ne décrivent certainement pas une «partie à boire». Le manuscrit du Congshu tang contient sept poèmes supplémentaires (quatre en tétramètres et trois en pentamètres) qu'on ne trouve nulle part ailleurs et qui sont reproduits sur les pages 78-81 de l'édition de Dai Mingyang. Les quatre poèmes tétramétriques ressemblent assez à ceux qui sont attachés au poème «Partie à boire», mais les trois en pentamètres me semblent trop pleins de clichés pour être de Ji Kang (ce n'est pas l'avis de Dai Mingyang, p. 81), et j'ai décidé de ne pas traduire ces sept poèmes qui ne se trouvent que dans le manuscrit du Congshu tang[93].

Le premier des six poèmes en tétramètres contenus dans toutes les éditions est cité, avec des variantes, dans *Taiping yulan* 770 (et non pas 617 comme le dit Dai Mingyang), p. 4a. Ce poème, ainsi que celui qui le suit, est un chant au bonheur de vivre en paix dans la nature.

1

Doucement les eaux qui coulent
S'entraînent les unes les autres et s'en vont.
Poussée au gré du vent, ma barque de cyprès
Tantôt va à la dérive, tantôt s'arrête.
5 Je sifflotte dans la brise fraîche
Et fais clapoter mes rames tout à mon aise.
Je jetterai l'aviron, lâcherai la perche,
Errant heureux toute l'année!

Comme d'habitude quand il écrit en tétramètres Ji Kang cite souvent le *Shi jing*: le vers 2 imite *Shi jing* 256 et les vers 3 et 4 sont presque mot à mot du *Shi jing* 176. Et il y a des échos aussi des *Chu ci*. Les deux premiers vers semblent contenir une allusion voilée au *Lun yu* 9, 16: «Le maître au bord d'un ruisseau dit: 'Il s'en va ainsi, sans s'arrêter jour ou nuit'», citation qu'on interprète d'ordinaire comme une description du temps qui passe. Si ces six poèmes forment un tout, cette citation pourrait être considérée comme une métaphore initiale (*xing* 興 en terminologie traditionnelle chinoise) qui introduit et inspire tout ce qui va venir. Ce premier poème, pourtant, et celui

---

[93] Dai Mingyang reproduit ces sept poèmes ensemble à la fin du chapitre consacré à la poésie de Ji Kang dans son édition, mais dans le manuscrit du Congshu tang les poèmes en pentamètres se trouvent à la suite des poèmes du frère de Ji Kang, très loin de ces poèmes intitulés «Partie à boire». Les trois poèmes en pentamètres sont très «taoïstes», à la manière des poèmes de cette époque, montrant, comme corollaire de la poursuite de l'immortalité, le mépris des «hommes vulgaires».

qui suit, semblent presque en dehors du temps : le poète ici, et les
canards dans le poème suivant, semblent tellement à l'aise dans l'univers qu'ils font corps avec lui et avec le temps qui passe.

2

Qu'ils sont menus ce couple de canards mandarins
   Qui nagent avec leurs ailes repliées.
Baissant la tête, ils mâchent les algues verdâtres,
   Confiant leur corps au vaste courant.
5 Le matin ils planent sur les rapides translucides
   Et le soir perchent sur les îlots merveilleux.
Bercés par les flots purs,
   Ils montent et descendent avec eux.

Ce deuxième poème répète le thème du premier, mais ici le poète
décrit des canards mandarins vivant à l'aise dans l'univers et se
laissant porter par le grand mouvement du temps. L'abstraction et les
grands thèmes philosophiques n'étant pas le fait des poètes chinois
d'ordinaire, Wang Fuzhi craint que des lecteurs superficiels ne cherchent à expliquer ces poèmes par une interprétation allégorique. Je
suis de son avis : il ne faut pas essayer de voir uniquement dans ces
poèmes des descriptions de courtisans qui se laissent aller au fil de
l'eau parce qu'ils ont été déçus dans leurs aspirations politiques. Ces
deux premiers poèmes font l'éloge de la vie «naturelle», du laisser-
aller taoïste au sein de la nature.

3

Mon chant se répand sur l'île des orchidées,
   Les sons harmonieux pressants et clairs.
J'ajuste mes cordes au mode de seconde clair
   Et laisse errer mon cœur dans la Grande Image.
5 Je me cultive dans l'obscurité
   Et l'écho de mes notes douces résonne.
Zhong Qi n'est plus là :
   Qui saurait apprécier ce que j'ai dans mon cœur ?

«Le mode de seconde clair» est ma traduction très imprécise des
mots *qingshang* 清商, un mode particulièrement triste et envoûtant

selon des textes anciens et médiévaux. Le terme «Grande Image» apparaît dans *Laozi* 35 et 41 où il est vraisemblablement une épithète pour le *dao*. Le binom que je traduis par «l'obscurité», *qingmei* 傾昧, est inconnu ailleurs; il s'agit sans doute dans ce vers 5 d'une méditation sur «le *dao* clair qui semble obscur» (*Laozi* 41). Les deux derniers vers font allusion à Zhong Qi (ou Zhongzi Qi), l'ami du cithariste Bo Ya, qui appréciait si bien les intentions de ce dernier dans sa musique (ce qu'il «avait dans son cœur»), que Bo Ya a cassé sa cithare quand Zhongzi Qi est mort (*Lüshi chunqiu* 14, p. 140 de l'édition Zhuzi jicheng). Ce poème ajoute une note de solitude à la série (si c'en est une) et montre le poète contribuant à l'harmonie universelle par sa musique.

4

Je range les cordes [de ma cithare] et laisse errer mes pensées,
    M'amusant à pêcher dans les abîmes neuf fois profonds.
Dans le fort courant à mille mesures [de profondeur],
    [Les poissons] que j'attire de temps en temps se suspendent à mon fil.
5 Que vous êtes beaux, Zhuangzi et Laozi :
    Tout en vous reposant, vous avez prolongé vos années !
En vérité vous vous êtes transformés en dragons,
    Libérant vos cœurs dans un élan immense !

Ce poème, dont le premier vers semble indiquer qu'il est la suite du poème précédent, est fait de deux quatrains, la pêche dans le premier quatrain, qui n'est autre chose qu'une méditation au bord de l'eau, menant naturellement à l'éloge des deux «pères» du taoïsme. C'est dans le *Shi ji* 63, p. 2140, que Confucius compare Laozi à un dragon, mais «le prolongement des années» pour lequel Ji Kang loue les héros taoïstes ici est, bien entendu, l'écho de ces propres préoccupations.

Dans le poème suivant le ton change abruptement.

5

Qu'il est sévère ce vent froid
    Qui se produit sur le fleuve et sur sa rive !
Je tourne le dos à la forêt fleurie

369

Et m'en vais à contre-courant à l'Ilot de Cinabre.
5 Tenant en moi-même la force *yang*, je cracherai des fleurs,
Marchant sur le givre sans m'affaiblir.
Mais hélas! mon regard intense voit
Toutes les plantes dépérir!
La douleur de mon cœur!
10 Qui connaît les ressorts obscurs [de la nature]?

La bouffée d'air froid avec laquelle ce poème commence est tout à fait inattendue. Ji Kang semble conscient que le paradis terrestre décrit dans les premiers poèmes était fragile, et que le givre de l'automne allait le détruire. Il y a encore des échos du *Shi jing* : les mots pour la «rive» dans le vers 2 et «l'Ilot» du vers 4 viennent du *Shi jing* 129, et le vers 8 vient, mot à mot, du *Shi jing* 204, mais ce poème se caractérise surtout par l'usage fait de la terminologie taoïste. L'îlot du vers 4 est fait de cinabre; la force *yang* du vers suivant et les «ressorts obscurs», *xuan ji* du dernier vers, suggèrent tous que le poète cherche une solution au dépérissement naturel qu'il voit autour de lui dans l'alchimie (nous savons qu'il était forgeron amateur : cf. *La vie et la pensée*, pp. 39, 53). Le terme «ressorts obscurs», autant que je sache, apparaît dans ce poème pour la première fois, et par la suite a pris un sens taoïste, associé à l'alchimie (comme dans le deuxième des quatre poèmes intitulés «Les taoïstes» de Zhang Yue, 667-730, contenu dans *Quan Tang shi* 87, p. 947 de l'édition de Pékin, 1960). Malheureusement Ji Kang ne précise pas davantage sa pensée, et dans le dernier poème revient à la description du paradis terrestre, gardant pourtant une note de mélancolie automnale pour la fin.

6

Qu'elle est belle cette profusion d'orchidées
Qui croît dans la plaine!
Leurs feuilles vertes sont denses,
Leurs belles fleurs luxuriantes.
5 Le parfum de ces plantes odorantes embaume,
Et, emporté par le vent, se répand partout.
Je conduirai jusqu'à la Salle du Poivre
Où les parfums exhalés imprégneront ma voiture tirée par un dragon.
[Mais] quand je regarde ces plantes automnales,
10 Je me sens désappointé, en train de déchoir.

J'aurais mieux aimé que l'ordre des poèmes 6 et 5 soit inversé, que ce sixième poème, dont les huit premiers vers continuent la description du monde idéalisé des premiers cinq poèmes, et dont les deux derniers vers seulement suggèrent un changement inexorable, introduise le vent froid, le givre et le dépérissement des plantes du poème 5. Mais, puisque nous ne sommes même pas sûrs que ces poèmes forment une série, peut-être qu'il vaut mieux les accepter dans l'ordre reçu. La «Salle du Poivre» du vers 7 (ou peut-être plus exactement la «Salle du Xanthoxyle», une épice chinoise qui tient lieu du poivre des pays tropicaux) était, sous les Han, la chambre des femmes de l'empereur dont les murs avaient été imprégnés de poivre pour que, à la chaleur, ils rendent une odeur agréable et bienfaisante (*Han shu* 66, p. 2885). Cette visite au palais des femmes impériales de jadis donne à cette promenade campagnarde l'allure d'un voyage au pays des immortels.

Mais la mélancolie automnale des derniers vers différencie ce poème des poèmes qui chantent les immortels traditionnels et cette note de douleur et de solitude se trouve aussi dans trois des quatre poèmes en tétramètres qui suivent, dans le manuscrit du Congshu tang, les poèmes que je viens de traduire. Le quatrième poème, qui, il faut l'admettre, clorait bien la série, est une «promenade des immortels» en bonne et due forme.

Le quatrième poème attribué au frère de Ji Kang, Ji Xi, l'est aussi, et c'est avec la traduction de ce poème que j'aimerais terminer ce chapitre. Dans les versions imprimées de l'œuvre de Ji Kang ce poème est composé de vingt vers tétramétriques avec un étrange changement de rime commençant au sixième vers. Luxun croit qu'à partir de ce sixième vers il s'agit d'un poème de Ji Kang et non pas de son frère. Je crois qu'il a raison, mais je trouve qu'on peut commencer le poème de Ji Kang au cinquième vers, ce qui donne un poème cohérent de seize vers.

[Poème sans titre]

Les fleurs abondent dans la forêt verte
  Où les oiseaux printaniers s'amusent en bandes.
Ému par cette scène, je me mets à penser longuement :

Comment pourrais-je ne pas méditer toujours?
5 Mais méditer toujours sur quel sujet?
Méditer sur une ascension vers la Cour Céleste.
Je monterai aux nuages, passant au-delà légèrement,
Confiant mon corps au dragon sans cornes merveilleux.
Au loin j'atteindrai le Jardin Mystérieux,
10 Lâchant les rênes à l'Étang Fleuri.
L'Arbre du Soleil brille la nuit;
Les poires sauvages pendent de leurs branches.
Regardant en bas, je me rincerai la bouche à la Source Divine;
Regardant en haut, je grignoterai des branches de jaspe.
15 J'abriterai mon cœur dans l'Origine Blanche
Où, depuis le début jusqu'à la fin, je ne dépérirai jamais.

J'adopte les leçons du manuscrit du Congshu tang dans les vers 2,
9 et 15, sauf que, dans le dernier vers je maintiens le 皓 des versions
imprimées. Je proposerai même une correction textuelle de mon
propre crû pour le vers 11: 若 pour le 華 du texte. Il me semble que
le texte actuel a été corrompu par le caractère 華 dans le vers précédent.
Le Jardin Mystérieux, nous avons déjà vu dans les monts Kunlun
(*supra*, pp. 342-343). L'Étang Fleuri du vers 10 serait un autre nom
pour l'Étang de Jade, Yao chi 瑤池, à mi-chemin entre le ciel et la
terre, dans le Kunlun, séjour de la Reine-mère de l'Ouest (plusieurs
textes cités par Dai Mingyang donnent cette variante). L'arbre du
vers 11 (si l'on adopte ma variante) est le célèbre arbre de l'ouest
où viennent se coucher les dix soleils (*Shanhai jing* 17, p. 7a); c'est
pourquoi il «brille la nuit». Les «poires sauvages» se trouvent aussi
dans le Kunlun, sont rouges, sans noyau, et ont la propriété d'empêcher la noyade de ceux qui les mangent (*Shanhai jing* 2, p. 18a).
La Source Divine et l'arbre de jaspe fournissent tous les deux des
nourritures de Longue Vie (pour la première, cf. Kaltenmark, p. 151,
et surtout *Huainanzi* 4, p. 57; pour le dernier, Hervouet, p. 202).
«L'Origine Blanche» semble une invention de Ji Kang. Ban Gu, à la
fin de son «Youtong fu» (*Wen xuan* 14, p. 20a) emploie les termes
utilisés par Ji Kang ici, mais dans un sens très confucéen et morali-
sateur. Le contexte ici nous demande de comprendre ce terme comme
une épithète pour l'origine première, unie et sans couleur, pour le *dao*.
   Comme dans les poèmes qui font suite à «Partie à boire» que nous
venons de lire, ce poème commence par une évocation des beautés

printanières. Cette fois-ci ces beautés inspirent au poète une méditation (vers 4 à 6), une méditation qui est en même temps un voyage
extatique dans le pays des immortels. Dans le taoïsme religieux ulté-
rieur ces voyages sont clairement décrits comme ayant lieu à l'intérieur
du corps du pratiquant[94]. Chez Ji Kang, et dans le taoïsme ancien
en général, le sens qu'il faut donner à ces voyages est moins précis.
Comme nous l'avons déjà vu (*supra*, pp. 340 et suiv.), Ji Kang écrit
dans une tradition poétique déjà bien établie de son temps quand il
se décrit en train de se promener avec les immortels. Mais ces prome-
nades sont entrées non seulement définitivement dans la littérature;
elles jouent aussi un grand rôle dans l'art et dans la religion. Les
miroirs de bronze et les encensoirs des Han décrivant les randonnées
des immortels sont bien connus; ils montrent que ce thème jouait un
très grand rôle dans la vie quotidienne aux alentours de l'ère chrétienne.
Les découvertes récentes des tombeaux de cette époque nous montrent
encore plus clairement la très grande importance religieuse que ces
voyages mystiques ou spirituels revêtaient pour les contemporains.
Certains tombeaux nous montrent des personnages montés sur des
dragons, recevant des recettes ou des fruits magiques des immortels,
chevauchant dans les nuages, comme dans les poèmes de Ji Kang
dont ils pourraient être les illustrations[95]. Mais les rapports exacts
entre ces aspects à proprement parler religieux des Chinois du temps
de Ji Kang et leurs œuvres littéraires restent à déterminer. Les Chinois
sont extrêmement discrets à propos de leurs croyances religieuses,
si discrets, en fait, que c'est la découverte toute récente de ces tombeaux qui nous révèlent beaucoup de croyances inconnues ou à peine
esquissées dans les livres. L'archéologie nous aidera peut-être à déterminer plus exactement le sens à donner à ces poèmes de Ji Kang.

[94] Cf. I. Robinet, *Méditation taoïste*, Paris, 1979, surtout pp. 259 et suivant.

[95] On trouvera une bonne mise au point sur les peintures murales de ces tombeaux
dans Hou Ching-lang, «Recherches sur la peinture de portrait en Chine, 2: À l'apogée
de la dynastie des Han (140-49 av. J.-C.)», à paraître dans *Ars asiatiques* 37 (1980);
cf. aussi Michael Loewe, *Ways to paradise: The Chinese quest for immortality*, Londres,
1979.

7

CONCLUSIONS

J'ai dit, au début de cette étude, que peu de poètes ont laissé une œuvre aussi monothématique que Ji Kang. Nous avons vu, dans tous les poèmes que nous avons lus, ou peu s'en faut, des allusions au taoïsme, aux immortels, aux pratiques psychiques ou diététiques qui font partie de la vie de l'adepte taoïste. Même dans les échanges de poèmes avec son frère ou ses amis ce thème apparaît constamment et semble montrer que des discussions sur le taoïsme ont fourni l'élément principal de leurs entretiens. Dans le troisième poème de Ji Kang en réponse aux deux Guo un désaccord sur le sens à donner à l'engagement taoïste semble même avoir précipité la rupture de cette amitié que les poèmes des Guo décrivaient comme une communion d'esprits très chaleureuse.

Dans son œuvre en prose, qui est beaucoup plus copieuse et, il faut l'admettre, plus variée, nous constatons aussi une couleur taoïste et un intérêt presque (mais pas tout à fait) omniprésent pour la façon de «nourrir la vie» d'un adepte taoïste, soit dans ses essais qui s'attaquent directement à ce problème, soit dans d'autres qui discutent des problèmes psychologiques ou même métaphysiques que l'engagement dans la voie de «l'immortalité» peut poser. Les rares fois où il aborde des problèmes politiques de front (dans le court essai «Remontrance du Précepteur Impérial», «Taishi zhen», ou dans ses poèmes en hexamètres sur Yao et Shun, par exemple), il insiste sur l'impartialité dénuée de sentiments personnels qui doit inspirer l'empereur, citant comme idéal les hommes du monde primitif avant l'invention de la culture et les complications inhérentes à la civilisation.

Dans sa vie privée, autant que nous puissions la connaître d'après les très rares sources qui en parlent, Ji Kang semble avoir vraiment essayé de vivre concrètement, dans la vie de tous les jours, la vie d'un homme près de la nature, près de la simplicité primordiale. Le *Shishuo xinyu* 2, p. 25a (qui cite le *Xiang Xiu biezhuan*), décrit ses activités de forgeron et de jardinier avec ses amis Xiang Xiu et Lü An, et pendant les années qu'il a passées en la compagnie de Sun Deng dans les montagnes au nord de Loyang, il a dû vivre, autant que cela se peut, la vie d'un «immortel» (*La vie et la pensée*, pp. 42-47). Dans sa lettre à Shan Tao, aussi, il se décrit un peu comme un sauvage, refusant de se laver la tête ou même de se lever pour uriner, et rejetant tout à fait la vie des convenances et du rituel qui incombait à un fonctionnaire chinois.

Les deux critiques littéraires qui parlent de l'œuvre de Ji Kang vers le début du VIe siècle mettent tous les deux l'emphase sur le fait qu'il est, lui ou son œuvre, franc, qu'il ne mâche pas ses mots. Liu Xie parle de «sa volonté pure et altière» et Zhong Rong du fait qu'il «dévoile trop ouvertement les fautes d'autrui et fait voir trop clairement le talent de l'auteur». S'il en est ainsi, si Ji Kang a décrit, dans sa poésie et dans sa prose, et a vécu dans sa vie même, son attachement au taoïsme et à la poursuite de l'immortalité, qu'est-ce que nous devons penser de l'opinion des nombreux critiques ultérieurs de sa poésie qui n'y voient qu'allégorie quand il parle des immortels? Voici ce que dit un critique à titre d'exemple, un critique à la fois très fin et très érudit, Liu Xizai 劉熙載 (1813-1881):

Ji Shuye [c'est-à-dire, Ji Kang] ... était un homme d'une haute tenue morale. Bien que dans ses ballades sur le thème de Qiu Hu [*supra*, pp. 333-342] il honore le Silence Obscure..., sa peine et son indignation extrêmes se trouvent en fait en dehors des mots; celui qui sait lire la poésie doit entendre cette vérité [qui se trouve en dehors des mots].

Liu Xizai est le porte-parole ici d'une grande partie de la critique traditionnelle qui ne voit dans les poèmes qui chantent les immortels qu'allégorie politique. Pour ces critiques le fait que Ji Kang chante les immortels dans ces poèmes montre ipso facto qu'il est triste: en tant qu'«homme d'une haute tenue morale» l'usurpation des Sima ne pouvait que l'attrister, et il nous montre cette tristesse allégoriquement en se disant désirer suivre les immortels, c'est-à-dire en rejetant ce monde corrompu.

Les faits que j'ai cités, tirés de la vie et de l'œuvre de Ji Kang, me semblent donner tort à ces critiques. Mais ces faits sont de l'ordre de ce qu'on appelle aujourd'hui en critique littéraire «intentionaliste», c'est-à-dire qu'ils relèvent des «intentions» de l'auteur qui ne se trouvent pas forcément dans l'œuvre elle-même (Liu Xizai le reconnaît lui-même quand il dit que «la peine et l'indignation se trouvent en dehors des mots»): Ji Kang, croyant fermement à la recherche de l'immortalité, ou, plus exactement, à la prolongation de la vie par les méthodes des adeptes de la Longue Vie (il nous le dit en tant de mots dans certaines de ses œuvres en prose; cf. *La vie et la pensée*, pp. 53, 83, etc.), ne doit pas se servir des immortels simplement comme figures allégoriques dans sa poésie. Ce raisonnement est faux, et encore plus faux (si cela est possible) lorsqu'il s'agit d'un auteur chinois. Les Chinois ne croyant pas que le monde soit régi par un Dieu absolu ou par un système de valeurs morales transcendantes et figées pour l'éternité, ont une capacité d'accomoder plusieurs croyances dans leur esprit à la fois; sans être moins constants dans leur moralité qu'un Occidental, le Chinois peut à la fois être bon «confucianiste», bon «taoïste» et, plus tard, bon «bouddhiste». Ji Kang pourrait très bien croire fermement aux immortels, et écrire des poèmes traditionnels où ils apparaîtraient simplement comme une allégorie cachant son désir de quitter un monde corrompu. Mais dans les poèmes des immortels Ji Kang ne fait pas que les citer en passant: ils apparaissent comme le résultat d'une ascèse, d'une série d'actions morales et physiques destinées à «nourrir la vie», à mener à la Longue Vie ou à l'extase mystique. Les ballades intitulées «Sur le chant Qiu Hu» dont parle Liu Xizai, justement, sont typiques: les premiers quatre poèmes prêchent l'ascèse, la pauvreté, la condition basse, l'abstention des exercices intellectuels et sexuels, ainsi que du vin. Dans le cinquième poème il arrive au bonheur mystique, «laissant errer son cœur dans le Silence Obscur». Ce n'est que dans les deux derniers poèmes que nous rencontrons les immortels et, venant comme ils le font après cette ascèse et cette exaltation mystique, les considérer comme l'expression du dégoût de la vie de la part de Ji Kang serait montrer une très grande insensibilité envers sa poésie. Et ces remarques sont également valables pour la fin de la série de poèmes écrits à son frère et, à un moindre degré peut-être, aux poèmes qui se terminent sur une apothéose qui consiste en la retraite dans les montagnes comme dans le poème «Aspirations».

Ces remarques sont valables aussi, à mon avis, même pour le court coda à la fin de son dernier poème, «Angoisse au cachot»: Ji Kang n'envisage pas la poursuite de l'immortalité comme un pis-aller, mais comme le but de sa vie. Voici ce qu'en dit Su Shi 蘇軾 (1037-1101):

Quand il a écrit «Angoisse au cachot» Ji Kang savait qu'il n'éviterait pas [la mort]. C'est pourquoi il dit dans la dernière strophe:
> Je cueillerai des fougères dans les replis des montagnes
> Laissant mes cheveux dénoués dans les grottes rocheuses,
> Sifflant longuement et fredonnant toujours des vers
> Entretenant ma nature foncière, nourrissant ma longévité!

Il se lamentait de ne pas pouvoir accomplir ce but. Sima Zhao, après avoir fait tuer Ji Kang, s'en est repenti [cf. *La vie et la pensée*, p. 50]; s'il s'en était repenti avant de l'avoir fait tuer, Ji Kang aurait évité [la mort] et je sais qu'il aurait fait disparaître ses traces parmi les hommes comme un lapin qu'on relâche se jette dans la forêt. Est-ce si difficile de cueillir les fougères, les cheveux épars dans le dos? (Cité par Hu Zi 胡仔, *Tiaoxi yuyin conghua*, 2ᵉ Série 1, Pékin, 1962, p. 5).

Je pense non seulement que Ji Kang croit sincèrement aux immortels qui hantent ces poèmes, mais que c'est dans l'expression très personnelle de ces idées religieuses en vers que nous devons chercher la principale originalité de sa poésie. Depuis les *Chu ci* les poètes ont exprimé des idées religieuses en vers, des descriptions de randonnées mystiques, des cérémonies religieuses, des chevauchées des chamanes, des rencontres avec des dieux et des déesses. Mais il me semble que ces descriptions, chez les poètes antérieurs à Ji Kang, restent assez impersonnelles: le poète ne nous décrit pas son engagement psychologique dans la poursuite de son salut. Chez Ji Kang nous voyons un poète qui raconte non seulement les bonheurs des randonnées mystiques dans les montagnes magiques, mais aussi les difficultés de l'ascèse qui y mène et les remords que ses propres fautes et péchés lui inspirent. Son introspection est beaucoup plus complexe que celle de ses devanciers, son dialogue avec sa conscience plus développé.

Dans l'évolution des formes poétiques, les poètes de l'ère Zhengshi (c'est-à-dire, Ji Kang et Ruan Ji, principalement) sont nettement en retrait de leurs devanciers de l'ère Jian'an. La virtuosité de Cao Zhi, l'invention prosodique de Cao Cao et de Cao Pi, et les poèmes des autres membres de la Pléiade de la fin des Han ont laissé un legs si considérable que Ji Kang et Ruan Ji semblent ne pas avoir senti le besoin d'inventer de nouvelles formes poétiques. Les vers de Ji Kang considérés les plus beaux sont en tétramètres, les poèmes «paysagistes»

VIII

(poèmes 9 et 14 de ceux envoyés à son frère aîné, par exemple), où il renouvelle, d'une façon quasi miraculeuse, la forme millénaire, héritée du *Shi jing*, qui n'avait servi, depuis des longs siècles, que pour des poèmes rituels ou des pièces de circonstance. Mais l'originalité de ces poèmes réside dans l'emploi d'un langage contemporain rehaussé par des emprunts du *Shi jing* et, en même temps, des *Chu ci*. Le résultat est nouveau, mais non pas au même degré que les nouveautés de ses devanciers dans la forme pentamétrique et d'ailleurs il n'a pas fait école.

Ji Kang, en se détournant de la vie extérieure et de la politique, pour s'occuper de son âme, est un poète marquant dans l'évolution de la poésie chinoise. Il innove et ouvre à cette poésie un domaine jusqu'alors négligé ou inconnu, mais que les poètes médiévaux ultérieurs allaient exploiter dans leur poésie métaphysique et paysagiste.

SUMMARY

Ji Kang (also called Xi Kang, A.D. 223-262) is well-known as one of the most original Taoist philosophers in early medieval China. He was also a poet of note and this article contains annotated translations of all his poetry. His work includes poems in pentameters, hexameters, in *yuefu* meters, and in Chu song style verse, but his best poems are in tetrameters, a form he was particularly fond of and into which he breathed new life. There are also many series of poems written to various friends and to his elder brother, some of which are very original in that they use different meters in the same series. In all his poetry, as in his prose, Ji Kang shows an almost single-minded interest in the pursuit of Taoist immortality, and some of his finest verse is devoted to descriptions of the quasi-mystical roamings of immortals in particularly beautiful natural scenery. In his autobiographical poetry Ji Kang shows himself time and again to be a man struggling with his own conscience, accusing himself of guilt and shame and making us feel that he is sincerely interested in achieving his religious salvation and that he, for the first time perhaps in the history of Chinese poetry, has managed to transcend political commitment and devote himself to the improvement of his own soul.

This translation of Ji Kang's entire poetic output (that is, the first chapter of Dai Mingyang's edition of the *Ji Kang ji*) rearranges the poems according to their subject matter, beginning with the poems written to his brother and to friends, continuing with poems on philosophical subjects (mainly Taoist im-

VIII

mortality) and ending with autobiographical poems, in particular his long swan-song, "Youfen shi", "Anguish in prison". The poems are given in literal translation. Each poem is followed by extended interpretations of allusions, of difficult passages and with emmendations when, as is often the case, there seems to be textual corruption. Reference is made to previous critical opinion when it is deemed interesting.

LISTE DES POÈMES TRADUITS

Dix-neuf poèmes donnés à mon frère aîné, bachelier, lors de son entrée dans l'armée 119
Trois poèmes présentés par Guo Xiazhou 144
Cinq poèmes présentés par Guo Xiashu 149
Trois poèmes en réponse aux deux Guo 153
Poème donné à Ruan Deru 162
Deux poèmes de réponse par Ruan Deru 165
Partie à boire 172
Poème sans titre 175
Dix poèmes en hexamètres 323
Sept poèmes en tétramètres sur le chant Qiu Hu 333
Immortels en promenade 342
Pensant à mes parents 346
Aspirations 348
Angoisse au cachot 354
Six poèmes en tétramètres 366
[Poème sans titre] 370

IX

Folk Ballads and the Aristocracy

Ever since I first read them a number of years ago I was struck by the folk poetry called "Nanchao yuefu" (Ballads of the Southern Dynasties) and surprised at how easy they were to appreciate, even for a Westerner. Most pre-Tang poetry written by literary men has always seemed to me to be difficult to get into, difficult to feel what the author was getting at. These literary poems were so intimately tied up with the poet's life, and his life so intimately tied up with the history of the times and in particular with the history of the court, with the life of the emperor, that the reader needs an enormous amount of historical baggage to be able to understand what is going on. Beginning with Qu Yuan in the fourth century B.C. and right down to the fourth century A.D. at least the vast majority of poetry that still subsists deals with the court and with the men who were at the center of the state and state politics seems to be almost all that interested the poets who wrote it.

With the Southern Ballads we are in another world — as far from the world of the court as it is possible to be and still be in China. These ballads are folk poetry, not court poetry, and the subjects they concern are every-day subjects: love mainly, forsaken women, merchants or sailors who must leave their lovers, young women engaged in raising silk-worms and who neglect their duties to indulge in amorous dalliance with their boyfriends, etc. Earlier poetry sometimes describes forsaken women or estranged lovers, but usually as allegories: the forsaken woman represents the poet who, like Qu Yuan, yearns to win back the good graces of his sovereign. But the Southern Ballads are not allegorical; they really describe human emotions experienced by ordinary people far from the court and the destiny of the nation. Or do they? Some of the ballads that seem most innocent, whose emotions seem simplest and most direct, are attributed to aristocratic authors, generals and princes of the blood who were in the center of politics and who were directly responsible for the destiny of the dynasty. How are we to interpret these unlikely attributions? I cannot pretend to have found the answer, but I think it is worthwhile to pose the problem and at least to attempt to imagine why these unlikely attributions have been made.

I would like to limit the corpus of poems I will discuss to one part only of these Southern Ballads: the "Xiqu" (Western Lyrics), a group of short poems almost all written in quatrains with lines of five syllables. I will leave aside a larger group of ballads called "Wusheng" (Wu Music), although they are probably the model for the "Xiqu" and are very similar to them. The "Wusheng" were written in or near the capital Jiankang (Nanking), the "Xiqu" in the middle basin of the Yangzi in what is now the province of Hubei and in its adjoining provinces. The "Wusheng" date, in their great majority, from the fourth century, and the "Xiqu" grew up after the waning of the "Wusheng" and date from the fifth century. There can be no doubt that the "Xiqu" grew out of the "Wusheng"; they resemble them very closely and are sometimes called "Wuge" (Songs of Wu) in old texts, but there are subtle differences in the poems that probably reflect the differences in geography and perhaps in society.[2] I

2   Most of the information I give here comes from Wang Yunxi, *Liuchao yuefu yu minge*, Shanghai: Gudian wenxue chubanshe, 1957, pp. 3-32.

Folk Ballads and the Aristocracy

will take most of my examples here from the "Xiqu" because they are much more often attributed to members of the aristocracy than are the "Wusheng."[3] There remain today about 470 of these Southern Ballads, of which about 140 are "Xiqu." They are all found in the most complete collection of ballads in existence, the *Yuefu shiji* of the late Northern Song scholar Guo Maoqian.[4]

Perhaps the best way to begin is to read a few of these poems in more or less literal translation so that you will be able to see why I put into doubt their attribution to aristocrats. Let us begin with the very first of the "Xiqu" that appears in Guo Maoqian's collection; according to Wang Yunxi the poem is one of the earliest of the "Xiqu," dating to around 430.[5] The poem is the first of five quatrains that bear the collective title of "Shicheng Music":

I was born and raised near Shicheng	生長石城下
And my window opens out to the watchtower on the town wall.	開窗對城樓
The young men in the town,	城中諸少年
As they pass in and out, come and pay me a visit.[6]	出入見依投

There are two translations of this short poem and one commentary on it in Chinese. Suzuki Torao and Anne Birrell translate the text that is given in the *Yutai xinyong* 10[7] that contains two variants, "gate" (*men*) for

---

3   I have been enormously helped in my study by the excellent as yet unpublished thesis entitled "The Western Songs (Xiqu) of the Southern Dynasties (420-
589) — A Critical Study" presented to the Australian National University in
1984 by Chan Man Sing. I would like to thank David Knechtges who very
kindly sent me a photocopy of the thesis.

4   My examples will be quoted from the Peking edition (Zhonghua shuju, 1979).

5   Cf. Wang Yunxi, *Liuchao yuefu yu minge*, p. 11.

6   Text in *Yuefu shiji* 47, p. 689.

7   Cf. Suzuki Torao, *Gyokutai shinyô shû* 3, Tokyo: Iwanami shoten, 1975,

"window" in line 2, and "handsome" (*mei*) for the plural in line 3. They also understand the last line of the poem more or less as I have. Suzuki has "The handsome young masters in the town drop in to honor me with their patronage as they pass in and out of the city wall"; Birrell has "Drop in as they come and go." The Chinese commentary by Zhang Houyu[8] understands the last line differently: "Every time the young men in the town pass before her window, they all gaze at it lovingly, unable to detach their eyes." He has perhaps allowed himself liberties with the grammar of the last line so as not to shock his feminine readers (since he is being published by the Chinese Women's Press). Such descriptions of sexual licence, of what certainly seems to be a woman selling or perhaps freely giving her charms to many men, are rare in the "Xiqu," although they are not uncommon in the "Wusheng." The four other quatrains under this title are delicate poems of sentiment and are more typical of the "Xiqu." I would like to translate the second of these five poems before discussing their authorship. It is put into the mouth of a young woman:

In the warm spring when all the flowers bloom,	陽春百花生
I pick some to stick as a crown in my headdress.	摘插環髻前
Twisting my fingers and stamping my feet to [the tune of] "Forgetting Sadness,"	捥指蹋忘愁
Together with [the one I love] we make the most of the years of our youth!	相與及盛年

The young lady in the poem (the vast majority of these poems, "Xiqu" and "Wusheng" alike, are spoken in the persona of women, and usually women in love) is in all probability participating in a spring festival, dancing on the green and perhaps participating in the stamping dances that are described in the first three of the four "Jiangling yue" (Jiangling

pp. 304-305; Anne Birrell, *New Songs from a Jade Terrace*, London: George Allen & Unwin, 1982, p. 269.

8 Cf. *Gushi jianshang cidian*, Peking: Zhongguo funü chubanshe, 1988, p. 1179.

Folk Ballads and the Aristocracy

Music) poems that also are "Xiqu."[9] The tune "Wang chou" (Forgetting Sadness) in line 3 is most probably another name for the tune "Mo chou" (Don't Be Sad), which is said to be derived from "Shicheng Music" in the *Jiu Tangshu* monograph on music. The monograph also states that the refrain that was sung with "Shicheng Music" contained the words *wang chou*.[10] There are three other quatrains under the same title "Shicheng Music," and all three depict scenes of parting between sailors (or perhaps river merchants) and their wives or lovers. There is a charming, naive freshness about all of them that sets them apart from literary poetry.

And yet, immediately before its remarks on the tune "Mo chou" the monograph on music of the *Jiu Tangshu* has this to say:

> "Shicheng" was written by Zang Zhi (d. 454). Shicheng is in Jingling (the present Zhongxiang, Hubei). Zang Zhi was once prefect of the commandery of Jingling[11] and looked out from the town walls and saw groups of young people singing at the top of their voices. This occasioned his writing of this piece.

The *Jiu Tangshu* would thus have us believe that Zang Zhi, a soldier, hunter and gamester who is nowhere mentioned as being interested in literature was inspired by what he saw and heard on the town wall to compose or perhaps transcribe these folksongs. On the face of it there is nothing impossible about a soldier indulging in poetry, as Cao Cao proved two centuries earlier. It is quite probable that the majority of the peasants who sang these songs were illiterate and, if the songs have reached us, some literate person must have written them down. And almost all the Chinese who have written on these poems whose works I have read repeat these remarks from the *Jiu Tangshu* and consider Zang Zhi to be the author of these five quatrains: Yu Guanying,[12] the members

---

9   Cf. *Yuefu shiji* 49, p. 710. See the *Yuzhu baodian* 10, p. 13a-b (Guyi congshu edition), by Du Taiqing (d. *ca.* 596), quoted by Chan Man Sing, "The Western Songs (Xiqu) of the Southern Dynasties," p. 89.

10   Cf. *Jiu Tangshu* 29, p. 1065.

11   Some time around 430; see *Songshu* 74, p. 1910.

12   Cf. *Han Wei Liuchao shixuan*, Peking: Renmin wenxue chubanshe, 1979 (first

IX

of the Department of the History of Chinese Literature of the University of Peking,[13] Zhang Yaxin,[14] Zhang Houyu,[15] and Chan Man Sing.[16] I have long since learned that it is dangerous to contest Chinese opinion on their literature, but I wonder if they are right in accepting the *Jiu Tangshu* attribution.

It would be relatively easy to accept the attribution to Zang Zhi of these poems if it were the only case in which a famous aristocrat is said to have created a category of Southern Ballads, but there are seven examples of this kind of attribution for the "Xiqu" and three for the "Wusheng," some of which are not at all easy to accept. The second "Xiqu" title given by Guo Maoqian is called "Wu ye ti" (The Crow Cried in the Night), and it is attributed to the famous literary patron, the Song prince Liu Yiqing (403-444) in the monograph on music in the *Jiu Tangshu* and to his cousin Liu Yikang (409-451) in the *Jiaofang ji* (*ca.* 760).[17] The latter attribution is accompanied by so many anachronisms and mistakes (some pointed out by Guo Maoqian) that it cannot be considered seriously. But there are also other attributions in other texts cited by Chan Man Sing. I would like to look into the various attributions in some detail because I think they will show us that it is impossible to know which,

published 1958), p. 241; it is true that Yu Guanying puts the fifth quatrain of the "Shicheng Music" (the only one he quotes) under the general rubric of "Anonymous," but he nevertheless repeats the *Jiu Tangshu* attribution to Zang Zhi in note 1 of his commentary.

13 Cf. *Wei Jin Nanbeichao wenxue shi cankao ziliao*, Peking: Zhonghua shuju, 1962, p. 366.

14 Cf. *Liuchao yuefu shixuan*, [Zhengzhou]: Zhongzhou guji chubanshe, 1986, p. 56.

15 Cf. *Gushi jianshang cidian*. See note 8 above.

16 On pp. 24-25 of his unpublished thesis mentioned in note 3 above.

17 On this work see Robert des Rotours, *Histoire de Ngan Lou-chan (Ngan Lou-chan che tsi)*, Paris: Presses Universitaires de France, 1962 (Bibliothèque de l'Institut des Hautes Études Chinoises, vol. 18), pp. XIII-XIV. The *Jiu Tangshu* 29, p. 1065, and the *Jiaofang ji* are both quoted in the *Yuefu shiji* 647, p. 690.

350

Folk Ballads and the Aristocracy

if any, of these various attributions is accurate, and this negative information will be a first step in delimiting the question I asked at the beginning of this article: why have historians gone so far as to fabulate such highly improbable scenarios in order to attribute so many of these popular songs to aristocratic authors?

The *Jiu Tangshu* gives the following account of how the song "Wu ye ti" was written and by whom:

> "The Crow Cried in the Night" was written by the Song Prince of Lin-chuan, [Liu] Yiqing. In 440 the Prince of Pengcheng, [Liu] Yikang, was transferred to Yuzhang (the present Nanchang, Jiangxi). Yiqing at the time was governor of Jiangzhou (the present Jiujiang, Jiangxi) and when [Liu Yikang] reached Mt. Lu[18] the two cousins met one another and wept. When Emperor Wen (Yikang's elder brother and Yiqing's cousin) heard about their meeting he was most unhappy and ordered [Yiqing] to return to his domicile [in the capital]. The latter became extremely frightened. One night a concubine heard a crow cry and she knocked on the door of his studio to say: "Tomorrow my lord will be amnestied." Within a year he was appointed governor of Southern Yanzhou (the present Yangzhou, Jiangsu) and he wrote this song. Thus the refrain of the song goes:

> He forces[19] the window, but to
>   no avail,   籠窗窗不開
> The crow cries at night,   烏夜啼
> And night after night I await
>   my lover's coming.   夜夜望郎來

> The song that has come down to us today does not seem to have anything to do with what Yiqing originally intended to convey in his song. [...][20]

---

18 The text reads *zhen* one of whose meanings is "principal mountain of a province"; see the pseudo-Kong Anguo commentary to the *Shangshu* 3, p. 14a (of the *Shisan jing zhushu* of Ruan Yuan). Liu Yiqing's capital was close to Mt. Lu, the most imposing mountain of the entire region.

19 Reading *long* 攏 for the *long* 籠 of the text.

20 *Jiu Tangshu* 29, p. 1065; this text is followed by the first of the eight poems contained under the title "Wu ye ti" in *Yuefu shiji* 47, p. 691. I have unfor-

To accept this explanation of the origin of the song one would first of all have to believe that the crow at this time in China was an auspicious bird. Certain legends do present the bird under more positive auspices than a reader of, for example, *Macbeth* or Edgar Allen Poe might expect. It was the symbol of the sun, the emblem of the Zhou dynasty and considered a bird that practiced filial piety by nourishing its mother, but it was also considered a bird of evil omen in both the *Shijing* 41 and 192 and the *Zhouli*.[21] The fifth poem in the series under this title would seem to describe its nocturnal cry as something sad and, one would have thought, unlucky:

Crows, at their birth, want to fly,	烏生如欲飛
To fly and fly, each in its own direction.	飛飛各自去
Thus separated from their loved ones, they have no peace of mind	生離無安心
And cry through the night till dawn.[22]	夜啼至天曙

Neither this poem nor any of the seven others grouped under this title have any relation whatsoever with amnesties of any kind, and only Nos. 3-5 mention birds crying: No. 3 is put in the mouth of a woman separated from her lover who hurries to write an answer to his letter when she failed to hear a bird cry during the day (not at night), and No. 4,

tunately not been able to consult the following article on "The Crow Cried in the Night": Fujii Mamoru, "U ya tei no seiritsu to sono denshô," *Shinagaku kenkyû*, 29, 1963, pp. 23-31.

21 See Wolfram Eberhard, *The Local Customs of South and East China*, Leiden: E.J. Brill, 1968, pp. 429-430, to which should be added Chenggong Sui (231-273), "Wufu," in *Quan Shanggu Sandai Qin Han Sanguo Liuchao wen*, "Quan Jin wen" 59, pp. 7a-8a, which depicts the crow as a filial animal.

22 *Yuefu shiji* 47, p. 691; translations in Marilyn Jane Evans, "Popular Songs of the Southern Dynasties. A Study in Chinese Poetic Style," an unpublished thesis presented to Yale University in 1966, p. 156, and Chan Man Sing, "The Western Songs (Xiqu) of the Southern Dynasties," p. 170. There is a commentary by Zhang Houyu in *Gushi jianshang cidian*, p. 1181.

Folk Ballads and the Aristocracy

perhaps the most beautiful of the eight, is the poem of a lover frustrated by, not a crow, but a shrike (*wujiu*), literally a "crow mortar," which gets its name from the tallow tree (*wujiu*) that is in flower at the time of the year the bird sings:

A fine bird indeed is the shrike Who says he knows when the day will break! For no reason he cried at the third watch And my lover has left, braving the darkness.[23]	可憐烏臼鳥 強言知天曙 無故三更啼 歡子冒闇去

In short, none of these poems is in the slightest relevant to Liu Yiqing's predicament and we are left wondering why it has been attributed to him. Chan Man Sing believes the attribution of this title to a musician-concubine in Liu Yiqing's household made by Xu Jian (659-729) in the *Chuxue ji* is more likely because the musician is said to have composed the song "beset with anguished thoughts."[24] Perhaps to show the utter futility of looking for which among all these highly unlikely attributions is correct, there is yet another given in the *Qinshuo* by Li Mian (717-788) who believes it to have been written by the daughter of He Yan (190-249) when her father was imprisoned.[25] The idea that a ballad of this type that

23 *Yuefu shiji* 47, p. 691; there is a translation of this quatrain and an interesting discussion of the theme in Chan Man Sing, "The Western Songs (Xiqu) of the Southern Dynasties," pp. 150-151, 196-198. There are commentaries by Zhang Yaxin, *Liuchao yuefu shixuan*, p. 57, and Zhang Houyu, *Gushi jianshang cidian*, p. 1181; see also Qian Zhongshu, *Guanzhui bian* 1, Peking: Zhonghua shuju, 1979, p. 104, for a discussion of this theme in world literature.
24 Cf. *Chuxue ji* 16, p. 386 of the Peking edition (Zhonghua shuju, 1962); Chan Man Sing, "The Western Songs (Xiqu) of the Southern Dynasties," pp. 26-30.
25 Cf. *Yuefu shiji* 60, p. 872; Chan Man Sing, "The Western Songs (Xiqu) of the Southern Dynasties," p. 26.

only appeared in the fourth century could be attributed to someone like He Yan's daughter who lived in the first half of the third century reduces the whole exercise to absurdity.

As I said earlier, seven of the prefaces to "Xiqu" songs in the *Yuefu shiji* attribute the creation of song titles to aristocratic authors. We have already seen two cases, one concerning Zang Zhi and the other Liu Yiqing (or others). I must admit that some of the five remaining cases seem quite plausible to me, in particular the poems attributed to two emperors, one to Emperor Wu of Qi (Qi Wudi), Xiao Ze (440-493), because the one rather prosaic poem ascribed to him corresponds in every respect to the conditions that are said to have inspired it,[26] and three to Emperor Wu of the Liang dynasty (Liang Wudi), Xiao Yan (464-549), because he was himself a poet and a man of letters and the historical background given corresponds to events in his life.[27] Of the three remaining titles, two are ascribed to men unknown elsewhere as poets and the poetry they are said to have written on the occasion said to have inspired it seems unrelated to it.[28] The poems by Liu Shuo (431-453), who has a dozen or so poems still in existence, correspond well to the description given to them and are quite possibly written by him.[29] Thus four, over half of the seven attributions given for "Xiqu," seem doubtful to me and require us to wonder why they have been attributed to such unlikely authors?

---

26 Cf. *Yuefu shiji* 48, p. 699; there are translations of the poem by me, in Roderich Ptak and Siegfried Englert, eds., *Ganz allmählich (Festschrift für G. Debon)*, Heidelberg: HVA, 1986, pp. 92-93; and Chan Man Sing, "The Western Songs (Xiqu) of the Southern Dynasties," pp. 32-36.

27 Cf. *Yuefu shiji* 48, p. 708; see the important discussion in Chan Man Sing, "The Western Songs (Xiqu) of the Southern Dynasties," pp. 40-43.

28 Cf. *Yuefu shiji* 49, p. 703 ("Xiangyang yue"), and p. 722 ("Xi wu ye fei").

29 Cf. *Yuefu shiji* 49, pp. 719-720; his other poems can be found in Lu Qinli, *Xian Qin Han Wei Jin Nanbeichao shi*, Peking: Zhonghua shuju, 1983, pp. 1213-1216.

Folk Ballads and the Aristocracy

The relation of popular and literary art is a complicated matter, in China as elsewhere in the world. It used to be said that many of the themes in Haydn's symphonies were copied by the composer from tunes he heard Croatian peasants singing as they worked in the fields around the Esterhazy estate in Hungary where he was the composer in residence, tunes that were still sung in the neighborhood a hundred years later. And then someone had the bright idea that it was the peasants who were singing tunes that Haydn had created and put in his symphonies. I suppose the thought behind this was that tunes good enough to have lasted so long must have been written by a genius and, as far as they knew, Haydn was the only one in the neighborhood. There is no way of proving these theories one way or another. The "Xiqu" and the "Wu-sheng" are obviously folk art; just as obviously, literate men have imitated them and, even in poems thought to be anonymous, lines taken word for word from literati poems can be found showing that in all probability some of these anonymous poems at least were written by literati.[30] Popular poems too have also been used by the literati for satirical or political purposes, so that extreme care must be made before an attribution is denied to be sure some hidden satire is not intended.[31] But I still believe I have shown that some at least of the attributions to aristocrats that one finds in the *Yuefu shiji* are erroneous. How can we account for this fact?

30 Among the "Xiqu," for example, the first line of the third of the "Qingcong baima" poems, *Yuefu shiji* 49, p. 711, is almost word for word from the famous "Fufeng ge" of Liu Kun and the third line of the second "Meng Zhu" poem, p. 714, is almost word for word from an imitation of Cao Zhi by Xie Lingyun.
31 In the *Nan Qishu* 26, p. 485, Wang Zhongxiong (*fl.* 500), the son of Wang Jingze, quotes No. 6 of the "Aonong ge" (*Yuefu shiji* 46, p. 668), to criticize his sovereign. There is no suggestion here that the poem was *written* by Wang Zhongxiong; he uses a ballad that in all probability dates from a century earlier and perhaps deliberately misquotes it so as not to offend the emperor.

The Southern Ballads, the "Xiqu" like the "Wusheng," are revolution-ary in the history of Chinese poetry. They represent something quite new, a kind of hedonism, an interest in aspects of every-day life that classical poetry and even earlier *yuefu* ignored completely. It should perhaps be remarked in passing that even earlier *yuefu* were published for the first time together with the Southern Ballads by Shen Yue (441-513) in the *Songshu* around 500. Before this period it was unthinkable that anyone would be interested in publishing any literature that was not concerned in some way with moral, social or political matters. The ballads we have been reading are precisely the kind of literature that was not considered worth preserving before Shen Yue's times and, I would suggest, attribut-ing some of them at least to aristocratic men, engaged in politics, and endowing them with satirical messages that show they were in fact not simply frivolous folk songs, but serious works by men seriously engaged in the service of the state, was a way of making them worthy of being read by gentlemen of the ruling class.

Folk Ballads and the Aristocracy

Chinese Characters

Aonong ge 懊儂歌
Cao Cao 曹操
Cao Zhi 曹植
Chan Man Sing (Chen Wancheng) 陳萬成
Chenggong Sui 成公綏
Chuxue ji 初學記
Du Taiqing 杜臺卿
Fufeng ge 扶風歌
Fujii Mamoru 藤井守
Gushi jianshang cidian 古詩鑒賞辭典
Guanzhui bian 管錐編
Guo Maoqian 郭茂倩
Gyokutai shinyô shû 玉臺新詠集
Han Wei Liuchao shixuan 漢魏六朝詩選
He Yan 何晏
Jiankang 建康
Jiangling yue 江陵樂
Jiangzhou 江州
Jiaofang ji 教坊記
Jingling 竟陵
Jiujiang 九江
Jiu Tangshu 舊唐書
Kong Anguo 孔安國
Li Mian 李勉
Liang Wudi 梁武帝
Linchuan 臨川

Liuchao yuefu shixuan 六朝樂府詩選
Liuchao yuefu yu minge 六朝樂府與民歌
Liu Kun 劉琨
Liu Shuo 劉鑠
Liu Yikang 劉義康
Liu Yiqing 劉義慶
Lu 廬
Lu Qinli 逯欽立
mei 美
men 門
Meng Zhu 孟珠
Mo chou 莫愁
Nanchang 南昌
Nanchao yuefu 南朝樂府
Nan Qishu 南齊書
Pengcheng 彭城
Qi Wudi 齊武帝
Qian Zhongshu 錢鍾書
Qinshuo 琴説
Qingcong baima 青驄白馬
Qu Yuan 屈原
Quan Jin wen 全晉文
Quan Shanggu Sandai Qin Han Sanguo Liuchao wen 全上古三代秦漢三國六朝文
Ruan Yuan 阮元
Shangshu 尚書

Shen Yue 沈約
Shicheng 石城
Shijing 詩經
Shisan jing zhushu
　十三經注疏
Songshu 宋書
Suzuki Torao 鈴木虎雄
U ya tei no seiritsu to sono
　denshô
　烏夜啼の成立とそ
　の傳唱
Wang chou 忘愁
Wang Jingze 王敬則
Wang Yunxi 王運熙
Wang Zhongxiong 王仲雄
Wei Jin Nanbeichao wenxue shi
　cankao ziliao
　魏晉南北朝文學史參
　考資料
Wen 文
Wufu 烏賦
Wuge 吳歌
wujiu (shrike, tree) 烏臼
Wusheng 吳聲
Wu ye ti 烏夜啼

Xiqu 西曲
Xi wu ye fei 西烏夜飛
Xian Qin Han Wei Jin
　Nanbeichao shi
　先秦漢魏晉南北朝詩
Xiangyang yue 襄陽樂
Xiao Yan 蕭衍
Xiao Ze 蕭賾
Xie Lingyun 謝靈運
Xu Jian 徐堅
Yanzhou 兗州
Yangzhou 揚州
Yu Guanying 余冠英
Yutai xinyong 玉臺新詠
Yuzhang 豫章
Yuzhu baodian 玉燭寶典
yuefu 樂府
Yuefu shiji 樂府詩集
Zang Zhi 臧質
Zhang Houyu 張厚餘
Zhang Yaxin 張亞新
zhen 鎮
Zhongxiang 鍾祥
Zhouli 周禮

X

XIE LINGYUN ET LES PAYSANS DE YONGJIA

Xie Lingyun 謝靈運 (385-433), le premier grand poète paysagiste de la poésie chinoise, a été dépeint dans sa biographie[1] comme un aristocrate hautain et dédaigneux. Il fut en effet pendant une année, de l'automne 422 à l'automne 423, préfet à Yongjia 永嘉 (l'actuel Wenzhou 温州 dans le Zhejiang) et on l'accuse de s'être montré indifférent aux paysans qu'il administrait. Il y a, pourtant, dans son œuvre, trois poèmes qui datent de cette époque et qui semblent prouver non seulement qu'il était loin d'être indifférent aux paysans, mais aussi qu'il assumait sérieusement son rôle de préfet et de fonctionnaire, en bon confucianiste. La traduction de ces trois poèmes le montrera clairement.

Xie Lingyun fut nommé préfet à Yongjia peu de temps après l'accession au trône de l'empereur Shao 少 à la fin du mois de juin, 422. Cette nomination était pour lui une rétrogradation, presqu'un exil, et elle mit fin, au moins temporairement, aux très grandes espérances qu'il nourrissait de devenir un des principaux personnages de la cour impériale. Il décrivit ses sentiments, souvent contradictoires, dans une série de poèmes écrits au moment du départ de la capitale (Jiankang 建康 , l'actuel Nankin) et au cours de son voyage à Yongjia.[2]

1. *Songshu* 宋書 67, p. 1743-1787, de l'édition de la Zhonghua shuju publiée à Pékin en 1974.

2. Ces poèmes se trouvent dans les chapitres 20 et 26 du *Wenxuan*. On les trouvera recueillis dans l'édition de Gu Shaobo 顧紹柏 , *Xie Lingyun ji jiaozhu* 謝靈運集校注 , [Zhengzhou?], Zhongzhou Guji chubanshe, 1987, p. 35-53. Cette édition est actuellement de loin la meilleure; mes références aux œuvres de Xie Lingyun seront

Une lecture rapide de ces poèmes pourrait faire croire que Xie Lingyun renonçait définitivement à la carrière d'homme d'État et qu'il s'apprêtait à se retirer loin de la cour pour toujours et sans remords. Mais une lecture plus attentive montre que ces poèmes contiennent des indices subtils de la grande contradiction qui sous-tend toute sa vie : son désir de servir l'État, et son désir de se retirer du monde pour mener une vie d'ermite toute consacrée à la méditation mystique. Il y dit à plusieurs reprises qu'il considère son poste comme un genre de retraite anticipée au bord de la mer qui lui permettra de parcourir les montagnes en jouissant des beautés de paysages inconnus. Mais il se lamente aussi, d'une façon allusive, de ne pas avoir été utilisé à sa juste valeur par les hommes au pouvoir.[3] Par ailleurs il cite le *Yijing* 易經 à l'occasion d'un danger encouru durant un passage de rapides. Cette citation même, qui est une métaphore des dangers encourus par les hommes politiques, prouve à mon sens que les pensées de Xie Lingyun sont encore très proches d'un passé politique dont il n'est nullement détaché.[4] Certes, Xie Lingyun réitère fréquemment son désir ardent de se retirer de la vie publique, mais ses plaintes répétées d'être séparé de ses amis restés à la capitale et les quelques allusions qui prouvent son intérêt persistant à l'égard de la vie politique montrent qu'il n'avait pas l'étoffe d'un véritable ermite, comme il voudrait bien nous le faire croire. Les poèmes qui décrivent ses rapports avec les paysans de Yongjia le montrent encore plus clairement.

La réputation d'indifférence à ses devoirs d'administrateur et aux malheurs du peuple qu'on prête à Xie Lingyun apparaît déjà dans la biographie écrite moins d'un demi-siècle après sa mort par Shen Yue 沈約 (441-513). Celui-ci décrit la vie de Xie Lingyun à Yongjia dans les termes suivants :

> Il y avait à Yongjia des paysages célèbres, tels que [Xie Lingyùn] les avait toujours aimés. Contrarié d'avoir été expulsé de la cour pour administrer cette commanderie, il passa son temps à se promener selon son bon plaisir. Il parcourut ainsi toutes les sous-préfectures de sa juridiction, restant absent des dix ou des quinze jours chaque fois... Quant à juger les procès du peuple, c'est ce dont il n'avait cure.[5]

faites à cette édition, appelée simplement par le nom de l'éditeur.

3. Dans les v. 11-14 de son poème « Yongchu san nian ... chu fa du » 永初三年 初發都 ; Gu Shaobo, p. 35.

4. Dans les v. 9-10 du poème « Fuchun zhu » 富春渚 ; Gu Shaobo, p. 45.

5. *Songshu* 67, p. 1753-1754, dans la belle traduction de Paul Demiéville reproduite de l'*Annuaire du Collège de France*, 63ᵉ Année, Paris, 1963, p. 330, dans *Choix d'études sinologiques*, Leiden, E. J. Brill, 1973, p. 335.

La lecture des poèmes écrits à cette époque qui décrivent les rapports de Xie Lingyun avec les paysans contredit ce jugement de Shen Yue.[6]

Le premier des trois poèmes doit dater de la fin du printemps 423, la période évoquée dans le v. 7 du poème.

種桑   La culture des mûriers

詩人陳條柯   Le poète du *Shijing* expliqua comment on [rabaisse] les branches [des mûriers pour les effeuiller],

亦有美攘剔   Et loua aussi l'art de les tailler.

前修為誰故   Pour qui les sages antiques œuvrèrent-ils de la sorte ?

後事資劜績   Pour que, après eux et grâce à eux, nous puissions filer la soie.

5 常佩知方誡   Je garde toujours gravé dans mon cœur le précepte : « [Faire comprendre au peuple] les règles de bonne conduite » ;

愧微富教益   Mais j'ai honte de l'avoir si peu « enrichi » ou « éduqué ».

浮陽騖嘉月   Quand les rayons du soleil dardent à la bonne saison,

執桑迫閒隙   On profite d'un moment de loisir pour cultiver les mûriers.

疏欄發近郊   Les tuteurs espacés partent des murailles de la ville,

10 長行達廣場   Et les longues rangées vont jusqu'à la bordure des champs.

曠流始涖泉   Les vastes cours d'eau naissent comme sources jaillissantes ;

洒塗猶跱迹   Les longues routes suivent les traces de petits pas.

俾此將長成   Que ces [mûriers] parviennent à maturité !

慰我海外役   Ils me consoleront de mon service au delà des mers ![7]

6. J'ai beaucoup profité dans ce qui suit de la conférence du professeur Yang * Yong 楊勇 de l'Université chinoise de Hong Kong donnée lors des journées d'études sur Xie Lingyun qui eut lieu à Beiyandang shan 北雁蕩山 et à Wenzhou en novembre 1991, conférence qui devait être publiée en 1993 en même temps que les autres conférences données à la même occasion.

7. Pour le texte de ce poème, voir Gu Shaobo, p. 70. Il y a une traduction anglaise dans J.D. Frodsham, *The Murmuring Stream : The Life and Works of Hsieh Ling-yün*, Kuala Lumpur, University of Malaya Press, 1967, p. 133 du vol. 1, commentaire p. 145-146 du vol. 2. Référence à cet ouvrage sera faite désormais par le nom de l'auteur suivi du chiffre 1 ou 2 selon qu'il s'agit du premier ou du deuxième tome. J'ai aussi comparé les textes donnés par Gu Shaobo avec ceux donnés par Lu Qinli 逯欽立, *Xian Qin Han Wei Jin Nanbeichao shi* 先秦漢魏晉南北朝詩 , Pékin, Xinhua shuju, 1983, p. 1168-1172, pour les trois poèmes de Xie Lingyun que je traduis dans cet essai.

Les deux premiers vers font allusion aux poèmes nᵒˢ 154.3 et 241.2 du *Shijing* 詩經 qui décrivent l'art très ancien en Chine de la sériciculture.

Les v. 5 et 6 font allusion au *Lunyu* 論語 11.25 et 13.9. Dans le premier passage un disciple de Confucius déclare qu'il veut rendre le peuple dont il a la charge « courageux et respectueux des règles de la bonne conduite »; dans le deuxième, Confucius lui-même déclare qu'il faut d'abord enrichir le peuple et ensuite l'éduquer. Enfin il y a sans doute une allusion au *Shijing* 304.2 dans le dernier vers du poème : « L'ordre régna au delà des mers »; en citant ces deux mots, Xie Lingyun évoque le vers entier. Avec ce vers du *Shijing* en tête le lecteur est amené à féliciter le préfet Xie de son bon gouvernement dans ce coin perdu « au delà des mers ».

Le poème n'est pas assez détaillé pour qu'on puisse savoir avec quelque précision comment Xie Lingyun s'y est pris pour cette « culture des mûriers ». Ce n'est guère que dans les v. 7 à 10 qu'il nous dit qu'elle a lieu pendant « la bonne saison », sans doute le printemps, et qu'il s'agit d'ériger des tuteurs[8] bien espacés dans de longues allées. Avec les allusions au *Shijing*, les six premiers vers du poème placent les travaux du préfet de Yongjia dans une perspective historique millénaire : il aide ses administrés à accomplir les actes préconisés par les Saints de l'Antiquité, en même temps que lui-même suit le précepte de Confucius d'enrichir le peuple. Le dernier vers montre on ne pourrait plus clairement toute l'importance qu'il accordait à cette activité en faveur des paysans.

Le poème suivant est impossible à dater avec précision, mais il semble probable qu'il fut écrit peu de temps après le poème précédent.[9]

---

8. Le mot que je traduis par ce terme, *lan* 欄, est utilisé dans le sens verbal de « tuteurer » dans le *Qimin yaoshu* 齊民要術 50, consacré à la plantation des arbres; voir le *Hanyu da cidian* 漢語大詞典 4, p. 1369, le sixième sens sous ce caractère. Frodsham 2, p. 145, cite le *Fan Shengzhi shu* 氾勝之書 qui donne le cinquième mois pour la date de *semer* les graines des mûriers. En fait la culture de ces arbres est assez compliquée; si mon hypothèse à propos des tuteurs est exacte, il ne s'agit vraisemblablement pas de semailles ici, mais de repiquage et de tuteurage, sujets traités en plus grand détail au début du chapitre consacré à ce sujet dans le *Qimin yaoshu* 45.

9. Tel est l'avis de Gu Shaobo, p. 86, n. 1; Yang Yong, « Xie Lingyun nianpu » 謝靈運年譜, in *Essays in Chinese Studies Dedicated to Professor Jao Tsung-i*, Hong Kong, 1970, p. 34, le date aussi de 423, mais dans sa conférence de novembre 1991, encore inédite, il le date du neuvième mois lunaire de 422. Pour le texte de ce poème, voir Gu Shaobo, p. 85-86; il y a une traduction anglaise dans Frodsham 1, p. 123, et un commentaire dans Frodsham 2, p. 126.

白石巖下 徑行田	Faisant l'inspection des champs sur le sentier en bas du mont des Pierres Blanches
小邑居易貧	À vivre dans une petite localité, on tombe facilement dans la pauvreté,
災年民無生	Et dans les années de désastres, le peuple n'a plus de quoi subsister.
知淺懼不周	Mes maigres connaissances, je crains, ne suffisent pas,
愛深憂在情	Mais mon amour [pour le peuple] est profond, et mon angoisse [pour lui] l'est aussi.
5 莓蓿横海外	De mauvaises herbes poussent dans tous les sens ici au delà des mers
蕪穢積頹齡	Et les champs en friche se multiplient alors que mes forces déclinent.
饑饉不可久	Je ne peux laisser la famine continuer plus long-temps :
甘心務經營	C'est de bon cœur que je me mets au travail !
千頃帶遠堤	J'encerclerai de vastes superficies par une longue digue ;
10 萬里瀉長汀	Je drainerai les terres au bord de la mer à l'infini !
州流涓澮合	Je ferai en sorte que dans les arrondissements les ruis-seaux et les rigoles coulent d'une façon ordonnée,
連綫塍埒并	Et que dans les communes les sentiers qui courent entre les champs soient réguliers et parallèles.
雖非楚宮化	Bien que les transformations ne puissent se comparer à celles des palais de Chu,
荒關亦黎萌	J'aurai aidé le peuple commun dans sa détresse.
15 雖非鄭白漑	Bien que [ces travaux] n'égalent ni le canal de Zheng [Guo] ni celui du [Maître] Bai,
每歲望東京	Tous les ans [les hommes de Yongjia pourront] regar-der [avec fierté] vers la capitale.
天鑒倘不孤	Si le ciel nous voit et ne nous délaisse pas,
來茲驗微誠	Ma faible sincérité doit porter ses fruits dans les années à venir.

Le mont des Pierres Blanches, Baishishan 白石山 (appelé Baishi-yan 巖 par Xie Lingyun), se trouve à une quinzaine de kilomètres à l'ouest de la ville actuelle de Leqing 樂清 , à environ vingt-cinq kilo-mètres au nord-est de Wenzhou. On peut facilement imaginer le préfet faisant un tour d'inspection[10] à quelques dizaines de kilomètres de son

---

10. « Tour d'inspection » traduit les mots *xingtian* 行田 . J'adopte la définition de Ye Xiaoxue 葉笑雪 , *Xie Lingyun shixuan* 謝靈運詩選 , Shanghai, Gudian

X

120

chef-lieu et constatant avec douleur l'état de délabrement dans lequel la région est tombée (v. 5-6), à la suite de catastrophes naturelles (v. 2). Les protestations de modestie du v. 3 n'empêchent pas le poète d'envisager des plans grandioses d'amélioration de l'agriculture (v. 9-12). Il déclare tout de même que ses travaux ne pourront pas rivaliser avec ceux du duc Wen 文 de Wei 衛 à Chuqiu 楚丘 (v. 13),[11] ni avec ceux de Zheng Guo 鄭國 et Maître Bai 白公 (v. 15) dont les célèbres canaux permirent l'irrigation sous les Qin et les Han Antérieurs d'une grande partie du sud de l'actuelle province du Shaanxi.[12] Les v. 14 et 16 sont obscurs. Je suis la suggestion de Gu Shaobo et remplace le caractère 亦 dans ce vers par un caractère homophone (au temps de Xie Lingyun comme aujourd'hui), 益. Dans le v. 16, les mots traduits par « la capitale » se lisent « capitale orientale » dans la plupart des éditions, et « la capitale [Jian]kang » dans deux monographies locales consacrées à Wenzhou. Huang Jie, suivi en cela par Gu Shaobo, suggère de substituer « occidentale » à « orientale », faisant de ces mots une allusion au *Hanshu* où on lit que les canaux de Zheng Guo et du Maître Bai permirent aux régions qu'ils irriguaient « de vêtir et de nourrir la capitale », c'est-à-dire Chang'an, « la capitale occidentale ». « Si le ciel nous voit » du v. 17 est une allusion au *Shijing* 236.4, et les deux mots à la fin du vers sont une allusion au *Lunyu* 4.25.

Xie Lingyun réalisa-t-il les plans grandioses qu'il nous dévoile dans les v. 9-12 de ce poème? Gu Shaobo croit que ces vers décrivent un rêve du poète qu'il ne put jamais réaliser; Yang Yong, dans sa conférence encore inédite, croit, au contraire, que les constructions de digues et de canaux dont parle ce poème ont bel et bien existé et qu'elles peuvent être comparées aux trois réservoirs construits à Baishi depuis quelques années. Il ajoute que le lieu-dit « Xie tian cun » 謝田村 qui se trouve à cet endroit « a sans aucun doute été nommé pour commémorer les aménagements splendides accomplis par Xie Lingyun ». Réalisations ou rêves,

wenxue chubanshe, 1957, p. 56. Il se réfère à un usage similaire de ces mots dans la biographie de Wang Xizhi 王羲之, *Jinshu* 晉書 80, p. 2102 (référence déjà donnée par Huang Jie 黃節, *Xie Kangle shi zhu* 謝康樂詩注, 1924, réimpression Taibei, Yiwen yinshuguan, [sans date], p. 81).

11. Le duc Wen avait restauré sa capitale détruite en 660 av. J.-C. à Chuqiu; voir *Zuozhuan* 左傳, Mingong 閔公 2, Couvreur 1, p. 228-229; voir aussi *Shijing* 50, une ode qui loue les travaux du duc à Chuqiu.

12. Voir *Shiji* 史記 29, trad. Édouard Chavannes, *Les mémoires historiques de Se-ma Ts'ien*, t. 3, p. 523-525 (réimpression Paris, Adrien-Maisonneuve, 1967), et *Hanshu* 漢書 29, p. 1685.

les projets décrits dans ce poème montrent que Xie Lingyun prenait à cœur les malheurs des paysans de la région de Yongjia.

Le dernier poème que je traduirai ne concerne pas directement les paysans de Yongjia, mais il est dédié aux gens du peuple et témoigne encore une fois combien Xie Lingyun prenait au sérieux son engagement vis-à-vis des plus humbles de ses administrés. Le « Pavillon du Nord » nommé dans le titre du poème se trouvait à quelques kilomètres au nord de Yongjia, adossé au fleuve.[13] Il s'agit vraisemblablement du lieu de débarquement de Xie Lingyun lors de son retour vers son domaine de Shining 始寧 au mois d'octobre 423, retour décrit en détail dans son poème « Chu qu jun » 初去郡 contenu dans le *Wenxuan* 26. Le premier vers fait référence à des employés subalternes qui vécurent sous la dynastie des Han Antérieurs, des gratte-papiers qui, par leur talent, surent monter en grade et occuper des postes importants dans la hiérarchie administrative.

北亭與吏民別   Au Pavillon du Nord je prends congé
         des employés de mon bureau et des gens du peuple

刀筆愧張杜   J'ai honte devant Zhang Tang et Du Zhou, ceux qui maniaient le couteau et le pinceau,

棄繻慚終軍   Et je rougis devant Zhong Jun qui a rejeté le sauf-conduit.

貴史寄子長   Dans mon estime pour l'histoire, je me remets à Sima Qian ;

愛賦托子雲   Dans mon amour pour les *fu*, je me confie à Yang Xiong.

5   昔值休明初   Jadis je vécus les débuts d'une ère éclairée,

以此預人羣   Qui m'entraînèrent à m'engager dans la vie sociale.

常呼城旁道   [Mais] j'en appelais toujours à ceux qui habitent en marge de la société,

更歌憂逸民   Et je chantais constamment ma douleur pour les hommes retirés du monde.

猶抱見素樸   Je cultivais en moi [le précepte de Laozi] de montrer ma simplicité naturelle,

10   兼弘擁來勤   En même temps que je m'efforçais de rester diligent.

定自懲伐檀   Mais à la fin j'ai pu vérifier l'authenticité de ce qui est dit dans le poème « Couper le bois de santal »

亦已驗惟塵   Et aussi dans celui qui parle de « poussière ».

---

13. Selon le *Taiping huanyu ji* 太平寰宇記 99, p. 3b, qui cite, d'autre part, les v. 25-26 du poème.

X

122

晚來聲餘荣	Sur le tard je me suis laissé entraîner à la recherche d'un restant de gloire,
憩泊甌海濱	Et je me suis reposé ici à Ou 甌 au bord de la mer.
15 時易速還周	Les saisons ont changé si vite que déjà une année entière s'est écoulée ;
德之難濟振	J'ai manqué de capacités et c'est avec difficulté que j'ai pu aider les sinistrés.
眷言徒矜傷	Je pense à vous, [peuple de Yongjia], avec affection, m'affligeant en vain [de vos malheurs] :
靡術謝經綸	Incompétent, je dus renoncer à essayer de régler vos problèmes,
焖乃卧沉病	D'autant plus que je fus alité à cause d'une grave maladie
20 針石苦微身	Et que les aiguilles d'acupuncture ont endolori mon corps.
行久懷丘窟	Quand on est loin de chez soi, on pense à son lieu d'origine,
景昃感秋旻	Et quand les rayons du soleil déclinent à l'ouest, on s'émeut du ciel automnal.
旻秋有歸棹	Sous le ciel automnal un bateau rentre au pays ;
昃景無淹津	Les rayons du soleil déclinent ; impossible de s'arrêter.
25 前期眇已往	Le passé est déjà loin derrière nous
後會邈未因	Et il n'y a pas de raison que nous nous rencontrions d'ici longtemps.
貧者闕所贈	J'aurais tant voulu vous offrir quelques cadeaux.
風寒護爾身	Le vent est froid : prenez bien soin de vous !

Le titre de ce poème nous dit que Xie Lingyun s'adresse aux petits employés de son bureau et aux gens du peuple, mais les quatorze premiers vers sont entièrement consacrés à son autobiographie. Peut-être qu'il pensait, consciemment ou inconsciemment, à ses employés quand il choisit les deux premiers mots du poème : « couteau et pinceau », *dao bi* 刀筆. Dans l'Antiquité, les scribes des *yamen* rédigeaient les documents officiels sur des fiches de bambou à l'aide de pinceaux et de couteaux pour gratter leurs erreurs. La honte dont il parle dans ces vers est néanmoins purement personnelle : il n'a pas eu la carrière d'un Zhang Tang 張湯 ni de son protégé Du Zhou 杜周, deux fonctionnaires qui servirent sous l'empereur Wu 武 des Han Antérieurs et qui, bien que de basse origine, atteignirent les plus hauts postes à la cour.[14] Zhong

14. Leurs biographies se trouvent dans le *Shiji* 122, p. 3137-3144 et 3152-3154, traduites dans Burton Watson, *Records of the Grand Historian of China*, vol. 2, New York, Columbia University Press, 1961, p. 426-437 et 448-450.

Jun 終軍 mourut vers l'âge de vingt ans en 112 av. J.-C. C'était un jeune génie plein de morgue. Quand il partit faire carrière à la capitale et que le garde-barrière lui présenta un laissez-passer, un morceau de tissu sur lequel on écrivait des caractères et qu'on déchirait en deux, afin de vérifier l'identité du voyageur à son retour, il le rejeta en déclarant qu'il reviendrait « un grand homme qui n'a que faire d'un laissez-passer ! »[15]

Les deux vers qui suivent évoquent deux des plus grands écrivains de la Chine ancienne, l'historien Sima Qian 司馬遷 (145-86 av. J.-C.) et le poète et penseur Yang Xiong 楊雄 (53 av. J.-C.-18 ap. J.-C.). Ce premier quatrain est la déclaration par Xie Lingyun de son aspiration à une carrière de fonctionnaire public. Les cinq personnages historiques qui y sont évoqués cumulent les vertus d'administrateur et d'écrivain qu'il lui faudrait pour une telle carrière, vertus qu'il dit modestement lui manquer.

Avec le cinquième vers commence le récit de sa vie. L' « ère éclairée » fait sans doute référence au fondateur de la dynastie des Song, Liu Yu 劉裕 (363-422), ou à la période de paix qu'il instaura. Xie Lingyun entra dans la carrière vers 405, avant l'avènement de Liu Yu qui eut lieu en 420, mais le terme qu'il emploie implique une allusion à un fondateur de dynastie. Le terme traduit par « vie sociale », *renqun* 人羣 , est emprunté au *Zhuangzi* 莊子 .[16] Dans les deux vers qui suivent, Xie Lingyun semble vouloir tempérer l'ardeur de son engagement en disant qu'il reste attaché à la vie érémitique malgré son entrée dans la vie politique. Le v. 9 est inspiré du *Laozi* 老子 19, un chapitre que le poète cite souvent. Cette allusion au *Laozi* montre que Xie Lingyun n'a pas l'intention de se laisser pervertir par les choses extérieures, qu'il entend rester fidèle à sa nature foncière. Dans le vers suivant, le poète souligne qu'il entend en même temps « rester diligent », en bon confucianiste.

Dans le distique suivant (v. 11-12) il fait allusion à deux poèmes du *Shijing*, n°s 112 et 206, poèmes allusifs qui mettent en accusation des ministres d'État paresseux, corrompus et de peu de valeur. Xie Lingyun vise, en particulier, les hommes au pouvoir, Xu Xianzhi 徐羨之 , Fu Liang 傅亮 et son propre cousin Xie Hui 謝晦 , qui destituèrent son protecteur, le prince de Luling, entraînant sa propre rétrogradation comme préfet de Yongjia. Il fait allusion à cette rétrogradation dans le distique suivant (v. 13-14) : il parle de ce poste comme constituant « un restant de gloire » « sur le tard » de sa vie (en fait il a trente-huit ans)

---

15. *Hanshu* 64b, p. 2819-2820.
16. *Zhuangzi* 13, trad. Watson, *The Complete Works of Chuang-tzu*, New York and London, Columbia University Press, 1968, p. 145.

dans le v. 13, et dans le v. 14 il traite ce même poste comme une occasion pour prendre des vacances au bord de la mer. Cette contradiction semble bien refléter son attitude envers l'année passée à Yongjia : un engagement réel et énergique pour servir le peuple et l'État d'un côté, et, de l'autre, une attitude hautaine et frivole d'enfant gâté à qui on demande une corvée qu'il considère en dessous de sa dignité. Il se peut aussi que l'indifférence à la chose publique qu'il affiche soit une façon de s'opposer à la dynastie qui mit fin aux Jin.[17]

À partir du v. 15 et jusqu'à la fin du poème, Xie Lingyun parle directement aux gens du peuple assemblés pour lui dire au revoir. Il s'excuse de ne pas avoir été à la hauteur de sa tâche en évoquant, comme il le fait souvent dans sa poésie, sa maladie chronique dont on ne connaît pas précisément la nature.[18] Dans les derniers vers du poème il annonce son départ pour son domaine de Shining, départ qui dut avoir lieu, comme c'est le cas dans tant d'autres de ses poèmes, le soir. Le fait même d'avoir écrit un poème adressé aux travailleurs subalternes de son bureau est assez frappant et ces quatorze derniers vers montrent en outre une réelle sympathie de l'auteur à leur égard.

Il nous reste à considérer un certain nombre de questions. Pourquoi Shen Yue dans sa biographie de Xie Lingyun donne-t-il l'impression que celui-ci est indifférent aux paysans ? Les trois poèmes traduits ici, dont aucun n'est inclus dans le *Wenxuan*, sont-ils authentiques ? Enfin, la question la plus importante : comment doit-on interpréter ces trois poèmes dans le cadre de la vie et de la pensée de Xie Lingyun ? La citation de la biographie de Xie Lingyun par Shen Yue (*supra*, p. 2), « Quant à juger les procès du peuple, c'est ce dont il n'avait cure », pourrait sembler inspirée du poème intitulé « Je lis dans ma bibliothèque » écrit en toute probabilité pendant son séjour à Yongjia. Ce poème prône « l'inactivité » taoïste (*wuwei* 無為) et contient les vers :

5 Dans les bureaux vides il n'y a plus de plaintes en justice ;
  Les cours oisives attirent les petits oiseaux.[19]

17. Voir Zhong Youmin 鍾優民, *Zhongguo shige shi : Wei Jin Nanbeichao* 中國詩歌史：魏晉南北朝, Jilin, Jilin daxue chubanshe, 1989, p. 234-237.
18. Paul Demiéville pense qu'il s'agit « probablement » du « diabète », *Choix d'études sinologiques*, p. 343 ; Frodsham 1, p. 32, opte pour la tuberculose pulmonaire suivant l'avis de Ye Xiaoxue, mais n'exclut pas non plus la possibilité du diabète (Frodsham 2, p. 148, n. 12).
19. Gu Shaobo, p. 61 ; le poème est contenu dans le *Wenxuan* 30 et traduit par Frodsham 1, p. 170, et Erwin von Zach, *Die chinesische Anthologie* (Harvard-Yenching Institute Studies XVIII), Cambridge, MA, Harvard University Press, 1958, p. 548.

Xie Lingyun se vante ici de gouverner en saint taoïste; il ne faut pas y voir un dédain du vulgum pecus et Shen Yue était sûrement un trop fin lettré pour se permettre une interprétation aussi tendancieuse.

Se peut-il que Shen Yue n'ait pas connu ces trois poèmes parce qu'ils n'existaient pas à son époque, parce qu'ils sont des fabrications d'un faussaire tardif ou parce qu'ils furent attribués à tort à Xie Lingyun par un éditeur peu soigneux? La première édition connue des deux premiers poèmes ne date que des Ming[20] et la première édition du troisième poème est encore plus tardive : une monographie locale des Qing.[21] Je doute néanmoins que ces poèmes soient apocryphes. Nous savons que Xie Lingyun laissa une production énorme qui se perdit peu à peu; il ne restait pas une seule collection de son œuvre vers l'an mille de notre ère. Tang Geng 唐庚 (1071-1121), dans sa sélection de poèmes des trois plus célèbres poètes de la famille Xie, *San Xie shi* 三謝詩, n'inclut qu'une dizaine des poèmes de Xie Lingyun parmi ceux qu'on trouve dans le *Wenxuan* et aucun autre.[22] Il est fort possible, sinon probable, qu'un certain nombre de ces poèmes « perdus » existent encore; que des rédacteurs de monographies locales en aient trouvé sous les Qing est loin d'être impossible.[23]

Mais la question la plus importante à poser est de savoir ce que ces poèmes nous révèlent sur les sentiments véritables de Xie Lingyun envers les paysans et surtout envers son mandat de préfet de la commanderie de Yongjia. Il ne cesse pas de nous dire, dans la quasi totalité des poèmes qui datent de cette époque, qu'il se sent irrésistiblement attiré par la vie d'un ermite taoïste, qu'il méprise le service public en général et le poste de préfet de Yongjia en particulier. Dans le v. 14 du dernier poème que nous venons de lire il parle, comme dans tant d'autres poèmes contemporains, de ce poste comme d'une espèce de « repos », de pré-retraite au bord de

20. *Gushiji* 古詩紀 57, p. 16b et 15b, édition *Siku quanshu*, Taibei, Taiwan Shangwu yinshuguan, 1983, vol. 1379.

21. *[Qianlong] Wenzhou fuzhi* [乾隆] 温州府志, p. 6a (réédition Taibei, Chengwen chubanshe, 1983, p. 2015).

22. Frodsham 2, p. 126, n. 4, prétend avoir trouvé une variante textuelle dans la version donnée par le *San Xie shi* du deuxième poème traduit ci-dessus, p. 3, « Faisant l'inspection des champs... ». Or, non seulement ce poème ne se trouve pas dans cette édition (au moins dans la version rééditée par le Shanghai Guji chubanshe, 1983), mais la variante qu'il dit y avoir trouvée (*min* 民 pour le *qing* 情 des autres éditions) n'est pas recevable du fait que *min* n'appartient pas à la catégorie de la rime du poème.

23. Pour l'histoire du texte des poèmes de Xie Lingyun, voir Gu Shaobo, p. 470-474 et 539-560, et Jin Kaicheng 金開誠 et Ge Zhaoguang 葛兆光, *Lidai shiwen yaoji xiangjie* 歷代詩文要籍詳解, Pékin, Beijing chubanshe, 1988, p. 326-329.

la mer. Il me semble que ces trois poèmes montrent sans l'ombre d'un doute que cette attitude désabusée n'est qu'une feinte, une réaction d'enfant gâté à qui on a refusé le poste à la cour qu'il désirait. Ces trois poèmes respirent la grande sollicitude d'un préfet attaché à ses administrés, un préfet qui s'efforce de secourir un peuple dans la souffrance. Le fait d'avoir réussi, comme le pense Yang Yong, ou simplement de l'avoir rêvé, comme le pense Gu Shaobo, est secondaire ; ce qui me semble important, c'est que Xie Lingyun prit tout à fait au sérieux son mandat. Quelle que fût la sincérité de son désir de « quitter le monde » et de vivre en ermite, lorsqu'il se trouva confronté à cette commanderie arriérée et loin de tout, il s'appliqua de toutes ses forces à remplir son devoir comme un confucianiste du meilleur aloi.

Peut-être peut-on aller encore plus loin dans l'analyse de l'attitude de Xie Lingyun vis-à-vis du service de l'État. Shen Yue nous dit, dans sa biographie du poète, qu'en 426, rappelé à la capitale pour des besognes purement littéraires et laissé à l'écart des vrais leviers du pouvoir de l'État, Xie Lingyun, dépité, « cessa d'assister aux audiences matinales. Il se mit à creuser des étangs [dans la banlieue de la capitale], à planter des haies, des bambous, des arbres, des potagers, faisant trimer [pour son propre compte] les corvéables de l'État sans plus observer mesure ni règle ».[24] D'autre part, chez lui dans sa propriété de Shining, Shen Yue nous informe que Xie Lingyun faisait travailler durement ses serviteurs : « Il y avait une foule d'esclaves et des centaines de dépendants attachés à la famille qui perçaient les montagnes, draguaient les lacs et à qui il donnait des corvées sans répit. »[25] Xie Lingyun ne semble pas éprouver pour ses serviteurs corvéables la sollicitude qu'il manifeste pour les habitants de Yongjia qui sont sous sa juridiction administrative. Est-il trop hardi de tirer de ce contraste la conclusion que Xie Lingyun se sentait attaché à ses paysans de Yongjia précisément parce qu'il était responsable d'eux en tant que préfet, qu'il était leur « père et mère », comme on dit en chinois d'un haut fonctionnaire, alors que, quand il s'agissait de serviteurs en dehors de cette relation administrative, il se sentait beaucoup moins concerné ? Yang Yong, lui-même originaire de Wenzhou (l'ancien Yongjia), nous informe qu'il y a plus de vingt toponymes dans les environs qui évoquent la présence du poète-préfet. Aucune autre célébrité ayant gouverné ce lieu n'a eu droit à autant d'égards.[26] Et Gu Shaobo

24. *Songshu* 67, p. 1772 ; dans la traduction de Demiéville, *Choix d'études sinologiques*, p. 348.
25. *Songshu* 67, p. 1775.
26. Conférence inédite, p. 7, et les notes 10 à 14. Les natifs de Wenzhou ne sont

nous dit que, quand il visita le site de Shining en 1982, les habitants ne connaissaient pas du tout Xie Lingyun, mais étaient très attachés à la mémoire de Xie An 安 (320-385), son arrière-grand-oncle.[27]

Ces divers éléments tirés de la biographie de Xie Lingyun et de la mémoire collective des habitants de Yongjia-Wenzhou et de ce qui fut Shining me semblent suggestifs. L'affection (le mot n'est pas trop fort) que Xie Lingyun éprouvait pour le peuple de Yongjia, et dont témoignent ces trois poèmes, ne se manifeste pas dans les rapports du poète avec ses compatriotes, ni avec les corvéables de la capitale. Quelle était donc l'origine de cette affection ? Ne provenait-t-elle pas tout simplement du sérieux avec lequel Xie Lingyun assurait son mandat de gouverneur, le mandat d'un homme profondément imbu des valeurs confucianistes ? Xie Lingyun était un homme complexe, et ces trois poèmes témoignent d'un élément de cette complexité qu'on trouve assez rarement ailleurs dans sa biographie ou dans son œuvre :[28] ils montrent le désir inné chez lui de servir l'État et d'accomplir de grandes œuvres pour le peuple. Qu'il fût attiré par la retraite taoïste, par la contemplation des paysages et la recherche de l'absolu mystique (bouddhiste ou taoïste, les deux se confondaient à son époque), ne fait pas de doute, pas plus que son adhésion à la philosophie « néo-taoïste » de Guo Xiang qui permettait aux aristocrates de jouir de leur situation de haut fonctionnaire et de l'expérience mystique tout à la fois — du beurre et de l'argent du beurre. Mais il ne peut y avoir de doute que quelque part dans son âme Xie Lingyun était aussi attiré par l'engagement dans la vie publique.

pas tous aussi enthousiastes. Hu Dian 胡甸 , « Jiewen Xie ke ai he zai » 借問謝客 愛何在 , in *Shi tan* 詩譚 (Wenzhou) 5 (25 septembre 1991), p. 1, ne trouve pas de trace de Xie Lingyun « dans le cœur des habitants de Wenzhou » aujourd'hui.

27. Gu Shaobo, p. 43, n. 11.

28. Voir l'ouvrage de Zhong Youmin cité plus haut, p. 124, n. 17, *loc. cit.*

Music Bureau, Liu Yao, to have his orchestra learn it, but, try as they may, they were unable to. Someone suggested in a memorial that the Buddhist monk Pao-yüeh was a skilled musician and the emperor ordered him to have them play it. Within a period of ten days they had already got it down pat. By imperial command the singer Ch'ang Chung was ordered to make his voice moving and evocative. The piece is still in existence. Pao-yüeh also presented two songs of his own.

The emperor often rode in his ceremonial boat sight-seeing on the Five Rampart River[2]. The sails on the boat were made of cloth from Yüeh [Chekiang] and the rigging of green silk; the ends of the punting poles were of brass and the punters were all dressed in pale yellow trousers made from Yü-lin [Kueichou] cloth. When their ranks were opened, they were made [to seem] to rise from the river fully clothed[3]. The palace buildings still survive at the Five Ramparts. The Ch'i dynasty used sixteen dancers [to perform this song]; the Liang, eight.

> Long ago, on a mission to Fan and Teng,
> High water stopped us[4] at Plum Root Isle.
> Moved by this memory, I try to recapture times past.
> My thoughts well up, but I find no words to express them.

I have been unable to discover just what event so struck emperor Wu that it inspired him to this emotional outburst years later. The only historical occurrence that took place at Plum Root Isle, Mei-ken chu, was a battle in 446 when Shen Yu-chih destroyed rebel forces aimed at Nanking (Chien-k'ang). The scene of battle was a place now called Plum Heights, Mei-keng, that was also called "Cash Stream", Ch'ien-hsi, because money was minted there during the Six Dynasties. It is located between Kuei-ch'ih and T'ung-ling in Anhui, on the south bank of the Yang-tze, some 175 km upstream from Nanking. At the time of the battle the future emperor Wu was prefect in Nan-k'ang, miles away in southern Kiangsi. The founder of the Ch'i Dynasty, emperor Wu's father, went on a campaign against the barbarians in "Fan and Teng" in 446 (Nan-Ch'i shu 1, p.4) when Hsiao was six years old[5], and Hsiao Tse himself was prefect of Hsiang-yang (which included the localities of "Fan and Teng") probably around 470. He was also active in the area when the future dynasts had to turn against Shen Yu-chih and others in 477. He then earned the comment from his father: "Tse is really a chip off the old block!" (Nan Ch'i shu 3, p. 44). In none of these cases was he a "commoner", and even less a merchant, since he came from an old family of army officers. The word translated by "high water", ch'ao, usually means "tide", but I doubt that the tide had much effect so many hundreds of kilometers from the sea. The word is often used in poems describing conditions even farther inland, so I believe it must be taken to mean "high waves" or something similar.

This is the only poem that emperor Wu has left us, which may seem strange for the man who reigned during the Yung-ming era, one of the most crucial and

The Image of the Merchant in
Medieval Chinese Poetry

Anyone who has read the *yüeh-fu* ballads that go under the title "Ku-k'o yüeh", "The merchant's music" (or "Ku-k'o le", "The merchant's joy"), has surely been struck by the disparity in the attitudes towards merchants expressed in these poems. I would like to discuss the small group of poems that go under this title, translating into English those that have never been translated previously or whose translations seem to me for one reason or another unsuitable, and then attempt to draw some general conclusions about them and about the portraits of merchants that appear in them.

The nucleus of the ballads about merchants can be found in the *Yüeh-fu shih-chi* 48, in the "Hsi ch'ü", "Western songs", section of the "Ch'ing-shang ch'ü-tz'u" division (pp. 699-709 of the Peking, 1979, edition). The title of these ballads, "Ku-k'o yüeh", is ambiguous. It could mean "The itinerant merchant's music" or "The intinerant merchant's joy". I believe that in the earlier ballads the title should be translated "The merchant's music" for the following two reasons. In the first place they appear in the *Yüeh-fu shih-chi* among other ballads with titles ending in the word *yüeh/le* in which it seems clear the reading should be "music" (e.g., "Mo-ch'ou yüeh", "Hsiang-yang yüeh"), in the second place, the earlier ballads do not really describe "joy" at all, but passion or emotion or simply sadness. When the titles are used, in the ninth century, by the poets of the New *yüeh-fu* movement there can be no doubt that they refer, often satirically, to the merchant's "joy", and I have changed my translation accordingly when I translate their poems.

The earliest ballad on this theme is said to be by the second emperor of the Southern Ch'i dynasty, the emperor Wu, Hsiao Tse (440-493), and there is a short paragraph describing the origin of the ballad quoted in the *Yüeh-fu shih-chi* from the *Ku-chin yüeh-lu*[1]:

> "Ku-k'o yüeh" was written by emperor Wu of the Ch'i dynasty. When the emperor was a commoner, he once visited Fan and Teng (northern Hupeh, near present Hsiang-yang). After he mounted the throne he wrote a song in which he tried to call back these past times. He ordered the head of the

inventive moments in Chinese literary history. But he does not seem to have
been very literary[6]: "Scholars are unable to run the state; all they do is read
books! To run the state all I need is a single Liu Hsi-tsung: what use to me are
Shen Yüeh, Wang Jung and the hundreds of others like them?" (*Nan shih* 77,
p. 1927). I believe we should look on this poem as something written in the
tradition of the founder of the Han dynasty's "Song of the Great Wind", as
a short work destined for ceremonial usage. I suppose it must remain a little
mysterious, at least until someone is able to discover its background, which I
have been unable to do. In any case, this first poem written under the title "The
merchant's music" is distinctly atypical, having, as far as can be seen today, nothing to do with merchants. But the fact that the emperor chose this title for
his unique poem does suggest that there was no bad feeling against merchants
at this time.

The two poems following, ascribed to Pao-yüeh, are much more typical of
the ballads that belong to this category and really seem to describe people of
the merchant class.

> You're going away on a three-mile trip
> I'll go with you for two and a half,
> And give you the pin that binds my hair
> To pay for your travel expenses!

> When there's a message-bearer, send me many letters,
> And when there's none, think of me in your heart.
> Don't be like a jug sunk in a well
> And leave me without a word once you're gone!

There is an undeniable folk-song, popular ballad authenticity in these two
quatrains, even if we do know they were written at court by a Buddhist monk.
The first, with its exaggerated pathos (the distances are so short), is still touching, and reminds me of certain pseudo-popular love songs in Paul Heyse's *Italie-
nisches Liederbuch*; the second relies on the adage-like quality of the third line
to give it a folk-like flavor. Both poems are full of naïveté and true to life, very
different from emperor Wu's emotional self-indulgence[7].

Later sources[8] also attribute two further poems of the same type to Pao-
yüeh, although the *Yüeh-fu shih-chi* treats them as anonymous.

> "The big boats, with their lofty prows,
> "Where did they leave from Yang-chou?
> "May I ask you, there on the big boat,
> "Did you see my beloved?"

> "When they first left Yang-chou
> "The boats set out from Smooth Ford Docks.
> "The weathervanes were like a bamboo forest:
> "Where could I have hoped to find him?"

As Yü Kuan-ying points out[9], these two poems are written as a question and an answer. The language is very dialectical. The word for "boat", *pien*, is a southern regional term, and the expression for "lofty", *k'o-e*, also seems otherwise unknown[10]: "Yang-chou" here refers to Chien-k'ang (Nanking) as it does in all the ballads written at this time, being called by the name of the province it governed[11]. *Po* in line 4 of the second poem is also dialectial[12], as is the word for "weathervane", *wu-liang*, and it, as so often in these poems, is to be taken as referring not only to the forest of masts in the harbor (wherever it was; I have been unable to identify Smooth Ford Docks, P'ing-chin po), but also to hint at the changeableness of the departing sailor's heart: "like a feather in the wind" (the weathervanes were made of cock feathers). Since this is a "Western song", Hsi ch'ü, the scene of these poems should be taken as being a port on the middle Yang-tze, in present Hupeh.

The following poem, by the last great poet of the Six Dynasties period, Yü Hsin (513-581), is very similar to these popular songs and takes as its theme the emotions of parting lovers. But it is much less straightforward, much more sophisticated.

The Merchant's Lyrics

The weathervane opens the way at the prow of the boat,
As the tall masts set out from New Bank.
He conjures up in his heart the person on the shore
And from afar, in the middle of the river, he beats the drum.

The weathervane's symbolism in this poem is less simple than in the preceding, for there is no clear expression of fickleness in it. "New Bank" is Hsin-p'u, a port established in the fifth century (and thus "new") southwest of the present K'ai in Szechwan[13]. I imagine the drum was beaten as a matter of course when a boat left a harbor, perhaps as a signal to warn other boats of its presence during the night or in bad weather, but here the sailor-drummer seems also to be expressing his passion to the "person on the shore"[14].

The last of the Six Dynasties poets to have written to this theme is again an emperor, the last sovereign of the Ch'en dynasty, Ch'en Shu-pao (553-604), a fairly prolific poet, known especially for his faintly erotic verses. His poem is really the first to treat the life of the merchants in a more general way.

The Merchant's Music

In the land of the Three Rivers he joins with associates
And never refuses to travel, however far it be,
Always on his figure-headed boat,
Often chasing the early morning tide.

The "Three Rivers" in line 1 probably allude to the ancient province of Yang-chou as it is described in the *Shang-shu*, ch. "Yü kung", as referring to the lower Yang-tze basin. Like Yü Hsin's quatrain, this poem also shows some attention to the alternation of tones (although both poets are guilty of the fault of "crane's knees", using the same tones in unrhymed lines), but the poems are otherwise quite different. It is the last Ch'en emperor's that sets the theme that will now be followed: the merchant as a distant wanderer and an indefatigable worker.

The poem with the same title by Li Po (699?-762?), insofar as a poem by Li Po can be said to resemble a poem by another poet, is fairly close to the last Ch'en emperor's[15]

> The seafarer rides on the wind of heaven
> Going with his boat to work in distant places.
> Like a bird in the clouds,
> Once gone he leaves no traces.

The term "seafarer", *hai-k'o*, is used fairly often in T'ang poetry to refer to the man who floated to the Milky Way on a raft. Li Po uses the term in this way in No. 13 of his "Ku feng" poems (*Li Po chi chiao-chu* 2, Shanghai, 1980, p. 116). In his "Chiang-shang yin" (ibid. 7, p. 480) it refers to the man on the seashore who could converse with seagulls (*Lieh-tzu* 2; A.C. Graham, *The book of Lieh-tzu*, London, 1960, p. 45). But in the other examples in his poetry, including this one, it refers simply to seafarers, and in two cases to seafarers who travel to the Isles of the Immortals (7, p. 497; 15, p. 898). Here, because of the title of the poem, the seafarer must be a merchant. Li Po portrays him romantically, in an apotheosis, like some Taoist hero who hurtles from one end of the universe to the other. Li Po treats merchants in other poems, in particular the famous "Ch'ang-kan ballads" (4, p. 326), and always with compassion.

In fact all the poems we have read treat the merchants with sympathy. It is only after the rebellion of An Lu-shan (755-762), and in particular in the circle of Po Chü-i (772-846) that the attitude changes dramatically. There are a group of poems, "New *yüeh-fu*", by Po Chü-i, Yüan Chen (779-831), Chang Chi (*chin-shih* in 799) and Liu Yü-hsi (772-842) and a prose work by the latter, that show extreme antipathy towards merchants as a class. These texts are all fairly long and have been well translated, in particular in the important series of articles on T'ang merchants by D.C. Twitchett[16], so I will not re-translate them in their entirety here. But I would like to quote some of the more violent passages to show that I am not overstating my case.

The earliest of the poems would seem to be Po Chü-i's "New *yüeh-fu*" called "The salt merchant's wife", since it is one of the fifty poems called "New *yüeh-fu*" that he himself says were written in 809 (*Po Chü-i chi* 3, Peking, 1979, p. 52). We realize that his attitude is inhospitable even before we read the poem because, in a list of the fifty titles that precedes the poems themselves in which each poem is described in a few words, he says (p. 53) of "The salt merchant's wife" that it shows "hatred for men who have succeeded purely by luck", *wu hsing-jen* (cf. *Tso chuan*, Hsüan 16, Legge, p. 330: "When many people succeed purely through luck, the state will be unlucky"). Here are the first lines of the poem:

> The Salt Merchant's Wife
> Has gold and silk a-plenty.
> No work in the fields for her, no silk worms, no spinning;
> She may travel in the four directions and still be "home",
> The wind and water her village, the boat her plot of ground.
> She was the daughter in a small family in Yang-chou,
> And married a great merchant from farther up-river.
> In her blue-black chignon, as she grew richer, the golden hairpins multiplied;
> And on her white wrists, as she grew plumper, the silver bracelets became tighter ...

Even without Po Chü-i's three-word description of this poem, it is clear that Mrs. Salt Merchant is not presented in a favorable light; her gold and silver ornaments, moreover, were actually illegal[17], and the following lines of the poem show that her husband robs the state of the salt tax that he should have given to it. In this poem Yang-chou is no longer Nanking, but the city that bears the name today which became an important center of commerce, especially for the salt trade, after the construction of the Grand Canal. The portrait of this over-dressed, over-fed, irascible nouveau riche matron is, alas, a caricature worthier of an anticapitalist propaganda movie than of a great poet.

* And the poem on the theme of "The mercant's joy" by Po Chü-i's friend Yüan Chen is even worse. It is found in the *Yüan Chen chi* 23, pp. 268-269 (of the Peking, 1982 edition), and is one of a series of ballads dated 817 (p. 254). It would seem to have been written in response to a poem on the same theme by Li Yü (cf. p. 262), a poem that no longer exists. It has again been translated by Twitchett (1968 article, pp. 81-82) and by A.C.Y.J. Palandri (*Yüan Chen*, Boston, 1977, pp. 82-84). There are many textual variants and many difficulties with this poem, not all of which have been cleared up by Ishida Mikinosuke in his excellent translation and study of the poem, "Gen Shin no gafu 'Kokaku raku' ni tsuite: Tôdai shôgyôshi no ichi shiryô to shite", in *Tôhô gakkai sôritsu jûgo shûnen kinen tôhôgaku ronshû* (Tokyo, 1962), pp. 1-9. I would like only to quote a few lines here to show the extreme animosity Yüan Chen harbors against merchants. In ll. 5 and following the tone is set. As a young merchant leaves home to begin his career,

> His father and elder brother set down the law:
> "Seek for profit, not for fame;
> "If you seek for fame, some things must be avoided:
> "Seek profit, and no holds are barred!"
> 10. He binds himself to his fellow merchants:
> "Lie when you sell: don't be sincere.
> "In all transactions be false,
> "Even to your own flesh and blood!"
> Then they go off together

Swearing allegiance to the death.
15 Once he has learned their market-place jargon,
He loses all feeling for his fellow villagers.

And when he goes back to sell fake baubles to the innocent girls from his home town he rakes up a profit ten times the money he put up for the merchandise (11. 23-24). He prospers, widens his market to include exotic jewels, Tangut horses, Tibetan parrots, asbestos from the South Seas, brocades from * Szechwan, slaves from Yüeh and from Central Asia. He becomes so rich, while still living economically, that, installed in Ch'ang-an, he is able to live in the same style as princes and to corrupt small officials who flatter him and run his errands. His two sons do business in timber and salt, and he himself, completely devoted to the search for profit, has become like a gigantic whale that no one dares to try to catch. His life has been one of "merchant's joy" and, with two sons to succeed him, there is no end in sight to the war for money he is waging.

Yüan Chen, like his friend Po Chü-i, presents us with a caricature here, as does their friend Liu Yü-hsi in his poem entitled "The merchant's lyrics", "Ku-k'o tz'u", which is dated to the period 806-814 when the poet was in Lang-chou (Ch'ang-te, Hunan) by Pien Hsiao-hsüan in his *Liu Yü-hsi nien-p'u* (Peking, 1963), p. 68. The preface and the beginning of the poem read:

> The merchants of the four corners of the world compete with one another to become the richest of all, and the salt merchants are the most notorious among them. It is said that "when the merchants win, the peasants suffer". Moved by this, I have written the following song.
> The merchants do not plan their trips beforehand:
> They go only where they can make a profit.
> They confuse the common people by mixing good with bad,
> And then seize every opportunity to manipulate their prices.

And the poem lists the attributes of the merchants: shrewd and calculating, attentive to the slightest possibility for gain, seeking good luck in Taoist temples or Buddhist monasteries, clothing their women folk in rich jewellery. * Rich as nobleman, they enjoy life wherever they go, and avoid taxes. The conclusion:

> Peasant, what are you doing,
> Painfully busying yourself with your pitiful ploughing?

Liu Yü-hsi's attitude towards the merchants corresponds very closely to his friends.   *

He is even more eloquent, and disparaging, in his prose piece "Kuan shih", "Observing the market-place". This has again been translated by Ishida Mikinosuke (*Wada hakase koki kinen tōyōshi ronsō*, Tokyo, 1961, pp. 61-71) and Twitchett ("The T'ang market system", in *Asia major*, 12 (1966), pp. 228-

230) and I would like to quote only a short passage which describes the merchants themselves. The whole piece is of great interest, especially since descriptions of this sort are so rare in the pre-modern period. Liu Yü-hsi dates his "observation" to 808[18] and he describes in some detail the disposition of and the animation in this southern market. He ends his piece with a description of the merchants:

> Their hearts within them stir, intent on profit; their avaricious eyes stare out without blinking. Those holding contracts and those attempting to monopolize the market meet together and attempt to force [the prices?] up. Crafty words represent things of bad quality as being good; deceitful hands ruin the weights and measures. An infinitesimal error gives rise to a torrent of vulgar language; they abuse and cheat one another: bad faith and treachery can be seen everywhere. Discordant noise is encouraged; smoke and dust increase; evil odors arise; cloth sandals pile up [?]. If one were to describe these men in a word [?]: they seem to have different forces driving them, but actually they are all the same ...

The profusion of bracketed question marks will show that this text is full of problems, many of which I don't pretend to have solved, but Liu Yü-hsi's attitude comes through clearly: he treats the merchants with the same disdain, depicts them as the same two-dimensional caricatures as his friends Po Chü-i and Yüan Chen.

There is also an undated poem on this same theme by Chang Chi. Arthur Waley said Chang Chi's ballads "have the same excellent social and political intentions als Po's, but have not even the modicum of poetry that Po manages to inject into his verse-tracts" (*The Life and Times of Po Chü-i*, London, 1949, p. 144), but I find Chang Chi's contribution to this theme a good deal less
* one sided than Po Chü i's (and thus better poetry). Chang Chi shows us how the merchants set out on their voyage with libations to the gods (1. 4), how they choose the richest among them as their chief who, night after night, counts their ligatures of cash and is the last to go to sleep (11. 7-8). The poem then describes (beautifully) the nocturnal landscape in the Tung-t'ing Lake region and the frenetic, dangerous race the merchants engage in to get to their destination before their competitors. It is only in the last two lines that we feel the criticism that is presumably the aim of the poem:

> The peasant, with his heavy taxes, suffers constantly;
> Let him give up his calling: he would do better to become a pedlar!

Another *yüeh-fu* by Chang Chi, "Yeh-lao ko", "The song of the old rustic", makes this same comparison, but more ferociously, contrasting the old rustic, who must eat acorns to survive because of the exhorbitant taxes he has to pay, with the rich southern merchants who feed meat to the dogs on their boats. The last two lines of Chang Chi's "The merchant's music" are close to the last two of Liu Yü-hsi's poem and make one conscious of the fact that all of these New *yüeh-fu* come from the same milieu and that they all date from, roughly speaking, the second decade of the ninth century (808-817).

Liu Yü-hsi has given us another group of three quatrains about merchants which probably dates from early in the next decade (822-824, cf. *Liu Yü-hsi nien-p'u*, p. 125) when he was in K'uei-chou (Feng-chieh, Szechwan). Since, as far as I know, they have not been translated before, since they are consider- ed representative of his best work (Pien Hsiao-hsüan and Wu Ju-yü, *Liu Yü-hsi*, Shanghai, 1980, p. 89), and since they give us another view of merchants by Liu Yü hsi, I would like to translate them here. The short introduction to these three quatrains again quoted from the *Ku-chin yüeh-lu* in the *Yüeh-fu shih-chi* 94, p. 1321, tells us that Liu Yü-hsi is here inspired by a popular ballad in the Hsi ch'ü tradition (to which "The merchant's music" also belongs) called "Ta-t'i ch'ü", a sub-section of the "Hsiang-yang yüeh" (*Yüeh-fu shih-chi* 48, pp.703- 706). During the Southern Dynasties these songs described the beautiful girls who lived in the wine houses on the Big Dike, Ta-t'i, on the Han River in I-ch'en (Hupeh) and who were frequented by passing merchants and sailors. But Masuda Kiyohide, in his *Gafu no rekishiteki kenkyû* (Tokyo, 1975), pp. 336-353, shows that during the T'ang the Big Dike was located some fifty kilometers upstream in Hsiang-yang. Liu Yü-hsi's quatrains are very close to the poems in the "Hsiang- yang yüeh" tradition (these are quoted by Masuda on pp. 348-352 of his book), but chances are he is describing a scene on the Yang-tze in Szechwan because he does not seem to have visited Hsiang-yang (unless he passed through on his way to Lang-chou in 805). Masuda suggests (p. 352) that "in these poems" Liu Yü-hsi "is probably thinking of the Big Dike in Hsiang-yang"; he certainly has written poems very much in the earlier tradition. The titles quoted in 1.3 of the second poem are popular poems, the first can be found in *Yüeh-fu shih-chi* 45, pp. 664-665, and in *Yü-t'ai hsin-yung* 10; the latter are a form of Szechwan folksong made famous by Liu Yü-hsi's settings (Kuo Mao-ch'ien, *Yüeh-fu shih- chi* 81, pp. 1140, and A. Waley, *op. cit.*, p. 167, follow an erroneous tradition in saying they date from Liu Yü-hsi's stay in Hunan, see *Liu Yü-hsi nien-p'u*, pp. 109-110). The first of these three quatrains is attributed to Li Shan-i in *Ch'üan T'ang-shih* 563, p. 6539. Kuo Mao-ch'ien has placed the quatrains under the heading "New *yüeh-fu*" because there was no old Hsi-ch'ü under exactly the same title. The poems are regulated *chüeh-chü*.

On the dike

[1]

The wine-house flags face one another on the big dike;
There are masts lined up below the dike, storeyed houses upon it.
At sunset the travellers struggle in their haste to cross over;
The sound of the oars, *yu-yat*, fills the mid-stream.

[2]

South of the river, north of the river, they look out at the misty
waves,
As night comes the travellers reply to one another in song:
"Peach leaf" tells of their love, "Bamboo branch" of their
grievances.
The water flows without limit; the moonlight is intense.

[3]

Surrounding the long dike the water ebbs and flows;
The wine shops and inns open one after the other.
As the sun goes down they raise the blinds and beckon to the mer-
chants;
The lofty great boats lower their sails and approach.

The merchants only appear tangentially in these verses, but their description,
more objective, as part of the river landscape, has allowed Liu Yü-hsi to avoid
caricature here. In the original Chinese these quatrains present unforgettable
pictures of the Yang-tze (or the Han-shui?) in the twilight; they are full of
rhythm and music.

The last poet I would like to translate is one who lives about a generation
after Liu Yü-hsi, towards the end of the T'ang dynasty, Liu Chia (*fl.* 867). He
has left two poems in his small corpus (which occupies the entire *Ch'üan T'ang
shih* 585) on this theme. The first has been correctly translated into French by
G. Margouliès in his *Anthologie raisonnée de la littérature chinoise* (Paris, 1948),
p. 202, but I shall translate it here into English because I think it revives the
earlier tradition which sees merchants in a more sympathetic light and thus
sets off the New *yüeh-fu* ballads as somewhat of an anomaly.

The Merchant's Lyrics

The merchant rises by lamplight
And still says he is setting out too late.
Through high mountains there are short cuts
That he takes in the dark, never fearing for a moment.
Brigands await in ambush by the road;
Wild beasts come to chase him.
His gold and jades are thrown to the four winds,
His empty bag fallen at the crossroads.

In Yang-chou he has a great house,
But his whitened bones haves no earth to receive them.
His young wife, on the day of his death,
Seated before her mirror, plays with blossoming branches.

Liu Chia's merchant is much closer to Li Po's (especially in his "Ch'ang-kan ballad") than to those in Po Chü-i's circle. He has, moreover, written another short poem which seems to be an answer to and a refutal of the New *yüeh-fu* ballads. His poem's title, "Fan ku-k'o le", "Against the merchant's joy", is reminiscent of Yang Hsiung's "Fan Li sao", "Against the Li sao"[19], and as Yang Hsiung writes against the attitudes of Ch'ü Yüan in the "Li sao", Liu Chia here writes against those who speak of "the merchant's joy".

Against the Merchant's Joy

Do not speak of the merchant's joy:
Merchants often are deprived of graves.
Their boats strike against wind and waves,
And they disappear entirely into the fishes' bellies.
It's only because the peasant's life is even harder
That they envy the [merchant's] state.

Liu Chia, in the last couplet, is echoing Chang Chi and Liu Yü-shi in the last couplets of their poems on the merchant's joy, but his meaning is quite different. Chang Chi and Liu Yü-hsi suggest that the peasants should give up working the soil to enjoy a life of ease as merchants; Liu Chia suggests that giving up farming may get them out of the fire, but becoming merchants will at best only land them in the frying pan. This short poem and its title show that the ballads written by Po Chü-i and his friends are somewhat of an anomaly in the tradition and that their extreme animosity towards merchants was a momentary phenomenon. Here we find a poet a generation or two later than them using a tone much closer to the tone we heard in the Six Dynasties and early T'ang poets.

How are we to account for this sudden eruption of anti-merchant feeling? The position of merchants in Chinese society has varied throughout history. Traditionally it is said that it was under the influence of legalist thought in the Han period that measures were first taken to prevent the merchants from wielding too much influence[20]. But, as Yang Lien-sheng says, "even under" the Han, "the attitude towards merchants was already ambivalent ... Under later dynasties of imperial China, the fate or merchants also tended to follow a zigzag course". And he continues, "A knowledge of the general historical background is necessary for the understanding of the merchants' position in a particular era because a meaningful evaluation can be made only by comparison with their position at other times[21]". It seems to me that even our pitifully small sample of ballads shows us the truth of these statements, and that we can actually see, in the attitudes expressed in these ballads, what amounts to a short "zigzag" in history. But is there anything in the "general historica background" that can account for these changes of course? I believe there is The "decay" of the T'ang dynasty after the An Lu-shan rebellion, so lamented by the Middle and Late T'ang poets, was actually a period of extraordinary economic expansion, due in part to improvements in agriculture. The weakening of central government controls, too, meant a weakening of restrictions and, "With the gradual removal of these formal restrictions in trade, the wealth of individual merchants began to grow to an unprecedented degree ... Trade boomed, and the merchants grew wealthy" (Twitchett, 1968, p. 78). And this expansion was extremely rapid; it took place within a few decades about the turn of the ninth century. I can only state it as an hypothesis, but I believe it is this "unprecedented" expansion of the merchants' power that precipitated a violent reaction on the part of the poets in Po Chü i's circle. And an aggravating circumstance is the fact that Liu Yü-hsi, one of the most outspoken of the circle, was a member of the reform government of Wang Shu-wen which was in power for five months in 805. Although it is notoriously difficult to determine political tendencies among Chinese literati, this reform group shows definite tendencies towards what today would be called a "planned economy", what some call "neo-legalism", and it is precisely this tendency (and not the more conservative "Confucians") who oppose laissez-faire liberalism, and the giving of freedom of action to merchants[22]. This, I think, could explain the anomaly. the extraordinary power attained by the merchants around the end of the eighth and the beginning of the ninth centuries provoked these poets, one of whom, at least, was of "legalist" tendencies, to a severe reaction against the merchants in their verse.

It seems impossible to me to see any "class consciousness" or class-inspired bias in this attitude against the merchants. The poets in Po Chü-i's circle were of course of the official class, but so were those who wrote sympathetically of the merchants. The lower classes, if we can believe a text found in Tun-huang that dates to this period called *T'ai-kung chia-chiao*, "Grandfather's family teachings", seem also to have been hostile to merchants:

> Marry not into a merchant's family;
> The way of the market-place is to take in profit:
> Don't become the neighbors of people like that![23]

Twitchett (1968, p.64), after complaining that the official historians are uniformly hostile to the merchants, says that, to find information about them, "We are thrown back upon casual information contained in literary texts ... above all, upon early ninth century poetry". For him "the principal shortcoming" of this material "is that it almost all derives from a very short period, roughly 780-845, and thus it gives little opportunity to detect secular change". Perhaps the poetry we have read can help remedy this shortcoming and let us see in greater depth the changes Twitchett's articles describe so well. And reading this short series of poems on a single theme will help us, too, I think, see that the poems by Po Chü-i and his circle, because of their polemical nature, their Manichaean insistence upon the unremitting blackness of the merchant's character, are artistically inferior to the earlier examples we read, in which the merchants are described with more sympathy as real human beings, good and bad[24].

Notes

1) A lost work by the sixth-century monk Chih-chiang; see Wang Yün-hsi, *Yüeh-fu shih lun-ts'ung* (Shanghai, 1958), p. 148, and M. Gimm, *Das Yüeh-fu tsa-lu des Tuan An-chieh* (Wiesbaden, 1966; Asiatische Forschungen, Band 19), p. 592. There is a reconstruction of the work in Wang Mo, *Han Wei i-shu ch'ao*, preface dated 1798 (repr. Kyoto, 1976), pp. 310-325, this paragraph appearing on pp. 320-321. This work and the poems which follow are all quoted from the *Yüeh-fu shih-chi* 48, Peking, 1979, pp. 699-702.

2) I don't know where this was. Pao-p'u-tzu speaks often of an immortal place called Five Ramparts, Wu-ch'eng (e.g., James R. Ware, *Alchemy, medicine and religion in the China of A.D. 320: The Nei P'ien of Ko Hung*, New York, 1981, p. 32), which is also mentioned as a place in the K'un-lun in other chapters (cf. Wang Ming, *Pao-p'u-tzu Nei-p'ien chiao-shih*, Peking, 1980, p. 9, n. 82). Is it too fanciful to see this as the name given to a river in one of the palace gardens in Nanking? The present Wu-ch'eng in southern Anhui is a later settlement, and the towns named Wu-ch'eng in the Middle Ages were in the north or in Szechwan.

3) This passage is not clear. It seems to describe some sort of aquatic floor show perhaps similar to the one presented impromptu in Lo-yang by the southerner Hsia T'ung before Chia Ch'ung (217-282); cf. *Chin shu* 94, p. 2429.

4) Variant from the *T'ung tien* 145, p. 758b (Kuo-hsüeh chi-pen ts'ung-shu edition, T'ai-pei, 1966 reprint), *chia chi:* "we rested our oars".

5) If his father's date of birth is correct, Hsiao Tse was born when the former was 13 years old, which "seems open to question", as Lu Ch'in-li says in his *Hsien Ch'in Han Wei Chin Nan-pei ch'ao shih* (Peking, 1983), p. 1377.

6) Ami Yûji, *Chûgoku chûsei bungaku kenkyû: Nan Sai Eimei jidai o chûshin to shite* (Tokyo, 1960), pp. 25-26, tries to prove the contrary, but I believe without much success.

7) The second poem is included in the *Yü-t'ai hsin-yung* with a variant, *k'o*, for the second word in line one, *hsin*. Anne Birrell, *New songs from a Jade Terrace* (London, 1982), p. 269, has misunderstood the first two lines of the poem, although they are well translated into Japanese in Suzuki Torao, *Gyokutai shin'ei shû* (Tokyo, 1975), pp. 305-306, whose translations she usually follows. Hsiao Ti-fei, *Han Wei Liu-ch'ao yüeh-fu wen-hsüeh shih* (Peking, 1984, originally published in 1944), p. 232, believes these two poems by Pao-yüeh actually depict the "times past" that emperor Wu tried to recapture. Not daring to describe his love affair, he commissioned Pao-yüeh to do it for him!

8) The *Ku yüeh-fu* 7 of Tso K'o-ming (*fl.* 1350) and the *Ku shih chi* 62 pu of Feng Wei-na (d. 1572).

9) *Han Wei Liu-ch'ao shih lun-ts'ung* (Shanghai, 1953), p. 60, points out that these two poems and a pair from a group called "Na-a t'an" (*Yüeh-fu shih-chi* 49, p. 714), are the only Hsi ch'ü songs written in dialogue form.

10) Lu Yu uses a similar term, probably echoing this poem, see below, note 24, as does Liu Yü-hsi, below, p.101, [3], l. 4.

11) See Wang Yün-hsi, *Han Wei Liu-ch'ao T'ang-tai wen-hsüeh lun-ts'ung* (Shanghai, 1981), pp. 41-43.

12) See Wang Yün-hsi, *Liu-ch'ao yüeh-fu yü min-ko* (Shanghai, 1957), p. 133.

13) See the *Chung-kuo li-shih ti-t'u chi,* vol. 4 (Shanghai, 1982), p. 34, (3) 2, for its place on the map.

14) The poem is also found in Yü-Hsin's works under the title "Ho Chiang-chung ku-k'o"; see Ni Fan, *Yü Tzu-shan chi-chu* (Peking, 1980), p. 372.

15) The poem bears the title "The merchant, ballad", "Ku-k'o hsing" in Li Po's works, *Li Po chi chiao-chu,* vol. 6 (Shanghai, 1980), p. 455.

16) I am thinking in particular of his "Merchant, trade and government in Late T'ang", in *Asia Major,* 14 (1968), pp. 63-95, and "The T'ang market system", *ibid.,* 12 (1966), pp. 202-248. The translations from poems by Yüan Chen, Liu Yü-hsi, Chang Chi and Po Chü-i can be found on pp. 81-86 of the 1968 article. Although Twitchett's translations are in the main quite reliable I have re-translated the passages I quote or paraphrase, modifying Twitchett's versions when I think they need it.

17) Cf. *Chiu T'ang-shu* 45, p. 1953; T'ung-tsu Ch'ü, *Law and society in traditional China* (Paris and The Hague, 1961), p. 140. It seems doubtful that these sumptuary laws were ever enforced.

18) This is the date determined by Ishida, p. 67, out of three given in textual variants (806, 807 and 808). He has chosen this date because the *Hsin T'ang-shu* 35, p. 917, says there was a drought in the general area concerned in this year, which corresponds with what Liu Yü-hsi tells us in his article. Twitchett, p. 229, chooses 807 which is the date given in the *Ch'üan T'ang-wen* 608, p. 10a.

19) Cf. D.R. Knechtges, "Two studies on the Han *fu*", in *Parerga* (Seattle) 1 (1968), pp. 18-29.

20) E.g. T'ung-tsu Ch'ü, *Han social structure* (Seattle and London, 1972), pp. 117 ff.; Sung Hsi, *Sung-shih yen-chiu lun-ts'ung* (T'ai-pei, 1962), p. 1.

21) "Government control of urban merchants in traditional China", in *Ch'ing-hua hsüeh-pao,* 8 (1970), p. 188.

22) Cf. Twitchett, 1968, p. 87; E.G. Pulleyblank, "Neo-Confucianism and Neo-Legalism in T'ang intellectual life", in A.F. Wright, (ed.), *The Confucian persuasion* (Stanford, 1960), pp. 106 ff.

23) Cf. P. Demiéville, *L'oeuvre de Wang le Zélateur* (Paris, 1982; Bibliothèque de l'Institut des Hautes Etudes Chinoises, Vol. XXVII), pp. 682-683.

24) There is a poem with the title "The merchant's joy" by Lu Yu, *Lu Yu chi* 19 (Peking, 1976), pp. 568-569, translation by B. Watson, *The old man who does as he pleases* (New York and London, 1973), p. 33. Lu Yu (1125-1210) follows the *yüeh-fu* tradition for this poem closely, but describes the riches of the merchants objectively, not to vilify them but to show their indifference to political hierarchy and to lament his own plight, that of a half-starved Confucian scholar dependent upon political favoritism to succeed.

Glossary

Ami Yûji 綱祐次

Chang Chi 張籍

Ch'ang Chung 常重

Ch'ang-te 常德

ch'ao 潮

Ch'en Shu-pao 陳叔寶

chia chi 假楫

Chia Ch'ung 賈充

chiang-shang yin 江上吟

Ch'ien-hsi 錢溪

Chih-chiang 智匠

Ch'ing-shang ch'ü-tz'u 清商曲辭

Chûgoku chûsei bungaku kenkyû: Nan Sai Eimei jidai o chûshin to shite 中國中世文學研究：南齊永明時代を中心として

Fan 樊

Fan ku-k'o le 反賈客樂

Fan Li-sao 反離騷

Feng-chieh 奉節

Feng Wei-na 馮惟訥

Gafu no rekishiteki kenkyû 樂府の歷史的研究

Gen Shin no gafu 'Kokaku raku'ni tsuite: Tôdai shôgyôshi no ichi shiryô to shite 元稹の樂府佰客樂に就いて：唐代商業史の一史料として

Gyokutai shin'ei shû 玉台新詠集

hai-k'o 海客

Han-shui 漢水

Han Wei i-shu ch'ao 漢魏遺書鈔

Han Wei Liu-ch'ao shih lun-ts'ung 漢魏六朝詩論叢

Han Wei Liu-ch'ao T'ang-tai wen-hsüeh lun-ts'ung 漢魏六朝唐代文學論叢

Han Wei Liu-ch'ao yüeh-fu wen-hsüeh shih 漢魏六朝樂府文學史

Ho Chiang-chung ku-k'o 和江中賈客

Hsi ch'ü 西曲

Hsia T'ung 夏統

Hsiang-yang 襄陽

Hsiang-yang yüeh 襄陽樂

Hsiao Ti-fei 蕭條非

Hsiao Tse 蕭賾

Hsien Ch'in Han Wei Chin Nan-pei-ch'ao shih 先秦漢魏晉南北朝詩

hsin 信

Hsin-p'u 新浦

I-ch'eng 宜城

Ishida Mikinosuke 石田幹之助

K'ai 開

k'o 客

k'o-e 珂峨

Ku-chin yüeh-lu 古今樂錄

ku feng 古風

Ku-k'o hsing 估客行

Ku-k'o tz'u 估客詞

Ku-k'o yüeh/le 估客樂

Ku shih chi 古詩集

Kuan shih 觀市

Kuei-ch'ih 貴池

K'uei-chou 夔州

Lang-chou 郎州

Li Po chi chiao-chu 李白集校注

Li Shan-i 李善尭

Liu ch'ao yüeh-fu yü min-ko 六朝
　　樂府與民歌

Liu Chia 劉駕

Liu Hsi tsung 劉係宗

Liu Yao 劉瑤

Liu Yü-hsi 劉禹錫

Lu Ch'in-li 逯欽立

Masuda Kiyohide 增田清秀

Mei-ken chu 梅根渚

Mei-keng 梅埂

Mo-ch'ou yüeh 莫愁樂

na-a t'an 那呵灘

Nan-k'ang 南康

Ni Fan 倪璠

Pao-p'u-tzu Nei-p'ien chiao-shih 抱
　　朴子內篇校釋

Pao-yüeh 寶月

pien 艑

Pien Hsiao-hsüan 卞孝萱

P'ing-chin po 平津泊

po 愽

pu 補

Shen Yu-chih 沈攸之

Sung Hsi 宋晞

Sung-shih yen-chiu lun-ts'ung 宋史
　　研究論叢

Suzuki Torao 鈴木虎雄

Ta-t'i 大堤

Ta-t'i ch'ü 大堤曲

T'ai-kung chia chiao 太公家教

Teng 鄧

Tôhô gakkai sôritsu jûgo shûnen
　　kinen tôhôgaku ronshû 東方學
　　會創立十五周年紀念東方
　　學論集

Tso K'o-ming 左克明

Tung-t'ing 洞庭

T'ung-ling 銅陵

T'ung-tien 通典

T'ung-tsu Ch'ü 瞿同祖

Wada hakase koki kinen tôyôshi ronsô
　　和田博士古稀記念東洋
　　史論叢

Wang Jung 王融

Wang Mo 王謨

Wang Shu-wen 王叔文

Wang Yün-hsi 王運熙

Wu-ch'eng 五城

wu hsing-jen 惡幸人

Wu Ju-yü 吳汝煜

wu-liang 五兩

Yeh-lao ko 野老歌

Yü Hsin 庾信

Yü Kuan-ying 余冠英

Yü-lin 鬱林

Yü-t'ai hsin-yung 玉台新詠

Yü Tzu-shan chi-chu 庾子山集注

Yüan Chen 元稹

yüeh/le 樂

yüeh-fu 樂府

Yüeh-fu shih-chi 樂府詩集

Yüeh-fu shih lun-ts'ung 樂府詩論叢

ADDENDA AND CORRIGENDA

I Immortality-Seeking in Early Chinese Poetry

p. 103, l. 10: delete the comma before the full stop
p. 105, fn. 13, l. 1: *for* Chuci *read Chuci*
p. 109, l. 17: *for* Henen *read* Henan
p. 110, fn. 27, l. 3: *for* 山 *read* 仙

II The Wang Ziqiao Stele

p. 77, l. 6: *for* Taiping jing *read Taiping jing*
p. 77, fn. 3: *for* Hou Hanshu *read Hou Hanshu*
p. 78, l. 6: *for* 麗 *read* 酈
p. 78, fn. 9, l. 3: *for* Shuijing zhushu *read Shuijing zhushu*
p. 78, fn. 9, l. 8: *for* italics *read* s p a c e d l e t t e r s
p. 80, l. 9: add a comma after 璋
p. 82, l. 4: *for* Wang *read* Wan
p. 82, fn. 22, l. 1: *for* Han social structure *read Han Social Structure*
p. 82, fn. 25, ll. 3 and 4: *for* Bielanstein *read* Bielenstein

III Ts'ao Chih and the Immortals

p. 21, fn. 29: *add* 2 *after Huai-nan-tzu*
p. 22, fn. 31, l. 7: *for* wih *read* with
p. 54, fn 129, l. 2: *for* 1 *read* 2

IV From Scepticism to Belief in Third-Century China

p. 311, l. 17: *for* occured *read* occurred
p. 311, last line: According to the *Jiankang shilu* 建康實錄, p. 188 (of the
        Peking: Zhonghua shuju, 1986 edition), Gan Bao died in 336.
p. 312, l. 5: *for* Jixianlu *read Jixianlu*
p. 312, l. 6: *for* Taiping guangji *read Taiping guangji*
p. 312, l. 14: *for* jun *read jun*
p. 312, l. 15: *for* guo *read guo*
p. 312, l. 17: *for* shennü *read shennü*
p. 312, l. 21: *for* zhenren *read zhenren*
p. 312, l. 26: *for* feixian *read feixian*
p. 312, l. 29: *add* a *after* is

p. 312, l. 31: *for* yunü *read yunü*
p. 312, fn. 5, l. 1: *for shinshü read shinshû*
p. 313, l. 8: *for* later *read* latter
p. 313, l. 30: *for* Soushenji *read Soushenji*
p. 313, fn. 14, l. 1: *for "Song for the Temple of Mt. Yu", "Yushan shennü ci ge" read*
"Song for the Temple of Mt. Yu", "Yushan shennü ci ge"
p. 313, fn. 14, l. 3: *for* Yuefu shiji *read Yuefu shiji*
p. 314, l. 1: *for* Jixianlu *read Jixianlu*
p. 314, ll. 2-4: *for* Yiwan leiju *and* Yiwen leiju *read Yiwen leiju*
p. 314, l. 10: *for* Jixianlu *read Jixianlu*
p. 314, l. 15: *for* thereareabetween *read* the area between
p. 314, l. 16: *for* hocuspocus *read* hocus-pocus
p. 314, l. 20: *for* zhangshi *read zhangshi*
p. 314, l. 21: *for* zi *read zi*
p. 315, l. 1: *for* Jinshu *read Jinshu*
p. 315, l. 2: *for* cishi *read cishi*
p. 315, l. 3: *for* zifu *read zifu*
p. 315, l. 22: *for* Ming *read* Min
p. 315, l. 11: *for* Jixianlu *read Jixianlu*
p. 315, fn. 21, l. 1: *for "Shennü zhuan" read* "Shennü zhuan"
p. 315, fn. 22, l. 1: *for "The Fu of T'ao Ch'ien" read* "The Fu of T'ao Ch'ien"
p. 315, fn. 22, l. 2: *for "The Divine Woman" read* "The Divine Woman"
p. 315, fn. 22, l. 3: *for "Shen-nü fu, The Song of the Goddess" read* "Shen-nü fu,
The Song of the Goddess"
p. 315, fn. 23, l. 4: *for* Quan shanggu sandai *read Quan shanggu sandai*
p. 316, l. 6: *for* of *read* for
p. 317, l. 13: *for "Shennü fu" read* "Shennü fu"
p. 317, l. 32: *for* Soushenji and the Taiping guangji *read Soushenji* and the
Taiping guangji
p. 317, fn. 28, l. 1: *for "Yangshenglun" read* "Yangshenglun"

V The Cold Food Festival in Early Medieval China

p. 52, l. 27: *for* of *read* or
p. 53, l. 26: *add* " *after full stop*
p. 61, fn. 23, l. 1: *for* Mitsu *read* Mitsuo
p. 79, l. 12: *for* defy *read* beg for

**VI Songs for the Gods: The Poetry of Popular Religion in Fifth-Century
China**

p. 1, fn. 3, l. 3: *for* vol. 1 *read* vol. 2
p. 3, last l.: *for* 苟 *read* 敬

p. 5, fn. 19, l. 2: *for* forthcoming), chap. 2, part 1. *read* 1990), p. 74

p. 8, ll. 5-7: see now Françoise Sabban, "Sucre candi et confiseries de Quinsai", *Journal d'Agriculture Traditionnelle et de Botanique Appliquée* XXXV (1988), pp. 197-198

VII Une fête chez Su Shih à Huang chou en 1082

p. 124, fn. 1, l. 11: *add*). *after* n. 3

VIII La poésie de Ji Kang

p. 155, l. 5: *for ceke read cike*
p. 171, l. 25: *for* Ji *read* Kan
p. 363, l. 11: *for* Wan Shi *read* Wanshi

IX Folk Ballads and the Aristocracy

p. 359, l. 4: *add comma after* aristocrats

X Xie Lingyun et les paysans de Yongjia

p. 117, fn. 6: As far as I know these lectures have not been published

XI The Image of the Merchant in Medieval Chinese Poetry

p. 97, l. 21: *for* mercant's *read* merchant's
p. 98, l. 7: *add* (?) *after* Tibetan
p. 98, l. 32: *for* women folk *read* womenfolk
p. 98, l. 38: *for* friends *read* friends'
p. 99, l. 28: *for* one sided *read* one-sided
p. 101, l. 37: *for* haves *read* have

INDEX

Two systems of romanization are used for Chinese words in the articles, Wade-Giles and the official Pinyin romanization now used in China and in most of the rest of the world. In this index Chinese words and names are given in alphabetical order only according to the Pinyin romanization. This is followed by the romanization that is used in the article referred to when it differs from the Pinyin. Chinese characters are given only when they do not appear in the texts of the articles referred to. Words in parentheses are given to explain Chinese terms whose characters do not appear in the index or to define in English terms that may be obscure.

An Lushan Rebellion: XI 96, 102
Anguo si [An-kuo ssu](monastery): VII 122-123
Anqi [An-ch'i]: III 19

Bai Juyi [Po Chü-i]: VII 130-131; XI 96-97, 99, 102, 103
Bai, Master (Bai gong): X 119-120
Baishi lei [Pai-shih lei]: VI 10
Baishi xiansheng [Pai-shih hsien-sheng]: VI 11
Balazs, Étienne: VII 122, 133
ballads, *see yuefu*
Ban Gu [Pan Ku]: III 24; VIII 328-329, 353
Ban Si: VIII 338
Baoxiang shanren [Pao-hsiang shan-ren]: *see* Zhuo Erkan
Baoyue [Pao-yüeh]: XI 93, 94
Baudelaire: VIII 122
Bian Qian: II 80
"Biandaolun" 辯道論 , "An Analysis of Tao[ism]": III 15-23
Birrell, A.: IX 347-348
Bo Ya: VIII 368
Book of Poetry, *see Shijing*
Boyi and Shuqi: VIII 352, 363

Cai Yong: I 109; II 78, 82; [Ts'ai Yung]: V 57
Canglang: VIII 355, 361-362
Cao Cao: I 111-113; [Ts'ao Ts'ao]: III 15, 18-19, 23, 25-26, 47; IV 315; V 56-57; VIII 333, 340, 347, 376; IX 349
Cao E [Ts'ao O]: VI 2
Cao Pi: I 111, 113, 117; [Ts'ao P'i]: III 15, 19, 25-27; VIII 110, 116, 120, 323-324, 341, 347, 350, 376
Cao Zhi: I 111, 114, 117; [Ts'ao Chih] III; VIII 120, 124, 127, 340, 376
Chan Man Sing: IX 347, 350, 353
Chang Zhong [Ch'ang Chung]: XI 93
Chang'e [Ch'ang-o]: III 22
Chaofu: VIII 352
Chen Chu [Ch'en Chu]: VI 4
Chen Jin: VIII 357
Chen Lin: IV 315
Chen Shubao [Ch'en Shu-pao]: XI 95-96
Chen Yanjie: VIII 111
Chen Zuolong: VIII 357
Chen Zuoming: I 116; [Ch'en Tso-ming]: III 25, 41, 50; VIII 116,

126, 131, 133, 138, 149, 155, 158,
337, 342, 344, 352, 365
Chen Shou [Ch'en Shou]: III 55; VIII
108
Chenggong Sui: I 116; IV 312
Chenggong Xing: IV 312
Chenggong Zhiqiong: IV 312 ff.
cherry apple [pommier sauvage]
(*pyrus spectabilis*): VII 123-125,
128-129
Chisongzi ("Red Pine Cone"): I 103,
106, 110; [Ch'ih-sung-tzu]: III 24,
28, 30, 40-41, 54; VIII 138
Chonger [Ch'ung-erh], Marquis of
Jin [Chin], Duke Wen: V 53-54,
76-77
Chu ge: : VIII 345-346
Chu Guangxi [Ch'u Kuang-hsi]: VI
11
Chuci:: I 103, 105-109, 114-115, 117;
[Ch'u-tz'u]: III 24, 28, 31, 36, 41;
V 54; VIII passim
Cinnabar Fields (*dantian*): II 79
Cinnabar Hill or Mountain: I 106,
109-110; III 41
Cinnabar Isle: VIII 369
cold food, *see hanshi*
Confucius: I 117; V 75; VIII 145, 152,
155, 330, 33, 351, 368; X 118
crows [corbeaux]: VII 130-131; IX
350-353

Da Xia: I 107-108
Dai Mingyang: VIII 113, 116, 131,
134, 149, 150, 171, 176-177, 359,
366
Dan shui: VIII 146-147
daojun [*tao-chün*]: VI 6
Daoshi: IV 312
Daoxuan [Tao-hsüan]: III 16
daoyin [*tao-yin*], gymnastics: III
18-19
Darwin, C.: V 65
"Dati qu" ["Ta-t'i ch'ü"]: XI 100

Dating: VIII 348-349
de Groot, J.J.: V 63-65
Ding Yan [Ting Yen]: III 15-16, 42
"Distant voyage", *see* "Yuan you"
Divine Woman, *see shennü*
Dong Zhongjun [Tung Chung-
chün]: III 18
Dongfang Shuo [Tung-fang Shuo]
III 16, 39; VIII 156-157, 327-329,
331
Dongpo [Tung-p'o]: VII 127, 130
dongtian [*tung-t'ien*]: VI 6
Dongwangfu [Tung-wang-fu]: III
24, 47-48
Dongye Huo: VIII 174
Dongyezi: VIII 173-174
Dou [Tou], Aged: III 17-18
"dragon taboo": V 54-56
drinking songs: III 46-47
Du Fu [Tu Fu]: VII 123, 125, 131
Du Gongzhan [Tu Kung-chan]: V
61-64, 71
Du Guangting: IV 311, 314
Du Yu [Tu Yü]: V 76
Du Zhou: X 121-122
Du Fu [Tu Fu]: III 56
Duo Guwutu: VIII 330

E, nymph [O]: III 35; [Ehuang]: IV
316
Eberhard, W.: V 67-68, 74
Ehuang, *see* E

Falin [Fa-lin]: III 15-16
Fang Dongshu [Fang Tung-shu]: III
56
Father King: I 110, *see also*
Dongwangfu
Fayuan zhulin: IV 312
feng and *shan* ceremonies: III 31-33
Feng Yan: VIII 335
filial piety: VIII 346-347
fire festivals: V 64 ff.
First Emperor of Qin: I 105-106; III

19, 21-22, 28, 39
Frankel, Hans H.: III 55
Frazer, James: V 65-67, 69-70, 71
Fu Liang: X 123
Fu Yue [Fu Yüeh]: III 16; VIII 147
Fusang tree: III 38-41
Fuxi: VIII 156-157, 348-349

Gan Bao: IV 311
Gan Shi [Kan Shih]: III 18-21, 26-27
Ge Hong: I 106; [Ko Hung]: III 25-27
Gœthe: III 57
Gouyi [Kou-i], Lady: III 16
Gu Kaizhi: VIII 112, 135, 137
Gu Shaobo: X 120, 126
Gu Yanwu: I 104
Gu Yong: VIII 323
Guan Zhong [Kuan Chung]: III 33
Guanqiu Jian: VIII 117
Guiguzi: VIII 174
Gujin tushu jicheng [Ku-chin t'u-shu chi-ch'eng]: VI 2; VI 14
Gujin yuelu [Ku-chin yüeh-lu]: VI 1; XI 92, 100
"Guke le (yue)" ["Ku-k'o le (yüeh)"]: XI 92
Guo Maoqian [Kuo Mao-ch'ien]: VI 1; IX 347, 350; XI, 100
Guo Pu: I 116; [Kuo P'u]: III 56
Guo Xiang: X 127
Guo Xiashu: VIII 116, 143, 148-153, 160-161, 373
Guo Xiazhou: VIII 143-148, 160-161, 373
Guoyu [Kuo yü]: VI 4; VIII 334

Han Anguo [Han An-kuo]: VII 131
Han Shixiong [Han Shih-hsiung]: III 20-21
Han Zhong: I 106; [Han Chung]: III 34-35
Hanshi waizhuan:: VIII 358
hanshi [han-shih]: V; VII
Haydn, F. J.: IX 355

He Chengtian [He Ch'eng-t'ien]: VI 2
He Yan: VIII 109; IX 353-354
He Zhuo: VIII 134, 176
He 和 [Ho], physician: III 53-54
Hebo [Ho-po]: III 35; VI 11
Heyse, P.: XI 94
Hidatsa Indians: V 65
Hong Mai: IV 315
Hong Yixuan: VIII 114
Hongya: VIII 348-349
Houtu ci [Hou-t'u tz'u] temple: V 76
Hu Kejia: VIII 358
Huainanzi [Huai-nan-tzu]: V 56; VIII 145
Huan Tan: I 108; [Huan T'an]: III 17-18; V 52
Huang Jie [Huang Chieh]: III 44; VIII 337-338
Huang Lao: VIII 342
Huang Xingzeng: VIII 113
Huangzhou [Huang chou] (Hubei): VII
Hui Shi: VIII 136

immortals: I-III passim; V 68; VI 7, 9; VIII 138, 340, 342-343, 374
Ishida Mikinosuke: XI 97
Itô Masafumi: III 56

Jade Maiden, see yunü
Jao Tsung-i: VIII 365
Ji Kang: I 114-117; IV 317; VIII
Ji Xi: VIII 117, 119, 123, 141-143, 356, 365, 370
Ji, Mount: VIII 351-352
Jia Chong [Chia Ch'ung]: VI 3
Jia Sixie [Chia Ssu-hsieh]: V 60
Jiang Ziwen [Chiang Tzu-wen]: VI 2,
Jiangbo [Chiang-po]: VI 10
"Jiangling Music": IX 348-349
Jiaofang ji :IX 350
Jie Zhitui [Chieh Chih-t'ui], see Jie

Zitui
Jie Zitui [Chieh Tzu-t'ui]: V 52
   passim
jie [*chieh*] (requite a god): VI 10
Jing Chu suishi ji [*Ching Ch'u sui-shih chi*]: 60
"Jiu ge": I 105
Jixianlu: IV 311-315, 317
Johnston, R. Fleming: V 67
Jushi [Chü-shih], in Central Asia: III 20

Kaltenmark, M.: V 68-69; VIII 138
Kanwu [*K'an-wu*]: V 64
Knechtges, D.: I 108
Komori Ikuko: III 51
Kong Rong: VIII 323-324
Kong Yan [K'ung Yen]: V 57
Kongzi jiayu: VIII 359, 363
Kou Qianzhi: IV 312, 317; [K'ou Ch'ien-chih]: VI 6
Kôzen Hiroshi: VIII 111, 122-123, 131

La Festival (All Saints): II 79, 82
Laolaizi: VIII 331
Laozi: I 109; II 82; [Lao-tzu]: 53-54; VI 6; VIII 129, 139, 147, 150-151, 325-327, 329, 332, 335, 336, 338, 354, 368; X 123
Lévi-Strauss, C.: V 69-71, 79
Li Bai [Li Po]: XI 96, 102
Li Chong: VIII 108
Li Daoyuan: II 78; [Li Tao-yüan]: V 74-76
Li Fengmao: VI 5, 16
Li Fu: V 64
Li Mian: IX 353
"Li Sao": I 105; XI 102
Li Shan: VIII 176, 357-358, 361
Li Shanyi [Li Shan-i]: XI 100
Li Si: VIII 335
Li Zhi: VIII 357, 361
Li Zhouhan: VIII 360

Lienü zhuan: VIII 330-331
Liexianzhuan: II 78; [*Lieh-hsien chuan*]: V 68; VIII 138
Liu An: III 16
Liu Jia [Liu Chia]: XI 101-102
Liu Lü: VIII 131, 134
Liu Shuo: IX 354
Liu Xie [Liu Hsieh]: III 23 fn 35; VIII 109-110, 374
Liu Xin [Liu Hsin]: 1V 17-18, 27
Liu Xizai: VIII 374-375
Liu Xizong [Liu Hsi-tsung]: XI 94
Liu Yao: XI 92
Liu Yikang: IX 350
Liu Yiqing: IX 350-354
Liu Yu: X 123
Liu Yuxi [Liu Yü-hsi]: XI 96, 97, 98-101, 102, 103
Liu Zhen: VIII 173
liubo [*liu-po*]: III 34-35
Liuxia Hui: VIII 330, 354, 360
Long Life: I 103; VIII 353, 375
Longyu [Lung-yü], princess: III 33, 35
Lü An: VIII 352, 356-361, 373
Lu Hui: V 57
Lu Ji: I 118
Lu Qinli: VIII 364-365
Lü Xun: VIII 356-358
luan (phœnix): VIII 120-121, 123
Luan Da [Luan Ta]: III 19, 21
Lucian: V 63
Luling, Prince of: X 123
Lunyu [*Lun-yü*]: VI 4; VIII 147, 152, 155, 329-330, 332, 336, 353, 359, 361, 366; X 118, 120
Lüshi chunqiu [*Lü-shih ch'un-ch'iu*]: V 54
Luxun: VIII 113, 149, 343

Ma Xulun: VIII 335, 337
Macbeth:: IX 352
Macrobius: V 63
Maspero, Henri: II 82

Masuda Kiyohide: XI 100
Mei Cheng [Mei Ch'eng]: III 55
Mencius: VIII 361-362
Meng Jiao [Meng Chiao]: III 56
merchants, attitude towards: XI
Mianju: VIII 175
mingjiao (Doctrine des Noms): VIII
353, 360
mirrors: III 24, 34
"Mo chou", *see* "Wang chou"
Moriya Mitsuo: V 71
mulberry trees: X 117-118

Nakamura Takashi: V 71-73
Nanchao yuefu, *see* Southern
Ballads
New *yuefu* [*yüeh-fu*]: XI 92, 96, 100,
102
Nie Zheng: VIII 153, 155
Nineteen Old Poems: I 111
Ning Yue: VIII 348-350
Niu Ai 牛哀 : III 21

Obi Kôichi: VI 17
osmanthus tree: III 44
Ovid: V 63-64, 77

Palandri, A.C.Y.J.: XI 97
Penglai, Mount [P'eng-lai]: III 38-39,
48
Perfect Man, *see* True Men
phœnix: *see luan*
Plutarch: V 77
Poe, E.A.: IX 352

Qie Jian [Ch'ieh Chien]: III 19-20, 23,
27
Qimin yaoshu [*Ch'i-min yao-shu*]: V
60, 63
Qin Ziyu: IV 315
Qincao [*Ch'in-ts'ao*]: V 57
qingming 清明[*ch'ing-ming*]: V 60-62,
67; VII 125 and passim
"Qiu Hu": VIII 333

Qu Yuan [Ch'ü Yüan]: III 24, 28-29,
48, 54; V 78; VIII 157, 341
Queen Mother of the West, see
Xiwangmu

Ren Fang: VIII 323
Rong Qiqi: VIII 171
Rongzhai suibi, see Hong Mai
Ruan Ji: I 114-117; [Juan Chi]: VII
131; VIII 109, 137, 161, 376
Ruan Kan: VIII 161-171, 327

San Xie shi:: X 125
Shan Tao: VIII 160, 345, 374
Shang shu: VIII 338; XI 95
Shanhai jing: VIII 147
shatang [*sha-t'ang*]: VI 8 and
Addenda
Shen Huaiyuan [Shen Huai-yüan]:
VI 11
Shen Youzhi [Shen Yu-chih]: XI 93
Shen Yu: IX 356
Shen Yue: X 116-117, 124-125, 126;
[Shen Yüeh]: XI 94
Shengxian gaoshi zhuan: VIII 363, 339
Shennong: VIII 156-157
"Shennü fu", "Divine Woman fu":
IV 315-317
shennü:: IV 312 ff.
"Shenxian ge" ["Shen-hsien go"]: VI
1, 5 ff.
Shi Le [Shih Le]: V 58-59
Shiba Rokurô: VIII 360, 362, 363
"Shicheng Music": IX 347-349
Shigezawa Toshio: V 71
Shijing: I 104; [*Shih-ching*]: III 37-38;
VI 4; VIII 125 and passim; IX
352; X 117-118, 120, 123
Shishuo xinyu: VIII 134-135, 143
"Shiyilun" ["Shih-i lun"]: III 25-27
Shuijingzhu [*Shui-ching chu*], see Li
Daoyuan
Shuo yuan: VIII 334
Shuowen jiezi, see Xu Shen

Si of Bao: IV 316
Sima Qian: I 104-105, 107; VIII 353;
    X 121, 123
Sima Xiangru: I 106; [Ssu-ma
    Hsiang-ju]: III 56; VIII 349
Sima Yi: VIII 117-118
Sima You: VIII 117
Sima Zhao: VIII 117, 356, 376
"Sixuan fu", see Zhang Heng
Song Changbai [Sung Ch'ang-pai]:
    III 36, 56
Song Yu: IV 315 fn 22, 317
Soushenji: IV 311-313, 317; [Sou-shen
    chi]: VI 10
Southern Ballads: IX 345-346, 350,
    356
St. Epithanius: V 63
stilts: III 38-39
Su Che: VII 126
Su Jun [Su Chün]: VI 10
Su Lin: VI 5
Su Qin: VIII 350
Su Shi [Su Shih]: VII; VIII 376
"Su-e" ["Su-o"]: VI 5
Sun Chu [Sun Ch'u]: V 57
Sun Deng: I 114-115; VIII 112, 354,
    360, 373-374
Sun Xingyan [Sun Hsing-yen]: III
    15-16
sun, festivals related to: V 65-69
Sunü, White Girl: III 22
Suzuki Shûji: VIII 362
Suzuki Torao: IX 347-348

Tai, Mount: I 110; [T'ai]: III 31-33,
    41; IV 312
Taigong jiajiao [T'ai-kung chia-chiao]:
    XI 103
Taiping guangji: IV 311-312; [T'ai-
    p'ing kuang-chi]: V 67
taiqing ("Grande pureté): VIII
    120-123, 147
Taiyuan [T'ai-yüan], Shanxi: V
    passim

Tang Geng: X 125
Tao Hongjing [T'ao Hung-ching]:
    VI 6
Taoist gymnastics, see daoyin
"Tian wen": I 105
Tonghou lang [T'ung-hou lang]: VI
    7
Tongwu: VIII 337
True Men (Perfect Man, zhenren 真
    人, immortal): I 105, 113; II 79-80;
    III 37, 42, 44-45; IV 312; VI 6
Twitchett, D.C.: XI 96, 97, 98, 103

von Zach, E.: VIII 360, 362

Waley, A.: VIII 339; XI 99, 100
Wan Xi: II 79
Wang Anshi [Wang An-shih]: VII
    122
Wang Bo: II 79
Wang Can: IV 315; VIII 347
"Wang chou": IX 349
Wang Fuzhi: VIII 126-127, 131, 133,
    347, 365, 367
Wang Mao: VIII 114
Wang Qiao: II 76-77; [Wang Ch'iao]:
    III 24, 34-35 (= Wangzi Qiao);
    VIII 339, 342-343
Wang Rong [Wang Jung]: XI 94
Wang Shao: V 73-74
Wang Shijie [Wang Shih-chieh]: VII
    132
Wang Shuwen: XI 103
Wang Su: V 75
Wang Wei 王維: VI 18
Wang Wengao [Wang Wen-kao]:
    VII 126
Wang Yi [Wang I]: 1V 28-29, 44, 48;
    VIII 120-121
Wang Yunxi [Wang Yün-hsi]: VI
    5-6, 7, 10, 15, 16; IX, 346-347
Wang Zhang: II 80
Wangzi Qiao ("Prince Qiao"): I 103,
    106, 110, 116; II passim; [Wang

Ch'iao] III 24, 28, 30, 40-41, 46,
    53-54; VIII 138, 339, 341
Wanshi 萬石: VIII 355, 363
Wei Juxian [Wei Chü-hsien]: V 76
Wei Qingshi [Wei Ch'ing-shih]: VII
    126
Wei Xiao [Wei Hsiao]: V 59
Wen (Jin emperor): IX 351
Wen of Wei: X 120
Wen Qin: IV 313
Wen, Duke, see Chonger, Marquis of
    Jin
Wenjiang of Qi: IV 316
Wenshi zhuan: VIII 357
Westermarck, Edward: V 67
White Stone Fort, see Baishi lei
Wu (Han emperor): I 105-107; III 19,
    21-22, 24, 28, 33, 39; V 76
Wu (Liang emperor), see Xiao Yan
Wu (Qi emperor), see Xiao Ze
Wu (Toba Wei emperor): V 65
Wu Jing [Wu Ching]: III 49-50
Wu Jun [Wu Chün]: VI 12
Wu Kuan: VIII 113
"Wu sheng": VI 1, 15; "Wusheng":
    IX
"Wu ye ti": IX 350-351
Wu Zixu [Wu Tzu-hsü]: V 78; VI 2
wuwei (inactivity): X 124

"Xi shi": I 107-108
Xia Qingjing [Hsia Ch'ing-ching]:
    VI 3
Xia Tong [Hsia T'ung]: VI 3-5
Xiahou Zhan: VIII 112
Xian Chao: IV 312 ff.
"Xian fu", see Huan Tan
xian, see immortals
Xiang Xiu: VIII 373
"Xiangyang yue" ["Hsiang-yang
    yüeh"]: XI 100
Xianmen [Hsien-men]: III 46
Xiao Tong: VIII 130
Xiao Yan: IX 354

Xiao Ze [Hsiao Tse]: IX 354; XI 92-93
xiao:: VIII 364
Xiaoshi [Hsiao-shih]: III 35
Xie An: VIII 112, 134-135; X 127
Xie Hui: X 123
Xie Lingyun: X
Xie, Mme: VIII 343
xing: VIII 366
"Xiqu" ["Hsi-ch'ü"]: VI 15; IX
    passim; XI 92, 95, 100
Xiwangmu: I 104, 107, 109; [Hsi-
    wang-mu]: III: 21-22, 24, 34-35,
    47; IV 311; VIII 340, 369
Xu Dashou [Hsü Ta-shou]: VII 132
Xu Gongchi [Hsü Kung-ch'ih]: III
    46-47, 49, 50
Xu Guang 徐光 [Hsü Kuang]: V 58
Xu Jian: IX 353
Xu Shen: I 103, 106; [Hsü Shen]: V
    56; (Shuo-wen chieh-tzu): VI 14
Xu Shi [Hsü Shih]: III 21
Xu Xianzhi: X 123
xuan ji: VIII 369
Xuanyuan, see Yellow Emperor
Xunzi: VIII 358
Xuyou: VIII 352

Yan Hui: VIII 332, 337
Yan Junping: VIII 354
Yang Guifei [Yang Kuei-fei]: VII 125
Yang Lien-sheng: XI 102
Yang Xiong: I 117; [Yang Hsiung]: V
    76; VIII 157, 328, 337; X 121, 123;
    XI 102
Yang Xiu: IV 315
Yang Yong: X 117, fn 6, 126
Yang Zhu: VIII 160
"Yangzhou" ("Yang-chou"=
    Nanking): XI 95
Yanzi (Zhuangzi): VIII 338
"Yelao ge" ["Yeh-lao ko"]: XI 99
Yellow Duke, Huanggong 黃公: III
    53-54
Yellow Emperor (Huangdi 黃帝): I

105, 109; III 32-33, 34, 36
Yezhongji [*Yeh-chung chi*]: V 57
Yi Yongchang: II 79
Yijing: IV 313; VIII 128, 136, 145,
    148, 174, 334, 335, 336, 359; X 116
Yin Xi: II 80, 82
yinsi [*yin-ssu*] ("excessive cult"): VI
    2, 13
Yiwen leiju: IV 314
Yongcheng jixianlu, see *Jixianlu*
You Mao: VIII 358
"Youth of the White Stone": VI 9-11
Yu Guanying [Yü Kuan-ying]: III
    46-47, 49, 50, 56; VI 8, 15; IX 349;
    XI 95
Yu Liang [Yü Liang]: VI 10
Yu Rang: VIII 153, 155
Yu Xin [Yü Hsin]: XI 95
Yu, Mount: IV 313; [Yü]: VI 18
Yuan Chen [Yüan Chen]: XI 96,
    97-98, 99
Yuan Shansong [Yüan Shan-sung]:
    V 75
Yuan Xian: VIII 331-332
"Yuan you": I 105-107; ["Yüan yu"]:
    III 28-29, 41, 46, 50
Yuefu shiji [*Yüeh-fu shih-chi*]: VI 1,
    15; VIII 120; IX 347, 354, 355; XI
    92, 94,100
yuefu: I 109-113; [*yüeh-fu*]: III 15,
    28-51, 49; VIII 120; IX; XI
yunü (Jade Maiden): IV 312; VI 7
Yutai xinyong: IX 347; [*Yü-t'ai
    hsin-yung*]: XI 100

Zang Zhi: IX 349-350, 354
Zengcheng: VIII 339
Zhang Dan [Chang Tan]: VI 4
Zhang Heng: I 108; VIII 128, 133
Zhang Houyu : IX 348, 350
Zhang Hua: IV 313
Zhang Ji [Chang Chi]: XI 96, 99-100,
    102
Zhang Liang [Chang Liang]: III 24,

54
Zhang Maoxian, *see* Zhang Hua
Zhang Min: IV 312 ff.
Zhang Pu [Chang P'u]: III 56
Zhang Qi: VIII 123
Zhang Tang: X 121-122
Zhang Xian: VIII 117, 176
Zhang Yan: VIII 361
Zhang Yaxin [Chang Ya-hsin]: VI 8;
    IX 350
Zhang Yi: 348-350
Zhang Yue: VIII 369
Zhao Daoyin [Chao Tao-yin], *see*
    Zhao *zun*
Zhao Futan [Chao Fu-t'an]: III 50, 56
Zhao Wenshao [Chao Wen-shao]:
    VI 12
Zhao Youwen [Chao Yu-wen]: III
    15, 31, 35, 36, 39, 50, 52, 55, 56
Zhao *zun* [Chao *tsun*] VI 5-6
Zhen gao: IV 312-313, 317 (Maoshan
    revelations)
Zheng Guo: X 119-120
Zheng Zizhen: VIII 354
zhenren, see True Men
Zhenzun [Chen-tsun]: VI 6
Zhiguai [*Chih-kuai*]: VI 7
Zhijiang [Chih-chiang]: VI 1
Zhong Hui: VIII 111, 350, 352,
    356-357, 359-360
Zhong Jun: X 121-123
Zhong Qi: VIII 368
Zhong Rong: VIII 110-112, 116, 124,
    374
Zhong, Mount [Chung]: VI 2, 11;
    VIII 340, 342
Zhou Ju [Chou Chü]: V 54-56
Zhou li [*Chou li*]: V 61-62, 66, 70,
    71-74; IX 352
Zhu Qian [Chu Ch'ien]: III 36, fn 78,
    40, 44, 50
Zhu Xuzeng [Chu Hsü-tseng]: III 44
Zhuangzi: I 105-106; [Chuang-tzu]:
    III 37, 53-54; VII 129; VIII 136,

140, 152, 158-159, 171, 338-339, 354, 368; X 123
Zhuo Erkan [Cho Erh-k'an]: III 37, 41 (= Baoxiang shanren), 50, 56
Zi ting: VIII 340
Zigong: VIII 332

Ziyu: VIII 354, 358
Zong Lin [Tsung Lin]: V 60-61
Zuo Ci [Tso Tz'u]: III 19, 26-27
Zuozhuan [Tso chuan]: V 53-54, 59, 61, 77-79; VI 4; VIII 175, 330, 334, 356, 359